Second Edition

Handbook of

SCADA/ Control Systems Security

Second Edition

Handbook of

SCADA/
Control
Systems
Security

Edited by

Robert Radvanovsky
Jacob Brodsky

CRC Press
Taylor & Francis Group
Boca Raton London New York

CRC Press is an imprint of the
Taylor & Francis Group, an **informa** business

CRC Press
Taylor & Francis Group
6000 Broken Sound Parkway NW, Suite 300
Boca Raton, FL 33487-2742

First issued in paperback 2020

© 2016 by Taylor & Francis Group, LLC
CRC Press is an imprint of Taylor & Francis Group, an Informa business

No claim to original U.S. Government works

ISBN-13: 978-1-4987-1707-6 (hbk)
ISBN-13: 978-0-367-59666-8 (pbk)

This book contains information obtained from authentic and highly regarded sources. Reasonable efforts have been made to publish reliable data and information, but the author and publisher cannot assume responsibility for the validity of all materials or the consequences of their use. The authors and publishers have attempted to trace the copyright holders of all material reproduced in this publication and apologize to copyright holders if permission to publish in this form has not been obtained. If any copyright material has not been acknowledged please write and let us know so we may rectify in any future reprint.

Library of Congress Cataloging-in-Publication Data

Names: Radvanovsky, Robert, editor. | Brodsky, Jacob, 1963- editor.
Title: Handbook of SCADA/control systems security / editors, Robert Radvanovsky and Jacob Brodsky.
Other titles: SCADA/control systems security
Description: Second edition. | Boca Raton : CRC Press, Taylor & Francis Group, [2016] | Includes
    bibliographical references and index.
Identifiers: LCCN 2015040115 | ISBN 9781498717083 (alk. paper)
Subjects: LCSH: Supervisory control systems--Handbooks, manuals, etc. | Automatic
    control--Security measures--Handbooks, manuals, etc. |
Technology--Risk assessment--Data processing--Handbooks, manuals, etc.
Classification: LCC TJ222 .H36 2016 | DDC 005.8--dc23
LC record available at http://lccn.loc.gov/2015040115

Visit the Taylor & Francis Web site at
http://www.taylorandfrancis.com

and the CRC Press Web site at
http://www.crcpress.com

In Memoriam

Dr. Wayne Boone

and

Dr. Harold Brodsky

Dedication

This book is dedicated to our families and friends who have been supportive in the development of this book. Their patience and understanding of our efforts are an author's best backing. Our thanks go to them during this time period ...

By failing to prepare, you are preparing to fail.

Benjamin Franklin

Know the enemy and know yourself; in a hundred battles you will never be in peril. When you are ignorant of the enemy, but know yourself, your chances of winning or losing are equal. If ignorant both of your enemy and yourself, you are certain in every battle to be in peril.

Sun Tzu
The Art of War

Contents

Section V: Conclusion

Foreword

Klaatu barada nikto

Increasingly, the services we rely on in our daily life, such as water treatment, electricity generation and transmission, health care, transportation, and financial transactions, depend on an underlying information technology and communications infrastructure. Cyberthreats put the availability and security of these services at risk.

Something wicked this way ...

The world faces a combination of known and unknown system vulnerabilities, a strong and rapidly expanding adversarial capability, and a lack of comprehensive threat and vulnerability awareness. Within this dynamic environment, both governments and private-sector companies are confronted with threats that are more targeted, more sophisticated, and more serious.

Sensitive information, including classified government data and proprietary data from private companies, is routinely stolen. This undermines our confidence in information systems security and the ability to protect our privacy. As bad as the loss of this intellectual capital is, we increasingly face even greater threats that could significantly compromise the accessibility and reliability of our critical infrastructure.

Malicious actors in cyberspace, including nation-states, terrorist networks, and organized criminal groups, are capable of targeting elements of the U.S. critical infrastructure to disrupt or destroy systems on which we depend. Stated motives include intelligence collection; theft of intellectual property, personal identity, or financial data; disruption of commercial activities; and cyberterrorism. Criminal elements continue to show increasing levels of sophistication in their technical and targeting capabilities and have shown a willingness to sell these capabilities on the underground market. In addition, terrorist groups and their sympathizers have expressed interest in using cyberspace to target and harm the United States and its citizens. Although terrorist groups and their sympathizers may lack their own purpose, tools and techniques are readily available for purchase through black markets. This generates a very real threat to the stability and resilience of our critical control systems.

Malicious cyberactivity can instantaneously result in virtual or physical consequences that threaten national and economic security, critical infrastructure, and public health and welfare. Similarly, stealthy intruders have laid a hidden foundation for future exploitation or attack, which they can then execute at their leisure—and at a time of great advantage to their cause. Securing cyberspace requires a layered security approach across the public and private sectors. The current reliance on perimeter defense as a single solution provides a false sense of security. Similar to the Maginot line, this approach is predicated on predictable actions on the part of our adversaries. Once the attacker figures how to drive to Belgium and the Ardennes, it is too late for the system. The landscape requires a fresh approach to defense in depth along with an active defense posture and capability.

Darmok, and jalad ... at tanagra

By investing in both public- and private-sector ventures, the government and industry can establish centers that serve as "always-on facilities" for cyberincident response and management. This enables the centers to provide "actionable intelligence" for asset owners, operators, and government agencies.

President Obama's *Cyberspace Policy Review* called for "a comprehensive framework to facilitate coordinated responses by government, the private sector, and allies to a significant cyber incident." With the federal government and private industry working together to develop joint incident response capabilities, these goals may be achieved. The approach requires vigilance and a voluntary public/private partnership in order to build the capability and relationships necessary to combat the growing cyberthreat.

In addition to identifying threats and vulnerabilities, specific work must be conducted by asset owners and operators with the assistance of the vendor community to develop mitigation plans to enhance security. This includes the need to evaluate the interdependencies across critical infrastructure sectors. For example, the electric, nuclear, water, transportation, and communications sectors support functions across all levels of government and the private sector. Government bodies and organizations do not inherently produce these services and must rely on private-sector organizations, just as other businesses and private citizens do. Therefore, an event impacting control systems has potential implications at all levels and could also have cascading effects on our ability to conduct commerce or generate life-giving services.

Assessing risk and effectively securing industrial control systems are vital to maintaining our nation's strategic interests, public safety, and economic well-being. A successful cyberattack on a control system could result in physical damage, loss of life, and cascading effects that could disrupt services for a prolonged period of time. We all must recognize that the protection and security of control systems are essential to the nation's overarching security and economy. A real-world threat has already emerged that significantly changed the landscape of targeted cyberattacks on industrial control systems. Malicious code, dubbed Stuxnet, was detected in July 2010. Analysis concluded that this highly complex code was the first of its kind, written to specifically target mission-critical control systems running a specific combination of software and hardware. The analysis quickly uncovered that sophisticated malware of this type has the ability to gain access to secure systems, steal detailed proprietary information, conduct reconnaissance, and manipulate the systems that operate mission-critical processes within the nation's infrastructure. In other words, this code can automatically enter a system, steal the formula for the product being manufactured, alter the ingredients being mixed in the product, and indicate to the operator and the operator's defenses that everything is functioning normally. Looking ahead, there is a deep concern that attackers could use the information about the code to develop variants targeted at broader installations of programmable equipment in control systems.

Lacking a silver bullet

Overcoming new cybersecurity challenges requires a coordinated and focused approach to better secure the nation's information and communications infrastructures. No single government agency has sole responsibility for securing cyberspace, and the success of our cybersecurity mission relies on effective communication and critical partnerships. Private industry owns and operates the vast majority of the nation's critical infrastructure and cybernetworks; therefore, the private sector plays an important role in cybersecurity.

Set within an environment characterized by a dangerous combination of known and unknown vulnerabilities, strong and rapidly expanding adversary capabilities, and a lack of comprehensive threat and vulnerability awareness, the cybersecurity mission is truly a national one requiring broad collaboration. Cybersecurity is critical to ensure that the government, businesses, and the public can continue to use the information technology and communications infrastructure on which they depend. We must continue to engage and collaborate in order to provide analysis, vulnerability, and mitigation assistance across the broad spectrum of industrial control systems. We must work closely with the international community in order to mitigate the risk on a global scale.

Seán McGurk
Global Manager, Intel Security

Synopses of chapters

This book is divided into five sections. The first four each consist of several chapters that represent groupings of topics, which emphasize those topics comprising functions within and throughout ICS environments; the fifth consists of conclusions.

These topics are categorically subdivided into unique and prioritized levels, beginning with Section I and its subsequent chapters, building up to Section II, and so on. Each subsequent section emphasizes a different meaning that is being conveyed such that it can be structured and remembered in an easy, cognitive fashion. A listing of each section and its corresponding chapters (with a brief summary of its description and function) is provided below.

Section I: Social implications and impacts

Chapter 1: Introduction

This chapter provides the basis for the entire book and describes some of the historical backgrounds of industrial control systems (ICS) and why it is important to critical infrastructures worldwide. There are some terms and definitions covering a brief synopsis of the intent of this book and what is to be expected from professionals who are emerging within the ICS security community.

Chapter 2: Sociological and cultural aspects

This chapter is more theoretical than most in that it identifies both background and emerging trends in the direction of the ICS security community. Some of the issues that continue to plague the ICS security community are the differences between the engineering and IT communities and the lack of proper coordination and communication between the two groups. This chapter reflects this current trend, along with other factors involving the paradigm shift from engineering to IT within the ICS security community.

Chapter 3: Threat vectors

This chapter outlines threat factors, both internal and external, to a given automated operation. Some of the factors include identifying motivational aspects and why an adversary would attempt to disrupt and perhaps even destroy a given automated operation.

Chapter 4: Risk management

This chapter applies both common and not-so-common risk methodologies and principles that can be applied to safeguard and secure an automated operation. The aim of this chapter is to provide a fundamental understanding of what risk is within the plant and how disruption can potentially cause near or completely catastrophic events to occur.

Chapter 5: International implications of securing our SCADA/control systems environments

This chapter provides an international perspective and implies that cybersecurity is non-border-specific; that is, the author of this chapter attempts to provide a representative picture of how events and incidents are related to one another for all critical infrastructures—worldwide.

Chapter 6: Aurora generator test

This chapter outlines the concepts surrounding the implications in terms of the types of physical damage and consequences that could result from a potential cyberattack. Additionally, this chapter provides a fundamental understanding of any engineering risks associated with the actual test and how it may be tied to cybersecurity.

Section II: Governance and management

Chapter 7: Disaster recovery and business continuity of SCADA

This chapter discusses methods for restoring and mitigating issues involving a *cyberincident*. Essentially, this chapter answers "what if" questions by providing a roadmap to the management of recovering automated operations to the state before the cyberincident occurs. The other half provides the "how" questions, discussing what would keep the automated operations going.

Chapter 8: Incident response and SCADA

This chapter outlines what steps should be performed as a result of a cyberincident; how management within the organization is informed; if regulated, how communications should be made to the regulating organization; and so on.

Chapter 9: Forensics management

This chapter identifies methods of determination of the events leading to a cyberincident; this includes best practices that should be applicable within any given automated operation and how this can assist the asset owner in deterministic analysis.

Chapter 10: Governance and compliance

This chapter outlines the importance and reasoning behind implementing a governance or compliance program and how it impacts SCADA and control systems environments. More critical infrastructure organizations are having regulatory requirements or guidelines imposed on them that limit or dictate the course of operation. This chapter will outline the challenges and issues (and perhaps solutions) encountered within those operation environments.

Chapter 11: Project management for SCADA systems

This chapter identifies and focuses on SCADA and control systems implementations and the challenges often associated with them. Unlike traditional projects, SCADA and control systems' projects are uniquely different, requiring more precision and cultural understanding of the expectations of a project manager.

Section III: Architecture and modeling

Chapter 12: Communications and engineering systems

This chapter outlines the necessity for good communications within and throughout the control systems environments, while at the same time outlining fundamental engineering concepts and reasons for those environments, as well as general impacts and interactions with business and IT systems' environments.

Chapter 13: Metrics framework for a SCADA system

This chapter provides a strategic "roadmap" for the development of a secured SCADA/control systems environment and what it entails.

Chapter 14: Network topology and implementation

This chapter provides some generic, non-industry-specific examples of how an ICS network is defined and configured. Examples are not specific to any hardware manufacturer and represent general rather than specific functions that encompass an ICS network. The chapter also provides more specific functionalities involved within an ICS network, identifies key component systems that are required to secure an ICS network, and discusses why these systems are important.

Chapter 15: Active defense in industrial control system networks

This chapter defines the concept of an active role: taking the defenders' greatest strength—their personnel—and empowering them to break down barriers of communication and technology to identify, respond to, and learn from potential adversaries. This provides a strategic approach to security.

Chapter 16: Open-source intelligence (OSINT)

This chapter broaches the topic of intelligence gathered not from closed or private sources, which can cost significant amount of time and effort, but through publicly available sources. These sources provide rapid performance and vulnerability assessments of potential attackers, giving a critical edge to both private- and public-sector current and future operations.

Section IV: Commissioning and operations

Chapter 17: Obsolescence and procurement of industrial control systems

This chapter identifies current issues with ICS environments and some of the issues that arise when ICS equipment is not sufficiently maintained and kept up to date.

Chapter 18: Patching and change management

This chapter follows the obsolescence chapter and discusses why it is important to patch ICS equipment. Many of the issues that most public utilities are currently facing today involve either obsolescence issues or, more specifically, the lack of patching of key and critical systems to plant operations. Recent malware outbreaks, such as what occurred with Stuxnet, have caused many ICS security professionals to reevaluate patching methodologies within their plant operations.

Chapter 19: Physical security management

Just because ICS equipment is located within a plant or secured facility, it does not mean that there are no insider threats. This chapter provides an insight into the physical localities of ICS equipment and discusses physical security as an integral part of the holistic management of a plant.

Chapter 20: Tabletop/red–blue exercises

This chapter discusses one of the aspects of how to conduct training exercises for SCADA/control systems and provides as close to "real-life" scenarios as possible. For a tabletop exercise, the chapter outlines what is involved and how and what to set up and configure for this type of exercise. For the red–blue exercise, it describes a current program offered through the U.S. Department of Homeland Security to owner/operators of SCADA/control systems by giving students a simulated example through the disruption of real systems without any consequence for or impact on real critical infrastructures.

Chapter 21: Integrity monitoring

This chapter outlines the data that are relied upon for accurate processing and also discusses how objectives such as access rights, the integrity of operations, and data and reporting must be both valid and consistent.

Chapter 22: Data management and records retention

This chapter outlines some of the emerging issues with "data overload," especially the logging requirements that are emerging for many cybersecurity regulations and compliance guidelines today. The issue is what data are important to retain and why organizations need to retain that data.

Section V: Conclusion

Chapter 23: The future of SCADA and control systems security

This chapter provides a "future thought" in terms of one or two possible directions that ICS security can go. The authors and editors identify 5- and 10-year directions and what might be different in the future.

Appendix I: Listing of online resources SCADA/control systems

Appendix I provides a comprehensive listing of known online resources specific to SCADA and control systems security, along with a brief summary of each of their functions and purposes.

Appendix II: Terms and definitions

Appendix II provides terms and definitions used by SCADA and control systems professionals within and throughout this community.

Acknowledgments

Some materials used in this book were taken from several very reliable and useful sources. Any information that may appear to be repetitive in its content from those sources was taken to provide a more introspective perception of what defines SCADA security.

The editors wish to thank the following organizations and individuals for their contributions:

United States Department of Homeland Security's National Cyber Security Division's Control Systems Security Program

United States Department of Homeland Security's Industrial Control Systems Computer Emergency Response Team (ICS-CERT)

United States Department of Homeland Security's Federal Emergency Management Agency (FEMA)

Idaho National Engineering and Environmental Laboratory (INEEL)

Sandia National Laboratories (SNL)

Pacific Northwest National Laboratory (PNNL)

United States Department of Energy's Office of Energy Assurance

United States Department of Energy's National SCADA Test Bed (NSTB)

Government of Canada, Public Safety Canada

Government of Lithuania, Ministry of National Defense

National Institute of Standards and Technology (NIST)

Seán McGurk, Intel Security

Editors

Robert Radvanovsky is an active professional in the United States with knowledge in security, risk management, business continuity, disaster recovery planning, and remediation. He obtained his master's degree in computer science from DePaul University in Chicago, and he has significantly contributed toward establishing several certification programs, specifically on the topics of critical infrastructure protection and critical infrastructure assurance.

Robert has special interest and knowledge in matters of critical infrastructure and has published a number of articles and white papers regarding this topic. Although he has been significantly involved in establishing security training and awareness programs through his company, Infracritical, his extracurricular activities include working for several professional accreditation and educational institutions on the topics of homeland security, critical infrastructure protection and assurance, and cybersecurity. He is the owner of, and one of the lead moderators to, the SCADASEC mailing list for supervisory control and data acquisition (SCADA) and control systems security discussion fora, while working as an active participant with the U.S. Department of Homeland Security Transportation Security Administration's Transportation Systems Sector Cyber Working Group as well as the U.S. Department of Homeland Security Control Systems Security Program's Industrial Control Systems' Joint Working Group. Both of these working groups are part of President Obama's Cyber Security Initiative.

Robert's first book, *Critical Infrastructure: Homeland Security and Emergency Preparedness* (released May 2006), is a reference work dealing with emergency management and preparedness, and it defines (in greater detail) what critical infrastructure protection is. His second book, *Transportation Systems Security* (released May 2008), was designed to educate mid-level management (or higher) about aspects of holistic security analysis and management of the transportation sector. His third book, *Critical Infrastructure: Homeland Security and Emergency Preparedness, Second Edition* (released December 2009), coauthored with Allan McDougall, further evolves and incorporates critical infrastructure assurance as part of the critical infrastructure protection model. His fourth book, *Critical Infrastructure: Homeland Security and Emergency Preparedness, Third Edition* (released April 2013), further evolves and incorporates newer aspects of the critical infrastructure protection model. His fifth book project involved coediting and cowriting a book on SCADA security with Jacob Brodsky, titled *Handbook for SCADA and Control Systems Security, First Edition* (released February 2013), and works cooperatively in maintaining and promoting the SCADA and Control Systems Security (SCADASEC) mailing list.

Jacob Brodsky has been interested in computers and telecommunications since childhood. First licensed in 1975, he still maintains his amateur radio license, call sign AB3A. In 1986, he began his career at the Washington Suburban Sanitary Commission (WSSC) as an instrumentation and telecommunications technician while attending evening classes at the Johns Hopkins University Whiting School of Engineering. He received a bachelor's degree in electrical engineering in 1991. Due to the economy at the time, he chose to stay at WSSC and has not regretted that decision one bit.

Jake has worked on every aspect of SCADA and control systems for WSSC, from the assembly language firmware of the remote terminal unit to the communications protocols and the telecommunications networks, including frequency-division multiplexing analog and digital microwave radios, the data networks, systems programming, protocol drivers, human–machine interface design, and programmable logic controller programming. In 1994 and 1995, Jake participated under a special temporary permit from the Federal Communications Commission to use spread spectrum on the air as an amateur radio licensee. As a result, he is also very much aware of the practical limitations behind the designs of spread-spectrum radio systems.

In 2007, Jake became a voting member of the distributed network protocol (DNP3) Technical Committee, and in 2012 he was elected chairman of the DNP user group. Jake has contributed to the National Institute of Standards and Technology SP 800-82 effort and to the ISA-99 effort. He is also a cofounder and moderator of the SCADASEC e-mail list. Jake is a registered professional engineer of control systems in the state of Maryland, and he has coauthored chapters on control systems for several texts, including *The Instrument Engineers Handbook Volume 3* (CRC Press, August 2011) and *Corporate Hacking and Technology-Driven Crime* (IGI Global, August 2010). His most recent writing effort was coediting and cowriting an edited book on SCADA security with Robert Radvanovsky entitled *Handbook for SCADA and Control Systems Security, First Edition* (released February 2013).

Contributors

This book was written with the community in mind; it brings about a sense of owner-ship, pride, and responsibility in our actions, thoughts, and movement. The contributors who are listed provided time and effort that they felt was relevant to this book, providing insight and expertise knowledge in areas of engineering, information technology, security, risk management, and more. The editors of this book would like to express their gratitude and to thank each and every contributor for their contribution toward this (and perhaps future) endeavors. Contributors' names are listed alphabetically.

Wayne Boone, CD, PhD, CISSP, CPP, CBCP, CISM, PCIP
Assistant Professor of International Affairs, Deputy Director, Canadian Centre of
  Intelligence and Security Studies (CCISS)

Dr. Wayne Boone was the coordinator and principal instructor of the infrastructure protec-tion and international security (IPIS) program at Carleton University in Ottawa, Ontario, Canada. He had over 33 years of asset protection and security (AP&S) experience in the areas of force protection, critical infrastructure protection, security risk management, physical security, operations security, and information system/SCADA security, first as an officer in the Canadian Forces Security and Military Police (SAMP) branch, then as a consultant with Precision Security Consulting, and finally as an academic, instructor, and technical adviser/leader in AP&S projects through his role as a driving force in Carleton University's masters of infrastructure protection and international security program. Wayne researched at the leading edges of thinking for AP&S governance and oversight within the public and private sectors. He was active in the conceptualization and develop-ment of internationally recognized certification programs in AP&S.

Vytautas Butrimas
Cybersecurity and IT Department Adviser
Ministry of National Defence, Republic of Lithuania
National Communications Regulatory Authority Council Member

Dr. Vytautas Butrimas has been working in information technology and security policy for over 26 years, starting from his work as a government computer specialist to his pres-ent role as vice-minister at the Ministry of Communications and Informatics, Republic of Lithuania, responsible for information society development. In 1998, Vytautas moved on to the Ministry of National Defense (MoND) as policy and planning director where he partici-pated in NATO membership preparations, managing a task force preparing Lithuania's first national military defense strategy. From 2001 to 2011, Vytautas served as deputy director of the Communications and Information Systems Service (CISS) under the MoND, where he led two task forces preparing the first MoND Cybersecurity Strategy and Implementation Plan, and he contributed to the creation of the MoND CERT. Serving from 2011 to 2014 as chief MoND adviser for cybersecurity, he was also a member of the working group that drafted the recently approved new law on cybersecurity. Vytautas has participated in NATO and national cybersecurity and crisis management exercises, which included critical infrastructure threat scenarios. In 2007 (and again in 2012), the president of the Republic of Lithuania appointed Vytautas to the National Communications Regulatory Authority Council (RRT-Council). Vytautas has contributed to various international reports and has written several articles on cybersecurity and defense policy issues. He currently serves in the MoND Cybersecurity and Information Technology Department as senior adviser.

Jim Butterworth, CFE, GCIA, GSNA, GREM, EnCE
Chief Security Officer
HBGary

Jim Butterworth joined Soliton Systems as chief technology officer. He leads Soliton's product development in the area of cybersecurity, incident response, malware analysis, and insider threats. In addition, he provides global executive guidance in all matters pertaining to cybersecurity for Soliton clients. He is a member of the Sacramento Chapter of the Association of Certified Fraud Examiners.

Robert M. Lee
Founder and CEO, Dragos Security

Robert M. Lee is a SANS Institute Certified Instructor, the course author of *ICS515—Active Defense and Incident Response*, and the coauthor of *FOR578—Cyber Threat Intelligence*. He is also the CEO of Dragos Security, a nonresident national cybersecurity fellow at the New America think tank, a PhD candidate at Kings College London, the author of the book *SCADA and Me*, and the writer for the weekly web comic *Little Bobby*. Robert gained his start in cybersecurity in the U.S. Intelligence Community as an Air Force cyberwarfare cyberspace operations officer, where he stood up and led a first-of-its-kind intrusion analysis mission focusing on the identification of national-level adversaries breaking into critical infrastructure sites.

Allan McDougall, BA, BMASc, PCIP, CMAS, CISSP, CPP
Director, Evolutionary Security Management

Allan McDougall is a 20-year veteran security practitioner within the public and private sectors. Following his service with Canada's combat engineers, he has held senior technical advisory positions within the Federal Public Service in the security community, including the Department of Fisheries and Oceans, Canadian Coast Guard, Transport Canada, and Canada Border Services Agency. He has established himself as one of the leading contributors to transportation system security theory and has coauthored several works (including with Robert Radvanovsky, *Critical Infrastructure: Homeland Security and Emergency Preparedness* and *Transportation Systems Security*), has published several white papers on topics such as the dissolution and fragmentation of transportation networks, and has spoken at a number of universities on the protection of supply chains and related asset protection and security topics. He has served as the chair, Supply Chain and Transportation Security Council with ASIS International and was a founding member and later president of the International Association of Maritime Security Practitioners. He is currently active in a number of industry and cyberrelated working groups.

Seán McGurk, B.ET, B.TE
Global Manager, Intel Security
Senior Vice President, Centre for Strategic Cyberspace and Security Science

Seán Paul McGurk is the global manager of critical infrastructure protection at Intel Security. He also serves as the senior vice president of the National Critical Infrastructure CSCSS/Centre for Strategic Cyberspace and Security Science, an independent research organization. McGurk holds undergraduate degrees in electronic technology and technical education. He is a member of the Information Systems Security Association (ISSA) and the Institute of Electrical and Electronics Engineers (IEEE). He has received numerous awards, including the 2011 Federal 100 Award and the 2010 and 2009 SANS SCADA Leadership Awards.

Bernie Pella, GIAC, GSLC
Principal Cyber Security Consultant, Schneider Electric, Global Cyber Security Services

Bernie Pella has more than 30 years' experience in the area of nuclear and process controls. He is currently a cybersecurity consultant for the Invensys Critical Infrastructure and Security Practice. Bernie has experience in implementing the process controls and engineering automation cybersecurity program at the Savannah River Site, a Department of Energy–owned nuclear facility in Aiken, South Carolina. He spent 19 years at the Savannah River Site in various engineering positions that included 10 years as a shift technical engineer, process controls engineer, plant engineer, and cybersecurity engineer. Bernie also obtained commercial nuclear and building automation experience after leaving the U.S. Navy in 1986. Bernie spent 8 years in U.S. Navy submarine nuclear power operations, assigned to the *USS Scamp*-(SSN-588) during a major overhaul, and he was on the commissioning crew of *USS Buffalo*-(SSN-715). Bernie is a member of the industrial control system Joint Working Group and has presented many different industrial control system topics at conferences over the last several years. Bernie used an extended study degree program and is a 2008 graduate of Excelsior College with a bachelor of science in technology.

Lt. Colonel (USAR retired) Darrell G. Vydra, B.Eng, MBA, CISSP, ISSMP, PMP
Founder and Principal, Vydra Consulting

Lieutenant Colonel (retired) Darrell G. Vydra graduated from the United States Military Academy in 1981 with a BS in General Engineering, was commissioned in the United States Army, and served on active duty for 11.5 years before he entered the United States Army Reserves in 1992. He served in a number of capacities and global locations during his 30-year career (platoon leader and battery commander in Germany, battalion commander at Fort Sheridan, IL, foreign military sales liaison officer to the Kingdom of Saudi of Arabia, deputy director of displaced persons and refugees in Bosnia and Herzegovina, chief of information operations in Afghanistan, and director of strategic marketing and professional development at CENTCOM at MacDill Air Force Base, FL). He mastered both project management and physical security practices and expertise as a military officer. He began his civilian career as a defense contractor, moved into private-sector jobs, and quickly moved into project management, sales/marketing, and engineering positions while earning an MBA from Florida Institute of Technology in Acquisition, Procurement and Life-Cycle Management and an MS from DePaul University in Telecommunications Systems Management. He moved into information technology (IT) security operations in the early 2000s and earned his CISSP and ISSMP from ISC2 and his later earned his PMP from PMI. He now works as a consultant for Energy and Utilities, namely project managing governance, risk management and compliance (GRC) projects.

Joseph Weiss, PE, CISM, CRISC, ISA Fellow, IEEE Senior Member
Applied Control Solutions, LLC

Joseph Weiss is an industry expert on the electronic security of control systems, with more than 40 years' experience in the energy industry. He serves as a member of numerous international organizations related to control system security and has published over 80 papers on instrumentation, controls, and diagnostics, including the book *Protecting Industrial Control Systems from Electronic Threats*. He is an ISA Fellow; managing director of ISA Fossil Plant Standards, ISA Nuclear Plant Standards, ISA Industrial Automation and Control System Security (ISA99); a Ponemon Institute Fellow; and an IEEE Senior Member. He has two patents on instrumentation and control systems, is a registered professional engineer in the State of California and a certified information security manager (CISM) and is certified in risk and information systems control (CRISC).

Jeff Woodruff, CD, CAS
Departmental Security Officer, Canadian Radio-Television and Telecommunications
    Commission

Jeff Woodruff is a 25-year veteran of the police, security, and emergency management fields and currently holds the position of departmental security officer for one of Canada's federal government entities. In this capacity, he manages the security program, safety program, business continuity program, and emergency management program. As a former military policeman in the security branch of the Canadian Armed Forces, he served two tours in Canada's Special Operations Command, providing close security support for a counterterrorism unit. His work in physical security and operational risk management has been widely recognized within the public service community, particularly among security practitioners and professionals.

Craig Wright, GSE CISSP, CISA, CISM, CCE, GCFA, GLEG, GREM, GSPA
Vice President, Centre for Strategic Cyberspace and Security Science

Dr. Craig Wright is a lecturer and researcher at Charles Sturt University and vice president of the National Critical Infrastructure CSCSS/Centre for Strategic Cyberspace and Security Science with a focus on collaborating government bodies in securing cybersystems. With over 20 years of IT-related experience, he is a sought-after author and public speaker both locally and internationally, training Australian government and corporate departments in SCADA security, cybersecurity, and cyberdefense, while also presenting his latest research findings at academic conferences. Dr. Wright holds the industry certifications GSE CISSP, CISA, CISM, CCE, GCFA, GLEG, GREM, and GSPA, and he is working on his second PhD on the quantification of information systems risk.

Steven Young, MBA, IEM, CHS-V, IAHSS
Security Strategist and Principal Consultant

Steven has 20 years of diverse experience in the financial, medical, pharmaceutical, manufacturing, and government industry sectors (law enforcement and defense). He is an expert in leading security audits, performing resilience architecture assessments, developing disaster recovery plans, investigating security incidents, and assessing business risks/threats. He has a BA from Loyola University and an MBA from the University of Notre Dame. He is published in several industrial and law enforcement trade journals. He has served as an information security consultant for the U.S. Navy, the U.S. Coast Guard, and the U.S. Federal Reserve. He is also a licensed investigator, specializing in data breaches in two states with reciprocity in several others.

Editors' notes

This publication offers an aid to maintaining professional competence, with the understanding that neither the editors, chapter authors, or publisher are rendering any legal, financial, or other professional advice.

Due to the rapidly changing nature of the industrial control systems (ICS) security community, the information contained within this publication may become outdated, and therefore the reader should consider researching alternative or other professional or more current sources of authoritative information. A significant portion of this publication was based on research conducted from several government resources, publications, and Internet-accessible websites, some of which may no longer be publicly available or may have been restricted due to laws enacted by that country's federal or national government.

The views and positions taken in this book represent the considered judgment of the editors and chapter authors. They acknowledge, with gratitude, any inputs provided and resources offered that contributed to this book. Moreover, for those who have contributed to the book's strengths and its characteristics, we would like to say "thank you" for your contributions and efforts. For any inconsistencies that have been found, we alone share and accept the responsibility for them and will gladly make corrections as needed.

One additional note concerns the evolutionary process that we are witnessing within this community. The evolvement concerns itself with the transition from a traditional perspective—that ICSs are "islands"—to the current moment, in which those very systems are now interconnected, either privately or via open communications mediums (such as the Internet); additionally, ICSs are being treated less as an engineered automation plant asset, and more as an information technology (IT) asset, and thus we are seeing the initial witnessed efforts of a paradigm shift from engineering to IT. Part of the reason for this paradigm shift is the lack of qualified process control engineers who are technically competent in ICS design and implementation; the other part is that the term "security" has a different meaning and context within the engineering community compared to the IT community, causing continued cultural differences between them.

As there have been very few publications dedicated to this community, efforts involving establishing best practice methods, metrics, and standards continue to evolve; thus, this book represents a work in progress. Although we realize that there may be some areas that are lacking or are weak in their dissertation, please understand that we are striving for as complete a book as possible. For example, there are currently no generally accepted performance-based auditing criteria. Therefore, we have eschewed the auditing chapter as we feel that merely confirming the purchase of equipment and training of personnel does not constitute a valid security audit. For this reason, auditing has not been included in this publication.

section one

Social implications and impacts

chapter one

Introduction

Jacob Brodsky and Robert Radvanovsky

Contents

Critical infrastructure consists of both physical and cyberbased systems (along with their assets) that are essential to an economic state such that the disruption or destruction of their operations would have a debilitating impact on the security, public health, and safety of that economy. This transpires worldwide. These systems (and their assets) provide essential, yet vital, products and services to our economies, which include products such as food and critical manufactured products, or services such as our electricity, water, and wastewater treatment facilities, chemical and oil production facilities, and transportation modes. All these are essential to the operations of economies and their governments. Threats in recent years have underscored the need to protect many of our infrastructures. If vulnerabilities in these infrastructures are exploited, our critical infrastructures could be disrupted, disabled, possibly causing loss of life, physical damage, and economic losses (U.S. General Accounting Office 2007). A majority of the infrastructures worldwide are owned and operated privately by corporations.

What are "control systems," and why are they important?

Generally speaking, most control systems are computer based. They are used by many infrastructures and industries to monitor and control sensitive processes and physical functions. Typically, control systems collect sensor measurements and operational data from the field, process and display this information, and relay control commands to local or remote equipment. In the electric power industry, they can manage and control the transmission and delivery of electric power; for example, by opening and closing circuit breakers and setting thresholds for preventive shutdowns. Using integrated control systems, the oil and gas industry can control the refining operations on a plant site as well as remotely monitor the pressure and flow of gas pipelines and control the flow and pathways of gas transmission. With water utilities, control systems can remotely monitor well levels; control the wells' pumps; monitor water flows, tank levels, or water pressure in storage tanks; monitor water quality characteristics such as pH, turbidity, and chlorine residual; and control the addition of chemicals. Control system functions vary from simple to complex; they may be used to simply monitor processes that are running; for example, from environmental conditions within a small office building (the simplest form of site monitoring) to managing most (or, in most cases, all) activities for a municipal water system or even a nuclear power plant. Within certain industries such as chemical and power generation, safety systems are typically implemented to mitigate a disastrous event if control and other systems fail.

Control systems were not always computer based. In fact, there are still many pneumatic control systems. Some are analog systems, based on operational amplifier circuits. Some are mechanical feedback systems and others are hydraulic; for example, the set point for many pressure-reducing valves is made by setting the position of a hydraulic pilot valve configuration.

In addition to guarding against both physical attack and system failure, organizations may establish backup control centers that include uninterruptible power supplies and backup generators (Library of Congress 2004).

Types of control systems

There are two primary types of control systems:

1. Distributed control systems (DCSs) are typically used within a single process or generating plant, or used over a smaller geographic area or even a single-site location.
2. Supervisory control and data acquisition (SCADA) systems are typically used for larger-scale environments that may be geographically dispersed in an enterprise-wide distribution operation.

A utility company may use a DCS to generate power and may use a SCADA system to distribute it (Library of Congress 2004).

Control loops in a SCADA system tend to be open, whereas control loops in a DCS tend to be closed. The SCADA system communications infrastructure tends to be slower and less reliable, and so the remote terminal unit (RTU) in a SCADA system has local control schemes to handle that eventuality. In a DCS, networks tend to be highly reliable, high-bandwidth campus local area networks (LANs). The remote sites in a DCS can afford to send more data and centralize the processing of that data (Radvanovsky and McDougall 2009).

Components of a control system

A control system typically consists of a master control system or central supervisory control and monitoring station, consisting of one or more human–machine interfaces (HMI) in which an operator may view displayed information about the remote sites and issue commands directly to the system. Typically, this is a device or station that is located at a site in which application servers and production control workstations are used to configure and troubleshoot other control system components. The central supervisory control and monitoring station is generally connected to local controller stations through a hardwired network, or to remote controller stations through a communications network that may be communicated through the Internet, a public-switched telephone network (PSTN), or a cable or wireless (such as radio, microwave, or wireless) network (Radvanovsky and McDougall 2009).

Each controller station has an RTU, a programmable logic controller (PLC), a DCS controller, and/or other controllers that communicate with the supervisory control and monitoring station. The controller stations include sensors and control equipment that connect directly with the working components of the infrastructure (e.g., pipelines, water towers, and power lines). Sensors take readings from infrastructure equipment, such as water or pressure levels and electrical voltage, sending messages to the controller. The controller may be programmed to determine a course of action, sending a message to the control equipment instructing it what to do (e.g., to turn off a valve or dispense a chemical). If the controller is not programmed to determine a course of action, the controller communicates with the supervisory control and monitoring station before sending a command back to the control equipment. The control system may also be programmed to issue alarms back to the control operator when certain conditions are detected. Handheld devices such as personal digital assistants (PDAs) may be used to locally monitor controller stations. Controller station technologies are becoming more intelligent and automated and can communicate with the supervisory central monitoring and control station less frequently, requiring less human intervention. Historically, security concerns about control stations have been less frequent, requiring less human intervention (Radvanovsky and McDougall 2009).

Vulnerability concerns about control systems

Security concerns about control systems were primarily historically related to protection against physical attacks or the misuse of refining and processing sites or distribution and holding facilities. However, in more recent years, there has been a growing recognition that control systems are now vulnerable to cyberattacks from numerous sources, including hostile governments, terrorist groups, disgruntled employees, and other malicious intruders (Radvanovsky and McDougall 2009). Without going into too much of a dissertation about recent malware outbreaks, such as Stuxnet and Duqu, the malware Stuxnet* alone has been one of the most heavily researched, discussed, and hypothesized of any known control systems malware to date.

Several factors have contributed to the escalation of risk of these control systems, which include the following concerns:

- The adoption of standardized technologies with known vulnerabilities
- The connectivity of many control systems via, through, within, or exposed to unsecured networks, networked portals, or mechanisms connected to unsecured networks (which includes the Internet)

---

* Stuxnet was considered a "worm," which is a self-replicating virus.

- Implementation constraints of existing security technologies and practices within the existing control systems infrastructure (and its architectures)
- The connectivity of insecure remote devices in their connections to control systems
- The widespread availability of technical information about control systems, most notably via publicly available or shared networked resources such as the Internet

Adoption of standardized technologies with known vulnerabilities

Historically, proprietary hardware, software, and network protocols made it rather difficult to understand how control systems operated, as information was not commonly or publicly known, was considered proprietary (in nature), and was therefore not susceptible to hacker attacks. Today, however, to reduce costs and improve performance, organizations have begun transitioning from proprietary systems to less expensive, standardized technologies that use and operate under platforms that run operating systems such as Microsoft Windows, UNIX, and LINUX systems, along with the common networking protocols used by the Internet. These widely used standardized technologies have commonly known vulnerabilities such that more sophisticated and effective exploitation tools are widely available and relatively easy to use. As a consequence, both the number of people with the knowledge to wage attacks and the number of systems subject to attack have increased (Radvanovsky and McDougall 2009).

Connectivity of control systems to unsecured networks

Corporate enterprises often integrate their control systems within their enterprise networks. This increased connectivity has significant advantages, including providing decision makers with access to real-time information, allowing site engineers and production control managers to monitor and control the process flow and its control of the entire system from within different points of the enterprise network. Enterprise networks are often connected to networks of strategic partners as well as to the Internet. Control systems are increasingly using wide area networks and the Internet to transmit data to their remote or local stations and individual devices. This convergence of control networks with public and enterprise networks potentially exposes the control systems to additional security vulnerabilities. Unless appropriate security controls are deployed within and throughout the enterprise and control system network, breaches in enterprise security may affect operations (Radvanovsky and McDougall 2009).

Implementation constraints of security technologies of control systems

Existing security technologies, as well as strong user authentication and patch management practices, are typically not implemented in the operation of control systems; additionally, most control systems are typically not designed with security in mind and usually have limited processing capabilities to accommodate or handle security measures or countermeasures (Radvanovsky and McDougall 2009).

Existing security technologies such as authorization, authentication, encryption, intrusion detection, and filtering of network traffic and communications require significantly increased bandwidth, processing power, and memory—much more than control system components typically have or are capable of sustaining. The entire concept behind control systems was integrated systems technologies, which were small, compact, and relatively easy to use and configure. Because controller stations are generally designed to perform specific tasks, they use low-cost, resource-constrained microprocessors. In fact, some devices within the electrical industry still use the Intel 8088 processor, which was introduced in 1978. Consequently, it is difficult to install existing security technologies without seriously degrading the performance of the control systems (or causing disruptions of entire control systems networks), thus requiring the need for a complete overhaul of the entire control system infrastructure and its environment (Radvanovsky and McDougall 2009).

Furthermore, complex password-controlling mechanisms may not always be used to prevent unauthorized access to control systems, partly because this could hinder a rapid response to safety procedures during an emergency or could affect the performance of the overall environment. As a result, according to experts, weak passwords that are easy to guess, are shared, and are infrequently changed are reportedly common in control systems, including the use of default passwords or even no password at all (Radvanovsky and McDougall 2009).

Current control systems are based on standard operating systems as they are typically customized to support control system applications. Consequently, vendor-provided software patches are generally either incompatible or cannot be implemented without compromising service by shutting down "always-on" systems or affecting interdependent operations (Radvanovsky and McDougall 2009).

Insecure connectivity to control systems

Potential vulnerabilities in control systems are exacerbated by insecure connections, either within the corporate enterprise network or external to the enterprise or controlling station. Organizations often leave access links (such as dial-up modems to equipment and control information) open for remote diagnostics, maintenance, and examination of system status. Such links may not be protected with any authentication or encryption (or if any exist, are considered rather weak as the individuals who configured the control systems environments wanted something easy to remember, since oftentimes they had to maintain and manage hundreds of similar devices throughout a given area of region). This increases the risk that an attempted external penetration could use these insecure connections to break into remotely controlled systems. Some control systems use wireless communications systems, which are especially vulnerable to attack, or leased lines that pass through commercial telecommunications facilities; in either situation, the method of communication performs no security methodologies whatsoever and, if there are any security measures implemented, they are capable of being easily compromised. Without encryption to protect data as it flows through these insecure connections or authentication mechanisms to limit access, there is limited protection for the integrity of the information being transmitted, and the process may be subjected to interception, monitoring of data from interception, and (eventually) penetration (Radvanovsky and McDougall 2009).

Publicly available information about control systems

Public information about critical infrastructures and their control systems is available through widely available networks such as the Internet. The risks associated with the availability of critical infrastructure information poses a serious threat to those infrastructures being served. This has been repeatedly demonstrated by graduate students from several academic institutions over the past several years, whose dissertations reported either partial or complete relevant and sensitive information about specifically targeted infrastructures; this information, if utilized, could provide threat vector methods of attack, allowing subversive communications into and throughout these infrastructures and their control systems' networks. A prime example of publicly available information is with regard to the electric power industry, in which open sources of information such as product data, educational materials, and maps (even though outdated) are still available, showing line locations and interconnections that are currently being used; additional information includes filings of the Federal Energy Regulatory Commission, industrial publications on various subject matters pertaining to the electric power industry, and other materials—all of which are publicly available via the Internet (Radvanovsky and McDougall 2009).

Recently, other more invasive methods of determination through commercial services that probe for specific Internet functions (such as web services) somehow found either partially protected, if not completely open, control systems directly connected to the Internet (ICS-CERT 2011a).

The use of readily available and generally free search tools significantly reduces time and resources required to identify Internet-facing control systems. In turn, adversaries can utilize these tools to easily identify exposed control systems, posing an increased risk of attack. Conversely, owners and operators can also use these same tools to audit their assets for unsecured Internet-facing devices (ICS-CERT 2011a).

Internet-facing control systems have been identified in several critical infrastructure sectors. The systems vary in their deployment footprints, ranging from stand-alone workstation applications to larger DCS configurations. In most circumstances, these control systems were designed to allow remote access for system monitoring and management. All too often, remote access has been configured with direct Internet access (with no firewall) or utilizing either default or weak user names and passwords. These default and common account credentials are often readily available in public space documentation (in some cases, even on the control systems' manufacturers' websites).

Control systems are vulnerable to attack

Entities or individuals with intent to disrupt service may use one or more of the following threat vector methods, which may be successful in their attack(s) of control systems (U.S. General Accounting Office 2004):

- Disrupting the operations of control systems by delaying or blocking the flow of information through the networks supporting the control systems, thereby denying availability of the networks to control systems' operators and production control managers.
- Attempting to or succeeding in making unauthorized changes to programmed instructions within PLC, RTU, or DCS controllers, change alarm thresholds, or issue unauthorized commands to control station equipment, which could potentially result in damage to equipment (if tolerances have been exceeded), premature shutdown of processes (shutting down transmission lines or causing cascading termination of service to the electrical grid), or disabling control station equipment.
- Sending falsified information to control system operators, either to disguise unauthorized changes or to initiate inappropriate actions to be taken by systems operators—that is, falsified information is sent or displayed back to system operators who

may think that an alarmed condition has been triggered, resulting in system operators acting on this falsified information, thus potentially causing the actual event.

- Modifying or altering control system software or firmware such that the net effect
produces unpredictable results (such as introducing a computer "time bomb" to go
off at midnight every night, thus partially shutting down some of the control systems, causing a temporary brownout condition; a "time bomb" is a forcibly introduced piece of computer logic or source code that causes certain courses of action to
be taken when either an event or triggered state has been activated).
- Interfering with the operation and processing of safety systems (e.g., tampering with
or denial of service of control systems that regulate processing control rods within a
nuclear power generation facility).
- Many remote locations containing control systems (as part of an enterprise DCS
environment) are often unstaffed and may not be physically monitored through surveillance; the risk of threat remains and may be higher if the remote facility is physically penetrated at its perimeter and intrusion attempts are then made to the control
systems' networks from within.
- Many control systems are vulnerable to attacks of varying degrees; these attack attempts
range from telephone line sweeps (aka wardialing), to wireless network sniffing (war-
driving), to physical network port scanning and physical monitoring and intrusion.

Consequences of compromised control systems

Some consequences resulting from control system compromises are as follows:

- Although computer network security is undeniably important, unlike enterprise network security, a compromised control system can have significant impacts within real-
world life. These impacts can have far-reaching consequences not previously thought
of, or in areas that could affect other industrial sectors (and their infrastructures).
- Enterprise network security breaches can have financial consequences: customer privacy becomes compromised; computer systems need to be rebuilt, and so on.
- A breach of security of a control system can have a cascade effect on other systems,
either directly or indirectly connected to those control systems that have been compromised; however, not only can property be destroyed, but people can be hurt or,
even worse, be killed (St. Sauver 2004).

False reports of vulnerabilities involving control systems

Not all situations are actual security incidents; in some rare cases, certain circumstances
can be expounded negatively almost as bad as the threats themselves, making for a
"false-positive" scenario in which there never was a given cyberincident, but is exacerbated due to press coverage and incorrect (or untimely) information gathered. For example, on November 10, 2011, the Illinois Statewide Terrorism & Intelligence Center (STIC)
issued a daily intelligence notes report entitled "Public Water District Cyber Intrusion."
As widely reported in the press, the report detailed initial findings of anomalous behavior in a SCADA system at a central Illinois public water district, and alleged a malicious
cyberintrusion from an IP address located in Russia that caused the SCADA system to
power itself on and off, resulting in a water pump burn out. ICS-CERT was made aware
of the report on November 16, 2011, and immediately reached out to the STIC to gather
additional information, in which ICS-CERT was provided with a log file; however, initial

analysis could not validate any evidence to support the assertion that a cyberintrusion had occurred (ICS-CERT 2011b).

ICS-CERT reached out to the affected entity, Curran-Gardner Public Water District, to gather detailed information, offering support and analytics to uncover what caused the pump to fail.* After detailed analysis of all available data, ICS-CERT, along with the FBI, found no evidence of a cyberintrusion into the SCADA system of the Curran-Gardner Public Water District in Springfield, Illinois. At the request of the utility and in coordination with the FBI, ICS-CERT deployed a flyaway team to the facility to interview personnel, perform physical inspections, and collect logs and artifacts for analysis (ICS-CERT 2011b).

There was no evidence to support claims made within the initial Illinois STIC report—which was based on raw, unconfirmed data and subsequently leaked to the media—that any credentials were stolen or that the vendor was involved in any malicious activity that led to a pump failure at the water plant. News of a potential cyberattack reached the media almost immediately and spread quickly worldwide. At the end of their analysis, both the Department of Homeland Security (DHS) and the FBI concluded that there was no malicious or unauthorized traffic from Russia, or that any foreign entities, as previously reported, had infiltrated the water utility. Analysis of what caused the pump failure has yet to be disclosed publicly (ICS-CERT 2011b).

The net result demonstrated several days of unnecessary time and resources expended in support and analysis by several organizations, in which many felt that the central Illinois water utility was penetrated, and, along with some conspiracy theorists, further complicated the situation by making false accusations that the entire scenario was a government "cover-up"—when, in fact, no threat, no intrusion whatsoever had existed.

Control systems community challenges

One of the more interesting challenges is how to address security-related issues within the SCADA/control systems community, and the sectors it supports, as SCADA/control systems enterprises do not operate in a context similar to that of their traditional IT counterparts. It is probable that one of the more significant aspects to control systems is the scope in which they dictate how issues are to be addressed (Radvanovsky and McDougall 2009).

Many technologies within the IT realm, such as SQL database transaction speeds, have traditionally been viewed by SCADA/control systems engineers as having inadequate speed for control system data storage purposes. Although the technology has made this operation outmoded (Moore's law), most opinions are difficult to shake, and thus many process control engineers continue to have difficulties accepting IT solutions within their environments. Based on some of the challenges mentioned in this paragraph, the problem is not so much a matter of data management as it is about trends and statistical analysis.

One of the larger problems is that forensics and evidentiary discovery practices are often associated with security management practices. Within control systems, these priorities are a little bit different from normalized systems, which are (usually) listed in the following order:

1. Safety
2. Availability
3. Security

---

* According to the ICS-CERT report, at no time were there any impacts to customers served by the water district due to the pump failure. Refer to ICS-CERT (2011b), p. xxii for the detailed report.

Note where "security" is listed: last. The reason for this is that IT-based architectures may be completely inverted from the priorities listed earlier, and thus there appears to be a conflict between what/how SCADA/control systems operate and (more importantly) how the corporation's enterprise defines its priorities. Several industries are currently attempting to either reach a compromise or figure out how both environments—IT and control systems communities—can work together. Observationally, in some industries, such as nuclear power generation, these environments may never coexist together—ever (Radvanovsky and McDougall 2009).

Some of the larger issues associated with control systems involve legacy architectures no longer supported, utilize equipment that cannot be taken off-line immediately or easily, and pose serious operational and financial risks to the companies using them. Unless these systems are interconnected with newer systems or are upgraded, there is no easy method of determining a plausible cause for any given event or incident. Outside of what may be found at the company's control center, there is little forensic data to be found, as control center computers do not lend themselves to traditional forensics analysis unless taken off-line or removed off-site. Given the nature of most control systems, if it is an ongoing operational need, it may be very difficult to remove the servers in question for an extended analysis.

Where does control systems security fit?

Of the more interesting discussions over the years, one of the more intriguing is where SCADA/control systems security fits into the overall picture. Some would like to think that SCADA/control systems security should be isolated and set apart from traditional IT-related security environments, whereas others feel that it should be combined. One perspective suggested an alternative: combining a set of interlocking circles, whereby the significant security practices, with SCADA/control systems security being the smallest and having an interconnecting function between the other two security practices, are *dead center* between significant IT and control systems practices. Although the exact number is not known, SCADA/control systems security practitioners have the smallest number of experts (even though this area is growing and evolving). To understand the scale of the number of IT security practitioners versus SCADA/control systems security practitioners, see Figure 1.1.

Future of control systems

As for where things are going, control systems will have to be segmented and configured so that high-risk sections of the control system will have to be carefully protected. These include several threats. First, ensuring that logging takes place in more than one part of a control system. When the gates of a dam are opened, there should be not only a digital signature of the operator who initiates the command at the master station from which it was sent, but also the signature of the operator at the RTU where the command was executed (Radvanovsky and McDougall 2009).

Protocols such as IEC-60870 and Distributed Network Protocol 3 (DNP3) have recently added secure authentication features to make this possible. The new specification can be found in IEC-62351.

The future holds much promise with protocols such as IEC-61850. However, it is an extremely complex undertaking that mixes many features into one layer. The maintenance management system is a nice feature with which to integrate the control systems' data, but

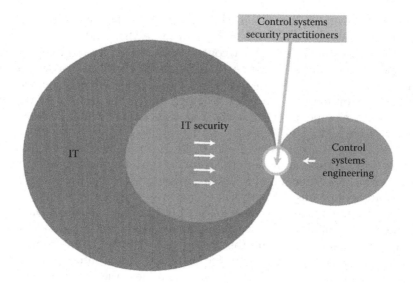

Figure 1.1 Comparative graphical representation of estimated total number of control systems security practitioners against other security practitioners. (Courtesy of Applied Control Systems.)

it may not be the best thing to place on the control systems' communications infrastructure. One of these operational elements is tactically significant and the other is strategically significant (Radvanovsky and McDougall 2009).

We may want to consider ways of segmenting and separating traffic for security reasons. This could entail reexamining the lower layers of the communications infrastructure.

SCADA/control systems' infrastructure needs to use a variety of ways to connect to remote stations. The goal is to avoid having common carrier problems disable a control system that it might depend on. Multiheaded RTU devices may be the future of many control systems.

Note the convergence of DCS and SCADA/control systems technologies. The SCADA/control systems concept originally grew from dealing with the constraints of high latency, low reliability, and expensive bandwidth. DCS concepts originally grew from the need to network everything to one central computer where everything could be processed all at once. DCSs are also getting smarter about how they distribute the functional pieces, and SCADA/control systems are handling closed loops more often as the communications infrastructure gets faster and more reliable (Radvanovsky and McDougall 2009).

This book provides a culmination of differing perspectives, ideals, thoughts, and attitudes toward securing SCADA and control systems environments. The thought is to provide a community-based effort toward establishing a strategy that can be established and utilized throughout the SCADA and control systems community. Although many of the chapters are all widely known and established within the IT, network, and security communities, to combine all three ideologies into one great big effort is a daunting task, and one in which we hope to achieve through community involvement through this book. Thus, this book is a living, breathing work in progress due to the quickly changing landscape of the SCADA and control systems security community.

References

Industrial Control Systems Computer Emergency Response Team (ICS-CERT). 2011a. ICS-ALERT-11-343-01—Control system Internet accessibility. http://www.us-cert.gov/control_systems/pdf/ICS-ALERT-11-343-01.pdf.

Industrial Control Systems Computer Emergency Response Team (ICS-CERT). 2011b. ICSB-11-327-01—Illinois water pump failure report. http://www.us-cert.gov/-control_systems/pdf/ICSB-11-327-01.pdf; http://news.infracritical.com/pipermail/scadasec/2011-November/thread.html.

Library of Congress. 2004. CRS Report for Congress. Critical infrastructure: control systems and the terrorist threat, CRS-RL31534. http://www.fas.org/irp/crs/RL31534.pdf.

Robert Radvanovsky and Allan McDougall. 2009. *Critical Infrastructure: Homeland Security and Emergency Preparedness*. 2nd edn. Boca Raton, FL: CRC Press/Taylor & Francis Group.

Joe St. Sauver. 2004. *NLANR/Internet2 Joint Techs Meeting: SCADA Security*. Columbus, OH: University of Oregon.

U.S. General Accounting Office. 2004. Critical infrastructure protection: challenges and efforts to secure control systems. GAO-04-354. Washington, DC. http://www.gao.gov/new.items/d04354.pdf.

U.S. General Accounting Office. 2007. Critical infrastructure protection: multiple efforts to secure control systems are under way, but challenges remain. GAO-08-119T. http://www.gao.gov/new.items/d08119t.pdf.

chapter two

Sociological and cultural aspects

Jacob Brodsky and Robert Radvanovsky

Contents

This chapter describes the current social aspects to implementing an industrial control system security program. Industrial control systems security is still in its infancy and, as such, there is resistance from many avenues. This chapter outlines the social hurdles, which the various groups are, and what concerns and motivates them.

It may be trite and pedantic to say this, but security begins and ends with people. This fact cannot be emphasized enough when dealing with industrial control system security. In the midst of all this high-tech gadgetry, too many act as if one could instill security with technology alone.

Although technical methods are the means to improving security, they ultimately require people to understand and use them. One can purchase many security technologies for a control system; but, unless the people who operate, maintain, and manage these systems know what to do with them, the return on the investment will be poor.

Security expenditures are not easy to justify. Responsibility for "security," specifically "cybersecurity," is not a very well-understood concept. By comparison, look at how safety works: Even if one were not responsible for a car accident, those who fail to put on a seatbelt are generally regarded as being partly responsible for the outcome. This sort of shared responsibility concept has only just begun to dawn on those who design and operate the security aspects of an industrial control system. Many operators still know little to nothing about how the control system gets data to them. They have no idea of what to do if the integrity is compromised. Many engineers still design systems without any of these features because "the customer didn't ask for it." Finally, many IT staff treat these control systems as if they were just another office application, where the computational service is the work product itself, instead of being a small part of the production effort.

Without a mandate to secure control systems, it is difficult to sell "security" to a company or a utility. The return on the investment is difficult to document. Some view it as an insurance policy; however, the data for this sort of approach is so thin that the risks and rewards are difficult to document. There are few laws mandating the accountability and reporting capabilities of a (potentially) compromised control system. Without prescriptive standards for recording near-miss metrics, and the resulting paucity of data in common form, few have any idea where to start, what to measure, or how to adjust to various situations.

Even if there is some sort of mandate for security, it is usually defined in terms of compliance instead of a performance approach. Without ubiquitous and standardized metrics, a performance-based approach is considered by many to be insufficiently developed to be regarded as usable. This leads to a "do it because we said so" compliance approach. Unfortunately, the compliance approach is usually an investment without people or training to back it up. Those who use this approach are probably expecting that practitioners will notice some metrics along the way and somehow start building a better performance-based approach. Owning all the tools does not make one a tradesman. Likewise, mere compliance alone will not make anyone more secure.

Like the issue of safety, security is easier to bootstrap in place if it is not sold as such. It can be an employee accountability system, self-integrity monitoring, improved diagnostics, or improved longevity (through better patch management), among many other things. An artful leader will carefully craft these features into a cohesive series of investments that coincidentally improves security.

Suppose that (somehow) these initial objections were overcome, and that an effort was underway to improve security. The logical thing would be to bring the IT security and engineering groups together to build something more secure. However, both professions bring biases to the table that makes working together very contentious. Furthermore, from the operational perspective, there may be significant ignorance of the issue, as it may not have been part of the assumptions behind the design or the operations of the plant. Operations staff need to be taught what to do with these security features and how to react to alarms that these new features will raise.

The fundamental change from older, hardwired automation designs to the newer, more highly networked systems is actually quite subtle. In the past, people had to stand in front of the equipment to operate it. There was very little remote operation capability, and where it did exist, it used an inherently trusted medium: the local telephone systems of the 1970s and 1980s. Engineers and operations staff assumed that those who could access the controls were either standing in front of machinery or were standing in a limited number of places where others could see and monitor their behavior.

Some thought was given to random, nonmalicious ignorance and mistakes; but beyond that, few considered the possibility of active malice on a plant. Malicious acts would tend to hurt the person who committed them, in addition to fellow employees and the public at large. It was presumed that everyone would have a sense of self-preservation.

Gradually, computer automation became more commonplace. Staffing levels were reduced. Operational processes were made more streamlined in an effort to save or conserve money. Eventually, as networking improved, the trend toward reducing staff became even more popular, until eventually one began to read articles about how an operator or engineer, running human–machine interface (HMI)* software from his laptop, was able to save the day for a plant many hours away. Few ever considered that the very features that

---

* HMI is software that displays information to an operator or user about the current state of an automated process, accepting and implementing any operator control instructions. Typically, information is shown using a graphical representation format (graphical user interface or GUI). HMIs are often considered part of a supervisory control and data acquisition (SCADA) system.

made this sort of rescue possible could also (potentially) provide a venue for sabotage for the plant from halfway around the world.

Engineering perspectives and their reactions

The first reaction from engineers when discussing an industrial security threat is incredulity. Why would anyone do that? They are used to the presumption that people might act in an ignorant manner, but not an actively malicious one. The idea that someone would want to destroy infrastructure seems foreign to those who have only concerned themselves with operating and upgrading that infrastructure over most of their careers.

A response to such concerns would be to discuss the possibility that someone from another social class/country/tribe/religion/etcetera might see an opportunity to hurt the economy of those considered enemies. Or, more likely, it could be a disgruntled contractor or employee who felt that he got a raw deal. The attack vector could be the very thing they used to make remote access possible. It could be a wireless link. It could be a logic bomb. It could be a modem left behind during the construction and testing phase. Unless the whole plant was built from the ground up just a few years ago, the chances are that there are lots of poorly documented "features" that could be exploited by someone with inside knowledge.

The goal is to get engineers to realize that any opportunity to control infrastructure from somewhere else or some earlier development work is a possible source of attack. People with malicious intent against infrastructure do exist. It may be necessary to rub some noses in this ugly reality. Despite the lack of any requirement to make reports of such incidents, there is already ample public evidence that such malicious behavior does occur.

The second reaction from engineers is pretty straightforward: It was not in the design criteria, so why bring this up now? The system does what it was designed to do.

The engineers have a point in this regard. Once upon a time, when these systems were designed, they were not presumed to be attached to any other networks. There was a certain trust because the extent of the network itself was presumed to have been limited. Unfortunately, others probably followed after the original design was completed and "made a tweak" that enabled remote access of some sort.

Again, it is useful to point out that fundamental assumptions behind the design criteria have changed. The systems were never designed for anything other than physical security. Furthermore, while it is not exactly effective for one to "bolt on security after the fact," we cannot ethically leave things as they are.

From a technical perspective, the network capacity and processor speed were selected without security overhead. Introducing that extra overhead may be possible, but full review and testing is needed. The IT security people should not secure the systems without the assistance of the engineering staff. This will become a significant discussion point later, when assigning scope and performance levels.

This is also an issue with how the design took place. Engineers, especially consulting engineers, typically work in a project delivery mode. The project is designed, there are reviews, the plans are bid for, construction takes place, and then everything is tested to ensure it does what it was designed to do. At that point, everyone washes their hands of the whole thing, turns it over to the operations staff, and then goes on to something else. The system is then expected to remain virtually untouched until the whole thing is depreciated enough to warrant upgrades. And then, the cycle continues all over again.

However, security is a continuous, ongoing concern. Project-oriented engineers may get flustered and bothered by this approach because it is not a performance metric for them. There has to be a retainer fee or a company account to which to charge the time they are going to have to spend to keep up with this stuff. Managers need to have this sort of contractual detail addressed before this objection comes up.

One way to deal with this problem, instead of contracting a firm to do this, is to hire control engineers and make them responsible for maintaining the infrastructure in conjunction with IT security. Note that this team of engineers and IT security could work under any of three major divisions: operations, engineering, or IT. It should be up to senior management to assess who has the staffing and budget to absorb these people and manage them in an appropriate manner.

Note for those who may be making this decision: Much has been written about this field for the chief information officer or chief security officer (CIO/CSO) executives. Sadly, too much of this advice has been conceived as if this was nothing but a gussied-up office system by those who have hardly even set foot on a working plant floor. The result is that many CIOs and CSOs carry some grave misconceptions over what a control system is or what it does. Do not automatically assume that a CIO or a CSO is appropriate for this task. Given this problem, another tactic is to simply acknowledge that this is an amalgamation of these three fields and to make the control systems security group independent of everyone else.

The third reaction identifies that the effort is an open-ended endeavor. Where do we stop? How do we set goals? The answer is that we as a society do not stop, but that we aim for the easy stuff first, and steadily improve from there. This is going to be a continuous process. We need to set priorities to handle the current system and figure out better designs for future systems. This may require depreciating existing assets faster than expected, and establishing different criteria for depreciation.

Managers should take note of this, and be ready to task technical staff with identifying those assets and accounting for the changes as early as possible. It is also worth noting that such security awareness is actually systems integrity monitoring and that, as such, it may have a great deal of utility for improving overall availability.

Note to those with high expectations: We must all learn to crawl before we walk. It is almost never prudent to impose full military-grade security on an existing control system overnight, no matter what fears the IT security people may have. It is dangerous, because there can be some side effects that may get in the way of critical or safety processes. Managers will encounter resistance if they push too hard. Following the inevitable accident, there will probably be testimony from license or certificate holders that these methods were not properly vetted before deployment.

To avoid this situation, ask, but do not push for better security. If there are significant objections or resistance from the people who hold licenses and certificates, particularly when the processes involve safety systems, take the time to discuss goals, methods, and timelines. These are the judgment calls we pay managers to make. It is imperative that all risks are laid on the table and discussed openly and honestly among all involved, and that the decision reasoning and outcomes are carefully documented for future reference.

The fourth reaction may be stated thus: "Well, if the Internet or remote access is bad, we'll stay away from it. Let's isolate, and all will be well." The problem with this attitude is that it will not stop malware on a flash drive or a contractor's laptop. It will not stop software logic bombs from those holding the control system hostage. More has to be done than simply isolating the networks. In any case, reporting requirements—although most are pretty minimal—are growing all the time. Engineers need to find ways to maintain some control even during periods of degraded security. This may include degraded performance strategies that do not rely on interconnections with other systems.

The fifth reaction may be stated as: "Where are the standards?" This is a good question, except that the standards are still very much a work in progress. We are going to have to forge ahead and help write better standards based on field experience. Right now, that field experience is mostly unreported or even hushed up. Many standards are underdeveloped because there is little experience to use to develop a sense of what good practice is.

It is difficult to gather field data on security systems, because there are sound reasons for not discussing incidents and accidents caused by this sort of thing. Until some sort of indemnity and limited liability is offered in return for making such reports, there is every reason to be concerned about potential lawsuits. There is a strong need for an anonymous reporting system so that everyone can learn from each other's mistakes. Defining and gathering this data is going to be one of the first tasks of the three-sided team of engineers, IT security, and operations.

Information technology perspectives and their reactions

On the other side, we have the offensive from an IT security researcher. Researchers often lack a familiarity with what they are attacking. Nevertheless, they are very good at it. Before getting started, IT security must be told, with strict authority, that the operators are ultimately responsible for everything that is officially in production. No potentially disruptive tests should be done without operations staff being aware of what is going on. There may be instances where life and limb are at stake. This is not just another office application. The product is real, and a backup cannot restore defective product.

The first reaction is: "You are relying on obscurity to protect this? There is no security through obscurity." This is true, mostly in very public arenas such as the Internet. However, in practice, there are thousands of points of data, with little understanding of the process at hand, and the automation systems that will protect key elements of the process. Real destruction (something that goes significantly beyond the nuisance level) will require subtlety. To get there, one will need specific knowledge of exquisite detail that very few besides another engineer would know. Turning things on and off rapidly may make a significant mess and trigger some downtime, but it usually does not cause a process to collapse catastrophically.

Security theory assumes information transfers without any sort of friction. That is not exactly true. While data can move that fast, the context and education to use that information do not convey so easily. The reality is that while obscurity is not security, it does represent a significant obstacle that may tip priorities from one aspect to another.

Thus, although an exposed HMI interface having an obscure backdoor password is a bad thing, a dial-up modem with access to a MODBUS interface with a remote terminal unit (RTU) may not be the worst thing in the world. The latter requires some understanding of what is present at the site to cause a problem. The former is much easier to abuse, because it includes metadata about what the site controls.

The second reaction is "What do you mean, I can't run a port scanner at full speed? An attacker would do that. This is really fragile stuff!" The answer is yes, this is all quite true, but there are some implicit assumptions here that they have not encountered before. This is where the concept of a real-time system and a near-real-time system needs to be explained.

Engineers know (or have some idea of) estimates of how much traffic should be on an industrial network. Process controllers are designed to go into a fault mode if they cannot see their remote input/output (I/O) within a very short period of time measured in tens of milliseconds. In an office, such delays might mean that a web page would take an extra few seconds to paint. Life goes on. For industrial controllers, however, this is cause for a fault condition. This is a design feature, not a failure.

The plant floor has advantages that offices do not have: First, it is possible to baseline the appropriate traffic levels and set alarms to show if there is too little or too much traffic to some surprisingly narrow margins. Second, the processes can be coordinated so that they do something sensible when too much traffic is encountered. This will require working in coordination with the engineers. When new systems are built, they will always be vulnerable to a denial of service attack, but with judicious network design and careful limits of scope, this should be an unlikely occurrence. Some designs have already planned for this problem because the engineers may know that network traffic capacity is tight.

It would be prudent to review this situation with the engineering staff to find out what is already in place and to integrate some form of operator alarms to handle this class of problem. New designs should have improved fallback control schemes to handle a saturated network on a programmable logic controller/distributed control system (PLC/DCS) or a supervisory control and data acquisition (SCADA) system. IT security will need to work with the engineering team to identify the risks and to help develop strategies to deal with this problem.

It may not be practical to remove denial of service attacks against control systems, but it is possible to detect the problem and limit the damage.

The third reaction is "Centralize all security into one great big glass room/box/ network switch for ease of monitoring." While it is indeed convenient to bring security together into one room, this is the sort of policy that works better in an office than on the plant floor. In an office, if the central security services are not available, nothing happens. The bureaucracy stops. This is not a good thing—there will certainly be a loss of money— but it is unlikely that someone will lose life or limb as a result.

However, if the security server denies access to a controller, if a single switch is misconfigured with everything, the process will continue to do something; perhaps that something will be very undesirable or even deadly, but it will continue with or without the control system. Inertial energy, chemical energy, thermal energy, and so forth do not magically disperse when the control system fails. The security systems need to be as resilient as the rest of the control system process. The IT security people will need to find ways to distribute security in a safe and resilient manner.

Managers need to make it abundantly clear that engineers work very hard to avoid single points of failure. After all that careful investment, there is not going to be one great big central thing that can fail at once and bring the whole operation to its knees. This is particularly true for license and key servers. The security systems will need to be distributed throughout the plant or SCADA system.

The fourth reaction is "We must push patches; there is no time to review anything." Once again, not so fast. Engineers, contractors, and senior operators tested things very carefully before turning them over to an end user; pushing a patch is indeed a very dangerous thing to do. Processes are typically broken up into parallel pieces. If possible, a patch will be deployed to a parallel segment of a process to evaluate it for stability, performance, and interoperability. If parallel segments are not available, then one of two common operations are possible: First, keep extra operators on-site to run things manually in case the update goes horribly wrong, or wait until a parallel segment is available, or until conditions are light enough that the infrastructure can afford to take a chance in case things go very badly.

Such conflagrations do not happen very often, but when they do, things can get ugly very quickly. Make sure the IT security people know that they are going to be given training so that they can help out with this effort and lend a helping hand in case a process goes awry. Note to managers: Care and ownership of one's actions is improved a great deal when staff has to not only admit to their misdeeds but also clean them up as well. The cost of training them with all the safety and process narratives will be greatly repaid in job performance.

The issue can be summarized by saying that patches should be pulled (by an operator and possibly others), not pushed, through the automation networks. This issue will become less of a problem as the development cycle for control systems focuses toward a more continuous, less disruptive, less project-oriented management.

That said, a policy where operations and engineering do not patch at all is unacceptable. Patching will improve the performance and life cycle of all parts of the control system. Evaluation of each patch release is something that everyone should be part of.

The fifth reaction is "Use strong passwords and authenticate everything." Few will argue with the authentication aspect, but strong passwords are often forgotten under stress. Use other methods for identity validation: biometrics or card/radio frequency identification (RFID) access (something you have/something you are [made of]). Passwords, if used, must remain very simple and easy to remember under stress. This limits their utility for obvious reasons. Locking people out in high-stress situations is a recipe for disaster, and besides, it is a security risk all by itself.

The sixth reaction is "The protocol is insecure by design." You can start and stop a controller with just one packet! We have got to fix this stuff! The answer is that protocols such as MODBUS, DF1, Profinet, or Common Industrial Protocol (CIP) were never designed to be exposed to untrusted or public networks. This is where we will need the expertise of the IT security specialists to help document the network topology, and set up virtual private networks (VPNs) where there is no other way to get the data from one place to another and back.

Eventually, some day, standards committees may include authentication in these protocols, but few are there now, and it takes time to do this correctly. The author knows this firsthand, from having seen the deliberations over the years that it took to develop a secure authentication feature set for the DNP3 (IEEE-1815).

The old joke about the civil engineer and the soldier rings true here: Engineers are paid to build things; soldiers are paid to destroy them. Similarly, engineers are paid to make things work; IT security researchers are paid to break things. Teaching them to chase a single goal with the same equipment is not easy. It is imperative that everyone focuses on the goal of making the system work more reliably. The security researchers need to recognize that their part of the equation is simply part of the whole control systems endeavor: making things more durable and reliable so that the system works better under adverse conditions. Engineers need to realize that the IT security researchers are not the enemy. By focusing everyone on the ultimate goal of better resiliency and reliability, we all win.

Finally, when these two groups understand each other, they will need to promulgate some actual user interfaces that the operations people can act on.

Operations perspectives and their reactions

Operators seek consistency. Usually, they do not like changing how things are done. With change, there will be complaints.

The first reaction from operations is that they probably had some very nice remote access in the past. Why should they not have access to their plant from the World Wide Web? It will be up to IT security, engineering, and management to decide how to make this work securely. One point worth making is that even if everything works in a perfectly secure manner (unlikely, but consider this for the sake of argument), we still do not know if the system is being accessed by the employee or perhaps a vindictive child or spouse, that the employee is not drunk or high, or that someone is not holding a family member hostage to force the issue.

When people have to be on-site to issue controls, one can use physical security to augment the other security features. Remote access defeats that layer of security. The operations staff needs to understand that something is needed to replace that implicit layer of security.

The second reaction is "What does this mean? What do we do when this stuff barks at us?" The immediate need is to explain that if you get alarm X from system Y, you call person Z and say the following things to them. This is, basically, how to call for help. However, underneath it all, this is a very important concern. The alarms and the systems designed by engineers and augmented by IT security will not be used by either of them. Real security begins on the front lines with the foot soldiers: operations. It is imperative that they understand what the new security features are, why they are needed, and what they can do for them. There is useful diagnostic and alert information embedded in those alarms that can improve recovery time from a bad situation.

Furthermore, this can be used to track when employees or contractors are jacked into the network. If the operations people were not notified, they have grounds for taking action against those who are not coordinating with them.

The third reaction is "What is this Big Brother stuff? I don't want my name on this stuff!" This comes out of an abundant distrust of the automation systems. Some of these very concerns were expressed when flight data recorders were first introduced to the airline industry.

The first issue is how the data will be used. Managers will need to be ready with policies that the operations staff will find reasonable. Nobody wants to be rated by the machines they work on. A reasonable compromise would be to use the data to improve training, for forensic purposes after an incident, and for preventing unauthorized intrusions.

An interesting side issue may arise when using biometrics such as fingerprint readers. This is where the IT security staff should explain the basics of what a hash function is, and how passwords and other access information are hashed before it is stored in the computer. This way, even if the hashed information is revealed, no one is likely to reconstruct the original fingerprint, retinal scan, or whatever token was used to access the data.

The second issue is one of job performance. It would be a mistake to think that a control system could tell you who is good at doing what. That is like having the autopilot rate the pilot. Management can use these systems to figure out who has done what, but they should not use it in any way for performance reviews. This point needs to be brought home to the operations staff.

The fourth reaction is "Why should we care how well this stuff works? If it breaks, we'll run things manually." The problem here is that, like modern airliners, the performance requirements are such that running things by hand for extended periods of time is no longer particularly safe or practical. Does anyone have an attention span good enough to keep a large furnace running properly by continually monitoring and adjusting the heat output, the air intake, and the fuel intake? We use automation because it is not financially feasible to staff places with lots of people to run things manually hour after hour, day after day.

Ultimately, as we become more reliant on the control system, we need to know how well the control system is doing its job. We need to know how healthy it is. And, if something is amiss, if a baseline of performance has changed, operators (and the IT security and the engineering staff) need to know. In other words, we need the operators to evaluate the control system continuously.

The fifth reaction is "What do you mean, we need to keep track of the contractors?" If they're incompetent we dismiss them! This flies in the face of reality. Contractors, or even company visitors, can leave all sorts of malware or back doors behind without even realizing they have done it. The people most likely to stumble across such anomalies are the operators themselves. IT security and engineering staff need to give the operators tools to track and hold staff accountable for what is left behind because they are the ones who will need to know what happened, and who to call to fix things.

The sixth reaction is one of resigned defiance: "Do what you must, but keep it out of our way, and don't get in the way of profitability." This is the most important point of all. This is often lost on everyone but the operators; the reason control systems exist is to improve quality, capacity, reliability, and availability. Whatever it does, a security system should not get in the way of these goals.

In other words, while security is important, it is no less important than the reliable and safe production of an inexpensive product on time. The purpose of security is to ensure that this can continue. As such, one point to make is that security systems can improve awareness of what is going on with the plant and its control system.

This is a primary selling point for SCADA and control systems' security features: self-integrity monitoring. The more we know about how well the control system is working, the better our processes can be controlled, and the more reliable our operation will be.

But, beyond that, there are some common issues of how to achieve that goal.

Penetration testing

If you do not attempt to penetrate the defenses, you will simply have to take the attestations of others that it will perform adequately when the time comes. Manufacturers can claim all sorts of things, but only by actually hiring someone to penetrate a system or product can you actually know where software flaws and other issues may be a problem.

That said, many IT security people prefer to perform penetration testing against real live systems, on the theory that this is the best way to find out at full scale whether the security system performs as designed. This can work in an office, where data can be backed up or restored in a jiffy. However, in a control system, there will be real product on the floor with real consequences. The machines may really come apart from a successful attack. Nobody really wants this to happen.

Just as we take samples of concrete and test them for strength during construction, we can test the individual pieces of a control system in a lab. Not surprisingly, many larger companies have such test labs, if for no other reason than to test integration of newer products on older systems. These labs could pull spares from stock and test them with the original running firmware against various security attacks.

Penetration testing can be a frightening, eye-opening experience. The author has personally observed a test where a safety integrity level (SIL) rated controller was attacked and frozen in its current state with a primitive local area network denial (LAND)* attack. Although a private security researcher may not get much traction with an original equipment manufacturer (OEM), the customers of that OEM usually do. The alliance between

---

* A LAND attack is best described as a denial of service. The attack consists of a TCP/IP packet with both the source and destination addresses of an SYN packet set to the victim's address. Unless the victim's software is able to recognize this attack, it will reply to itself endlessly. It was first reported on November 20, 1997.

customer and security researcher is thin at the moment, but it has every reason to grow and prosper in much the same way that insurance companies evaluate how crashworthy a vehicle is by actually purchasing one and destroying it.

Penetration testing also depends on how well chosen the access methods are and how easily they can be cracked. In the case of a certificate authority (CA) server, it has to be properly configured with up-to-date software that cannot be easily corrupted. As long as there is a backup CA server, it should prove fruitful to attack one to see what expectations an end user can have of it.

An alternative to attacking live equipment is to try out an attack on a virtualized platform of some sort. This is a brand-new approach that has not received much attention until now, because of issues regarding time of day accuracy in the guest operating system. However, even if the original software is working on real hardware platforms, one can still test the entire system on a virtualized platform in a private LAN.

These results should be shared with care. Above all, they need to be reported to a computer emergency response team (CERT)* agency and kept confidential, not only for the duration it takes to effect a patch but also for a certain time thereafter, to give the end-user community time to patch the most critical parts of their systems.

Network mapping and scanning

In and of itself, tools such as NMAP,† used for scanning and discovering network nodes and open ports, are not bad. However, the commonplace defaults for such tools are toxic for a control system or SCADA network. It is not uncommon for older equipment to be running with 10 Mbit half-duplexed hardware, and for that equipment to seize up in the presence of more than 3 Mbps of traffic. Recall that in the earlier days of networking, it was more commonplace to use a hub instead of a switch and that, because collisions were repeated to all ports on the hub, it was expected that networks would be incapable of more traffic than 30% of 10 Mbps or 3 Mbps.

Thus, when these devices were exposed to full duplex switches that could spew a sustained 10 Mbps of traffic, the equipment would often go catatonic or worse, even over-writing parts of their flash memory. There are documented cases where a nuclear power plant (Browns Ferry Unit 3) had to SCRAM‡ the reactor because they lost control of the cooling water pumps. The problem was believed to be someone accidentally inserting the wrong cable in a switch. This caused a significant broadcast storm to be propagated toward both 10 Mbps interfaces that happened to be the motor controls for the cooling water pumps.

---

* CERT agencies may go by different names in different countries, but the ultimate purpose is pretty universal: They are agencies that track computer problems and assist with negotiating a well-known outcome with the manufacturer. At some point, they will publish the links to the fix. This is very helpful to those with software and firmware from many vendors who seek one source for easy resolution and tracking of outstanding problems. Typically, CERT agencies are supposed to share information with each other, although some may have an easier time dealing with their domestic software firms than others.

† The NMAP tool is a program designed to scan a series of IP addresses or port numbers to see what responds. This tool is very useful to confirm that only the appropriate services at a network address are online or that no extraneous services are enabled. It is also useful for discovering hidden or forgotten addresses on a network.

‡ The acronym SCRAM has traditionally been used to refer to an immediate, emergency shutdown of a nuclear reactor. Though it is unknown what the acronym actually means, it has been used to describe a sudden and abrupt halt or shutdown of any given critical operation, and not necessarily associative with nuclear power generation.

The astute reader may be wondering why this older equipment has not been updated yet. The problem is that it is often embedded in large, expensive, and critical pieces of equipment. One does not just replace the interface of such equipment without a significant engineering and recertification effort. The network interface may have been state of the art when it was designed. Unfortunately, such equipment is purchased and financed with the expectation that it will last for 20 years or more.

A careful scan of the network (eliminating port scans in sensitive areas) would be educational. Also note that default speeds for port scanning are set with typical office computing platforms in mind. Usually, there are software switches that can slow down the scan to something that can reasonably coexist with the rest of the control system. The IT security and engineering staff will have to establish guidelines for where, when, and how often such scans should be done.

Nevertheless, these scans are invaluable. Often, old network equipment thought to be removed is still online. Scanning will find it. Sometimes one can find network ports open to control equipment that nobody has documented. This is where it is wise to scan a few spares and then make some inquiries to the OEM.

The more manufacturers that hear this sort of thing, the less likely they will be to think that they can "hide" a back door in a product simply by not documenting a port number.

Some features include web servers that were either not turned off or were poorly documented in the first place. It is not uncommon for plants to receive entire skids of equipment containing an embedded PLC with metered pumps. The PLC's primary interface may be known, but there may be others that are not. Those interfaces can be used for attack.

Traffic monitoring

It is common practice in the office world to use smart switches that can be queried to obtain statistics on how much traffic is coming from what port and can segment traffic in two groups of virtual LANs (VLANs) so that broadcast traffic does not go everywhere. It has done wonders for office computing performance and it can do the same for a working control system. However, there are some features that should be used with care.

First, because this is a switch, not a hub, one does not hear all the traffic all the time. One only hears traffic addressed to that specific port. A broadcast or multicast packet or an address with the Internet protocol (IP) address of something on that port is the only traffic to be expected.

It is commonplace for security staff to monitor traffic from various ports and VLANs. However, one must ensure that the switch backplane speeds and port speeds are up to the task. In an office, one would not usually notice a slightly slower web browser or a slower database response caused by network congestion, but on a busy control system, it would be noticed.

Second, while intrusion detection tools for Nessus and other open-source packages are available, they still are not as familiar with commonplace industrial protocols. Furthermore, not everything runs on Ethernet media. There are still RS-485 serial networks, long-distance twinaxial networks, and many more unique interfaces, such as HART.* It is important that such networks be identified, documented, and reviewed regularly, because the intrusion detection tools are simply not available for these interfaces.

* For information on the HART protocol, see http://www.hartcomm.org.

Who are the threats?

Most security people like to discuss the infamous man-in-the-middle (MITM) attacks because they are impersonal, or an evil hacker lurking in a basement somewhere. This is an easy sell because we have all imagined sociopaths like this before. And, although they do exist, they are comparatively rare.

A variant of this popular theme are the nation-state actors. The infamous Stuxnet malware was probably developed by a nation-state with resources. The only thing worth mentioning about nation-state threats is that if the control system is too difficult to act on, there are usually other methods. Someone with a decent hunting rifle could do significant damage to a substation before anyone could respond. The old joke about running from a bear applies; you do not need to run faster than the bear, you only need to run faster than your fellow campers. Likewise, if physical security and background checks of contractors and personnel are not maintained, having super-high-security cyberassets are not going to make much difference. In other words, to defend against nation-state actors, you need all security to be up to that level, not just the "cyber" part.

This brings us to the most common and the most insidious actors: insiders. There is a saying in the business—the most dangerous people on an industrial site are usually standing right next to you every day. While we commonly invoke an "evil" third party as the rationale for installing security, the most numerous and dangerous threats are actually the employees themselves.

Imagine a contentious situation regarding a union, and negotiations are not going well. Would it be outrageous for someone to have an "accident" which would cause significant damage and financially force the issue with the company executives? How would you stop a situation like this?

Imagine a contractor who thinks he was cheated on his last job with this customer. He installs a logic bomb in the controller code he wrote. How would you stop a situation like this?

Imagine a sociopath with a need to prove himself. He sets up a dangerous situation and then shows everyone how he "saved the day"—only, it does not go so well.

The reason why employees and contractors are so dangerous is because they know the process intimately and think they can weasel their way around the process. A hacker living in his parents' basement might not know what to do with an old dial-in modem used for a MODBUS connection to a PLC in the field. But these people just might.

It is imperative that someone develop extensive code review and storage systems for the PLC equipment in every control system. It is also useful that there be more than one system available to download and upload code from a controller. The reason for this became apparent with the infamous Stuxnet malware attack. The application environment was attacked in such a way that it would silently insert extra code into a controller. Since that code was both downloaded and uploaded from the same development work stations, nobody would have a chance to notice the extra software this malware inserted. Source code control systems (SCCSs) can mitigate this problem.

Engineers, particularly those who integrate embedded devices for control systems, like to think in terms of a project-oriented approach. They tend not to think of the whole life cycle of the software. The long-term value of an SCCS for configuration data is often lost on them. The IT departments, on the other hand, tend to get very bureaucratic with the SCCS and its features, requiring extensive training and complex models to manage software versions.

Somewhere between these two extremes is a happy medium. Someone who inserts a logic bomb in an embedded device can be discovered through review of the SCCS. Patches can be reviewed very easily with the aid of an SCCS to show all of the configurations that a patch is likely to face in the field. The ultimate goal for an SCCS is to have a clear, unambiguous record of what is supposed to be in the control system embedded devices.

Summary

Control systems security is not simple, nor is it easy. This chapter represents distilled experience of having dealt with the mindsets that various professions bring to the fore. Many behaviors are defensive and bureaucratic. We cannot afford knee-jerk reactions to these perceived threats. Management planning is key to bringing these professions together in a productive manner. Those who throw people into a meeting room with no guidance have no reason to expect good outcomes any time soon.

chapter three

Threat vectors

Jim Butterworth

Contents

Cyberspace operations

Cyberspace consists of many different nodes and networks. Although not all nodes and networks are globally connected or accessible, cyberspace itself continues to become increasingly interconnected and warehoused in the cloud. Computer networks make possible geographic travel, although electronically, at the speed of light, able to circle the globe in milliseconds.

We can isolate our networks using protocols, firewalls, encryption, and physical air gaps between network segments; however, the very purpose of the network is to interconnect; to accomplish efficiency, data sharing, and collaboration. Therein lies the challenge for a mature nation as they plan for sustainability to operate among the threat actors, fight through probes, reconnaissance, and successful incursions into their computer networks, computers, and data stores.

This chapter serves as a primer for building and maintaining a robust cyber operations capability that meets the growing threat to national networks, critical infrastructure, and a nation's most precious commodity … the information necessary for e-commerce, public service, finance, and defense. There is not a single industry that is not touched by cyberspace; therefore, it is incumbent on the stewards entrusted to protect it with vigilance, speed, and decisiveness.

Scoping threat vectors

The employment of cyber capabilities serves to enable, protect, and ensure continued operations in and through cyberspace. Such operations include computer network operations and activities to operate and defend a nation's interests globally. The types of people, process, and technology employed to attain these operations change at an alarming pace, as is required to remain in cadence with the myriad of threat actors placing you directly in their crosshairs.

The traditional military industrial complex philosophy of leveling the playing field does not apply in cyberspace, where but a few talented and determined foes can penetrate and wreak havoc on a company, a critical system, an intelligence agency, or even a government itself. Recent news stories highlight the anonymity that these threat actors can use to attain their goals, making the task of defending exponentially more difficult to achieve.

Globalization of the battlefield

IPv6 was driven out of necessity as the world simply ran out of addressable space. As global presence grew and nations moved their information online, seeing the benefit of an interconnected world, Internet assigned numbers authority (IANA) was forced to look into the sunset of IPv4 and devise a means to usher in a seamless means to remain connected.

Legacy network protocols, operating systems, applications, and equipment will remain connected, which is unavoidable. These older devices are reliant upon IPv4 to communicate, and are most likely incompatible with the IPv6 standard. While IPv6 has been available for several years, it has not gained wide acceptance by the networking community. A global consortium* recently announced their goal to accelerate the deployment of IPv6 at the Internet level by having several thousand Internet Service Providers, edge device manufacturers, and application developers to make IPv6 the default protocol, instead of relying on IPv4 as the default protocol.

The primary benefit to an IPv6 standard is the increased address space. Initial reports that IPv6 would usher in tighter security controls have proven false, with many reviewers reaching the conclusion that IPv4 with IPsec configured could be just as secure as the IPsec configuration within IPv6. Additionally, IPv6 traffic could be tunneled through an IPv4 message header, further solidifying IPv4's continued reliance.

If IPv6 eventually makes its way onto the world stage as the default protocol, legacy devices and applications will require modified sockets in order to communicate. If the operating system manufacturers have publicly stopped supporting aging operating systems, who then will be tasked with modifying the underlying network layer to ensure

---

* "Internet Society" and their test day entitled "World IPv6 Launch," which was initiated on June 6, 2012. Refer to http://en.wikipedia.org/wiki/World_IPv6_Day_and_World_IPv6_Launch_Day and http://www.internetsociety.org/ipv6/archive-2011-world-ipv6-day.

operability with IPv6, and who will conduct the code review to ensure there are no gaping holes or potential flaws that could grant unauthorized access?

Critical infrastructure protection and threat vectors

The lion's share of legacy networks exists in the industrial control systems (ICS) industry, largely due to the continued reliability and safety of these systems. The unintended consequence lies on our inability to patch, update, or conduct a technology refresh without the cooperation of vendors, service providers, and governmental agencies to ensure adequate funding exists, regulations and standards are put in place and enforced. Of paramount importance is that any infrastructure upgrades must be designed with security intrinsically baked into the ICS of tomorrow. In the United States, the Federal Energy Regulatory Commission (FERC) and North American Electric Reliability Corporation (NERC) have recently updated their CIP guidelines. In June 2011, the National Institute of Standards and Technology released Special Publication 800-82, Guide to Industrial Control Systems (ICS) Security. This is an example of where regulations and compliance are leading the development of advanced supervisory control and data acquisition (SCADA)/ICS technologies, such as Smart Grid.

Considerations must be made to not only design secure systems (programmable logic controllers, remote telemetry units, intelligent electronic devices) but also ensure the point-to-point communications protocols between them are not left to "off the shelf" distributions of Bluetooth, 802.x, infrared, or other network layer protocols. A determined foe will exhaust every possible avenue to gain entry, looking for devices that have embedded wireless wide area network (WWAN) antennas and processors, bridging wireless protocols with an external device designed to negotiate and proxy communications between these mediums, checking online repositories of exposed devices, the list of potential access points extends far beyond what is traditionally viewed as such. With just a bit of research and creativity an attacker can, with relatively low-tech and affordable modifications, decide to survey and lie in wait for the opportune moment to seize access to a system they can use as their base of operations against you. Cyberattack is designed to be clandestine and stealthy, and rest assured that future threats will rely upon bleeding edge exploit development, requiring defensive measures on par with the "art of the possible" to an attack enabler. A shining example of this are Stuxnet and Flame, both having been in clandestine operation for years without detection. Although the underlying payloads were designed for different purposes, Stuxnet, designed to induce uncontrollable failure in nuclear enrichment centrifuges, and Flame, designed to collect intelligence that would enable future operations. Presuming both of these payloads have been in operation for several years, it should make the reader curious about what undetected payload is currently operational and what its intended purpose is.

Computer network operations

How does a nation build and retain a talented and mature cyber workforce? It is this author's opinion that successful cyber operations are 65% human skill, operating 35% advanced technology solutions. Overreliance on automated detection, executive dashboards, and solutions that are only as efficient as yesterday's threat will certainly ensure continued vulnerability to the threat of tomorrow. Terms such as "advanced persistent threat" are good for categorizing a determined foe and make for good PowerPoint slides.

It misrepresents, however, the nature of the problem. Malicious code is a vehicle used to carry out computer network operations and is always designed by a human.

Automation in information processing enables vast amounts of computer instructions to be computed, culled, analyzed, and reported. The process, however, is wholly reliant on human interaction in order to program the algorithms that the process will use. This is an important consideration in that in all computing operations it takes human ingenuity to enable it. In computer network operations, it takes human skill to attack, exploit, and defend. Human knowledge that is aligned to a specific goal in mind, whether originating from nation-state efforts, privatized cyberterrorist groups, or random hobbyists using your network as their proving grounds. The end result is the same; unwelcome access, influence, and the ability to potentially cripple operations.

Computer network operations: Defend

Defense is more than collecting and aggregating the infinite alerts and events that automated sensors generate. Proper defense is not about keeping the adversary out; rather, it is about being able to successfully sustain critical operational functions while running in a degraded status. Stoic watch floors full of monitors and dashboards, "alive" and displaying the health of a network make for fantastic visions of advanced operations yet can convey a false sense of security. Their implementation oftentimes falls short of being able to detect, dynamically adjust, and provide real-time access to the information and access necessary to fend off or fight through an ongoing attack. Look for vendors and providers that are willing to open application programming interfaces (APIs) to share information and alerts in near real time, so that your frontline defenders can close the time gap from detection to subsequent action.

Computer network operations: Exploit

The art of digital exploitation can take either passive or active forms. Human involvement in cyberspace will leave traces. Despite the growing use of applications designed to provide anonymity such as virtual private server (VPS) networks, proxy servers, and bulletproof noncompliant servers located around the globe, they introduce a diplomatic and legal challenge the likes that will not be addressed or solved any time soon. National legislation takes years to adopt, and international treaties take decades to reach, leaving the defense of cyberspace to the owners of the systems and network themselves, employing the knowledge and expertise resident within their own teams.

The exploit operations gained from exhaustive and thorough digital analysis of discovered malware, internal characteristics of code structures, behavioral analysis, and the digital footprints in the sand left on an exploited host pay tremendous dividends in getting you closer to solving the person behind the keyboard problem. Who is your attacker? What is their motive? What is their technological capability? Can you maneuver within their attack cycle to mitigate the impact and sustain operations? Is the attacker using deceptive techniques themselves, such as planting flags, to throw you off in another direction? Cyberwarfare is similar to asymmetric warfare where a force of unequal size and firepower can successfully engage in conflict with a superior force. A control system engineer's responsibility is the daily care and feeding of the process under their charge, not to conduct cyber or asymmetric warfare with an intruder. Furthermore, engaging in tactics to disrupt the adversary on anything except an owner's systems could be construed as offensive in nature and subject the defender to legal action. Asymmetric warfare calls for an equal application of unconventional measures to equalize and tip the scales in your favor, if not tip completely knock the scale off the hinges. The defender's inability to take decisive measures gives the edge to the attacker. If analysis revealed the public location of the attacker's pass through server, it is highly probable that the server is the property of an unwitting party and any attempt to access would be unlawful. The attacker is keenly aware of the legal framework and privacy laws in the United States and routinely operates both domestic and international points of presence in order to exacerbate and cross the jurisdictions of investigating agencies.

To successfully defend, you must learn as much as possible about your primary adversary and threat against your interests. Simply penetration testing public-facing sites to find potential entry points does not yield enough information about your adversary's weaknesses. You must employ human skill and expertise; dare I say the "art of human hacking?" Behind every virus, Trojan, worm, remote access Trojan (RAT), botnet, dropper, or exploit payload is the person who built it. They are responsible, and the human psyche is far easier to exploit and manipulate than thousands of lines of evanescent code in memory, designed to operate from a segment of memory that is configured at runtime as a temporary clipboard that will never cache its contents to disk. The growing talent of open-source intelligence collection yields a tremendous amount of valuable information; however, there is no business argument that makes a person of this skillset valuable, save the information they can provide to security teams.

Computer network operations: Attack

The single-most important element of these operations is nonattribution. As outlined in the earlier section, even your "developers" may tend to reuse structures and routines in their custom efforts. All too often, these highly specialized groups of experts live within a black world, keeping their operations tightly locked down in the interest of nonattribution. To introduce a paradigm shift from this approach, imagine if skilled exploit/defense analysts were able to "have a go" at the result of a payload. This is similar to war-gaming exercises, where military forces play out their continuity of operations plans and adapt according to the environment, and unforeseen circumstances. It affords them an opportunity to hone their craft before they need to use it. Code reuse in malware is common due to its modular construction and reliance upon the x86 architecture. Application exploit development is reliant upon specific memory offsets of an application given a specific patch level. Once an application is patched, the memory allocation of the vulnerable point may change, rendering the exploit inoperative. This is not the same as the payload that is delivered and installed following a successful exploit. The exploit is designed to enable access, while the payload is designed to retain access. What the analyst would expect to see will differ depending on what class of malware it is. Getting back to the human in the loop, the malware coders are not waking up every day designing new innovative ways to exploit the x86 architecture. Once an operational payload is designed, they will continue to repurpose to functional blocks within other payloads. Collecting digital intelligence on the code assembly and structures can reveal patterns that can be used to identify and correlate other processes with these functions built in.

Digital intelligence

Digital information takes many forms, depending on their medium and placement within the OSI model. This could vary widely from standard radio frequency transmissions used in computing like Bluetooth/Wi-Fi, it could be the cellular networks we are continuing to increase our bandwidth and hence computing mobility atop. To be proficient at analyzing the many artifacts that fit the category of digital intelligence, an analyst must be adept at Unicode, Code Pages of many languages, file compression techniques, encryption schemes, hexadecimal encoding, byte offsets, file signatures, code bit shifting, identify the list of file formats, file and byte offset math, communication and messaging encapsulation protocols, keying and encryption algorithms, and many more—the requirements are staggering.

Types of sources of digital intelligence

We deal in both static and dynamic computing environments, composed of petabytes of stored files from standard computing assets and users, all the while expecting to be able to detect and handle any alert that triggers a threshold. Different uses and gems are derived from the many differing types of data. Are you dealing with memory resident malware that is designed to never write to disk? To ensure evanescent memory code is properly preserved, the responder needs to ensure that their memory-imaging tool is able to preserve the entire memory space, including the kernel-protected area. Failure to do so will result in smear, where recompiling memory introduces ghosts where instructions pointing to specific memory locations no longer exist, rather have been allocated and are in use by another process. Once the plug is pulled, the traces of the code disappear when the 5Vdc is removed from the memory chips.

Methods and procedures

How you gain access to intelligence is as varied as the types of digital intelligence that exist and equal in scope to the medium being chosen. RF exploitation requires advanced receiver technology. To secure digital communications at all points between transmission and reception, system designers will use techniques such as spread spectrum, encryption standards that use a combination of key-based or time-based authentication, compression or obfuscation of the data stream, and even point-to-point tunnels that use a master certificate authority to remain in sync. In the case of malicious code, in an effort to thwart reverse engineering of their code, authors will use packing schemes that obfuscate the contents of their code at rest. Oftentimes, these packers use a salt or some other form of bit shifting in order to scramble the data stream. Decryption of proprietary packers and encryption algorithms requires hefty computing resources, best adopted in a parallel computing structure for expedient results. As stated earlier, if a malware specimen is going to execute its payload, it will have to unpack itself into normal programming language. This is the point where the code is at its most vulnerable. Many analysts rely upon static code review of a binary or executable exported off of a system. The most accurate and telling time to analyze, however, is on the infected machine, as the payload is already resident.

We tend to traditionally view collection of digital intelligence as a row of lab computers, connected to source and destination hard drives, imaging the cell phones, video cameras, removable drives, CD/DVDs, hard disks, etc., that are all part of an intelligence effort. This will never be replaced, and analytic process advancements are being developed and fielded by vendors to assist the investigators in ascertaining the raw intelligence in a smooth process, in a fraction of the time. Using multiprocessors and multithreading of computing resources makes this possible.

Methods and procedures: Collection

When you do undergo collection operations, ensure that your process is commensurate your end goal. Clandestine or black bag collections require far more consideration than fear of being detected by your target. Oftentimes there are electronic, physical, and human interaction aspects to these types of operations. "Smash and grabs," concealed as a traditional crime of thievery, gains you the hard evidence. Passive taps, snarfing the airwaves, there are many creative and successful methods to collect intelligence. I would submit that the easiest method is directed against the human target, which as our own analysis of internal intrusions would prove time and again. The weak link and primary target in cyberattacks continues to be the end user. This is largely a result of the success the attacks have had when the end user is targeted as the attack vector. Exploits still require that they are executed in order to run, and one very effective method to accomplish this is to deceive a human operator.

Methods and procedures: Open source

Astroturfing is a phenomenon that has grown tremendously in the past few years. With the rise of WikiLeaks and groups such as Anonymous, LulzSec, and other organized #AntiSec movements, it is more important than ever to monitor these groups and be able to identify Astroturfing when it happens. This allows your organization to get ahead of the curve, plan your message accordingly, and handle any blow back from disinformation campaigns.

Methods and procedures: Deception

Pirate Pad, TOR, VPS, Proxy, Trac phones (amateur) ham radio, and personal management all have an inherent flaw. On the Internet, as much as they would like us all to believe, there is no such thing as true anonymity. A packet is structured and delivered, a fake e-mail account used to deliver a single message, has an originating IP that was used to sign up. It is a matter of putting talented open-source analysts at work, collecting as much information as they can about your threat. You're on their watch list, why shouldn't they be on yours?

Honeypot and honeynet technologies have their place in a defense-in-depth architecture. It is far easier to catch a bee with honey than it is with vinegar. In order for them to give the appearance that there is an entire infrastructure behind them, these technologies tend to rely upon virtualization, and modern malware is designed to recognize virtualization and either self-destruct, or will have built-in routines designed, upon detection, to invoke a harmless behavioral signature that will leave the sensors to weigh it as a benign low-level threat.

Computer incident response teams

Intrusions, sabotage, data theft, information exposure, and code manipulation will continue to occur in cyberspace. The geographically separated, yet electronically connected, world of cyberspace makes responding to these incidents, a sometimes-difficult task to achieve. Speed, mobility, and global omnipresence on our own heterogeneous networks require that we establish and maintain an infinite digital reach into our assets.

Field operations

There are times when response teams must deploy on-site, due to either an air-gapped network or as protective measures, such as creating isolated virtual local area networks (VLANs), are put in place to ensure the safety and operability of the rest of the infrastructure. Data on a network, unless specifically logged, do not remain for after action analysis. Data in memory are most certainly volatile, and as time passes the likelihood and possibility of operating system overwrites, fragmentation, or other computing actions introduces risk into the preservation process.

Development of flyaway kits, rapid response teams, forward operating or staging locations of equipment, or placing into the network/system administrators hands the tools, capability, and knowledge to preserve information rapidly, prior to taking protective and defensive measures. This statement presumes the incident will not cause further harm to personnel, endanger lives, or amount to a mission kill if you have to temporarily isolate or take down a system.

Understanding that TCP/IP is a connection-oriented protocol, once a computer network connection is terminated, or isolated from communicating, the connection will be torn down as a part of the protocol. This means that a response team may lose the ability to collect the volatile information on process connections, who and what is connecting inbound/outbound, and other information relating to an ongoing attack. In a control system environment, where there are as many measurement and test mnemonics as there are true control signals, the loss of any signal may cause a sensor placed as an interlock to invoke a safety circuit that prevents overload. Interfering with status signals can be as effective as interfering with the actual control signals themselves.

There has been decades of exposure within the IT industry to computer forensics and the necessity to preserve data using industry-accepted methods. Preservation is very critical for field operations, as it will take time for rapid response teams to deploy and arrive on-site.

Remote operations

Technology has also advanced to the point where it is completely feasible to conduct an entire investigation remotely. Software exists today that allows forensically sterile reach into your end points; to preserve and analyze data far faster than a response team can physically deploy on-site.

There is also a benefit to having these sensors and capabilities pre-deployed, in that your ability to seize on a critical alert, event, or other anomalous behavior can immediately be re-acted upon, thereby lowering your overall risk. Our assets will always be vulnerable. Determining the patch status of the operating systems across your enterprise is a necessary process in determining your vulnerability to the threats that are known today. It is called a zero day for a reason, and some of the nastiest exploits are yet to be discovered and are currently installed on many networks, around the globe, without regard for any specific industry.

Support to response teams

Incident response teams will need back-end support, either through passing back malware to specialized labs and expertise to conduct reverse engineering on a piece of suspiciously behaving process or driver, or providing remote access to the repository of evidence being collected so that remote examiners or analysts can begin to operate in parallel, using distributed processing technology to cull through and extract the necessary information to respond to the threat.

Support efforts can best be thought and planned for as master-, journeyman-, and apprentice-level skillsets. Some of the more advanced cyber-elite skills require a few master-level experts. Incident response requires a journeyman who has a breadth and depth of knowledge of computer network topology, ports, and protocols, and a varied exposure to operating systems from a forensic perspective. Finally, apprentice-level skills could be considered as imaging teams, evidence custodians, incident yeoman, and analysts using automated processes and procedures to extract actionable intelligence and data from evidence repositories.

Malware and emerging threat actors

Recent highly publicized events have run the gamut from highly developed and sophisticated attacks to exploitation of embarrassingly basic lack of patching to attain breach success. Attack vectors range from application exploits, the tried and still true structured query language (SQL) injection, introducing logic flaws during code execution, bypassing internal authorization mechanisms, escalating privileges, or exploiting the end user to allow the attack to begin from within the house instead of going through the front door.

Malware: Delivery

All too often an incident responder will uncover during an investigation a rogue file or e-mail attachment. This is typically something a very adept journeyman can identify and recognize as a threat. However, what is oftentimes the case is that they have stumbled upon the delivery mechanism, or "the dropper," which is designed as a single-use bullet to make an outbound connection to a transient location somewhere on the Internet, controlled by your attacker. Upon successful exploit, the victim system/user's computer will make an outbound connection, shimmed either via DynDNS, DNS2TCP, or straight out SSL or HTTP, to download the actual payload necessary for the attacker to begin their operations.

Dropper analysis will usually yield where, by IP or URL, the payload was retrieved from, but a swift adversary will have ensured their own anonymity and survivability by using an unwitting public-facing exploited server as a temporary base of operations. They have thousands of exploited computers at the ready, enabling them to quickly shift the landscape and render your investigative efforts dead in the water. Once the delivery of the payload is successful, they will oftentimes discontinue the use of that exploited server, hedging their bets that your investigative team will be unable to gain access to it in order to conduct analysis. Both law enforcement and legal involvement take time, and it gives the attacker ample opportunity to change their modus operandi, erase their tracks, and carry on with the next phase … launching the payload and establishing a foothold in your network.

Delivery can be accomplished by a variety of means, many of which rely upon the deception of a human in the loop. USB drives dropped in a parking lot, or handed out at conferences; crafty e-mail attachments, social engineering a user in their private life on Facebook, LinkedIn, or some other social networking (SN) medium, with the expressed purpose of figuring out the means which will yield the highest likelihood of success. Unfortunately, it is my opinion that the user represents the greatest threat to our ability to intercept and stop delivery. The user vulnerability reaches further than a lack of education. Although we can desire so, they are not expected to be the front line of defense against an attack. User education will stop some attacks, and when it does, the attacker will up the ante and begin to target our public-facing application and back-office developers, researching and singling them out as humans, knowing they contain the information required to do great harm.

Malware: Payload

The payload is the "sauce" that makes persistent access possible. They are usually stealthy in nature, deceptively designed to conceal their true purpose, hence making identification and eradication very difficult. Understand that the professional attacker is not going to rely upon the standard, already been analyzed and signatures written for, methods of retaining control over your machine(s). They adapt their tools and methods with target specificity in mind.

They can employ packing techniques, bit shifting of data at rest, obfuscation on the wire, hiding in plain sight, and a myriad of other deceptive and oftentimes troublesome tactics for our investigative teams. The "Holy Grail," however, is memory visibility and analysis in real time. Code must execute in memory, leaving the code itself exposed for our own analytic capabilities.

Memory detection and analysis is the digital battlefield of today and tomorrow. For a malicious piece of code to work, it must be running and to do so will occupy memory space. To occupy memory space is to interact with the host operating system kernel to achieve the desired outcome. There are only so many commands, structures, calls, routines, etc., that an operating system uses, and unless the malicious code has the ability to dynamically change the underlying kernel upon reboot, and there are instances of rootkits out there that can and have accomplished this in the real world, the fact remains that the malicious process itself is exposed when it is running in memory. It is also important to understand one last point with regard to malicious payload.

It can be designed as a single-use payload, designed to detect the presence of certain conditions and therefore launch; it can be designed to sleep and awaken at certain cycles; it can be designed to accept normal DNS query/response traffic to reconfigure itself. A payload can be a logic bomb, or a RAT designed to provide continued stealthy access into your network. Determining payload purpose is a master-level skill, and there are very few individuals that can accomplish this in support of a real-time investigation.

Malware: Command and control

Presuming the payload is designed for continued RAT access, the attacker must then establish a means to command and control the payload, all the while remaining undetected and nonattributable. Most control mechanisms of payload are noninteractive, meaning a command will be either sent or retrieved by the payload, and reconfigured on the fly to execute the revised operational request. The essence of command and control (C&C) is low and slow. One would tend to think that it would be beneficial for an attacker to configure their payload to operate during "non-peak" hours, to avoid detection. Yet what better way to conceal a single connectionless user datagram protocol (UDP) packet than to determine peak traffic times on your perimeter and configure the payload to sneak out a single, well-crafted domain name system (DNS) query? The attacker just needs to issue single commands to the payload, which is automated to perform internal reconnaissance, collection of data, further penetration, privilege escalation, exploit du jour.

Threat trends

While it is commonly known that many nations have either expressed interest in or have already developed advanced cyber operations capabilities, the threat landscape is by no means limited to the adversarial nation-state attack. In many regards, a more serious threat is the rise of the #AntiSec movement, as their intention is public disclosure and media exposure. Astroturfing is not likely to subside any time soon, and it is a more likely scenario that due to the lack of law enforcement action, or legal implications to the perpe-trators of recent highly publicized attacks, this underground movement will be viewed by many individual or splinter groups as an unregulated frontier to carry out their motives. As it stands today, they are largely correct in their assumptions that the international dip-lomatic community lacks the integrated and collaborative efforts to remove their cloak of anonymity and render swift justice in an unregulated and widely interpreted swath of "privacy rights," erring on the side of preserving an individual's right to privacy with regard to their activities on the Internet.

In the absence of global leadership and cooperation in this domain, an organization is essentially left to defend itself and take the necessary action to protect their assets. Participation in the Internet is voluntary and connecting a computer online, storing your data in the cloud, or otherwise taking advantage of the interconnected world we now live in is an essential way of life today, and it is prudent to remain vigilant and responsible for what an organization chooses to place or expose online.

chapter four

Risk management

Wayne Boone (revised by Allan McDougall)

Contents

What is risk?

Risk is an inherent part of business, and even life in general. It is something that we live with on a daily basis. That is because there will always be some form of obstacle or impediment that stands between us and achieving our objective(s). It can be as simple as traffic standing in the way of our crossing the street or as complex as working through interconnected regulatory requirements to succeed in international business. We also tend to respond to risk on a daily basis. We use resources such as people, time, consumables (gasoline, paper, food, water, electricity, etc.), buildings, equipment, information (including information systems), and processes or procedures to overcome obstacles (threats and vulnerabilities, as we will discuss) and reduce the potential for failure. We may make decisions to have other persons handle tasks to which they appear more suited. We may use different tools or better quality materials in our production. We may insist on more reliable information from those providing assessments. All this is to say is that we tend to take steps to avoid risk, to reduce its impact on our lives or to reduce its probability of occurring. Since we cannot anticipate all impediments and make preparations to overcome them, there will always be some uncertainty that we will succeed. According to Cardenas et al. (2009, p. 1434), "obtaining perfect security is impossible." One might even argue, given the economic lessons over the last 10 years, that attempting to achieve perfect security can be disabling for a nation and its economy. For the purposes of this chapter, that uncertainty can be considered to be risk, and dealing with residual risk is risk management. "Protecting SCADA systems is a tricky task" (Gold 2008, p. 39) and requires as close to "100% proof against both modern and old security threats" (p. 40). Considering the environment in which supervisory control and data acquisition (SCADA) systems typically operate, mission success defined as service delivery according to mandates, regulations, policy, and, perhaps most importantly, user expectations would indicate that what is being "done" has a relatively high value and, therefore, there may be more uncertainties that could potentially impede success. The business of identifying these uncertainties or risks that can impact commodities or services supported by SCADA systems is an ongoing task. Personnel take steps to see that such risks are identified, analyzed, assessed, and treated in some manner to reduce them to a level that is acceptable to those senior management individuals accountable for service delivery. This cyclical process can be considered to be risk management. How an operation approaches the issue of risk management can be the determining factor between significant success and catastrophic failure. The challenge is that "risk" and "management" are both terms that are terribly overused in a number of contexts. This chapter will address the concept of "risk management" from an asset protection and security (AP&S)* perspective.

Objective of this chapter

The objective of this chapter is to explain the AP&S risk management process at a conceptual level as applied to SCADA systems and their supporting environments. The individual elements of risk management will be covered, including mission analysis (what business you are trying to do), scope (how much you are trying to do and in which environment), asset valuation (what useful or needed things that you will use to do something and what deliverables or results you are trying to produce or achieve), threat assessment (what or who are the "bad guys" who want to prevent you from doing what you want to do), vulnerability assessment (what are the "holes" or weaknesses in your assets that could let the bad guys in), risk analysis (how bad is it in general if the bad guys exploit the holes), and, finally, risk assessment (how bad is it *to us*) as it applies to risk management. Ultimately, the extent of risk management that is conducted is an expression of management's decision of how it wishes to address or treat identified risks. This chapter stops short of the development of specific security safeguards, controls, and countermeasures (which can be considered synonymous). As a caveat, this chapter is not meant to be a primer on AP&S risk management. There are several excellent books and articles

---

* AP&S is an inclusive term that has been coined in critical infrastructure protection (CIP) literature and is equally applicable in information system and corporate security environments. This term acknowledges that protection of assets is often inadequate, since this concept does not include assurance, continuity, and resilience in many people's lexicon. Also, security as a term often connotes the traditional security guard in a physical environment, another limiting concept. AP&S refers to all measures taken through the risk management life cycle, including mission analysis, asset valuation, threat assessment, vulnerability assessment, risk assessment, and, thereafter, safeguarding implementation to protect against, mitigate the effect of, deter, absorb, isolate, respond to, recover from, and restore all services and capabilities after an attack or major interruption to operations.

that focus on risk assessment for the practitioner, and the harmonized threat and risk assessment (HTRA) produced by the Royal Canadian Mounted Police (RCMP) and the Communications Security Establishment Canada (CSEC) provides tactical guidance for those who are required to conduct threat risk assessments (TRAs). While practitioners will enjoy reading this chapter as a refresher of basic principles, both they and line managers will benefit more from the conceptual treatment of this topic, along with some lateral thinking and application of the principles. In this manner, it is intended that practitioners will hone their analytical skills, and managers will better understand the significant level of effort and resources that go into establishing and maintaining an effective risk management program. The overall expectation is that they will collaborate in their mutual interest to protect valued assets supporting mission success.

AP&S risk in theory

Risk itself can be challenging to define, since perspective factors highly into how it is approached. In the financial community, for example, addressing risk can lead to both positive outcomes (profit) and negative outcomes (losses). In the AP&S context, the concept of risk generally refers to negative or undesirable outcomes, which must be addressed to ensure mission success. Generally, AP&S risk can be described in terms of the exposure of an organization to losses that result from a threat agent exploiting a vulnerability to cause injury to some asset. This is often expressed by the following expression:

$$R = f(M, AV, T, V)$$

where risk (R) is a function (f) of mission importance (M), asset values (AV), threats (T) in terms of their capability, opportunity, and intent (COI) (will be explained), and vulnerabilities (V). While not strictly mathematically sound, if the mission is more critical operationally, the threats are more dedicated, and/or the vulnerabilities (gaps or holes) are greater, then the risk is greater. Conversely, if the mission, commodity, or service provided is less important to clients, if the assets used are not valuable in terms of their according to availability, integrity, or confidentiality (AIC),*—in that order of importance according to Cardenas et al. (2009)—if no threat is inclined or able to attack, or if there are no gaps in the assets' protective posture, then, arguably, there is no risk. Any increase to one of these factors (without corresponding decreases in other categories) leads to an increase in risk and must be addressed.

AP&S risk management is not an exact science; rather, it is considered more of an art, because it is ultimately a qualitative process. Even supporting quantitative approaches (such as *annualized loss expectancy*) are based on a range of assumptions and subjective decisions rendered by people with varying amounts of AP&S training, education, experience, and critical logic. For example, it may be challenging to determine the full hard (financial) and softer (maintenance, performance, opportunity, etc.) costs associated with a valve that actuates as part of a pipeline. Does it include the replacement, installed, or

---

* In traditional AP&S parlance, confidentiality or protection from unauthorized disclosure of sensitive information or other assets is paramount, followed by integrity and availability. However, when discussing SCADA systems and national critical infrastructures (NCIs), availability is considered the most important security function, followed by integrity (protection from unauthorized modification), and then confidentiality; while it is important to protect the privacy of individuals and the sensitivity of information such as intellectual property operating data, and so on, this is less important than having services accessible on demand and of an assured quality.

initial price of the valve, or the prices associated with a component part, or its calibration, or its removal of service? What are the costs associated with not doing something else when working toward getting a valve up and running, which could include requirements analysis, approval, choice of product, procurement, shipping, and arranging installers who may have to learn about the product, with supervision of installation, quality assurance, and testing? Notwithstanding this complexity of determining hard and softer costs, a valve is relatively simple. Now, consider the value of a key operating official or the chief executive officer (CEO) of the company. That individual's value could be based on their salary dollars, the cost of hiring a new person, lost opportunity costs associated with going in a certain corporate strategic direction, or in the value accrued by the CEO's support for the AP&S risk management program (which would include the provision of capable staff and other resources). These examples indicate the overall qualitative nature of AP&S risk management, supported by some supporting quantitative risk assessments. Typically, discussions and decisions become more quantitative and fiscally oriented as one ascends the "corporate ladder" (what is the bottom line?) as busy executives discuss relative numbers. Unfortunately, when expressing AP&S risk, the best that can be presented is a relative assessment, such as that provided by a Likert scale of, for example, negligible, very low, low, moderate, high, very high.* In all cases, assessment criteria and assumptions for each scale must be very clearly defined and communicated to those who conduct the assessment and to those who receive the reports if the risk management advice is to be successfully communicated.

There is a tendency today, in the era of fiscal restraint, to have to show some measurable empirical value. One must be cautious with this approach, as there are a range of risks that are dealt with on a preventive basis that cannot be easily defined in this manner. Consider that many laws hold executives accountable with respect to whether or not their organization has taken all reasonable steps to prevent harm. What is the dollar value of taking steps to meet this accountability? That may be calculable. What is the dollar value of the possibility that senior executives may face incarceration for failing to maintain their duty of care? That may be more difficult to calculate—the only certainty is that the senior executives will certainly want a voice in that matter.

Generally, risks are defined in terms of the *likelihood* of a threat exploiting a vulnerability to impact negatively on the AIC of assets supporting business activities, production, or service delivery, and the resultant *impact* to the organization.[†] Lowrance (1976) uses the terms *probability* and *severity* in defining risk, and Cardenas et al. (2009) uses the terms *likelihood* and *consequences*, but these may all be considered synonymous with likelihood and impact. It is at this point that confusion may emerge with respect to the concept of risk. When considering likelihood, one is dealing with probability. Probability can be described in terms of the number of times a specific outcome or condition occurs given a total number of events. For example, flipping a two-sided coin leads to a probability of 50% as long as all the flips are random. Typically, deliberate attacks and accidents affecting entities supported by SCADA systems are not random, in that conditions must be in place for the attack or incident to occur; nor are natural events such as hurricanes or floods completely unpredictable. Therefore, AP&S risk management is based on an accurate assessment of probabilities of negative events occurring, and taking appropriate mitigative action.

---

* A tip for providing more precise risk assessments is to use an even-numbered scale (typically four or six). This addresses the tendency to take the "safer" middle value instead of conducting more in-depth information gathering and analysis.
[†] As found in the *Protection of Assets Manual* Section 1.3.0 (ASIS International, n.d.).

Appropriate, in this case, refers to those measures that mitigate risk to a level acceptable to senior management and within the confines of what is considered to be legally acceptable.

A consideration here is that probability tends to be analyzed, assessed, and communicated in terms of simple individual risk events, without considering the effect of interrelated or aggregated outcomes on (potentially) complex systems. Consider weather events, and the concept of the 100 year storm. In many cases, people may look at the name and think that the storm need be considered in terms of a frequency of once per 100 years. There may be a tendency to discount this threat event thereafter, based only on history. However, with climate change, some areas have suffered a number of these 100 year storms over the past decade and there are new parameters defining what the 100 year storm may look like. This indicates that historical frequencies of threat events require continual reassessment for applicability in a certain industry, geographical location, or operating environment. From updated risk assessments may arise the requirement for changes to safeguards to ensure the AIC of valued assets supporting mission success.

The second consideration is how to describe the impact to the organization. This will be described further in the section "Scope of risk management," but it is important to understand that impact can be influenced by the perspective, location, and mission of those impacted. If you are driving a car that becomes involved in an accident, your impacts may be described in terms of health (you and those in the vehicle with you) and in terms of the costs associated with property damage. To the driver behind you who is caught in the traffic disruption, the impact may be more aptly measured in terms of the delays suffered waiting for the accident to be cleared and potentially lost earnings (such as could result from missing a meeting or a deadline to provide a service or product). Since time is an asset, it is being consumed without apparent return on investment.

Some aspects of impacts can be quantified; others can be assessed only qualitatively, and some others may be assessed as a hybrid of the two. Quantifiable impacts typically are more clearly measurable and demonstrable—as long as they can be assessed against an agreed scale or set of specifications according to a standard, "a set of useful metrics" (Zhu and Sastry 2010, p. 4)—if you will. Quantitative impacts utilize a specific number of units within that scale (e.g., dollars, number of products produced, or amount of service provided), which can be compared and, given the same conditions of a risk event, can be repeated. Other impacts are less quantifiable. Consider the loss of an employee in an accident. How does one measure the impact of such an event when the value of the asset is so difficult to quantify? It is certainly different if you are the parent or spouse of that individual, as opposed to a disinterested researcher or loss-prevention specialist analyzing the victim as part of a statistical group. How is the value and impact affected if the individual had a significant amount of corporate or technical memory that had not been written down? Outcomes of civil actions fall into qualitative impacts because of subjectivity and perspective applied to a factual event. Probability, in this case, is a result of precedent, common law, or a standardized means of calculating injury, which provides some degree of predictability.

What is certain in AP&S risk management is that risks are ultimately qualitative and must be acknowledged as such by both AP&S analysts and senior management. Many definitions, therefore, are not necessarily the most easily utilized. One of the clearest and most operationalized definitions within critical infrastructure protection (CIP) can be found in the Masters of Infrastructure Protection and International Security (MIPIS) program at Carleton University's AP&S risk management course—that the risk to an organization can be described in terms of a factor associated with "a threat agent exploiting a vulnerability to cause damage to an asset supporting a mission, resulting in some form of loss of AIC,

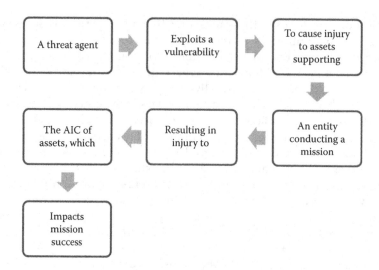

Figure 4.1 Description of AP&S risk broken down.

in turn resulting in operational impact to the mission." This structure of risk assessment fits into the concept of risk management well, in that it identifies and examines the major elements that lead to the losses to an organization. This is shown graphically in Figure 4.1. Note that each step can be isolated for analysis. More information on this will be presented later.

What does mission success mean?

Before one can answer this question, it is important to understand fully what is meant by mission. The mission of an organization is often simple to understand at the highest level; it may even be expressed as a motto on a poster or coffee cup, but such typically flowery and fluffy language may not define adequately what product, commodity, or service is provided, how much of it, how important it is to the community, region, or nation, and how reliably it is to be provided. To properly analyze the mission and draw salient conclusions for effective risk management, it must first be understood to the requisite level of detail. This is a matter of returning to first principles, and can be answered by two simple questions. The first is "why are we here?" and addresses the strategic level. The answer to the first question may be to provide a service (if part of a federal department) or it may be to generate wealth for the business owners in the production of commodities or products (if a privately owned enterprise). The motivation can be both monetary and more altruistic or patriotic, especially when considering those national critical infrastructures (NCIs)* supported by SCADA systems, for which the meeting of national objectives on security, sovereignty, economic prosperity, or health and safety may be their mandate. A follow-on question in this case may be "what do we do to help?"

The second question involves "How do we do that?" and exists at the operational level. The answer to this question describes the key activities or business lines of the enterprise. For a manufacturer, it may be to "deliver high-quality product X capable of meeting or exceeding the requirements of Specifications A–E for a specified period of time at a

---

* NCIs are those goods and services that have a very high AIC requirement based on their contribution to national objectives.

reasonable cost on client demand." From this mission statement, the various supporting, complementary, and interrelated activities within the organization can be identified, further decomposed, and analyzed at the tactical level. It is at this level that AP&S-relevant observations can be made and risk management-relevant conclusions be drawn.

The mission statement may be derived from the requirements of a parent organization, and may or may not be customized or interpreted for a subsidiary or regional facility. In those cases, the parent organization's mission statement is reviewed and the specific supporting business lines (operational) or functions (tactical) performed by the subsidiary organization are linked directly to the higher (strategic) mission statement. A critical path for expressing delivery mandates is thus formed.

Mission analysis

Once the mission statement has been captured and isolated, mission analysis can be undertaken. This is necessary to identify the indicators of mission success. Once again, this is a matter of asking simple questions and working toward detailed answers. Information to answer these questions is typically gleaned from reviewing business and AP&S documents, interviews, and site visits (observation). From the strategic mission statement, key business lines will emerge, such as those subordinate organizations in our example that prepare to build the product, fabricate the product, ensure the quality of the product, market the product, deliver the product, and support both employees and corporation. Each of these business lines should have its own mission statement or summary of key business functions, ideally linking functionally and understandably to the higher-level mission statement. By identifying each of the qualifying elements that are used to define a successful outcome, analysis will begin to lead to some AP&S-relevant findings that will contribute to risk assessment and overall risk management. An effective method is to ask the question, "So what?" from an asset valuation, threat, or vulnerability perspective. Since the overall objective of risk management is to apply an appropriate level of protection to assets in support of mission success, a lot of the answers to "So what?" will indicate that the AIC of an asset needs protecting. In our example, the organization must deliver a "high-quality product" (refining the goal toward something more achievable) that "meets or exceeds the requirements of Specifications A–E," specifications being precise, measurable, and consistent with both functional and quality criteria. From the statement, it can also be shown that the product must be deliverable on demand (transport the product) and must be produced for a reasonable cost (considering the costs to train, equip, supervise, and compensate employees within the business lines and to purchase all raw materials and consumables). Some examples of emergent considerations for AIC for each business line are broken down as follows:

- Prepare to build the product—so what? Need a
  - Trusted supply chain
  - Quality raw materials
  - Trusted staff to process invoices
  - Secure site to store materials
  - High-quality equipment, consumables, and processes (e.g., billing, receiving, etc.)
- Build the product—so what? Need a/an
  - Secure and safe facility
  - Trusted staff to build the product
  - Trusted, repeatable processes

- Effective supervision (by people) and monitoring (by information technology (IT) and SCADA systems) of all activities
- Ensure the quality of the product—so what? Need a
  - Trusted staff performing as trained and reporting deviations
  - Input materials that meet requirements right up to the time of use
  - Secure sight with an eye toward preventing unauthorized activity or unwanted (such as counterfeit) materials
  - Trusted and routine reporting lines
  - Trusted policies and procedures that permit interruption of operations for quality reasons
- Market the product—so what? Need a
  - Current assessment of business intelligence
  - Protected customer database
  - Trusted vendors
- Deliver the product—so what? Need a
  - Trusted and protected supply chain
  - Trusted transportation personnel and vendors
- Support both employees and corporation—so what? Need a/an
  - Set of processes for fair treatment
  - Honest and fair recruitment processes
  - Credible and sustained awareness, training, and development
  - Efficient and accurate remuneration processes
  - Trusted processes for advancement based on merit
  - Protected and safe working environment

These decomposed subsets are business processes that require assets whose AIC must be assured through a risk management program. This analysis will provide the framework for further risk-related analysis and assessment. Also, by taking this approach, the tasks (tactical) and objectives (operational) that need to be met to achieve the ultimate goals expressed in the mission statement (strategic) can be isolated and analyzed. From the statement given earlier, the measurable criteria are defined in "Specifications A–E." The criteria that are used to measure whether or not the objectives are being met could then be defined in several ways, for example:

1. Must meet functionality and quality requirements.
2. Must do so in a way such that the client is not left waiting.
3. Must take into account elements such as cost. In this manner, we can validate the strategic role of the business, as expressed in its supporting business lines and functions.

Ethical or moral considerations

Some persons confuse "why" an enterprise exists by attempting to overlay moral, ethical, or altruistic dimensions (social responsibility) onto government or private industry enterprises, typically in favor of a personal or group agenda. While this is appropriate to an extent, it can be taken too far. The first clear goal of a private industry business is to generate wealth for its stakeholders. This is a key difference between the private sector and the public sector. In the private sector, the focus is on wealth, whereas, in the public sector, the focus is (hopefully) on delivering a quality service function to improve the lives of the population. In both cases, it should be clear that the first goal is to be able to achieve the mission (and thereby generate wealth and provide needed services) as effectively and efficiently* as possible, regardless of personal preferences and beliefs.

There is an important risk management nexus to the ethical or moral dimension of an enterprise. In AP&S doctrine, all advice provided is considered to be apolitical and "politically incorrect." All recommendations for, and application of, approved safeguards must be apolitical in that they must map only to meeting the residual risk levels approved by senior management and are consistent with industry best practices, training, and education. According to Chittester and Haimes (2004, pp. 4, 5), "the level of acceptable risk depends on the critical nature of the system's mission and the perspectives of the individuals or groups using the information." They are politically incorrect in that they are statements of the supportable facts and do not get looked at through the lens of ensuring appropriate representation of demographic groups, and so on. It should be clear to the reader that this does not translate into "being abrasive," but only clinical in application.

In this manner, AP&S risk managers may find themselves in a temporary dilemma between, on the one hand, limitations on safeguard implementation that are imposed by senior management (after all, all protective safeguards have an inconvenience or hard cost associated with them) and, on the other hand, their best assessment of the most appropriate safeguards to be implemented to meet the residual risk targets approved by senior management. Fortunately, this is easily resolved. The primary role of the AP&S practitioner is as an adviser to senior management on residual risk. If the adviser communicates successfully to senior management the residual risk and any concerns after approved safeguards are implemented, even if that residual risk is higher than that which the AP&S practitioner considers prudent based on training, education, experience, and industry best practices, then the practitioner's job is done. It should be clear that there is a legal threshold here—if the AP&S practitioner notes that there is a clear violation of law or something being done that jeopardizes the life safety of the population, he or she may well be compelled to act, even without management support. This is a difficult call to make, and usually only made once within an organization, but it should be clear that the AP&S practitioner cannot simply hide behind management accountability when there is a clear and verifiable risk in this context.

Once the practitioner has expressed those concerns and senior management has acknowledged the advice provided (and thereby accepted the residual risk in question), the dilemma is resolved. Assumption of AP&S risk is a management function, not a technical one; the practitioner simply works within the residual risk targets set by senior management and implements the approved safeguards. An ethical consideration emerges only if the protective posture becomes too ineffective for the AP&S practitioner to tolerate, after which there is no choice but to vote with one's feet and seek alternate employment.

AP&S risk management in support of business and social responsibility

It is important to remember that all enterprises, public or private, manage risks every day. There are many types of risks, including financial, cultural, legal, business, partner,

---

* If one differentiates effective (doing the right thing) from efficient (doing things right), then it may be argued that private industry attempts to maximize efficiency (reduce overheads, maximize and exploit capabilities of staff, operate as a meritocracy) in its goal toward effectiveness (mission success being fiduciary). Government, on the other hand, focuses on effectiveness in reflecting Canadian values over pure operational efficiencies. Merit may take second place to hiring for gender equality, ethnic diversity, bilingualism, and so on.

operational, sales, and reputational, to name a few. Haimes and Chittester (2005, p. 1) note that "Prudent management of any business, whether in government or the private sector, calls for making cost-effective decisions regarding the investment of resources. Investing in the assessment and management of risk associated with cyber attacks, and thus, with information assurance, is no exception." AP&S risks to the AIC of valued assets contributing to mission success are just others to be managed within the overall process of enterprise risk management (ERM), which is a senior management function. All risk management programs exist only to support business lines, which, in turn, exist only in support of mission success, however defined in the enterprise's mission statement.

The alignment of business activities with societal norms (including ethical, altruistic, and moral) occurs on at least three levels. The first of these is the *legal* or *regulatory* level. While the business seeks to generate wealth, the government (representing and protecting the people) sets in place certain constraints and restraints* that limit how the business can achieve that goal. These are generally defined in terms of *criminal* acts between the individual and the state when the business does not act honestly. The second layer can be described as *civil* constraints and restraints—generally defined in terms of *negligence* and *tort* between individuals. In these cases, the company's failure to take all reasonable steps to prevent harm to another can lead to costs associated with *civil liability*. A third element involving social and cultural norms is a matter of projecting and protecting a *positive brand*. This brand is important if an enterprise wishes to be perceived as a positive and contributing member (or at least not as a destructive member) of the community, the region, and possibly the nation. Compliance and conformity with these and other societal norms such as environmental consciousness, charity, and community support refine what are considered to be acceptable boundaries for corporate activities, meeting objectives, and achieving goals.

A paradigm case of business and social accountability rests with those NCIs assuring national security, sovereignty, economic prosperity, and the health and safety of citizens. Overwhelmingly privately owned, these NCIs comprise those physical or logical networks that, if destroyed or disrupted, would cause serious injury to those assets supporting the NCIs' missions and also to those national objectives that have been deemed to be essential to our way of life. This includes transportation, energy, water, manufacturing, government, IT, and telecommunications; essentially, all services, goods, and commodities that are provided in the quantity, time, and quality that is consistent with the populace's expectations.

While the private sector owns and operates a significant portion of the critical infrastructures of the nation and is responsible for the provision of these essential goods and services contributing to national objectives, it does not follow that these enterprises have become accountable directly to the populace for the provision of uninterrupted, high-quality goods and services. As noted earlier, the primary role of private industry is to generate wealth for its stakeholders. The concept of making a reasonable return on investment while working in service to the nation is not inconsistent or in conflict. The burden of compliance for a private enterprise is simply to operate within the various legal, civil, and social constraints and restraints and to produce the goods and services in a quantity, quality, and timeliness outlined in contracts with the government. The government retains all accountability to its citizenry for meeting national objectives. Communicating to the

---

* A constraint is considered something that must be done; for example, all products must be sold by year end. A restraint is something that may not be done; for example, there must be no casualties or injuries during construction of a new production line.

NCIs the expected levels of performance, including standards of protection of the AIC of supporting assets, is a government responsibility and one to which the AP&S practitioner contributes significantly within the NCIs' risk management programs. While responsibility for the provision of a capability can be delegated, accountability for results cannot. This is especially true in the cases of government oversight of its NCIs. Supervision of performance, periodic monitoring and auditing, setting training standards, timely communication of threats, and information on vulnerabilities or changes to mandatory requirements are all essential elements of accountability.

In summary, following industry best practices for AP&S provides a secure and safe operating environment for the enterprise, and also contributes to legal compliance, protection from civil law suits, and a positive brand. In this manner, the AP&S risk management program definitely contributes to ERM and mission success, however defined.

Scope of risk management

As discussed earlier, when considering the basic elements of risk, the perspective and expectations of the individual or organization affected by the risks is important to understand. Consider the issue of critical infrastructure and who is responsible and accountable, both for individual service provision and in aggregate. In comparison, if one asks a citizen who requires a specific good, commodity, or service who is responsible for ensuring that the service is available and of expected quality and quantity, the reply will likely be "the company, of course"—the result of the service agreement between the individual and the company.

Regarding the provision of critical infrastructure services, the private company may fully understand and appreciate the expectations or service-level agreements with government if they are stated explicitly (which, in many cases, they are not, due to a lack of governmental oversight mechanisms). Companies, ever mindful of the financial bottom line, may prioritize how those services are to be achieved and to what extent they are achieved—particularly in the case of widely distributed services. Finally, as noted earlier, the government may require that the company providing critical infrastructure services comply with legislation and regulations to ensure that the service is available to some quantifiable extent (typically a percentage of "uptime" and "quality of service") and hopefully take steps to ensure that those criteria are met. In each of these cases, the concept of scope factors significantly. Clear delineation of roles and responsibilities, agreed to by all stakeholders, is essential to agreement on the scope of services provided, to provision of service, and to reducing any gaps in the protective posture of the NCI providing those services. The AP&S risk management program contributes to ensuring the provision of services and, ultimately, the mission success of the NCI. Risks within the NCI and among NCIs (since they are interdependent in many cases) may be influenced significantly by the actual ability to meet enough of the mandated or expected (by government) demand for critical services for the organization to remain viable, if not profitable. Finally, from the government perspective, a risk necessarily has a much larger scope, perhaps regional or national, in which case it may focus on and manage the ability of many companies to maintain an appropriate level of a critical service within a community—requiring the elimination of any one company as a single point of failure (SPOF) in the provision of an essential service to an individual, a community, a region, or a nation.

Thus, it can be seen how the extent to which scope can define how risk will be assessed and managed; scope becomes a limiting factor. From the corporate perspective, it may be communicated that the risk is being assessed in relation to the *ability of the corporation to remain viable*, if not profitable, in meeting its service delivery mandates from government. From the government perspective, the risk may be assessed twofold: first, in relation to the *trust of the community that a certain service will be available* on demand and to an appropriate quantity and quality to meet collective needs, and second, in relation to the *ability of the government to ensure, through service-level agreements (SLAs) and oversight, to continuity of service* in the expected quantity, time, and quality, to all citizens requiring it. From the individual's perspective, the risk may well be defined in relation to his or her *trust in the delivery and quality of that service at the home.* Each of these statements implies a reassessment of, and perhaps changes in, the company's objectives to be met and the goals to be achieved.

The reason that scope and perspective have been emphasized to such an extent in any chapter on risk management is that inadequate consideration of these two elements by risk analysts, senior management, and other stakeholders has led to misunderstanding of risk management recommendations and subsequent decisions that did not protect adequately the assets supporting the provision of critical goods and services. In short, clearly understanding how perspective and scope shape the focus of any risk assessment will be a very positive and significant step toward being able both to present and to argue a case for a protection posture—be it at more senior management tables, with peers, other NCIs, government oversight bodies, or the public being served. To assist in communicating or transmitting the existence of risks in the control system domain, four basic steps are offered:

1. Express the risk at the equipment level, describing the impacts in terms of the losses of its immediate functions. This level is perhaps best understood by the operators and engineers, both of whom must "buy in" to the risk assessment to convince line managers/supervisors and senior management.
2. Extrapolate the assessed impacts associated with a specific loss of function in terms of how they would affect the local system. This will get the attention of line managers and regional managers, who are responsible to headquarters or the main office for meeting AIC requirements.
3. Communicate how the local or individual system's loss would translate to the larger system of systems at a corporate level. This moves the risk into the strategic level and, by definition, becomes a senior management concern from a purely business perspective.
4. Finally, identify any potential outside issues associated with impacts at the community, regional, or national levels. This will concern senior management from an ethical, moral, or societal perspective, which is also their responsibility as a good corporate citizen.

This layered, bottom-up approach to scoping and expressing risks to mission success capitalizes on many strengths, including the analytical skill of the AP&S practitioner based on his or her training, education, and experience coupled with a growing collection of like-minded stakeholders through the tactical (operator), operational (line or regional manager), and strategic (senior decision-maker) levels of activity. An example of this approach, when considering the valve that helps mix a certain chemical into paint to help it bond more effectively onto metal, follows:

- Based on the assessment by capable engineering and design staff, there is a significant risk that this valve would not function as intended (integrity risk) and would likely not mix the needed chemical into the paint (availability risk). The engineer or operator would likely be the first to notice this.

- This loss of service would result in paint that would appear to be bonded appropriately to the metal during a quality assurance check but would become less bonded when exposed to water, thereby causing the paint to chip prematurely (integrity risk). This would not come to light until noticed after time by the consumer.
- The premature chipping of the paint would become a quality of vehicle issue in the eyes of the consumer, devaluing the company's product in terms of being competitive against similar makes and models (a business risk). Social media and word of mouth would communicate this risk to the community, to the region, and perhaps to the nation.
- As a result of this, one could reasonably expect a drop in sales (perhaps evolving into a business survival risk). However, it would not likely impact the safety systems on the vehicle and, therefore, would not likely gain the attention of the government regulator from a vehicle safety perspective. Nonetheless, senior management quickly becomes implicated if a bottom-up approach is adopted to scope and communicate risk.

This approach is effective, applicable in any system, is repeatable, and gets a clear, validated message to senior management regarding key risks. It presents a clear and logical link that allows the individual conducting the risk assessment to identify *what was assessed* and how findings relate to the *local, system, corporate,* and *outside* objectives and goals.

Asset value

As noted, assets of several types are necessary to achieve mission success, whether in service delivery or the production, processing, movement, or storage of commodities or products. These assets have value in terms of AIC, which means that they must be accessible on demand in sufficient quality and quantity and that they must be protected from unauthorized modification and unauthorized disclosure. They also have monetary value in that they must be purchased, installed, maintained, operated, updated, and finally disposed of. This monetary value is of interest to us, and also to a threat agent who would steal the asset, render it unusable to us, or corrupt its utility so that it is untrusted thereafter. Perhaps the most valued assets when considering SCADA systems are pieces of information; therefore, "data collection, control, communication, and management, which are essential for the effective operation of large-scale infrastructures, are being performed by SCADA systems. These work remotely to improve the efficiency and effectiveness of the control, operations, and management of critical physical infrastructures" (Chittester and Haimes 2004, p. 2).

Asset valuation

Asset valuation is, simply, the process of determining how important (qualitatively and quantitatively) an asset is to mission success in terms of AIC and, also, how important the asset is to a potential adversary. This will indicate how likely it is that an adversary will attack an asset, which is a key step in threat assessment, discussed later in the chapter. Quantitative asset valuation focuses on the total cost of ownership of an asset throughout its life cycle. Qualitative asset valuation focuses on what exactly the asset does in the various processes leading to mission success, and how critical the asset is to completing a process. Several examples are cited in the following.

It is important to keep the issue of perspective and scope in mind during the asset valuation process. The reason for this is simple. Consider the panel through which electricity enters a home. To an individual, it may be a critical part of the home's infrastructure, in that if it fails or catches fire, this results in a catastrophic situation—an absence of power, which, depending on the time of year, can be deadly or extremely costly. From a community or regional perspective, a similar type of panel can be more valuable if it is contributing to the recovery of electrical services after a blackout as part of the community that sells electricity back to the grid through alternate means (such as solar). This panel could also be more valuable to keep up and running and in good operating condition, since a failure could cause a fire resulting in damage to an infrastructure on which many households depend, or injury to several workers due to higher voltages involved and the technical complexity of the system. At the level of the federal government, a fire in an individual home may be significant if it reveals a design flaw in the panel that could affect a larger part of the population, all of whom trust the government to oversee the implementation of standards to ensure that vendors provide products that work correctly and meet the expectations of citizens. Government oversight action could include triggering a recall of the equipment or direction to the company to conduct emergency repairs. Thus, it is indicated that it is important to keep in mind the consideration of perspectives and scope in asset valuation.

Asset valuation in support of mission success

The achievement of goals and objectives is the result of work completed and the resultant provision of services or the production of goods and commodities. This is usually the product of processes that are brought together in systems. These processes can be defined in terms of the following:

- The creation, transmission, processing, and protection of information to make informed decisions, whether it is to open a valve or to open a regional office.
- The efforts of personnel to analyze information from all sources and make informed decisions to take some kind of action, such as overriding the automated opening of a valve, responding to an anomaly, or hiring new staff.
- The equipment and supplies that are consumed in the process, such as petroleum oils and lubricants (POL), stationery, toner cartridges, shop supplies, or light-emitting diode (LED) light bulbs.
- The physical equipment that provides the service, builds the product, and actuates or measures an action. It also includes the occupation and use of building spaces appropriate to the work being conducted. Examples include the switches in a rail yard, navigation systems for ships, satellite communications among road carriers, specialized diagnostic equipment, and the environmentally controlled buildings and offices in which this equipment is found, such as hospitals, power stations, emergency operations centers, and IT server rooms.
- The implementation of formal (hopefully written and understood) supporting activities, including policies, standards and procedures, training programs, and oversight mechanisms, all of which are intended to assure consistent, timely, high-quality services, commodities, and products.

All of the foregoing are assets, which are shown nested in the following in relation to the processes that they support (Figure 4.2).

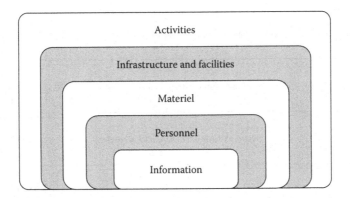

Figure 4.2 A taxonomy of asset usage.

Within the CIP doctrine, these asset groups can be organized according to the mantra of *personnel, materiel* (objects and consumables), *infrastructure and facilities,* and *information and activities.* For the sake of brevity, this will be referred to as the "unique level" in that it deals with a singularity—one person, one asset, one building, one piece of information, or one supporting activity. This is essential for effective risk assessment and management.

Many of these will also be the product of work or will require services that support them. This is the case with various forms of control systems. Again, the business of business is to generate wealth, not to operate a control system. The purpose of the control system is to help the company generate that wealth effectively, efficiently, and safely. So, when we are discussing the security around control systems, we are looking at an infrastructure that most likely supports an organization's critical path (but may not, depending on what business line it supports), but is, itself, often interpreted as being *critical infrastructure* because of the impacts associated with public safety (Figure 4.3).

The first layer identifies a general business line; for example, production operations (the assembly line). There are a series of discrete business functions comprising that business line; for example, each of the stations that prepare (paint, fold, drill, etc.) components to be assembled further down the line. Several automated systems (infrastructure and activities) contribute to the production process by performing a specific task or process. Each of the systems and processes, as one descends in the diagram, is an asset, and supporting the processes are additional assets as shown. Personnel oversee processes and intervene as necessary. Information is passed, analyzed by systems, and overseen by people. All processes take place in facilities and hopefully follow written procedures to produce, activate, actuate, move, or provide something (activities). Material is consumed, IT and telecom networks support communications and information exchange. Individual components (infrastructure) consume materiel, send information, are managed, changed, or maintained by people, reside in facilities, and perform a function that is essential to the provision of a mandated good or service.

Considerations for asset valuation

The valuation parameters of these assets can be refined in a number of ways. Remaining true to the business model, the values of the assets must be linked directly to the business processes and service delivery/production mandates that they support. Again, scope and perspective must be considered in asset valuation, since a misstep can lead to significant errors in the subsequent assessment or management of risk; some assets may turn out to

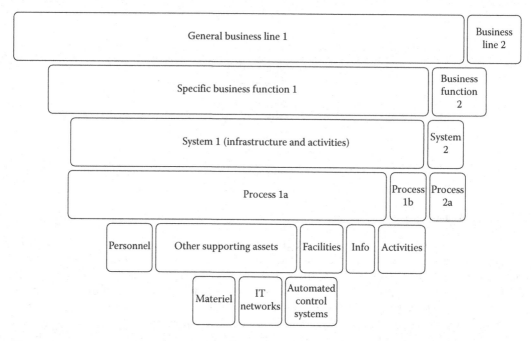

Figure 4.3 How assets support business functions.

be overprotected, which is inefficient, while others may be underprotected, which is ineffective. One approach involves identifying assets according to the following:

- At the unique or individual asset level, how does the loss of the asset affect the availability of the service (in terms of drops in production, etc.) or the integrity of the service (in terms of quality)?
- At the unique level, what are the confidentiality concerns associated with the unauthorized disclosure or loss of control over information that is directly related to the asset?
- How would these losses at the unique asset level affect the larger system, community, regional capability, or corporate entity (SLAs, legal or regulatory contracts, reputation, etc.)?

For example, in further consideration of the valve mixing a chemical into the paint for a piece of metal, one might argue that the loss of the valve entirely could lead to a shutdown of the painting line for a period of 5 h while it was replaced. The cost of this disruption would be, approximately, the cost of replacing the part, any installation/testing/calibration costs, and the lost production time while employees stood idle and no processing is being conducted (in the absence of redundant systems). Some of these costs may be recovered from returning the part for refurbishment or repairing in-house (reducing the costs associated with having to purchase a new part). The loss of the line, however, means that certain items may not be delivered on time, which is a cascading effect of the risk. Again, scope factors significantly here—the focus starts tactically or locally, but quickly rolls up to the level of the company. In this case, one might consider any penalties for late shipment, the potential losses associated with customer cancellation, or the loss of credibility or reputation in terms of the ability to deliver a product. Finally, downstream costs may involve having to repair vehicles that are found to have unacceptable paint jobs, the cost of protecting the brand, and the potential losses of brand value.

It is important to appreciate the nexus between the disruption and the value of the asset. It is not linear. When one considers how that component affects the system, including how its loss affects the process both upstream (toward the start of the process) and downstream (toward its final outcome), one may observe a *cascading* impact, because it acts like a house of cards—remove one card and the overall structure (system) begins to topple. The value of the asset, once compromised, must also be understood in terms of the overall impact at the unique asset, process, system, corporate, and societal levels. As with our chemical valve in the painting process, the monetary cost at a unique level may be rather insignificant (a couple of dollars), but it may be much more significant at a corporate level (many individual sales lost, representing thousands in lost profits, damage to reputation, etc.).

This becomes even more profound when dealing with safety systems. Consider the various measurement tools that activate safety systems in the nuclear industry. If those fail (*en masse*—this is very conceptual), then the unique cost may only be a few hundred dollars. If the item fails and, as a result, the safety system fails to prevent a significant radiation leak, then the impact could be measured in the millions of dollars in terms of liability to the company and much more in terms of the loss of territory and citizens within the affected area.* These can be referred to as *escalating* impacts, in that they operate differently at unique, process, system, corporate, and societal levels.

In summary, the proper valuation of assets, considering their importance in terms of AIC to the enterprise as well as the adversary or threat, is an essential component to be considered in the risk management process. Assets have value only to the extent that they support the operations of the enterprise. Once this has been determined, the AP&S risk analyst can compare these findings with those of the mission analysis and begin to formulate ideas regarding the extent of existing risk and to visualize appropriate safeguards to mitigate those risks to a level acceptable to senior management. The next step, the assessment of threats, will further paint the risk picture.

Threats: Introduction and categorization

The concept of threats is reasonably straightforward; it is their assessment and treatment that become complex and, possibly, complicated. A threat can be defined generally as any condition or action, typically negative, which can cause injury to the AIC of an asset by exploiting some vulnerability. For example, a thief may take advantage of a weak lock to steal items or a heavy snowfall may cause damage to the structure if there is a weakened roof. The challenge is often that individuals and organizations alike often fail to take the time to actually (1) identify potential threats in sufficient detail, (2) analyze how those threats tend to operate in terms of their COI to act, or (3) assess the threats relatively qualitatively, having limited understanding of the full impact or effects of a threat event. Chittester and Haimes (2004, p. 2) describe threat as "the intent and capability to adversely affect (cause harm or damage to) the system by adversely changing its states."

Threats within the AP&S domain are often grouped into three broad categories—the deliberate, accidental, and natural. Within the CIP specialty of AP&S, a fourth threat type

---

* This is why safety systems often rely on layers of protection in terms of redundancy—to prevent a single asset from failing and allowing for a catastrophic impact. Within the nuclear industry, there are multiple layers of controls that are overlapped and layered to ensure that these kinds of events are extraordinarily rare.

is emerging in the literature, that of deterioration. This phenomenon is interesting, because it can be considered either a risk (a result of a threat exploiting a vulnerability) or a threat (which can exploit a vulnerability to cause a risk). As a risk, deterioration can be considered the result of a threat exploiting vulnerabilities; for example, in the case of bridges the threat could be natural (exposure to the elements), man-made (salting roads), or accidental (construction staff cutting corners, incorrect maintenance), and major vulnerabilities could be inadequate inspections or a lack of spending on preventive maintenance. The result, that is, the risk, is then the deterioration. Since all AP&S risks are expressed in terms of their effects on the AIC of assets, deterioration can be considered both an integrity and an availability risk. However, deterioration can also be considered the first link in a chain of cascading risks; for example, in the case of a deteriorated bridge, when it could cause an accident if it fails, and thereafter cause a disruption in transportation, supply chains, and manufacturing (and possibly IT/telecom if conduits are routed across the same bridge).

As a threat, deterioration (or more specifically, a deteriorated infrastructure) can exploit the same vulnerabilities to cause the same cascading risks noted earlier. For the purposes of this chapter and follow-on study, deterioration will be considered a threat.

Deterioration (or alteration) in the *Dictionary of Civil Engineering* (Kurtz 2004) refers to defects or (negative) changes in the texture of a work resulting from mechanical, physical, chemical, or atmospheric causes (threats). The *McGraw-Hill Dictionary of Engineering* (2003) definition is, perhaps, more precise, referring to a decline in the quality of a structure over a period of time due to chemical or physical action of the environment. From the *ASTM Dictionary of Engineering Science and Technology*, 10th edition (2005), deterioration results in a need for repair due to physical or mechanical breakdown, and is a permanent impairment of the physical properties. The constant in all these is that the infrastructure no longer maintains the same robustness and resilience that it was intended to maintain, meaning that, as the demands placed on it approach its overall capacity, the likelihood of failure increases at what can be described as an increasingly unpredictable rate. Given the current state of infrastructure, the understanding of deteriorating structures is an increasingly important area of study to the AP&S practitioner.

Threats can also be described as failure scenarios when applied to SCADA systems. According to Bobbio et al. (2010, p. 1346), "A failure scenario consists in the identification of the sequence of adverse events that have produced an anomalous and undesirable behavior …, the identification of services that have been impaired (in terms of continuity, readiness, performance, response time) during the sequence of adverse events and the set of interconnected networks that … have contributed to their degradation."

There are several characteristics that distinguish threats in general and apply to these four threat types, including COI. Again, while not mathematically sound, it can be argued that if one or more of these are missing, then the attack or the threat event will not likely be successful.

Capability refers to the extent to which the threat agent possesses the knowledge, skills, abilities, and resources to launch an attack, including "ability and capacity to attack a target and cause adverse effects" (Chittester and Haimes 2004, p. 2). Opportunity refers to how possible it is to get close enough to the target to launch an attack. This includes the receipt of information regarding vulnerabilities of the target's assets; routing information of targeted IT systems for cyberattacks; transportation, infiltration, and exfiltration (if required) routes for physical attacks, and so on; essentially, anything that can get the threat agent into the proximity of the valued assets to be attacked. It may also be referred to in terms of the attacker having the time and space to commit the attack without fear of response or disruption. Intent is, perhaps, the most difficult to gauge, and refers to the level of commitment of the adversary to actually launch an attack, including "the desire or motivation of an adversary to attack a target and cause adverse effects" (Chittester and Haimes 2004, p. 2). Intent can result from cultural, ethnic, criminal, or religious indoctrination, the influence of a charismatic leader or family member (as in the Khadr case), or peer pressure.

Another challenge with intent involves the conditions that operate at the fringe of rationality, such as we find with those with significant mental challenges or that have been radicalized. In these cases, the ability to protect the infrastructure using deterrence and similar factors is often offset by the attacker's willingness to trade everything for success. This reveals another vulnerability or gap in our own defensive posture—the ability to assess the potential of violence that may or may not be present in a certain environment. This is the subject of ongoing efforts, and has resulted in a number of tools (such as the WAVR-21 assessment and similar structures). The challenge is that such tools are still at the point where those using them must possess significant education if there is to be an assurance of effectiveness.

In addition to categorizing threats by type and by characteristics, AP&S analysts also group them as being either internal or external (Cardenas et al. [2009] refers to them as outsider and insider attacks). An internal threat, such as an employee, contractor, or authorized visitor, has some or great knowledge of the organization, including its operational processes and its security posture. An internal threat has been granted access privileges to physical and electronic assets, and therefore possesses both capability and opportunity to launch an insider attack. According to Gold (2008, p. 40), "70% of attacks tend to be internal to the organization concerned. This is especially true with SCADA-based systems."

From a protection perspective against internal deliberate threats, corporate efforts typically revolve around ensuring the loyalty and reliability of the insider through background checks, appeals to patriotism or to "the team," or routine supervision and fair compensation to minimize any intent to launch an attack. The latter two, however, are areas of constant pressure—particularly as supervisors' workloads (including administrative tasks) increase and economic pressures continue to cause organizations to look for opportunities to adjust their balance sheets. An external threat has no legitimate access to assets, and must therefore build the capability, opportunity, and intent (COI) before attacking. In the case of deliberate external threats, all are developed with the assistance of intelligence which is typically gathered through reconnaissance of the target facility and information gathering from insiders and other knowledgeable people. This can occur accidentally through social engineering or deliberately through bribery, extortion, blackmail, subversion, or threats. In the current environment of standardization, there is a growing vulnerability that an attacker can identify a less protected area and, based on the need for compliance with a standard only, gather useful information for an attack against a more sensitive location.

The deliberate attack involves a willful intent to cause direct harm against assets to impact the AIC of an enterprise. The accidental attack does not involve intent, but rather negligence, inattention, distraction, fatigue, or overwork. In the case of the latter, there could be an intent by senior management or line managers to overtask or overwork their employees, thereby introducing the conditions for an internal or external accidental threat to occur and cause harm directly; that is, a hazard. This can lead to additional issues, such as legal liability, particularly where the demands placed on the organization move further and further away from the expected maintenance and operations of the equipment and processes.

A natural threat causes harm without intent by its nature and often affects the environment in which the entity operates, particularly within the realm of control systems. It may

Threat types	External	Internal
Natural	Earthquake, tornado, flood, tsunami, tropical storm, hurricane, thunderstorm, blizzard/snow/ice storm, hail, volcano eruption, landslide, erosion, wildfire, high wind, extreme temperature, disease, drought, animal attacks, meteorite, asteroid	
Deliberate	Terrorism, crime, sabotage, subversion, hostile military action, insurrection, state- or corporate-sponsored espionage (personal or electronic), cyberattacks, political activism, hoaxes, poisoning	Employee sabotage, theft, strike, work action (work-to-rule, slowdowns, stoppages, delay of access)
Accidental	Cut cable or water pipe (backhoe threat), wildfire, spill of dangerous material, poisoning	Error, loss or improper use of equipment, improper maintenance, slips and falls, spills, flooding, fire, poisoning
Deterioration	Erosion, rust/corrosion, weather fatigue	Wear, neglect, stress/structural fatigue, aging equipment or material

Figure 4.4 Threat categories.

also affect the area surrounding the infrastructure, meaning that the ability to respond to the event can be deteriorated significantly. Consider a serious storm—individuals needed to respond to an event may not be able to reach the facility. This is also a concern for business continuity planners who, from time to time, need to explain that plans may need to remain at the employee's home where they can be accessed if the facility cannot be.

Deterioration, as a threat, can be deliberate (e.g., willful decision not to maintain an infrastructure) or accidental (e.g., inadequate or nonroutine inspection or maintenance). The former case is a particular vulnerability where budget cycles and politics are linked— the cost of the maintenance of the infrastructure may lead to deficits, which, in fiscally restrained periods, are not politically acceptable. In the latter case, there will typically have been a change in some aspects of the infrastructure; for example, in the case of a bridge, it could be increased traffic, use of a new type of ice melter, different paving techniques or materials, a different paint type, and so on. Figure 4.4 summarizes the threat types and offers additional examples.

Analysis of threats

As noted earlier, analysis answers the question, "How bad is it?" Regardless of the threat under analysis, one must consider the likelihood of a threat agent exploiting a vulnerability to cause injury to an asset (risk), and the general impact of a successful attack. Threat assessment takes it one step further, and answers the question, "How bad is it to us?"; that is, the results of applying threat analysis to the assets, processes, systems, and enterprises under risk assessment. One method to conduct further threat analysis is described in the following.

Understanding that the threat is the act or condition that provides the vector or path for injury to be caused to an asset, it is now useful to consider further the nature of the threat agent. He or she can be described in terms of what they actually *do* to cause the injury to the asset—such as a burglar committing a theft or an IT cracker breaching the firewall of a corporate enterprise system. From the commission of the act, which has a certain likelihood based on the COI discussed earlier, three important elements for threat analysis emerge:

1. The threat itself in terms of the nature of the injury involved and resultant impacts (such as theft leading to unauthorized disclosure or loss of assets)
2. The threat agent performing the actions that lead to the threat manifesting itself (such as the burglar committing the act of theft)

3. The threat vector that describes the physical or logical path that is taken by the threat agent to successfully launch an attack (which will be discussed more in the section on vulnerability)

Challenges to threat assessment

In applying these three elements to the realm of control systems, one needs to be cognizant of the various different kinds of threats at the unique asset, system, and corporate layers. It is not sufficient simply to be cognizant of one form (say physical or technical) and ignore the others; this could lead to an incomplete assessment and introduce gaps (vulnerabilities) into the protective posture due to incomplete risk assessment. This is particularly true when dealing with high-availability systems in organizations that may be involved in operations with a significantly potential insider threat; for example, that of an employee or another given full and unmonitored access privileges to controlled areas and sensitive assets. These kinds of insider threats may become particularly grave because, as mentioned, they will typically have advanced or extensive knowledge of operations (and the controls that protect them), access to sensitive, high-value or other significant resources (such as keys or token to gain access, money and negotiables, and control consoles), and abilities to launch an attack and cause an impact (having often been trained specifically on the system, understanding the extent of monitoring and auditing of security-related events that take place, and provided with lists of what not to do). They may also act on behalf of an outside individual with ulterior motives, such as through the introduction of a USB device in return for money, where the attack is intended to cause other forms of harm.

To counter this, it is often proposed that the various members of the operations and AP&S (e.g., the corporate, IT, and continuity staffs) communities maintain routine liaison to share threat information regularly and as events occur, so as to generate a clear picture of likely threats to organizations that are similar in location, lines of business, size, sensitivity, value of assets, and so on. This information sharing is a necessary element of threat analysis, but is often defeated due to stovepipes within organizations or convoluted reporting chains. The premise is that all threat information is simply data, and the more the better, whether it is received from open (public, nonsensitive) or closed (private or government, sensitive) sources. At the highest sensitivity levels of information regarding a specific threat in terms of its COI, it is often the source of the information that leads to the closed and sensitive classification of the information, and not the content. Some information from open sources can be factually the same as from closed sources; it is the confirmation from trusted sources that verify the accuracy of the information, which better contributes to risk assessment and choice of safeguards under risk management. Typical closed sources include confidential informants, interception of signals such as telephone conversations, imagery from satellites, collated reports featuring analysis and assessment of COI that are prepared by the military and lead security departments, and so on.

A typical weakness (vulnerability) in the threat assessment process is the reluctance of some government agencies, private enterprises, and individuals to share information, regardless of the operational requirement to do so bidirectionally with public and private industry, especially in the case of NCIs that are working in the national interest. As discussed, some information is highly sensitive based on the source, even though the content is much less sensitive, or even unclassified. In other cases, the reliance on open sources without checking to determine whether or not the information is reliable and credible swings the vulnerability pendulum to the other extreme—where too much information (some of it just noise) clouds the situation. Private industry requires only an assurance from the government of the veracity and accuracy of the information, not the source. Information can also be "anonymized," that is, stripped of specific names and locations while retaining the essence of the threat details, likelihood assessment, and impact assessment. This, however, can pose challenges, as organizations move toward an increasing integration of geographic information systems to plot events in attempts to detect patterns or areas of concentration. Periodic operational security awareness sessions and reminders will go a long way to ensure that even the redacted or stripped threat information is protected from those without formal access approval, requisite security clearance, and the need to know. While the greatest fear of government agencies may be unauthorized disclosure by private industry, there is a reciprocal fear. Private industry, in many cases, is afraid of at least two things: first, that the government will fail to protect adequately their intellectual property and trade secrets from competitors; and second, that the government, learning more about the workings of an individual enterprise (including NCIs, interestingly enough), may impose additional regulations, policies, or taxes that could impede the freedom of the enterprise to operate. A subset of this is that private-sector enterprises, often already regulated, are rather reluctant to share vulnerability information with their regulators—particularly where the regulator entrenches its position with an "enforce everything" rule. Without the mutual confidence to share and protect each other's information, the threat assessment process remains incomplete.

A key concept relating to the sharing of both threat and vulnerability information is that of trust. As alluded to earlier, trust is essential to information sharing, comprehensive threat analysis and assessment, accurate risk assessment, and the appropriate, cost-effective implementation of safeguards. It is interesting to consider that all trust is personal; individuals will not typically share information unless there is mutual, personal confidence that the recipient actually needs the information, that sharing contributes to the common good (an integrated protection posture within and among enterprises, especially NCIs), and that the information will be protected adequately. That is why relationship building is so important among threat analysts; it is more likely to guarantee a continual flow of threat information. How is trust earned? The author suggests that, from an AP&S perspective, first and foremost, be good at your job. This requires training, education, and experience in your AP&S specialty. With demonstrated competence comes confidence from your peers. Also, you will be more able to communicate your information requirements to your peers, as well as to your and their senior management, making reasoned arguments based on a full understanding of protection requirements at the strategic, operational, and tactical levels. If the respective senior managers open the conduits, it remains only for the line managers, intelligence staffs, and AP&S analysts to begin sharing information of mutual interest, knowing that it is valued and both the source and information will be protected. In this manner, threat assessments will have more quality, which will contribute to the quality of the subsequent risk assessment.

The threat analysis effort focuses on one very basic question—"What or who is attempting to injure (deliberately) or is responsible for the injury of persons, materiel, facilities, infrastructures, information, and activities?" The focus of this question is always on operations and determining what injurious influences may occur (proactive), have been detected (alarms and indications), have occurred (reactive), may have shown indicators, or may be emerging within the physical and logical realms of operations. This approach has two benefits if supported by effective information sharing. First, it keeps the various groups aware of what kinds of threats are present in the environment so that they can take a more holistic approach to prevention, preparation, mitigation of vulnerabilities, and preparations for response to a threat event. Second, it increases the number of "eyes and ears" that can give the overall organization the ability to detect the approach or presence of a threat. This is called situational awareness in AP&S doctrine and is based on the following principles:

- All stakeholders understand and comply with baseline security safeguards and additional safeguards implemented as a result of a TRA. This means that they understand the residual risks to operations, and work within those boundaries. It also means that they understand what constitutes "normal" behavior in the operating environment—"business as usual," if you will—especially with respect to physical and logical access to valued assets.
- Knowing what constitutes business as usual, all are able to identify anomalies in operations, which are "not business as usual," and understand that it is their responsibility to challenge unknown persons conducting reconnaissance, attempting unauthorized access, and isolate or cease all unknown processes (within their levels of expertise and pursuant to policy and by following formal procedures).
- Since all anomalies to operations are likely to have an AIC nexus, reporting all such unusual incidents to line managers and to departmental or company security officer staff.

Through establishing technical and professional competence in AP&S, especially in threat assessment, as well as developing situational awareness and instilling mutual trust within an enterprise, among like enterprises, and also among collaborating enterprises (such as NCIs), more threat data will be made available to all, more comprehensive collation and analysis will be conducted by individual groups of threat specialists, more accurate and useful results (assessments) will be produced, and more threat products (threat assessments, intelligence summaries, etc.) will be shared among operational stakeholders. This will permit more accurate risk assessments to be conducted of individual facilities, infrastructures, and enterprises, which, in turn, will result in more informed decision making regarding the implementation of safeguards. The overall result will be a more appropriate cost-effective protective posture, and one which will lend itself to integration of safeguards within and among facilities and infrastructures, and among enterprises (government and private industry). Continued trust and the trusted sharing of useful products will be considered a success, and in business, as in threat assessment, success breeds success. More and better products will be shared by more and better threat analysts.

The terms of reference, charter, or "marching orders" for such a group of AP&S threat analysts would be straightforward to establish (assuming that all practitioners understand their roles, as discussed earlier). One key requirement (after trust) is courage on the part of both practitioners and senior management to open up their fingers and give up their tenuous hold on sensitive information in the outdated and mistaken impression that "knowledge is power" in AP&S, especially in threat assessment. While this concept may still be valid in politics, the author opines that it has no place in risk management, especially with respect to NCIs. Given the consequences of a breach or a successful attack on national objectives, in most cases the restrictive and exclusive "need to know" principle must be replaced with the more inclusive (within the threat assessment cohort) "need to share" principle, subject to the caveats and anonymization techniques discussed earlier.* Once the technical competence of the potential recipients of threat information has been established, and once trust is instilled, it remains only for the managers to park their egos and start the bidirectional information flow in strict conformance with the details of the information-sharing agreements among the group.

The goal is to achieve a broad representation of the AP&S and operational communities that can be influenced by threats. The ideal is to have each of the major organizations represented at the group by staff who are cognizant of the information-sharing requirements, authorized to speak about sensitive matters regarding the organization, and, most importantly, authorized to share threat information with all members of the group. As an example of the potential dynamics of such a professional body of threat analysts, individual representatives of the group could provide a routine and periodic overview (in real time) of what their organization has been contributing to operations and the challenges that they have faced. This would indicate the requirement to meet regularly to exchange ideas and information. In defining, describing, and analyzing those challenges, the speaker would use the framework of deliberate, accidental, natural, or deterioration threat types, taking into account both logical and physical domains. For example, the human resources organization may report that the online application system used to provide the initial screening of applicants (a personnel security measure) has shown signs of becoming unstable periodically (which might result in a false positive in showing a person to be trustworthy when he is not). The engineers responsible for the control system may indicate that they have been experiencing a much higher rate of replacement activities due to damaged equipment in a certain area, and the two seemingly disparate items may very well be collated and analyzed to determine that a deliberate threat event has occurred. It is important, in these meetings, that the information presented is accurate and critical (i.e., based on observation and analysis), nonaccusatory (this is not about performance reviews), as comprehensive as possible, and, perhaps most importantly, useful to others.

Part of the outcome of such meetings is a more defined and explained threat in terms of knowledge, skills, abilities, adaptability, resources, intent, commitment, and proximity. What is being established is a standardized, deterministic, and consistent approach to describing, collating, and analyzing threats to promote clearer understanding for subsequent assessment. With a clear understanding of threats, the analyst can then compare them to vulnerabilities to determine the further likelihood of a threat event taking place as it exploits those vulnerabilities.

In summary, threats are the most uncertain element in the risk equation, since, unlike the mission, assets, and vulnerabilities, the organization does not "own" the threats. Further, there is no apparent limit to the intent of a threat actor to launch an attack. Therefore, it is essential that the fullest picture as possible be amassed by threat analysts. It is clear that they cannot do this in isolation; they must collaborate and share threat information, unencumbered by outdated concepts of security clearances and other impediments to bidirectional information flows. Threat data can be sanitized through various methods, after which it will require courage on the part of senior management to release it. All recipients must be trusted to use the threat information responsibly, to share it with trusted colleagues, and to protect it appropriately throughout its life cycle. In this manner, the most accurate and current threat picture

---

* It should be clear that the need to share is based on operational requirements for an organization to be given access to information; it is not the simple act of making all information available to everyone.

will be possible, which will, in turn, improve the quality and utility of the subsequent risk assessment.

Vulnerabilities

A vulnerability, as put forward in the MIPIS program and other credible institutions that have a strong risk management approach, is described as a gap, weakness, or "lack" of something in an asset. These gaps are inherent in states of the asset (Chittester and Haimes 2004, p. 11) and in many cases of SCADA systems are the result of not seeing "security as a major integral part of the system" (Patel and Sanyal 2008, p. 401). These weaknesses can be exploited by a threat to cause a loss to the AIC of valued assets supporting the mission. This potential for loss is a risk, the extent of which must be assessed and safeguards applied to mitigate it. Since security and protection can never be absolute, and since not all risks can be mitigated completely (due, in great measure, to the uncertainty in assessing threats), there will always be some risk remaining. This is residual risk, which is assumed by senior management to be part of the cost of doing business. So, vulnerabilities are a key component of the risk equation, and also of risk management. Fortunately, vulnerabilities are perhaps the easiest to mitigate.

The primary reason that vulnerabilities can be mitigated is that they are "owned" by the enterprise. This is a key element, as asset values are likely relatively stable and threats are often outside of management control. All vulnerabilities are inherent, or else emerge, typically as an act of omission, not commission. All vulnerabilities exist or reside in assets, which are owned or controlled by the enterprise; specifically, senior management. Therefore, senior management has full control and discretion over addressing vulnerabilities in their enterprise. Since, by definition, vulnerabilities are a weakness, inadequacy, or lack of something that presents a "hole" to be exploited by a threat, they must be expressed in negative terms. The treatment of vulnerabilities has often proven difficult, however, because they are not approached clinically, dispassionately, and critically, but often in terms of a more accusatory approach that tends to devolve into unproductive, or even defensive, entrenchment of organizations. Figure 4.5 demonstrates a possible hierarchical structure around vulnerabilities.

The subjects of fragility and deterioration, however, are beginning to challenge this approach. In these cases, there can be vulnerabilities that emerge as the result of direct actions. For example, an increasing loading is a direct act that puts additional strain on an item and brings it closer to failure. These conditions, however, are often the result of systematic or management decisions, not just individual acts.

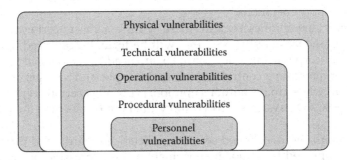

Figure 4.5 Taxonomy of nested vulnerabilities.

A fundamental vulnerability in any organization concerns the personnel (the inner layer of the taxonomy), and this may be the reason for organizations "circling the wagons" against the vulnerability analyst when he or she starts discussing weaknesses of individuals. While the intent is not personal, many people find it difficult to hear that they are not yet capable, even though it is true. Starting at the bottom of Figure 4.4, typical personnel vulnerabilities include the following:

- Lack of proper security clearance prior to being granted access to sensitive information. This results in a security breach in all cases.
- Lack of or inadequate technical training prior to assuming duties. This results in a capability gap while the individual learns "on the job," making errors and possibly causing accidents along the way.
- Ego and inability to acknowledge that one is not yet capable. This vulnerability can lead to anger, resentment toward the AP&S staff, and the hiding of other vulnerabilities. Without the maturity and courage to disclose fully the extent of additional training, education, and experience required, personnel will not be able to improve their operational capability.
- Inadequate supervision. Some senior managers in organizations think (erroneously) that "a manager can manage anything" and put untrained, uneducated, and inexperienced personnel in charge of competent practitioners. These managers simply do not have the capability to manage, guide, and correct technically competent staff, especially in AP&S. Another instance of inadequate supervision occurs when managers simply do not follow up on the activities of their subordinates and do not know what or how much work is being done; quality assurance often does not even make the cut as a business function.
- Lack of security awareness program. While senior management is ultimately accountable for protecting the assets supporting mission success, all personnel are responsible for protecting the assets entrusted to them as part of displaying due care. If they do not know what is expected of them to protect sensitive information, high-value equipment, the secrecy of how they operate, or to physically protect themselves, then there will be insufficient assurance of the AIC of assets, which could impact operations.

It is important that personnel vulnerabilities be addressed first, since many of the other vulnerabilities could cascade and be exacerbated due to weaknesses at the level of the individual. It must be stressed that these are not typically *personal* weaknesses, or individual flaws, but *personnel* weaknesses, which are institutional. There is no intent in vulnerability analysis to impugn any individual, but only to identify gaps that could be exploited by a threat. Vulnerability analysts are, after all, corporate resources whose primary role is to support operations.

If personnel vulnerabilities remain, there will be some uncertainty as to whether effective policy, standards, and procedures will be formally captured, or whether they will remain in the "corporate memory" or in "Sam's head." If no one but Sam understands how to operate or maintain a control system, for example, and Sam gets hit by a bus, this represents a SPOF, which, in the author's opinion, is the most serious type of vulnerability when discussing SCADA systems. Procedural vulnerabilities include the following:

- Lack of or outdated distributed security policies, standards, and directives. Policies should be approved by senior management as an expression of the importance of protecting valued assets that support operations. It is preferable that all key security policies such as corporate (physical, personnel, operational), information system, emergency management, and continuity of operations security policies be contained in one document. This assists in addressing any vulnerabilities associated with conflicting or incomplete direction.

- Inconsistent or conflicting procedures. At the process level, it is critical to ensure consistent, repeatable performance by all operators; otherwise, an apparently minor lack of attention to an anomaly could escalate very quickly to affect the whole process.

If the correct performance of individuals cannot be assured in light of inadequate training and procedures, then there could be significant operational impact. Operational vulnerabilities include the following:

- Lack of alignment of individual operational processes. This could result in one process working against another, thereby introducing more operational vulnerabilities.
- Lack of training in hazard and accident prevention.
- Inadequate personal protective protection equipment. This is either a personnel or an operational vulnerability and could lead to injuries which could render key personnel unavailable to do their jobs.
- Lack of cross-training of personnel. This could lead to SPOFs if key personnel with unique knowledge or skills are unavailable for work.
- Lack of communication among and within business lines. The classic "silos" impede information flow, understanding, and overall operational effectiveness, and could introduce "holes" in the overall corporate posture that could be exploited by an internal or external threat.
- Lack of operational security, which typically means maintaining the confidentiality of the workings of the organization, from strategic direction, to operational-level business lines, to tactical operation of equipment. It also refers to maintaining an operational focus to work activity and ensuring that no actions are taken which could affect the efficiency, reputation, or credibility of the organization.

Vulnerabilities in the first three types could start to have compounding effects on operational effectiveness; when technology is added to the mix, it can become even more serious. Technical vulnerabilities include the following:

- Lack of hardening of IT systems supporting operations. Hardening includes antimalware, intrusion detection or protection systems, disabling all unnecessary ports and accesses to the system, timely and complete patch management, encrypting open communications where warranted, and continuous monitoring of activity to identify anomalous actions.
- Lack of physical separation of IT systems and lack of integrated management. According to Haimes and Chittester (2005, pp. 3–4), "The need to store business information has added a new function to SCADA: the management information system (MIS). MIS enables managers and customers in remote locations to monitor overall operations and to receive data that facilitates the making and review of high-level business decisions. The ... SCADA—the engineering process control subsystem and the MIS—could be in conflict at times ... the PCS has dominance ... integrating security into the SCADA system more difficult. The situation is further complicated by company hierarchy; ... the MIS is under the control of the chief information office, while the PCS is controlled by engineering." "This integration of SCADA networks

with other networks has made SCADA vulnerable to various cyber threats" (Zhu and Sastry 2010, p. 2).

- Inadequate configuration management. Doctrinally, all changes to an approved system have security implications; accordingly, if all changes do not go through a formal assessment process for operational and security concerns, then new vulnerabilities or instabilities in the network or control system could be introduced.
- Inappropriate clipping levels. These settings, to determine when an anomaly should set off an alarm, could lead to more vulnerabilities, and possibly an attack, if they are set too openly.
- Infrequent maintenance. Not checking and maintaining equipment regularly could lead to failures, which may affect operational schedules.

Finally, if vulnerabilities exist in overall operations, the attitude of line personnel and management could be transmitted to the physical posture of the organization. Physical vulnerabilities could include the following:

- Inadequate physical access control. This could include leaving doors and windows insecure (including propping doors open for smoke breaks), not challenging unknown individuals, and so on.
- Lack of defense in depth. This could include not having perimeter fencing, signage, or reception areas.
- Not physically locking and controlling valued assets, such as IT systems, negotiables, IT server rooms, control rooms, consumables such as fuel, high-value equipment and spare parts, and so on.

Thus, it is seen that vulnerabilities do not exist individually or in a vacuum; rather, they can spread and either introduce new ones or exacerbate the magnitude of existing vulnerabilities. The greater the number, type, and extent of the vulnerabilities, the greater potential exists for threats to launch a successful attack, resulting in risks to the AIC of valued assets, with consequent operational impact. As with threats and asset valuation, vulnerability treatment is another instance where practitioners and professionals must consider the needs of operations first.

It is important for the vulnerability analyst to understand the concept of a temporal vulnerability, one that changes over time, such as the fragility of infrastructure in different seasons or the ability of an individual to withstand fatigue when working long hours. Most temporal vulnerabilities are a result of deterioration, whether accidental or deliberate, of a capability, as indicated in the aforementioned examples. When paired with deterioration as a threat, the risk is potentially compounded.

Understanding how these vulnerabilities emerge is critical to understanding risk. Consider a physical example of a building completely surrounded by a deep ditch over which persons take a footpath. If the threat is a vehicle-borne improvised explosive device (VBIED) that cannot get close to the facility because of the ditch, what changes in the vulnerability to this kind of attack can be discerned? There are questions to be answered here; for example, can the truck use the footpath or use bridging materials that may be readily available that can be used by the truck to cross the gap? At the same time, perhaps the driver of the truck is aware of the physical obstacle from previous reconnaissance, and will also bring materials that can be used to breach the obstacle. To counter the potential for a threat to exploit a vulnerability, the individual must understand the potential threat event and the extent to which conditions that are observed reduce the means, opportunity, or motive of the threat agent to launch an attack. This can be triaged by using a hasty method of linking the capabilities, opportunities, and intent associated with the threat to the means, opportunity, and intent facilitated by the environment (i.e., vulnerability).

While this approach is applicable directly to physical networks, it is also applicable to logical networks. IT equipment may be susceptible to threats exploiting vulnerabilities and causing risks that involve destruction, disruption, or corruption of equipment. At the logical level, it may include opportunities for malicious or otherwise disruptive information to cause havoc with the system, through exploiting such vulnerabilities as a lack of separation (from other networks, from other sensitivities of information, or other operating environments), inadequate hardening controls (such as firewalls or intrusion detection systems), or even inadequate training of personnel (which could cause accidents).

The description and representation of a vulnerability, therefore, must map directly to the threat (which can exploit it to cause a risk) and to an asset (which both houses the vulnerability and is impacted by the risk should a threat successfully exploit a vulnerability). This link can be analyzed in terms of the following:

- *The capabilities gap*: Describing how the vulnerability facilitates access by the threat to the asset to gain some capability desired by the threat agent (such as hijacking an IT transaction or service).
- *The opportunity gap*: Describing how the time and space available to the threat agent to exploit a vulnerability has been changed so that the attack has a greater probability of success.
- *The intent gap*: Describing how conditions found would reasonably lead an attacker (based on past tactics, motivation, and similar factors) to conclude that the rewards associated with successfully exploiting a vulnerability outweigh the risks of failure, of being identified as the attacker, or of being apprehended.

This description would also benefit from an understanding of the organizational breadth and depth associated with any vulnerability. Although all vulnerabilities are "owned" by the enterprise, since they map directly to assets used to achieve objectives, there are differing parameters that describe the mitigative effect that the organization can exert on the vulnerability to address it. These parameters can be described in descending order of effect as follows:

- *Span of control*: Exists when AP&S analysts in the organization have full, direct contact with the asset, have full authority from senior management (typically in policy), and have the technical capability to change that asset's structure, location, magnitude, or environment to reduce the exploitability of the vulnerability. This is the most effective situation in terms of being able to respond to the detection of a vulnerability because all decisions are reached internally at the lowest operational level and are most likely to be in line with the requirements, objectives, and goals of the organization.
- *Span of influence*: Exists when there is less direct control by specialist AP&S staffs, when decisions must be coordinated among various business line owners within an organization, or when vulnerability mitigation decisions must be coordinated with one or more other organizations. This situation seeks to acquire the range of action as per the span of control parameter, but must also ensure that the concerns of the other organizations are addressed. The AP&S analyst must influence the other organizations' operations and AP&S staff that vulnerability mitigation actions are

in the best interests of all. *Memoranda of understanding* or *agreement* are often used to establish the acceptable ranges of action in a specific case of vulnerability mitigation, taking into account all operational, financial, and cultural impacts of any measures taken.

- *Span of awareness*: Exists when processes are in place to identify and analyze vulnerabilities, as well as take preparatory steps toward mitigation, such as communicating their existence and assessment of magnitude to all stakeholders or hiring technically capable consultants. In this parameter, the organization cannot yet influence the environment or vulnerability, but has detected it to the point where it can begin to respond. The use of *bulletins, technical advisories,* and other communiqués issued by the intelligence section within the organization's security group could fall within this parameter.

- *No influence*: Exists where the organization relies on assets owned by another organization, or is not authorized or not technically able to access the assets to identify, analyze, or take mitigative action against vulnerabilities. No formal or informal relationship exists between the organizations and there is no trust established between them. Uncovering potential vulnerabilities is typically the result of an investigation of operational or performance impacts that are not otherwise explainable. Many organizations operate with areas in which they have no influence or awareness, especially in distributed operations having little direction from the center. This includes distributed and decentralized IT infrastructures. In all instances of this parameter, there is an absence of formal policy, hierarchy, or architecture; also typically missing is a cadre of trained operations or AP&S staff. This situation is best described as chaotic, nondeterministic, and inefficient. Staffs are not aware of the mission of the enterprise, nor of its main objectives, and are incapable of taking action on behalf of the mission in the absence of information or authority. In this parameter, it is the role of vulnerability analysts, supported by their AP&S managers, to identify the presence of vulnerabilities and commence building the relationships, understanding, and trust with the various business line owners and senior management to establish spans of awareness, influence, and, ultimately, control.

It is important to remember that these parameters must all "roll up" to the highest and most effective span of control parameter before trusted change can be effected; specifically, the taking of mitigative action to minimize the magnitude of the vulnerability.

Once the relevance of the vulnerability to the organization is established with respect to mission threat and asset, the vulnerability analysis (how big the gap is) has evolved into a vulnerability assessment (how significant the gap is to my operation). The focus of the vulnerability assessment is on taking the technical and operational details of the vulnerability (in terms of how it functions) and determining their relevance to the assets involved and the threats identified. It is at this point that we can begin to see the formation of the overall risk picture. The second part of the vulnerability assessment involves identifying the relevant level of control that the organization can bring to bear on the vulnerability.

In summary, vulnerabilities are weaknesses, gaps, or "lack of" something in an asset that could be exploited by a threat agent to cause a risk to the AIC of that asset, and thereby have a negative impact on mission success. Vulnerabilities are perhaps the best element of the risk equation on which to focus protection efforts, since they are typically within the physical, logical, and operational control of the enterprise.

Risk assessment and management

Once risk has been analyzed ("How bad is it?") and assessed ("How bad is it to us?"), something has to be done about it. The application of safeguards by security professionals, and the assumption of residual risk by senior management, is what risk management is all about. The management processes of "defining security roles of personnel, establishing rigorous management processes, … implementing security policy [at the] technical, operational, quality, and system [levels]" (Patel and Sanyal 2008, p. 401) all contribute to risk management. To be most effective, risk management must be proactive (Schneier 2003), as it deters, prevents, protects against, and mitigates adverse events before they occur. According to Patel et al. (2008, p. 483), "Risk assessment is … usually the most difficult and error prone step in the risk management process." That is why it is essential that risk analysts be trained, educated, and experienced to achieve usable results.

Risk management applied

As described in the introduction to this chapter, risk is a function of mission, asset values, threats, and vulnerabilities. Having objectives to achieve (mission), there will be some deliberate, accidental, natural, or deterioration elements (threats) that can exploit weaknesses or gaps (vulnerabilities) in an asset to cause an unwanted impact or uncertainty of a negative result that can affect the AIC of an organization's assets, thereby affecting mission success. Risks, once identified, analyzed, and assessed, must be treated; specific safeguards will be discussed in the next chapter. Applying risk management is simply putting into place the programs that can implement safeguards and treating with the residual risk, since "there is no such a thing as perfect security or prevention product … [which would be] extremely expensive both in economic and operational sense but also technically and socially infeasible. The arm-race between protections and attacks is a continuous up-hill battle" (Zhu and Sastry 2010, p. 2). The remainder of this chapter will cover those programmatic elements which serve to apply risk management to an enterprise.

One key step, often overlooked, is identifying the actual owner of the risk. Only this individual has the ability to make decisions on what courses of action are to be taken and where the triggers and thresholds for further action are going to be set. Too often, one looks at the risk management decisions to see that detached committees, working groups, or even individuals have essentially usurped the risk owner's role, diminishing his or her ability to maintain their accountability. There is a significant need to ensure that those making recommendations understand who owns the risks and collaborates with those risk owners to understand the basis of previous decisions.

Once risks have been assessed, they must be treated in a programmatic manner. Chittester and Haimes (2004, p. 10) suggest that three questions can assist in decision making:

1. What can be done and what options are available?
2. What are the associated trade-offs in terms of all costs, benefits, and risks?
3. What are the impacts of current management decisions on future options?

The answers to these questions will drive the programs for risk management, of which there may be many. Each contributes to mitigating (or reducing) and thereafter managing (maintaining) risk at a level acceptable to senior management. These components are introduced in the chapter offering a deeper treatment of safeguards and countermeasures.

Figure 4.6 Nested risk taxonomy.

Effective risk management is indicated by the presence of processes and capabilities in the organization's AP&S program that will continually address the categories of risk (Figure 4.6).

These risks are nested in a suggested order of priority. As noted earlier, all risks map to some loss of the AIC of valued assets. Since employees and staff are arguably the most critical asset to meeting mission objectives, risks to them are considered to be the most significant. Trusted and capable personnel can mitigate all other risks; conversely, untrusted or incapable staff can exacerbate all other risks, thereby having the most serious impact on mission success. Risks to personnel most frequently result in absenteeism due to injury through accident or workplace violence, or reduction of productivity due to errors, inadequate motivation, training, or supervision. Processes and capabilities within the AP&S program that would be appropriate to manage these risks include the following:

- An AP&S policy suite (policy, directives, standards, procedures, guidelines)
- An AP&S awareness program, including rewards for compliance and sanctions for noncompliance
- Periodic spot checks by AP&S staff (also an operational process)
- An occupational safety and health program
- An emergency response program

Having addressed personnel risks programmatically, arguably the next most important risks for the organization to manage are technical risks, since technology (IT, telecom, SCADA, etc.) permeates virtually all organizations, although with the advent of voice over IP (VOIP), the line between IT and telecom is becoming blurred. Technical risks typically result in unauthorized disclosure or modification of sensitive information, denial of IT service, equipment malfunctions, incorrect processing sequences on the production line, and so on. Processes and capabilities within the AP&S program that would be appropriate to manage these risks include the following:

- An information system security program that features a policy suite; monitoring (real or near real time) and auditing (periodic snapshot) of security-related system activity; hardening; and certification and accreditation of all IT and telecom systems

Once a trusted cadre of staff is established and trusted systems are implanted, the next set of risks to be addressed programmatically is procedural. Risks could result in errors affecting operations, or in not taking correct and corrective action on the processing line, with resultant work stoppages. Processes and capabilities within the AP&S program that would be appropriate to manage these risks include the following:

- A process mapping program that formally records all business processes, interdependencies, and steps to operate
- Formal written procedures that can be used to teach and evaluate the performance of AP&S practitioners

The next set of risks concern the physical environment or "protective shell" of any operation. Risks could result in unauthorized access to the facility and subsequent risks to availability as a result of theft of assets, sabotage of equipment, injury to staff, and so on. Risks from damaged equipment, especially IT and telecom, could accrue from unreliable heating, ventilation, air-conditioning, or refrigeration systems. Processes and capabilities to address these risks could include the following:

- Formal access control programs that feature electronic access control systems, wearing of badges, or challenging of all unknown persons or those without badges
- Regular maintenance programs for heating, ventilation, air-conditioning and refrigeration (HVACR) systems

Finally, operational risks affect the overall ability of the organization to meet its service delivery or production mandates. These are perhaps the most significant risks, and also the "umbrella" risks under which all the previous risks contribute. Operational risks could arise from the unauthorized disclosure of intellectual property or trade secrets, from production impacts in not getting services or products to the customer on time, and so on. Reputational, financial, and branding risks could also be included within operational risks. Processes and capabilities to address these risks could include the following:

- Routine reporting programs to senior staff for both operational and security-related incidents, followed by programs of formal, collaborative analysis of incidents
- Employee indoctrination and awareness programs to inculcate all with a sense of operational focus

Superimposed on all of these risk treatment programs are security intelligence and incident investigations programs. The former serve to provide current threat information as part of the risk management process, while the latter serve to validate all components of the overall risk management program. Both will contribute to determining the most appropriate safeguards to implement, as will be discussed in the next chapter.

Risks, by their nature, are imprecise, potential, and unverifiable until they are realized. Thereafter, they can be analyzed and adjustments made to the security posture. Part of the challenge in corporate-level risk management is that both senior management and line employees seek refinement and detail in the guidance and advice that they are given—but do not understand that this refinement and detail does not necessarily produce an exact value of return on investment. Senior managers want a quantitative expression of security return on investment, but this is not a linear relationship of X dollars providing Y protection from risk. As noted earlier, risk management is an art and not a science; the majority of threats contributing to risks are nontechnical, so it is not possible to apply quantitative, technical solutions to address all risks. This reality is quite unsatisfying to busy senior managers who are most comfortable in comparing values in spreadsheets. In some cases, this is why security risk management gets short shrift in ERM; it is less predictable, therefore easier to disregard in the short term. If not considered, however, security risks will very likely be realized in some form, and will have a significant effect on operations. Line employees, likewise, often demand clear proof and justification for implementing safeguards, which in all cases pose some inconvenience. They often cite a lack of historical precedent; so, if it has not (yet) happened here, why worry? Unfortunately, this is one of the fundamental challenges to an AP&S practitioner, that of "selling" the product of security in the absence of a direct impact nexus. Successful advisors are able to take security incidents that have befallen other organizations and extrapolate or apply them to the reluctant organization. But, it is acknowledged that precision in the likelihood or impact of the future risk events is not possible.

It may also be that the senior management team lacks the necessary mindset and openness to listen actively to reports on current security risks, which typically fall outside of routine risk management ranges and thresholds—itself a significant corporate vulnerability. The fundamental point to understand with risk is that it must be an honest and, as far as possible, accurate reflection of the conditions as they are found or expected. This requires trained, educated, experienced, and convincing AP&S specialists to meet those criteria, and also "a common language for risk management that may be used for describing risks" (Stoneburner 2006, p. 485).

The goal, therefore, should be to remain true to scientific principles where such principles can be applied (typically to the technical threats, vulnerabilities, and risks), but understand that there will be several risk types where scientific principles either do not apply or cannot provide the necessarily level of refinement. Once that point has been reached, then the practitioner must be able to put forward a reasonable, defensible, and confidently logical argument as to why a certain selection or decision is put forward for consideration. Reasoned arguments emerge as a result of considering risk from both historical data and also from making reasonable forecasts or predictions based on a strong situational awareness and currency with threat and intelligence information in the industry. Too often, a program manager or other administrator will argue that there is no threat (and therefore no risk) because there are no statistics or reports associated with the risk. Sophists tend to use this argument because it fits their own agendas—usually associated with making the case that nothing needs to be implemented (thereby reducing inconvenience) and no additional funding needs to be expended. A lack of historical data does not mean that the organization is not at risk. It can mean, simply, that no attack has taken place *yet*; or it can mean that no monitoring or auditing processes are in place to capture the information necessary to identify risks. It can also mean that the risk is defined differently or categorized differently within an operational system, perhaps under performance or quality of service parameters. It could also be a case of lack of communication among the various risk analysts in an organization; when risks are considered independently or in isolation among the various business lines and systems in an enterprise, the risk is often only partly identified within the organization, not fully understood in terms of the various impacts among business lines, and, therefore, not addressed with an integrated, strategic, business perspective. Finally, it can also mean that the risk under consideration is the result of something very infrequent (with, therefore, a lack of records) or something very new (such as emergent technology). In an effective risk management program, the practitioners conduct "worst-case" analysis (low-likelihood/high-impact events) and remain current on the technology, including threats and vulnerabilities.

Effective risk management means being able to synthesize all of the work mentioned earlier and accomplish four things. These are the following:

1. Ensuring that the relationships between mission, asset, threat, and vulnerability are mapped appropriately to the operations and requirements of the organization. This means being able to link those relationships among all business lines within an

enterprise to the requirements of parent organizations and other subsidiaries, and to all upstream and downstream stakeholders, especially customers and clients.

2. Ensuring that this approach is used consistently and appropriately for all forms of risk—documenting challenges in arriving at conclusions where they arise. Integrating risk management among all of these entities requires a deterministic, formal approach. This will provide a common picture from which to operate securely.

3. Ensuring that management has agreed to scales that can be used to communicate the outcomes of the risk assessment process in a meaningful and actionable way. Haimes and Chittester (2005, p. 1) remind us that "business and government still insist, and justifiably so, on the need for a way to evaluate, with some metrics, the efficacy of risk assessment and management associated with cyber attacks on telecommunications and supervisory control and data acquisition (SCADA) systems." Determining risk is but an intermediate step in risk management, and has value only to the extent that it will result in mitigative measures, which will be discussed in the next chapter. Again, consistency of terminology, of degree or significance of threats, vulnerabilities, or risks, is key to mutual understanding and integrated, cost-effective program implementation.

4. Ensuring that management communicates target residual risk, or risk appetite, early in the risk management process. By imposing any conditions that would result in senior management's nearly automatic conclusion that a level of risk is too high to accept, AP&S analysts will be able to efficiently determine appropriate safeguards and not waste time on risk management strategies when the appetite for risk is low. One method of assisting senior management in determining their risk tolerance is to provide the results of the vulnerability assessment, so that management understands how much influence it has on reducing the risk, since it "owns" the vulnerabilities more than the other elements of the risk management equation.

This last factor is linked directly to how management will choose to treat the risks that it faces. Options will be influenced by a number of factors. The first may be the level and nature of risk and how it translates into losses (in terms of AIC) to the organization. The second major factor will be the span of control that the organization can exert over the assets, threats, and vulnerabilities involved. This will guide the specific risk treatment actions that are taken by the company's senior management. These can be described in terms of the following:

- Directly *mitigating* the risk in terms of reducing any one of the values associated with asset value, threat, or vulnerability through various steps, including:
- Reducing the individual asset value by eliminating single points of failure (hot spares, inventory) or increasing the resiliency of infrastructure (redundancy), thereby reducing potential losses.
- Taking steps to reduce the threat in an area by engaging specially state-approved bodies that can engage in law enforcement or similar activities, and by sharing threat information among stakeholders and neighbors. This may result in an overall improved protective posture that will reduce the intent for a threat to act in a specific area.
- Addressing vulnerabilities by reducing the means, opportunity, motive, or perceived benefit to the attacker.
- *Sharing* the risk among organizations through the formation of communities that, through their collective efforts, have a greater impact than if they acted independently for the same level of effort. Councils, industry associations, and working

groups may contribute to understanding in this respect. Thereafter, through formal contractual agreements, individual senior managers can accept shared risk, especially in operating integrated systems, programs, and services.

- *Transferring* the risk to another entity, through either contracting out the requirement to return risk levels to acceptable levels, or having another party assume responsibility for dealing with the consequences of the event, such as an insurance company or a contracted security guard force. It should be reemphasized that this approach does not absolve senior management from accountability for decisions as to how those risks are treated. Transferring risk may still leave the organization open to a range of legal actions (in terms of failing to take all reasonable steps to prevent harm) or to a loss in terms of branding, reputation, and so on.
- *Accepting* the risk, where those accountable have made an informed decision that the level of risk to the AIC of operations does not conflict with the organization's requirements, nor does it represent potentially unacceptable losses. According to Haimes and Chittester (2005, p. 2), "The level of required information assurance, or conversely the level of acceptable risk, depends on the critical nature of the system's mission," which maps back to the section on mission analysis.
- *Avoiding* risks through changing locations of operations that place adequate time and distance between the operations of the organization and identified key threats, so as to make them less relevant.
- *Ignoring* the risk by choosing to reject the arguments offered by trained, educated, and experienced AP&S risk analysts. This is never considered to be prudent or demonstrative of due diligence, both necessary qualities of senior management. This approach could lead to legal issues such as negligence or failing to act in line with an appropriate duty of care.

The concept of the span of control also factors significantly in terms of determining how the organization wishes to respond. Where there is adequate span of control, the organization may decide to act unilaterally and inform its various stakeholders. This is efficient and, as long as the advice of trusted and capable AP&S analysts is taken, the most effective course of action. As this span of control diminishes, such as would happen where an agreement exists regarding the use of distributed and networked assets, the restrictions on unilateral freedom of action decrease.* This is where carefully defined and crafted agreements become important, as they reduce the potential for friction among interested or implicated organizations that can occur where expectations are less than clear. Where there is little more than a span of awareness, the organization may be limited to taking steps to learn more about potential risks so that cogent arguments can be made to influence, and then control, treatment of risks. In all cases, however, the degree of control that can be exerted is a factor of capacity to respond effectively to the identification of risks and implement appropriate controls.

Managing more complex risks

Part of the value in taking a formal and deterministic risk management approach lies in the ability it gives security practitioners to put forward consistent and understandable recommendations to senior decision makers regarding the management of risk, regardless

---

* This is perhaps most prevalent in NCIs, with multiple ownership, operational responsibilities, distances involved, and complexity of architectures.

of how complex, complicated, integrated, new, or diverse. Often, it may be a simple case of reiterating the regulatory or policy requirements to comply with relevant and appropriate best practices. This compliance, however, should not be interpreted as leading to effective or appropriate security in the wider sense, since compliance with baselines is the lowest form or protection; there will typically be peculiar threats and vulnerabilities that are not addressed adequately by general baselines. These are identified and assessed in a TRA, so additional safeguards would be based on that same TRA. This is the essence of threat-risk-based security. Baselines may provide overprotection in some cases, but in many more cases provide underprotection. It is in analyzing the delta of protection requirements and proposing risk-based safeguards that the AP&S practitioner provides the real value added to a protection posture.

Compliance with baselines as a risk management approach is safe and defensible by security managers ("I was just following policy"), but does not provide the value added, or expected, by accountable senior management. It may demonstrate "institutional" due care for assets, but in most cases not appropriate due care, given the diverse threats and vulnerabilities in many systems and enterprises. While the line manager may escape scrutiny with this argument, the senior managers will not. Although a rules-based compliance approach to AP&S addresses known and set questions and then applies predictable, sound, proven generic controls to address known and generic (if not current or emerging) threats and vulnerabilities, in many contexts this approach would itself constitute a vulnerability, because it introduces a gap in analysis. It does not allow for the identification and analysis of new missions, assets, threats, or vulnerabilities that can lead to risks. And, since compliance-based safeguards are typically open-source industry best practices, they will be well known by an adversary, who can study and analyze them to determine the best threat vectors (routes to the asset), strategies for vulnerability exploitation, and specific targets of an asset in terms of AIC; for example, destruction of a production line, denial of service attack on a SCADA system, corruption of data through masquerading, or stealing company secrets. It also leads to an attacker being able to engineer his or her way through the existing baseline safeguards—understanding that attacks need not always be technical, since social engineering may have a greater potential for attack success if baselines only are employed. Security awareness programs mandated by baselines are typically not current, not taken seriously, nor is it assured that all employees participate if a threat-risk-based approach is not implemented, because there will be little new or captivating threat or vulnerability information to pique their interest. If it is relatively certain that a company has not implemented threat-risk-based safeguards above baselines, then that company increases its susceptibility to attack, since it is seen as a weak link.

Complex risks may be described as those that feature the following:

- Emerging technology as the attack vector or as the target.
- Multiple and diverse threat sources; for example, a physical, social engineering, and concurrent cyberattack, or a distributed denial of service attack.
- Extreme motivation and disregard for collateral damage on behalf of the threat agent; for example, terrorists, criminals, the deranged, state-sponsored actors, or the excessively greedy. These risks could result in extensive property damage or contamination.
- Multiple and diverse assets targeted, perhaps concurrently.
- Multiple offices or production facilities targeted, perhaps concurrently.

Complex risks require complex analysis by well-trained and capable AP&S analysts, preferably those who have the trust and authority of their senior management to conduct extensive, often intrusive, and normally time-consuming analysis. Complex risk analysis also typically requires extensive coordination and liaison among stakeholders at all levels; this will require authority from senior management to "sidestep" routine (and bureaucratically inefficient) chains of command or reporting relationships. Trust by senior management in the technical, operational, and corporate capability of the risk analysts is essential for complex risks to be addressed adequately. Both AP&S practitioners and line managers can collaborate and actually break the chain of events that lead up to complex risks.

Consider a basic cyberattack on a discrete (unconnected) computer network such as a traditional SCADA system. This attack may be broken down into a series of steps, much like the processes used by the organization's own operations, and may include the following mental analysis on the part of the adversary:

- I must be able to identify where the system is housed and gain some level of access to it.
- I must determine if the assets that I want or those that I want to impact are actually there, and if the attack will meet my objectives.
- I must confirm the level of protection that is afforded those assets and if that level of protection changes with time or other factors.
- I must be able to pass through the perimeter controls, typically comprising a fence and a guard post, perhaps with some closed-circuit video equipment.
- I must be able to get into the building, hopefully without alerting anyone.
- I must be able to get past the receptionist (perhaps using social engineering).
- I must be able to gain access to the restricted area in such a way that I remain undetected for 15 min, which I estimate is required to launch the attack.
- I must be able to turn on one of the workstations.
- I must be able to use my cracking tools on the workstation to escalate my privileges and gain access to the files that I want to steal or corrupt to the operating systems or applications that I want to infect or change.
- I must be able to locate the files.
- I must be able to download the files without being detected or that provides me with 10 min before a response is made so that I can escape.
- I must be able to leave the restricted area with my USB key without being detained.
- I must be able to leave the facility.
- I must be able to download the file from my own computer.
- I must be able to break through any encryption placed on it.
- I must be able to exploit this information for my own purposes.

In thinking like an adversary and decomposing an attack into individual threat vectors, the AP&S risk analyst can isolate

- The business processes that could be affected
- Intermediate or final assets targeted
- Types of complementary or contributing threats that could be brought to bear
- Different vulnerabilities that may be exploited in isolation, concurrently, or in succession to bring the attacker closer to the targeted assets

This case study is not intended to be an in-depth coverage of safeguards, but is, rather, an illustration of how risk management processes can be effective if utilized by capable practitioners in a deterministic manner. From this decomposition, there emerge several points along the threat vector where the attack can be disrupted. For example, the attacker may have to pass through physical access control points at various stages of a layered defense that would prevent him or her from ever reaching the computer terminal. Similarly, even if the adversary makes it to the terminal, the USB ports can be disabled as part of workstation hardening to prevent the use of removable media. The terminal might involve technical controls, such as strong identification/authentication procedures that do not allow a terminal to operate unless the username and a complex, routinely changed password are entered. There may be a program of random searches of the person to prevent the unauthorized removal of media. And the list goes on. By fully understanding how the attack is likely to take place given the nature of the threat, the next step is to reduce vulnerabilities through the manipulation of means, opportunity, and motive or intent for the threat agent to act. The organization may also seek to manipulate the adversary's perception of the asset value through implementing stringent safeguards; for example, requiring highly sensitive documents to be stored on-site only on hard media, copied to prevent destruction, and stored off-site in secure locations after being strongly encrypted, requiring special software to open them. By manipulating the values of assets, threats, and vulnerabilities, risk analysts can either break the attack chain or reduce the impacts associated with an attack to acceptable levels.

This decomposition approach for complex risks also allows for a degree of efficiency to be realized. By comparing various threat models and vectors, analysts can identify overlaps that could allow the organization to apply a single safeguard that mitigates a number of different threat vectors. Some care must be taken to ensure that there is an appropriate balance of redundancy and resiliency (key elements in establishing layers of defense) in the security controls on the one hand, and efficiency and minimization of inconvenience on the other. In essence, the security practitioner must be able to work across the various communities in his or her organization to balance not only an appropriate number and type of controls, but also an appropriate level of operational impact within the organization. What is important is that doing nothing is not a preferred option when the mission is important and when valued assets are involved. Regardless of whether the threat is natural, deliberate, or accidental, action is preferred. This also applies to deterioration as a threat. Monitoring of deterioration of a facility or infrastructure and assessment of its extent drives one of three management decisions: do nothing, rehabilitate, or replace (Morcous et al., 2003). Maintaining current inventories, infrastructure condition databases, and maintenance data, along with having trained inspectors follow inspection intervals consistent with projected deterioration rates, are essential to addressing deterioration. These can all be considered programmatic activities, and are indicative of the components of an effective risk management program.

Risk management: Pulling it all together

In the management of risk, we have looked at the risk assessment and management processes in detail and then identified how those various elements interact. This interaction is important, not only in determining the nature and level of risk, but also in terms of later analyzing different attack vectors (a threat plus the route that it takes to exploit a vulnerability) that can be subjected to certain safeguards or controls so as to deter or disrupt the attack. Having identified these points, the concept of spans of control has been introduced in terms of the organization's ability to add, change, or remove factors that can impact the likelihood or gravity of a threat event. Finally, we have looked at communicating risks (including their elements) to overcome the challenges associated with analyzing threat events that cascade through systems or that escalate toward higher levels of impact. The next step is for the practitioner and management to decide on the controls that will be considered appropriate to the identified risk, and that mitigate risk to a level acceptable to senior management in terms of operational impact and tolerable in terms of social and cultural norms. Hentea (2008, p. 4) refers to this as "the process of assigning priority to, budgeting, implementing, and maintaining appropriate risk reducing measures." In all cases, it is senior management who ultimately decide the safeguards that are implemented and who is accountable for the residual risk to operations.

References

ASIS International. (n.d.). *Protection of Assets Manual.* Available online. Alexandria, VA: ASIS International.

Bobbio, A., Bonanni, G., Ciancamerla, E., Clemente, R., Iacomini, A., Minichino, M., and Zendri, E. (2010). Unavailability of critical SCADA communication links interconnecting a power grid and a telco network. *Reliability Engineering and System Safety*, 95(12), 1345–1357.

Cardenas, A. A., Roosta, T., and Sastry, S. (2009). Rethinking security properties, threat models, and the design space in sensor networks: A case study in SCADA systems. *Ad Hoc Networks*, 7(8), 1434–1447.

Chittester, C. G. and Haimes, Y. Y. (2004). Risks of terrorism to information technology and to critical interdependent infrastructures. *Journal of Homeland Security and Emergency Management*, 1(4), 1075–1075.

Gold, S. (2008). Look after your heart. *Infosecurity*, 5(8), 38–42.

Haimes, Y. Y. and Chittester, C. G. (2005). A roadmap for quantifying the efficacy of risk management of information security and interdependent SCADA systems. *Journal of Homeland Security and Emergency Management*, 2(2), 117.

Hentea, D. M. (2008). Improving security for SCADA control systems. *Interdisciplinary Journal of Information, Knowledge, and Management*, 3(12), 4.

Kurtz, J. (2004). Chapter D–D1/D2–Dynstat apparatus. *Dictionary of Civil Engineering: English–French.* New York: Kluwer Academic/Plenum.

Lowrance, W. W. (1976). *Of Acceptable Risk: Science and the Determination of Safety.* Los Altos, CA: William Kaufmann.

Morcous, G., Lounis, Z., and Mirza, M. (2003). Identification of environmental categories for Markovian deterioration models of bridge decks. *Journal of Bridge Engineering*, 8(6), 353–361.

Patel, S. C., Graham, J. H., and Ralston, P. A. S. (2008). Quantitatively assessing the vulnerability of critical information systems: A new method for evaluating security enhancements. *International Journal of Information Management*, 28(6), 483–491.

Patel, S. C. and Sanyal, P. (2008). Securing SCADA systems. *Information Management & Computer Security*, 16(4), 398–414.

Stoneburner, G. (2006). Toward a unified security/safety model. *Computer*, 39(8), 96–97.

Zhu, B. and Sastry, S. (2010). SCADA-specific intrusion detection/prevention systems: A survey and taxonomy. In *Proceedings of the First Workshop on Secure Control Systems (SCS)*. Stockholm: Team for Research in Ubiquitous System Technology.

chapter five

International implications of securing our SCADA/control system environments

Vytautas Butrimas

Contents

Introduction

As someone* occupied with government information technology (IT) and national security policy for the past 25 years, I have worked in a changing cyber security environment that started from dealing with the first hackers invading our IT systems with viruses such as the "Michelangelo" virus of 1991 to worrying about cyber criminals, socially motivated hacktivists, and possible activities of "cyber terrorists" to state-sponsored cyber attacks, not limited just to IT systems. The appearance of Stuxnet† and the "denial of computers" attack perpetrated against energy company Saudi Aramco strongly indicated that critical infrastructures (CIs) that support national economies and the well-being of modern society were now new targets for cyber attacks. Additionally, the extensive expansion of the capabilities of modern industrial control systems (ICSs) made possible by the advances in information and communication technologies (ICT) and their application to the management of complex systems running CIs has introduced, together with increased efficiencies and cost savings, serious dependencies, and vulnerabilities. Vulnerabilities that, due to a lack of understanding of the interrelatedness of increasingly complex systems, have given rise to unintentional incidents. Vulnerabilities that, if known by the "bad guys," may be exploited to execute intentional cyber related attacks, attacks which are now possible due to the entry of IT into the formerly isolated and proprietary world of ICSs (supervisory control and data acquisition [SCADA] systems). The new threats emanating from cyber space have provided new and broad challenges that range beyond the national level to the international level. CIs today have a cross-border or international dimension. Failure at a national level can affect a connected neighboring country. While some worthy and effective efforts are being made by national governments and industry in terms of laws, regulations, and standards, they fall short in meeting the international dimension of today's cyber threats. SCADA and ICS environments can no longer be considered safe from today's dynamic threats emanating from cyber space. This chapter will address implications of any changes to cyber space environments that have taken place within the last few years that now require international responses in the form of self-restraint, acceptance of responsibility, and cooperation. Possibilities for moving forward into the future—at an international level—will also be discussed.

In the past 5 years, a new concern has developed for the cyber security of CIs belonging to the energy, transportation, water, manufacturing, and telecommunications sectors. The public appearance of Stuxnet in 2010, and its subsequent analysis, revealed it to be a nation-state manufactured cyber weapon targeting specific control systems belonging to CIs, indicating that the cyber security environment had changed in a significant way. Up until then, the protection of the confidentiality, integrity, and availability of electronic data generated, transmitted, and processed in information systems was the key focus of the work of IT security professionals. The threats emanating from cyber space used to be a collection of "the usual suspects"—cyber espionage, cyber crime, and computer hackers. Policies were developed to ensure security of the chosen objects which needed to be protected from the perceived threats emanating from cyber space.

---

* Evaluations and ideas presented within this chapter exclusively belong to the author and is not considered an official position of the Ministry of National Defense of the Republic of Lithuania or any institution with which the author is associated.

† Stuxnet is cyber related malware discovered sometime in June 2010, and was designed to render industrial programmable logic controllers (PLCs) inoperable; in this case, the malware specifically targeted Siemens Series 7 devices.

From 2001 to 2011, I was responsible for information and communication security (INFOSEC/COMSEC) at the Communications and Information System Service under the Ministry of National Defense in Lithuania. The years 2001–2004 were especially intense, as my service was tasked with the IT and telecommunications work to join NATO in 2004. We had to demonstrate that we had fully implemented INFOSEC/COMSEC (later to be called "information assurance" and popularly called "cyber security" today) policies before anything was allowed to connect our national IT and communications infrastructure to NATO's systems. However, no NATO security policy or anything in my experience up until then ever provided even an inkling of an idea that there were other CIs that were just as vital to national defense and our ability to perform as a member of the NATO alliance. In late 2010, I was asked to write about the state of the cyber security of our energy infrastructure. It was assumed that this would be an easy task, thinking that IT systems were the same as those used in the energy sector. Needless to say, the writing of "The cyber security dimension of critical energy infrastructure" (Butrimas and Bruzga, 2012) proved to be both a humbling and very enlightening professional experience. CI protection is not just about information security and protecting documents, but about the reliable and secure monitoring and control of the real-time processes found in the energy, transportation, utility, and manufacturing sectors vital to the economy and the well-being of society. While disruptions to information systems could lead to one form of danger, disruptions to the control systems of CIs were potentially far more serious to a nation's national security and could affect other nations as well. Failure of an electric grid, gas pipeline, or traffic control system had cross-border or international ramifications that required international cooperation. This all seemed clear enough to me after writing the white paper; however, it was soon realized that there was a problem. This realization was not shared among any of my IT and security policy colleagues in government nor with colleagues in any other governments. Cyber security was basically understood in terms of the confidentiality, integrity, and availability of electronic data found within the information systems of governments, banks, businesses, public websites, and the computers of private individuals. The vulnerability of CIs and ongoing processes found within, for example, the electric grid used to supply power for those information systems and computers to operate were not within scope of government security policy makers. In fact, to those involved in developing government cyber security programs and strategies, ICS did not even exist. In discussing what needs to be protected, the term critical *information* infrastructure was used. Nobody seemed aware of the other critical (non-information-centric) sectors that were vulnerable to intentional and unintentional cyber incidents.

The alarm which should have sounded in the international community after the first appearance of malicious state cyber activity directed at the CI of another state went unheeded. This situation, with some exaggeration, is similar to what would have happened had the world continued to concentrate on fighting organized crime while ignoring the invasion of Poland or the Japanese surprise attack on Pearl Harbor. Governments did take steps at the national level to address the newly exposed vulnerabilities of CIs to cyber incidents and attacks. The U.S. Department of Homeland Security (DHS), in addition to establishing a national computer emergency response team, US-CERT, also created a dedicated CERT for ICSs. While national-level efforts were underway, the international borderless dimension of cyber space required new efforts at the international level to deal with vulnerable cross-border interdependencies exposed by this new threat. However, the efforts at the international level on cyber security policy among states and within international organizations continued to focus on dealing primarily with cybe rcrime and the antics of socially motivated hacktivists. This resulted in a dangerous gap between efforts to formulate national policies and efforts to formulate a comprehensive international cyber space and security policy. Recognizing and dealing with this gap has created a very broad challenge, not only at the national level for industry and government, but internationally as well. National efforts were not enough in protecting a system that was interrelated and interdependent with other systems in cyber space. Gas pipelines, power grids, and submarine communication cables today cross borders and reach across to other continents. A failure in one section of the grid can ripple and cascade across to affect other networks and systems belonging to CIs in other countries. Additionally, those same national systems are vulnerable to external attacks originating from other parts of the world. Management of these global-level complexities can only be done through international cooperation.

2010–2014: The security environment of cyber space changed for CI and ICS: Stuxnet, Saudi Aramco, Snowden, Havex-Dragonflies, and Bears Oh My

In terms of the cyber security of ICSs and the CIs they support, we live in a "post-Stuxnet world" today. One may ask what is so unique about this malware that was discovered years ago when thousands of new pieces of malware are discovered every day? Without going into technical descriptions (Langner, 2013), Stuxnet was the first publicly known (Russell, 2004) nation-state-developed malware which was specifically targeted against the control system of a critical industrial process. The malware effectively deprived operators of the "view" and "control" of centrifuges belonging to a controversial uranium enrichment facility. It achieved this by intercepting and inserting false data sent to the operators telling them that systems were functioning normally, when, actually, they were not. To put it more simply, the effect was similar to what would happen to a driver of an automobile whose mechanisms were manipulated to steer the car over a cliff. The driver feels no alarm nor reason to take action since the view of the road they see ahead is "normal." Even if they tried to take action to save themselves, they would find that they had no control of the steering wheel, brake pedal, or engine.

The appearance of Stuxnet can be said to be the equivalent of a "Hiroshima moment" for cyber security and international relations. The first known execution of a cyber attack by one nation-state against the CI of another nation proved that conflicts among states were now being executed in the cyber domain. It was recognized that this technology was now being applied to disrupt and destroy machinery and industrial processes. This operation, which was probably politically motivated (to keep Iran from making atomic weapons) also introduced a new problem of cyber weapons coming into the hands of lesser-skilled hacktivists, criminals, and even terrorist groups (Simonite, 2012). Unfortunately, the Stuxnet code made it to the Internet where it could be freely copied and analyzed. The methods could be studied and the code adapted to execute new and destructive cyber attacks. The makers of Metasploit also seem to have taken notice of Stuxnet, as new versions now have modules that apply to ICS (Selena, 2012). CIs that were, up until then, largely living in their own isolated world of closed communications networks and obscure proprietary technologies became a new area of interest for hackers. For example, SCADA/ICS began appearing at popular hacking conferences as a topic of interest. The website of Black Hat Asia 2014 featured a course on "attacking SCADA" at the top of the list. The course is intended to "provide students with the knowledge that they need to safely perform penetration testing *against live SCADA environments*" (Parker, 2014). Shodan is also being used to search for connected ICSs. One individual has even published, in their Twitter feed, screenshots of control system workstation panels that they stumbled on. They can also be accessed on Google,* and provide inspiration for others to seek out and even try to "touch" the controls of a critical system exposed on the Internet.

Not just hackers and governments were seeking ways to exploit the newly exposed vulnerabilities and do physical harm to ICSs of national CIs. For the first time, it was plausible to think about the possibilities of true "cyber terrorism." This technology was now available to terrorists groups lacking the skills to develop their own cyber weapon of mass destruction (WMD). The apparent success of the Stuxnet operation contributed to not only a new recognition of the vulnerability of CIs, it also provided the international security policy community with a new problem: what to do about nation-states playing cyber games with each other's CIs?

The implications of this new form of malicious cyber activity should not be lost on anyone. It raises the issue of whether one can trust the safety and reliability of systems used to monitor and control critical processes that are now so vital to our economies and societies' well-being. This is far from the concerns raised by distributed denial of service (DDOS) attacks on websites executed by hacktivists, the theft of financial information by cyber criminals, or the stealing of industrial secrets by industry competitors or spies. At the same time, it must also be remembered that the impressive work that led to the development of Stuxnet was supported by espionage and intelligence assets that only a nation-state could have provided. Details of the operations of the targeted facility had to be fully understood to develop and execute the cyber attack that was Stuxnet, and to ensure that the attack would not execute anywhere other than at the facility that was targeted. As one commentator on Stuxnet has said, the intelligence was so good "they knew the shoe size of the operators working at the plant" (Langner, 2011). One asks the question: is it OK to allow this kind of malicious cyber activity to continue without some kind of international response to punish the perpetrators, or at least agree on some rules of the game? International criticism of the Stuxnet operation was muted. Perhaps some thought it served some useful purpose in keeping Iran from making an atomic weapon. What is little appreciated is that the majority of potential targets for Stuxnet-type attacks are not in just the Middle East, but in the developed countries found in Europe, North America, and parts of Asia that are developing modern CIs—potential targets that are far less protected (not located in underground facilities) and more vulnerable (more possibilities for penetration) to Stuxnet-type attacks.

Saudi Aramco

In December 2012, another nation's CIs were cyber attacked. Saudi Arabia's oil company, Saudi Aramco, experienced a targeted cyber attack on its computer systems. This cyber weapon, called Schamoon, succeeded in executing a "denial of computer" (DOC) attack, wiping clean over 30,000† computer hard drives belonging to servers and workstations. The attack appeared to have been limited to the administrative part of the company and not the CI parts involved with the production and processing of oil. Although the attack did not affect the ICSs, it did cause havoc for the management of the business of the company. Even pipeline operations are dependent on management's world of contracts and timetables. As one commentator said, the

---

* https://www.google.com/search?q=dan+tentler+shodan+screenshots&rls=com.microsoft:lt-LT&tbm=isch&tbo=u&source=univ&sa=X&ei=RNBZVO_vH-eM7Abr8oAQ&ved=0CEEQsAQ&biw=1323&bih=662.
† Curiously, 30,000 is the same number used in describing a similar attack that occurred in South Korea.

company must have had a difficult time without this special information when there were orders to be processed and tankers waiting in the harbor when this attack occurred (Eugene Kaspersky Press Club, 2013). For the Saudis, this cyber attack was taken as an attack that threatened not just its critical energy infrastructure but its economy (AL Arabiya News, 2012). Although there was no conclusive proof, it was suspected that another government's cyber power was responsible (Perlroth, 2012a). The lack of international response further reinforced the message that cyber attacks are an attractive and highly effective tool to inflict damage on an adversary at low cost in terms of liability, preparation, delivery, and minimal collateral damage. The problem is getting worse, as there were indications that these attacks were counterstrikes in retaliation for earlier attacks (Perlroth, 2012b).

From Snowden to Sandworm

The next key event indicating a change was taking place in the cyber space environment occurred a few months after the Saudi Aramco cyber attack. This was the revelation of government electronic spying and surveillance by former U.S. National Security Agency (NSA) employee/contractor Edward Snowden that began in May 2013. Taking aside the issues of the breaches in the privacy of persons and government leaders which were raised by Snowden's revelation, it is the intelligence gathering and surveillance capabilities possessed by governments exposed by Snowden that are worthy of comment here. The revelations indicate that government capabilities include possibilities not only for passive measures to collect intelligence information, but also for active measures once a system's software or hardware has been penetrated by one of the catalog of available tools (Applebaum et al., 2013). These capabilities go beyond just massive monitoring of worldwide telecommunications traffic, but also penetrating the hardware and software supply chain, making the offensive capabilities truly worldwide in scope. If one recalls how much intelligence was required to develop and execute Stuxnet, the capability to develop a successor is more than feasible. In fact, it may be just too tempting not to do so, especially if one is the leader of a nation whose efforts to achieve a foreign policy objective by traditional means is continually being frustrated. The possibilities of making use of these intelligence gathering and surveillance capabilities combined with the proof of concept that was Stuxnet make for a very dangerous "cyber cocktail" capability with implications for the future of the cyber security of ICSs. The "Eye of Sauron" (to paraphrase *The Lord of the Rings*) has focused its attention on ICSs. Just one example of this at the time of this writing (November 2014) comes from one of the first published analysis of "Sandworm" which indicates that "Sauron's Eye" is looking for where ICS equipment manufactured by GE and Siemens is located (Hultquist, 2014). This reflected similar activity that most likely took place during the development of Stuxnet to meet the specifications of its Siemens-based warhead and location of its intended target.

Havex/Dragonfly/Energetic Bear

The cyber event of the summer of 2014 was the Havex (aka Dragonfly, Energetic Bear) malware attack. It illustrates an unsettling trend regarding a new ICS attack vector (which, in this case, are watering-hole attacks* on vendor websites) and the sinister nature of cyber

---

* A "watering-hole attack" is an attack method used against a target of a specific group (organization, industry, or region). Through this method of attack, the attacker guesses or observes which websites the group most often uses and infects one or more of those websites with malware; the eventual outcome is that one or more members of the targeted group become infected with the malware.

espionage. According to reports from the DHS industrial control systems computer emergency response team (DHS ICS-CERT), (Alert, 2014) this reported malware targets the software/firmware download websites of manufacturers of industrial control systems. Compromised vendor software that customers download from these sites may allow attackers to access customer networks, including those that operate CIs. Commentators are comparing this malware to Stuxnet, as they also indicated that the sophistication demonstrated and the choice of target pointed to nation-state involvement (Perlroth, 2014). This is really bad news, especially to those in the energy industry and other sectors of CIs. One respected colleague in the ICS world commented that "this is the tip of the iceberg." The news gets worse. According to an analysis conducted by Symantec, this malware not only provided a platform for conducting cyber espionage activities, but also provided the "attackers the ability to mount sabotage operations against their victims," and if the attackers had used the sabotage capabilities available, "could have caused damage or disruption of the energy supply in the affected countries" (Symantec Security Response, 2014). This should cause many who tend to accept cyber espionage as being part of traditional spying to pause and consider its ramifications. In cyber space, the cyber spy wears two hats. To remove the spy hat and put on the saboteur black mask only requires the press of the <ENTER> key. This is not about the spying of Mata Hari; it is about the activities of the cyber space spy/saboteur equivalent of James Bond. If James Bond gets the order to kill someone, he will, and has all the resources of the state and "Q" to help him inevitably succeed in his given mission.

In terms of the cyber exercise in which I participated in 2012, one of the difficulties encountered was finding ICS specialists to deal with solving a problem presented in the scenario. Specialists from traditional national CERTs with Microsoft Windows, Cisco, and Linux certifications were available, but what was lacking were ICS specialists with engineering diplomas who were more familiar with the affected equipment.

The problem of unintentional cyber incidents in CI

It is not enough to worry about protecting critical systems from intentional cyber attacks. Many readers of this chapter perhaps are also aware that unintentional cyber incidents also take place within ICS space. One of the causes of unintentional cyber incidents in ICSs comes from the great success in terms of better management and cost savings coming from digitalization of control equipment and entry of IT into ICS environments. IT's strengths of automation and remote management have allowed for the creation of complex systems of systems, providing integrated services over a wide territory. However, together with the good side of all this, there is also a bad side in terms of new vulnerabilities and potential points of failure. The term "cyber fragility" has been used to describe this situation in much depth by Ralph Langner in his book, *Robust Control System Networks* (Langner, 2012). The IT security professionals coming to work in ICS environments are new to this environment, and do not always understand the ICSs they are hired to secure in the same way that the ICS engineers who designed and operate them do. This false sense of "I know what I am doing" can have surprising and potentially dangerous outcomes. A good example is the emergency shutdown of the reactor at the Hatch nuclear power plant in 2008, which was caused by a software update on a single computer belonging to the control system. This was a complete surprise for the administrators, who had to question whether they were adequately knowledgeable about their operating environment to do their jobs. There are other surprises to consider coming from honest software programming errors.

Dangers of programming errors affecting the heart of cyber space: Heartbleed and Shellshock

In addressing vulnerabilities arising from the complexity of modern ICSs, there is also the issue of software programming used to enable our use of cyber space. The Heartbleed bug is a programming error in a popular OpenSSL library that is used for providing cryptographic services such as Secure Sockets Layer/Transport Layer Security (SSL/TLS) used to ensure secure communications over networks (Heartbleed Bug, 2014). "By attacking a service that uses a vulnerable version of OpenSSL, a remote, unauthenticated attacker may be able to retrieve sensitive information such as secret keys. By leveraging this information, an attacker may be able to decrypt, spoof, or perform man-in-the-middle (MITM) attacks on network traffic that would otherwise be protected by OpenSSL" (Homeland Security, 2014). If one considers that this vulnerability, which was exploitable for 2 years before it was discovered, was bad enough, how about a programming error in another vital part of cyber space management that was only discovered after 20 years. This is what happened with the discovery of the Bash shell vulnerability popularly called Shellshock. This is about a vulnerability discovered in the Bash interface shell used to access the depths of operating systems. Personal computers that used Bash could be subject to attacks using this vulnerability. However, this shell program is also used in networks that monitor and control processes found in CIs (Saarinen, 2014a). Bugs and patches to these well publicized vulnerabilities resulting from programming errors of long ago soon became available after they were disclosed. The problem is that it is likely that many more such unknown errors are waiting to be discovered. The vulnerabilities yet to be discovered in the software that runs our critical systems seem to be endless. Microsoft issues vulnerability patches every month. In November 2014, it issued a record number of fixes during its "Patch Tuesday" (Saarinen, 2014b).

One of the most important things to remember in terms of unintentional incidents stemming from cyber fragilities of ICSs in the context of this article is that knowledge of these vulnerabilities can be used by the "cyber samurai" to plan and execute cyber attacks on ICSs. Attacks and incidents that perhaps occur unintentionally are difficult to investigate due to a lack of ICS forensic capabilities. As ICS industry opinion leader Joe Weiss indicated that a major cyber incident in ICSs is likely to happen; however, we will probably never know whether it was achieved with malicious intent or not (Elinor, 2010).

Something wrong at the international level (United Nations and European Union) in terms of dealing with changes to the cyber security environment

One would think that for the international community there have been enough alarms and wake-up calls for action to be generated. What has been their response to the examples of malicious cyber activities of states listed above? In September 2010, I attended the UN-mandated Internet Governance Forum (IGF) in Vilnius. In the midst of concerns to preserve privacy and open access to the Internet, there was no attention given to some of the unsettling events occurring in cyber space during the previous 5 year mandate of the IGF. Estonia pulled out its national Internet plug after it had experienced a cyber attack in 2007, and, later, cyber was attacks were used to compliment a traditional armed attack during the Russian–Georgian war of 2008. News about Stuxnet had first appeared in IT professional circles 4 months earlier. Regardless of these unsettling actions, indicating that nations were engaging in malicious cyber activities, the IGF meeting simply concentrated on concerns of digital rights of privacy and universal access to the Internet. In the fall of 2013, the European Union held its Information and Communication Technologies conference (ICT 2013) in Vilnius. Once again, there was very little appreciation for what had happened in cyber space during the previous two summers (e.g., cyber attack on Saudi energy company Saudi Aramco in 2012 and revelations on the extent of government electronic spying and surveillance in 2013). Stuxnet, the attack on Saudi Aramco, and Mr. Snowden's revelations about the large-scale surveillance activities of governments raised serious security issues for the international community to address. However, in response, very little was being done about it in international fora and by organizations created to promote international security and peace. For some reason, perhaps thinking that some other organization will tackle the problem or just not being aware of what was happening, these fora were not considering the unsettling trends in cyber space. I suspect that what is really missing is an appreciation of the technological implications of the dynamic threats to ICSs emanating from cyber space. The UN-appointed Group of Governmental Experts on Developments in the Field of Information and Telecommunication in the Context of International Security is dominated by ambassadors and diplomats, working mostly for arms control agencies and ministries of foreign affairs. No one who can be called an ICS opinion leader who could address the implications of IT technology on modern ICSs is listed in the annex list of group members. I will return to the issue of IT bias in terms of dealing with the cyber security of ICSs later in this chapter.

A few words about Internet governance, the multistakeholder myth, and the ITU

The UN's International Telecommunications Union (ITU) organized the World Conference on International Telecommunications (WCIT) at the end of 2012 in Dubai. This was a most interesting conference, as the ITU tried to foster some updates to the way world telecommunications were to be regulated. For example, there were proposals to update the regulations to include something that was missing from the last time the regulations were approved in 1989: the Internet. While the WCIT meetings failed to reach an agreement on an updated set of telecommunications regulations to cover the Internet, it illustrated another issue: the growing divide between East and West in regard to Internet governance issues. It was evident that there was a growing concern among non-Western nations—in particular Russia and China—over the West's domination (in particular by the United States) of the way the Internet was managed. Democracies tended to support a multistakeholder approach (minimal government involvement) to Internet management, while more authoritarian governments sought more government controls over content and use. While Internet freedom advocates were joyous over the failure of the "UN to take over the Internet," (Klimburg, 2013) a dangerous split remained between East and West over the management of cyber space (Gewirtz, 2012). It also represented another failed opportunity by the international community to raise and deal with the issue of the malicious activities of states in cyber space. The West's position in favor of a decentralized "multistakeholder" approach to Internet governance sounds dishonest in the face of the malicious cyber activities of states in cyber space. Some of the very same states fighting to keep the decentralized multistakeholder model were also taking advantage of the assumed trust behind this system of governance by engaging in malicious behaviors in cyber space. This was similar to cowboys saying that they should be free to roam the prairie without the restrictions that could be enforced by sheriffs, while, at the same time, they engaged in cattle rustling. The multistakeholder model depends very much on a certain degree of trust among the stakeholders. The model will be discredited further if stakeholders choose to take advantage of this trust by engaging in cyber misbehavior, as seen in the case of the penetration of Belgacom. This serious intrusion on a key telecommunications provider in Europe and a major manager of international submarine cables has been linked to the work of a friendly nation that promotes multistakeholderism (Koot, 2013). Those that argue that the ITU should stay out of Internet governance are sounding more like outlaws calling for fewer sheriffs. Maybe it is not such a bad idea that the ITU is trying to address a problem that is not being addressed elsewhere—the malicious activities of states in cyber space. Those that are against the ITU's efforts at governance seldom indicate which alternative organization should address this issue.

Approach of NATO

In the last week of April 2007, I attended a NATO Cyber Security Workshop co-sponsored by the U.S. Department of Defense (DoD) and Microsoft held in Redmond, Washington. It was an excellent workshop for becoming familiar with NATO's approach to cyber security and vision for the way ahead. It also featured presentations from Microsoft on the virtues of the recently released Windows Vista operating system for the military. Microsoft also announced its Government Security Cooperation Program and invited NATO member governments to join. There were interesting aspects to the announced program. It was revealed that China had just signed (Russia had previously signed) on to the program and had been given access to Microsoft operating system source code. Although it was mentioned by this author, there was no reaction to the apparent contradiction between publicized cyber incidents associated with these two countries and providing them with access to one of the most popularly used and bug-filled operating systems in the world. Later, a presenter from Estonia came up to the podium and announced that he would depart from his planned presentation because "my country [was] under cyber attack." There we were, all the top NATO cyber security practitioners sitting in one place; yet, upon hearing this announcement, we could only look at each other in amazement. No one had any idea what to do, since there were no official policies or agreements in place that could address what had just happened. Later, NATO did come up with a cyber defense concept and offered to sign memoranda of understanding (MoU) with individual member states that included the possibility of sending "rapid reaction teams" for cooperation in cyber defense, which Lithuania signed in 2010.

This meeting of private industry, government, and NATO illustrated a lack of a comprehensive and coordinated policy toward cyber security. Microsoft's providing access to its operating system source code to nations with bad reputations for abusing cyber space seemed to contradict efforts being taken to improve the security of cyber space by Microsoft and the workshop participants.

NATO and other international organizations have different understandings of what needs to be protected and from what cyber threats. Protecting communications and information systems from cyber attacks by establishing CERTs is not enough to deal with protecting what is truly critical from the threats emanating from cyber space today. A good example that illustrates this comes from a 2014 summer conference held in Vilnius, commemorating Lithuania's joining NATO in 2004. I asked Mr. Sorin Ducaru, the NATO Assistant Secretary General for Emerging Security Challenges, "Has NATO evaluated what would happen to its ability to perform its mission if the critical infrastructure that it and member states depend upon to function was degraded by a cyber incident or cyber attack?" To illustrate, I reviewed what happened to the Carmel tunnel in Israel (part of the main highway to the seaport of Haifa) in the fall of 2013 (Hamadia, 2013). The operators were forced to close the 6 km tunnel for 2 days because a cyber attack knocked out the tunnel video camera surveillance system, fire control, and air-conditioning systems. This was not a "denial of service" but rather a "loss of view and loss of control" of critical processes required to ensure safe and efficient operation of a tunnel. I asked him to imagine the impact, in terms of a military operation, of the closing of a key transportation link for a military convoy of supplies that is forced to stop and wait for a tunnel to be declared safe? What effect would such a delay have on a nation's ability to participate in a mission and how would that effect NATO's operations? A tough question, and perhaps too tough to answer in a question and answer session after a long day. However, the Carmel tunnel cyber attack has one point that is missed by many. The "first responders" to the attack site did not come from a traditional CERT. They came from Cyber gym,* an organization that specializes in the security of ICSs. It was Cyber gym that determined what had happened and had the skills to contain and manage the incident. A CERT staffed with Windows/Linux/Intel/CISCO certificates hanging on their office walls did not have the skills to deal with an attack on an ICS in the Carmel case. This is an important point that needs to be considered, for it is a mistake to think that it is enough just to have a cyber security program with CERTs to deal with an attack on a website or malware on an information system. Sadly, this seems to be the mindset and set of assumptions behind the concept of CERTs. To deal with the full range of cyber threats to IT and ICSs, the appropriate range of skill sets is also required. Policies developed at the governmental level in focusing on the threat to IT systems are not enough to deal with the cyber threats of today. All parts of the cyber defense structure need to be accounted for. As with building a house, it needs not only a strong roof and walls, but also a good foundation.

The NATO summit in Wales conducted in September 2014 did include more attention on cyber defense. However, ambiguities continued to remain in terms of the alliance's understanding of what needs to be protected, from what cyber threats, and how to address them. In reading the published summit declaration in terms of cyber defense, NATO's chief focus is on protecting its own networks while the responsibility for protecting national systems are left to the nations themselves (Wales Summit Declaration, 2014). However, NATO does seem to recognize the possible threats from cyber attack on the CIs of its members, and will include consideration regarding an alliance response on a "case by case basis." What were not addressed were cyber attacks on the CIs of member states by other allies. Cyber attacks or intrusions performed by allies directed at the telecommunication sectors of Belgium and Germany (Müller-Maguhn, 2014; Gallagher, 2014) have been reported in the press. If it was proven that a cyber attack was successfully executed against the CIs of a fellow ally, would Article 5 of the NATO treaty be invoked?

Some hopeful signs have appeared during the time of this writing (November 2014) from NATO that it may be "getting it" in terms of cyber securing CIs. In October 2014, the newly accredited NATO Energy Security Centre of Excellence in Vilnius held the first tabletop exercise of its kind that included cyber attacks on the energy sector in one of the exercise scenarios (NATO, 2014). The participants of nine countries, including partners from Qatar and the United Arab Emirates, all concluded that the exercise was very useful. The lessons learned will be used to organize a full-scale exercise in the future. On the other hand, NATO may still be in a situation of the left hand not knowing what the

---

* http://cyber gym.co.il/, "Cyber Gym™ is the global leader in cyber defense solutions for critical and sensitive production, governmental, infrastructure and utility organizations including Finance, IT, TELECOM, ICS and SCADA environments."

right hand is doing. Soon after the above-mentioned NATO tabletop exercise, I attended the Innovative Energy Solutions for Military Applications (IESMA) 2014 conference sponsored by the NATO Energy Security Centre of Excellence and the government of Georgia, and supported by the NATO Science for Peace and Security Programme. It was an excellent conference on the latest and greatest innovative applications of technology applied to energy efficiency. Unfortunately, the word "security" was missing not only in the vendor's exhibit hall and product brochures, but also in the words used in the panels and discussions (IESMA, 2014). In a short intervention during the question and answer period, I tried to point out the dangers of innovation based on "insecurity by design." The excellent new products and savings of energy from technical innovation in the energy sector are made possible by advances in information and telecommunication technology. These technologies have a vulnerable side which is exploitable by malicious actors. Cyber security must be considered right from the beginning of the design phase before providing this new equipment to soldiers, sailors, and airmen going into harm's way. The high officials from NATO, including the department responsible for emerging threats, stated that technology was a separate issue from security, and that this was the reason why security was not being stressed at this conference; simply put, security was too big an issue to cover. It made no difference to this kind of thinking, even after pointing out that the energy sector has experienced multiple and serious intentional and unintentional cyber incidents. To this audience, the wake-up calls of Stuxnet, the attack on Saudi Aramco, the Idaho National Laboratories 2007 "Aurora" experiment, Black Energy, and Sandworm never existed.

This also brought home that there was a divide in the fundamental comprehension between IT and ICSs. An official NATO response to one comment indicated that one of the exhibitor's products (a deployable energy management system) sent its unencrypted data over the Ethernet, Bluetooth, wireless, and to smart phones; a NATO official said that encryption (if really needed) was "no problem." Another said that the equipment being discussed belonged to much smaller systems (found in mobile bases) and that the vulnerabilities being pointed out are not that easily exploitable. Later, during the coffee break, I approached the first official and tried to explain that encryption is not to be taken lightly when designing a control system that is to be run in real time. Encryption could cause unexpected problems.

OSCE (2015) makes an attempt at confidence-building measures for states to follow in cyber space

In May 2011, during the Lithuanian chairmanship of the Organization for Security and Co-Operation in Europe (OSCE), I was invited as "Lithuania's national cyber security expert" by the Lithuanian Ministry of Foreign Affairs to an OSCE conference on cyber security. During this conference, the OSCE decided to apply its expertise in arms control to cyber space. It subsequently created an informal working group (OSCE, 2012) to develop proposals for confidence and security building measures (CSBMs) for states to follow in cyber space. This was an exciting moment for me, as I actually participated in some of these early discussions, which took place from the summer of 2011 until the fall of 2012. While many proposals were discussed, nothing that would in any way put limits or restraints on malicious state activities in cyber space could be discussed. I know this, because I was one of those who made such a proposal (Digital Dao, 2012). Sitting in the meetings, it was noticed that while many able representatives from member nations were in attendance, they were mostly career diplomats whose experience in working with IT and (cyber)communication issues varied greatly or was based on previous work in nuclear or conventional arms control issues. Some nations only sent their local OSCE mission representatives, who mostly sat quietly, while others sent higher-level diplomats, who rigidly maintained an approved policy position rather than engage in an open discussion of the issues involved. It became clear that there was a significant lack of general, shared knowledge about the technical aspects of cyber security and its application to a foreign policy issue. Something very important was missing in these discussions on CSBM proposals. No one wanted to mention or discuss what Stuxnet represented, nor its implications. Here was an example of one nation's malicious cyber activities being directed at the CIs of another nation. This destabilizing activity was even being practiced by some nations represented in the workgroup. In fact, raising the issue of restraint by states while eliciting some nodding of heads by some representatives immediately raised concerns for cyber superpowers, who were publicly declaring in other communications and fora that cyber space was considered an "operational domain." The hostile reaction to any discussion on restraint and transparency seemed almost childlike, as if some valued toy was going to be taken away by a parent. It represented another failed opportunity in another international forum to deal with an obvious topic that no one wanted to discuss.

The OSCE, however, did come out with a curious document, called *Guide on Non-Nuclear Critical Energy Infrastructure Protection from Terrorist Attacks Focusing on Threats Emanating from Cyberspace* (OSCE, 2013a). It was curious for two reasons. One was the distinction being made between cyber threats directed at nuclear and nonnuclear power plants. As one colleague from the ICS world remarked to me, both nuclear and nonnuclear power plants use the same control systems and are equally vulnerable to cyber incidents and attacks. It really begs the question: Shouldn't we also be very concerned about what would happen to a nuclear plant if its control systems are hit by a cyber attack? The full plant failures resulting from loss of power to run control systems leading to reactor meltdowns (such as occurred at Fukushima, Japan) can be caused by a cyber event and not just by earthquakes and tsunamis. Another curious part of the guide was the use of the cyber terrorist model. Throughout the time of the writing of this guide, and after it was published, there was little evidence of "cyber terrorism" executed by what many consider to be terrorists of the "Al-Qaeda" brand. On the contrary, cyber attacks on critical energy sectors pointed to nation-state, not terrorist, involvement. I did manage to become a member (and stay to the end) of the task force and contribute to preparing the guide, but was unsuccessful in changing the title of the guide and including the activities of states as one of the sources of cyber threats. I was successful in reducing the IT bias contained in the early drafts of the guide by successfully proposing that, in addition to ISO 27000 standards, that more relevant standards for ICSs and the energy sector be included, such as IEC 62351 and IEC 62443. Language addressing the peculiarities in cyber security practices found in both the IT and ICS realms also found a place in the text. For example, this statement about risk: "Risk needs to be understood with an appreciation for the peculiarities in security practices found in the ICT and Industrial Control System (ICS) realms" (OSCE, 2013b).

A bias toward protecting IT and information systems from cyber criminals, hacktivists, and "cyber terrorists" seemed to be the only point policy makers had in common. This bias, or lack of awareness, was contributing to the lack of ICS language in legal instruments on cyber security. This was not the first time I noticed this missing element at a meeting on cyber security.

Closer to home: Experience in dealing with cyber security questions in Lithuania

In Lithuania, analogous experiences applied in dealing with national cyber security issues. Meetings were held in our government to discuss preparation for cyber exercises. Scenarios were proposed and one of them was to include a cyber attack on Lithuania's electric grid. One representative from a participating government ministry said that such a scenario was totally impossible, as our grid was "not connected to the Internet"! To someone aware of Stuxnet, this is a disturbing statement coming from a government official participating in the development of our national cyber security policy. In another cyber exercise scenario discussion, it was proposed that a Stuxnet-type cyber attack would result in lost electric power to half of the capital city of Vilnius. The exercise leaders agreed with this, but only on the condition that the location of the Ministry of National Defense would not be in the part of Vilnius experiencing the blackout. If this happened, the communications center used for the exercise would not be able to be used in the exercise. To this, I could only reply that one can only hope that if real conflict took place, our enemies, in executing a cyber attack on our electric grid, would also be sure to leave the ministry's power supply untouched. I ran into similar differing levels of understanding when working on various national task forces dealing with cyber security issues. The lack of a general base of knowledge about cyber security made it very difficult to answer fundamental cyber security policy questions such as:

- What needs to be protected
- From what cyber threats
- How to protect them

There was also reluctance, when discussing the cyber security of CIs, to invite representatives from the electric, gas, and other utilities. One can imagine how difficult it was to develop realistic scenarios that included a cyber attack on the electric grid or pipelines without the participation of national or regional operators.

In considering the responses of governments and international organizations to the increasingly sophisticated and dynamic threats emanating from cyber space, it is difficult to understand the presence of these "blinders" when seeking to determine what needs to be protected and from what threats. In spite of growing evidence of the attacks on increasingly vulnerable CIs, the emphasis continued to be focused on protecting government and business information systems from cyber criminals, hacktivists, and cyber spies. This is quite ironic, for if you ask anyone working in government or in an international security organization about the importance of CIs, the reply would be that it is very important. One would think that the main purpose behind the work of government officials is to ensure that the people they serve are protected from harm from malicious cyber incidents and not the other way around.

Why is the cyber security of ICSs/SCADA not being included in the discussions on securing cyber space and CIs? Reading the documents produced by these organizations, their understanding of cyber security appears to be lacking. Cyber threats tend to be characterized as external, in terms of outside attacks by criminals and targeted espionage attacks by states or state-sponsored actors on IT systems. CIs are mentioned but the fundamental understanding is basically IT based. The cyber vulnerabilities and exploits in the energy sector seem to be unconsciously lumped together with vulnerabilities, exploits, and attack vectors associated with traditional IT attacks (DDOS, spear phishing, social engineering, etc.). Targeted attacks on control systems of the Stuxnet variety (not to mention the unintentional incidents that take place) do not seem to be factored in. It is a mistake to assume that those writing the documents and making statements on cyber security and cyber defense in these organizations have ICSs in mind. Terms like SCADA, representatives of manufacturers of these systems, engineers, and the awareness of designers of SCADA's different approach to cyber security and specific cyber threats rarely appear. The assumptions do not fully apply to ICSs and, therefore, the documents dealing with the problem and the strategies to address them only cover part of the issue. This is similar to the realization I faced when writing the above-mentioned article on the cyber security dimension of critical energy infrastructure. This erroneous assumption coming from an IT bias is quite common when cyber security based on IT is so dominant.

I will use one anecdote to illustrate what I mean by IT not seeing ICSs. In Lithuania there is a very well-known painter, Aloyzas Stasiulevičius. He has had a long and successful career as a painter. His unique place in Lithuanian painting comes in part from his main theme that he uses over and over again—the city of Vilnius. He paints the same scenes in different ways and in different colors, but the theme is almost always Vilnius. The story goes that one weekend, Lithuanian painters gathered in a national park by the beautiful Lake Aisetas. Great paintings were accomplished, with depictions of lakes, forests, and wildlife scenes. When they came over to look at Stasiulevičius, who was painting beside a lake, they all remarked at his work—"Look, it is Vilnius!" IT cyber security specialists seem to be stuck with the same vision when they approach ICS cyber security. They see just the IT part and do not notice that ICSs are different. This mindset tends to dominate so much that, when policies are created for ICSs, there is so much that is missing. A good example of this is the integrated management system policy of the Slovak Republic's electricity transmission system operator Slovenskaelektrizacnaprenosovasustava a.s. (Integrated Management System Policy, 2014). Among the standards listed, only ISO 27000 is listed for information security management. There is no mention of any standards having to do with operating ICSs; for example, no mention of IEC 60870 and ISA 99/IEC 62443 (ISA99 Committee, 2015). If the writers of these documents and designers of critical systems are not aware of these relevant ICS standards, then they are just left out by default. The result is that much is missing from these documents that could be used to prevent and limit the possibility of a bad event occurring in CIs. The bottom line is that these efforts do not result in ensuring that everything that is truly critical is protected.

What is considered to be critical infrastructure seems so obvious, but ...

The dependence of our economies and well-being of our societies on a safe, reliable, and increasingly hi-tech-based infrastructure consisting of energy, finance, telecommunications, transport, and other utility sectors has been recognized by governments for a long time. The availability of the services provided by these sectors, if disrupted or discontinued for longer than a few hours, would have damaging effects on the economy and society. That is why their availability at all times is considered critical. The United States, among other countries, has a good understanding of what a CI is and what it means to its national security. This goes as far back as November 9, 1965, when President Lyndon Johnson, in a letter, cited a report on the blackout of 1965 which took place on that date. He wrote in his order for the preparation of the report, "Today's failure is a dramatic reminder of the importance of the uninterrupted flow of power to the health, safety, and well-being of our citizens and the defense of our country" (Federal Power Commission, 1965). This early recognition in 1965 by the U.S. government of the importance of CIs is further reinforced today in the existence of the DHS ICS-CERT, which is probably the one of the few nationally-backed CERTs of its kind dedicated to the cyber security of industrial control systems which form the backbone of today's CIs.

While the 1965 blackout was not the end result of a cyber incident per se, it was caused by an unintentional "programming error"* in one of the electromechanical links (a relay) belonging to the internationally operated electric grid providing electricity to the north-eastern United States and parts of Canada. The important message in terms of this article is that after the 1965 blackout, the U.S. and Canadian governments, as well as industry, after careful analysis of what was wrong with the system, implemented remedies at national and industry levels to ensure that such a failure would not easily reoccur. This included creation of the Northeast Power Coordination Council,† which would later become affiliated to what is known today as the North American Electrical Reliability Corporation (NERC), and the passage of the Electric Reliability Act in 1967. This resulted in more rational management and in improved reliability in the power industry, as well as setting the stage for developing the more complex and interconnected power systems of today. It also resulted in making management systems more complex and vulnerable to new threats from cyber space.

As long as the scope of affected systems is limited to one nation or is inside an isolated system, this model, in terms of local measures taken by industry, government, and a cooperative neighbor to prevent another blackout or failure in CIs, falls short in the changed cyber security environment of today. Today's threats in cyber space have a global or borderless character. The interdependence of CIs crosses borders. A cyber attack or incident leading to a failure of CIs may have its origin in another country or as a result of a political conflict among nations.

Much has been covered so far about the response of governments and the international community to the growing cross-border cyber based threats. What has been the response of industry, especially from the various CI sectors?

Response of industry

In talking about the public–private partnership between governments and CI sectors, the lessons of Stuxnet and the Saudi Aramco incident have not been learned. My experience as a guest speaker for a conference where energy sector representatives from industry and government participated serves as one illustrative example. In May 2014, I was invited to speak at an energy sector conference in Vilnius, sponsored by the Estonian Chamber of Commerce. It was opened by the Prime Ministers of Lithuania, Latvia, and Estonia. Participating were representatives from governments and private energy companies in Lithuania, Latvia, Estonia, Sweden, Poland, and energy-related NGOs.

What surprised me most was that, until my session, there was no mention of the word "security" in any of the presentations. Terms like "critical infrastructure bottlenecks" were used to describe the lack of transmission capacity on the grids or pipelines between countries. Polish industrial boiler manufacturer Rafako (2015) gave a vendor brochure-type presentation, filled with pictures of their products, descriptions of their experience in providing turn-key systems, and of sites where their products were installed. One picture showed a "condenser," a two- or three-story high cylinder-shaped object sold to nuclear power plants. Generally, security as a problem was only mentioned in the context of "supply"; for example, in terms of what could happen if Russia stopped fulfilling its gas supply contracts. Other

---

* The relay was mistakenly set to trip at a much lower power level than could be safely transmitted by the capacity of the power lines.
† https://www.npcc.org/default.aspx.

presenters covered the financial aspects (market forecasts) and the online bidding and selling of energy. China was cited as an "island of economic stability" in the East.*

My presentation (allowed for just 15 min) came after lunch, when the prime ministers and some of the morning presenters had already left, and I asked the audience to recall the huge condensers that were shown earlier. I pointed out that they were controlled by things called program logic controllers (PLCs)[†] and belonged to complex systems of monitoring and control called SCADA. These "systems of systems" have now, for various reasons, become vulnerable to unintentional and intentional cyber incidents that have caused major damage and loss of life. Nobody said they had heard of "Aurora" and were equally clueless about both the Google incident and the Idaho National Lab experiment.

In terms of "bottlenecks" and "problems with infrastructure," I asked them to imagine that one day, while looking at their online market transaction screens, they suddenly found that the screen had "frozen" or that a network/server error message ("try again later in about an hour") appeared while they were trying to make a bid. This could happen because of an attack on a website that hosts the online transaction system (I believe servers for the Nord-Balt Energy Pool Spot Market are located in Oslo, Norway). What would they do when something went wrong with the operation of the pipeline or electric distribution system, resulting in an interruption in the supply of gas or electricity? These incidents may be caused by unintentional or intentional failures in the control systems that are used to run devices that form these CIs. I also told them that classes are now being offered at Black Hat with titles like "Hacking SCADA" (Parker, 2014).

Cyber security in the sectors belonging to a given CI seem to be understood in different ways. A very interesting study on the cyber fragilities of traffic light control systems came out, which contains a surprising finding illustrating how some manufacturers in the industry look at cyber security: "A clear example can be seen in the response of the traffic controller vendor to our vulnerability disclosure. It stated that the company *has followed the accepted industry standard and it is that standard which does not include security*" (Ghena and Beyer, 2014). Similar perception problems exist in other critical sectors. In looking at air traffic control (ATC) systems, the willingness to implement solutions for improved resiliency of ATC systems to a cyber attack hinges on cost, and in some cases, a certain state of denial. As Camilleri writes in his study of the cyber preparedness of the aviation industry, "Most are already familiar with many of the issues of unencrypted radio communications. As most aerospace and defense contractors also originally developed the same civilian equipment for military aviation systems, they are also aware of the solution to these problems—simply to encrypt all communications traffic in air between aircraft, as well as on ground. But the FAA and airline industry argue otherwise" (Camilleri, 2014).

At the NATO IESMA 2014 conference I described earlier above, I made a point of visiting the vendors' and manufacturers' (including Honeywell, BAE Systems, Bredenoord) exhibition hall and asking about the connectivity and security of their equipment. I was provided with a lot of information about the way the equipment can be accessed over Ethernet, Bluetooth, wireless, smartphones, and even remotely over the Internet. The manufacturer's representative at the booth did not include any presentation on how secure their products were from threats emanating from cyber space. A heating, ventilation, and air conditioning (HVAC)[‡] vendor expressed surprise over hearing that the Target

---

* Which provoked a question from me: "What about Japan?"
† A digital computer used for automation of typically industrial electromechanical processes, such as control of machinery on factory assembly lines (https://en.wikipedia.org/wiki/Programmable_logic_controller).
‡ https://energy.ces.ncsu.edu/heating-ventilation-and-air-conditioning-system-hvac-defined/.

Corporation's financial system was cyber attacked through the company building's HVAC system (Target Hackers Broke in Via HVAC Company, 2014). Most vendors were very interested in learning more about what Stuxnet was. I spelled out the word to several vendor representatives who said they would investigate this and respond back to me. I suggested that the first question they asked their engineers back home was whether they had heard of Stuxnet and if they had read any of the analysis published by Ralph Langner. I told them that if their engineers answered negatively to those questions, then some attention and enlightenment would be in order for the good of their esteemed company's products.

In dealing with the malicious cyber activities of states, neither the international community nor industry appears to have a coherent understanding of the serious implications of the new threats emanating from cyber space being directed toward a CI. In international fora described above, there is either a reluctance to talk about any limitations on these activities, or they are not even recognized as an issue (some other organization's problem to deal with). The examples of the energy and airline industry used above may not be representative of the views and understanding of all the sectors of CIs as a whole, but without government leadership in fostering and in coordinating an effective international response, the threat to CIs from debilitating cyber attacks continues to exist.

Since Stuxnet (and other similarly produced malware that has followed) was the work of a nation-state directed at the CIs of another nation-state, the level of response required to address this kind of attack is beyond the local capabilities of a national government, regulatory body, or industry. Efforts to address this new form of cyber attack have to come from efforts of national structures in coordination with other members of the international community. As a former White House policy director, Jason Healy, remarked in his book, *A Fierce Domain: Conflict in Cyberspace 1986–2012*, "as Smart Grid and other technologies interlink the Internet with real infrastructure—made of concrete and steel, not silicon—the consequences of attacks will be far worse, especially from more covert nation-state conflicts … a further trend, which suggests that there will be more covert disruptive conflicts between governments, as each nation realizes its own advantages in disrupting adversaries on-line" (Healey, 2013, pp. 85–86).

Recommendations

Short/medium-term and long-term recommendations

In terms of making recommendations, a parallel two-track approach will be used: one for the immediate and short term and the other for the long term. I would like to borrow a term from the practice of medicine which has been useful in helping us to understand cyber space in the past (e.g., the use of the term "virus" to describe the actions of malicious software). My wife is a rheumatologist and she treats many patients using a two-track method by first prescribing symptom-relieving medication to reduce the immediate pain and discomfort felt by the patient. This addresses the immediate concern of the patient to feel better right away. However, the path to a cure also requires attention to the disease process, which will continue regardless of the effects of the short-term pain medication. For this reason, she also prescribes another drug (a disease-modifying antirheumatic drug [DMARD]) that treats the actual disease over a longer period of time. I will propose some solutions to the international issues of protecting SCADA systems in the same way, by proposing short-term solutions (providing immediate relief of "symptoms"), which can address some of the immediate concerns over dealing with current threats emanating from cyber space, and long-term solutions (cyber security "DMARDs") that can address core issues to ensure the reliability and safety of these vital systems, which form the technical platforms we depend on for our modern economies and way of life.

Short/medium term

Proposals for addressing the misbehavior of states in cyber space

1. Commitment to restrain from malicious cyber activities directed against critical civilian infrastructure (financial, energy/utility, transportation, and telecommunications).
   Rationale: The desire to protect national economies and civilians from financial loss or physical harm should be common to all nations. Certain state activities in cyber space can lead to misperceptions and instability in relations among states. For example, the placement of "logic bombs" or "back doors" in a nation's CI infrastructure can be mistaken for "preparation of the battlefield" activity and could lead to rapid escalation of tensions. Cyber activities directed against the CIs of another nation-state can also have significant cross-border and even regional effects, due to the integration of financial systems, power grids, pipelines, and other modern CIs.

   Something similar has already been mentioned in other proposals made by representatives of both Eastern and Western countries. One comes from the nation closely associated with Stuxnet. Richard Clarke, former adviser on national security for several U.S. presidents, has applied his extensive experience in nuclear arms control issues to the realm of cyber space in his recent book, *Cyber War*. Read his proposal for a cyber war limitation treaty (Clarke, 2010). Language prohibiting the use of cyber weapons against CIs is also included in the Shanghai Cooperation Group proposals for an international code of conduct sent to the UN in 2011 (Ministry of Foreign Affairs of the People's Republic of China, 2011).

   Restraint is not enough of a pledge; it also requires an acceptance of responsibility to meet one's obligations, which leads to Proposal 2.

2. Commitment to national cyber space liability: States agree to accept responsibility for malicious cyber activities taking place within their cyber space jurisdictions or transiting through them.
   Rationale: Nations need to agree on minimum obligations to secure their national cyber space. Emphasis should be placed on the state's obligations to react to incidents originating from or transiting through their cyber space jurisdictions. Nations should ensure, for example, that national internet service providers (ISPs) and law enforcement agencies take appropriate steps against individuals, groups, and/or information and communication technology equipment found to be participating in a cyber attack. This also implies that nation-states agree to develop a capacity for dealing with cyber security matters. This means establishing appropriate laws and structures (national CERTs, law enforcement organizations, etc.) needed to implement the commitment.

   This is also not a new idea. Scholars in the United States have been discussing the merits of nation-states accepting responsibility for what goes on in their cyber jurisdictions. Examples of this policy thinking include Chris C. Demchak and Peter Dombrowski's paper covering cyber borders and jurisdictions. They argue that cyber space is no longer a public commons or prairie where all can roam and do as they wish. There is so much development and interest at stake for a nation's security that the establishment and control of "cyber borders" is an important step toward ensuring protection of their CIs from cyber based threats (Demchak and Dombrowski, 2011).

Related to responsibility and liability is the problem of attribution. The level of difficulty to carry out cyber attacks and the probability of getting caught must be raised higher. The establishment and control by a nation-state of its cyber borders will make it more difficult for cyber attacks to pass unnoticed. However, the unsuccessful effort up until now of placing the blame needs to be shifted from trying to identify who is actually attacking to identifying "what nation, if any, is responsible" (Healey, 2013, p. 265). It is the nation-state that should be held responsible for ensuring the control of its cyber borders and for making sure that malicious cyber activity originating or transiting through its cyber jurisdiction is monitored and controlled. The full burden of responsibility for reacting to and investigating an attack should not be placed on the victim but on those closest to and capable to react to the incident.

3. Monitoring of implementation of agreed commitments as listed: Nation-states agree to create a coalition of willing experts and institutions to monitor and advise on violations of these two agreements.

   Rationale: Some means must be available to monitor and inform participating nation-states of malicious cyber activities taking place or transiting through their cyber jurisdictions. An institution consisting of experts that can monitor and provide objective evaluation of violations to commitments should be established. This will provide for a capability to apply pressure on nations that are slow or reluctant to act on reported malicious activity taking place in their cyber jurisdictions.

Again, this is nothing that should be new to anyone working in international relations; this is not naive idealism. In questions where the need is recognized and where it really matters, nation-states have banded together and signed international agreements and conventions. This has been especially so with prohibiting the use of weapons of mass destruction. One possible model for dealing with the production and use of cyber weapons by nation-states is the International Convention on Chemical Weapons. Still perhaps remembering their use in World War I, and in recognition of the advances in technology that could facilitate the use of chemical weapons and amplify their potential for harm, a convention entered into force in 1997. Over 190 nations have signed it, representing most of the world's population. Associated with the agreement, the Organization for the Prohibition of Chemical Weapons (OPCW) was created to monitor and follow up implementation of the convention (OPCW, 1997). The convention on chemical weapons can serve as a useful model when considering implementation of the three above-mentioned proposals.

The Asia Pacific Computer Emergency Response Team coalition (APCERT) offers an example of regional cooperation. APCERT is made up of CERTs and ISPs from Japan, China, and South Korea. APCERT treats "the Internet and its health as a connected common shared infrastructure" (Ito, 2011). The coalition has been successful at addressing cyber incidents arising from political conflicts among its members.

One example of an ad hoc, yet effective global response to a perceived common threat in cyber space, is the work of the Conficker work group in 2008–2009. Governments appear to have failed to recognize the growing danger to the Internet from the creator of the Conficker worm, and the growing number of infected computers that could be commanded into action at any time. The fight to save the Internet from this new and potentially destructive worm was taken up by a group of volunteers that included private subject-matter experts, Internet service entrepreneurs, and nongovernmental organizations. This core group of individuals was able to muster enough cooperation worldwide to analyze, monitor, and defuse the Internet bomb that was Conficker (Bowden, 2011). These are just a few examples of what a motivated international community can do.

One caveat regarding the cooperation of CERTs in terms of this chapter is that the CERTs need to have wider functions to include ICSs—or include the creation of a separate CERT—that focuses primarily on ICS issues, as was done by the United States. In remembering the Carmel tunnel cyber incident, to have a CERT staffed with IT specialists is not enough to respond to an emergency. Specialists familiar with ICS-specific cyber security concepts are needed to form the core of these ICS CERTs.

In addition to monitoring and informing of violations of confidence-building agreements, the institution proposed above can also undertake some useful risk assessments of current vulnerabilities and provide advice and best practice information on reducing the level of risk. Assessing the risks and planning for the worst can pay off in a big way when a real disaster happens. A good example comes from the response to the events after 9/11 by the U.S. financial system. The tragedy in the loss of lives and the physical destruction to CI sectors of electric power, communications, and transportation (the closing of civil aviation used to send checks within the check clearing system) that took place could have had far-reaching catastrophic effects on the United States as well as linked financial systems of the world. This additional scenario of disaster did not take place because the Federal Reserve System was able to make use of plans already made during preparations for the Year 2000 bug (Daily Kos, 2014).

Long-term recommendations

Education is a lifelong process, and is first on this list of long-term recommendations. The gap in knowledge between the IT cyber security practitioner, with his Windows Certified diploma, and his ICS colleague, with a formal engineering educational diploma, needs to be closed. The IT practitioner who is entering the ICS world and calling for application of his security practices needs to understand the system to which he is applying those practices. The ICS engineers need to understand why the IT practitioner is so concerned about the cyber security of his control systems. A whole IT/ICS cross-training approach that provides for a better understanding of the risks needs to be made part of the curriculum for the training of both future IT and ICS practitioners. From page 64 of the above-mentioned OSCE guide: "Risk needs to be understood with an appreciation for the peculiarities in security practices found in the ICT and Industrial Control System (ICS) realms."

One solution for addressing the international aspects of securing ICSs from threats emanating from cyber space is to add a voice that, up until now, has been missing from policy making at national government levels and debates going on in international fora and conferences—the voice of the ICS professional community. Too often, these policies and debates are dominated by leaders with degrees in political science and law. Information on the technologies being discussed and on the implications of their misuse is missing from meetings of international organizations. Appreciation for ICSs has also been lacking at the UN-sponsored IGF in 2010, and at the Cyber Budapest conference in 2012. Cyber Budapest is a good example of CI protection being discussed in a superficial way. The panel dedicated to CI protection featured only one representative from an operator of a CI—and that person came from the public relations department. The voices and views of ICS engineers continue not to be heard at conferences, and will

continue not to be heard until this community is invited and decides to actively participate in these meetings. In part, the lack of this voice is responsible for the emphasis on
fighting cyber crime and socially motivated hacktivism. Excessive concerns over web
defacements and the embarrassments that occur over such cyber incidents would be put
into proper perspective if a description of the cyber fragilities of CIs and the potential
for disruption to our economy and social well-being were pointed out and explained by
an operator of an electric grid or gas pipeline. Unfortunately, this information does not
enter the debate dominated by policy leaders with nontechnical degrees coming from
judicial, law enforcement, or foreign affairs backgrounds, who are concerned more with
maintaining a rigid official policy position such as a multistakeholder model for Internet
governance.

There is also the problem of IT dominance in terms of understanding and appreciating the peculiarities of ICSs. IT cyber security bias tends to shut out any consideration of
ICS cyber security questions. ICSs do not even appear to be considered, as national cyber
security policies and laws are made that omit references to ICS by default.

It appears as though it is assumed that IT is used everywhere, such that IT used in
CIs will automatically be covered. Unfortunately, this is not the case in practice. From
personal experience, it took a great deal of persuasion to even include a definition of ICSs
in Lithuania's cyber security law. IT bias acts like a horse blinder (a narrow focus on a
particular issue) that keeps policy-making activities on a narrow track. One example of
government policy with a narrow focus is *NIST Special Publication 800-150 (Draft) Guide to
Cyber Threat Information Sharing*, issued for comment in November 2014.

In reading a cyber security-strategy-related document such as this National Institute
of Standards and Technology (NIST) draft, I ask three questions:

1. What is to be protected?
2. From what threats?
3. How will selected assets be protected?

From reading the introduction (Chris et al., 2014), I concluded that the answers to my
three questions in terms of this cyber security policy document are

1. What to protect?—intellectual property and government secrets
2. From what threats?—criminal groups
3. How to protect?—establish better interconnectivity (threat information sharing)

It appears that the writers of the NIST document have never heard of threats emanating from cyber space that can affect ICSs. They seem unaware or unaffected by the
implications of events such as Stuxnet, Black Energy, and Sandworm. Perhaps this is all
covered in other documents, but to a casual reader, this may lead to the simple and no-
brainer conclusion that "this is all that needs to be done." The appendix at the end of the
NIST document with examples of cyber security scenarios also appears to indicate a lack
of imagination in regard to what is at stake and what could happen to ICSs that support
the operations of what is called a CI.

Policy makers who continue to work with these IT blinders risk leaving issues pertinent to ICS cyber security out of their final product. How may we "open up" the cyber
policy cabal dominated by political science, law, and IT security specialists and add ICS
professionals as equals to the debate on cyber security policy at the national and international level?

Call for a consilium*

To borrow another term from my wife's profession, a cyber security *consilium* of technology professionals is needed. My wife tells me that when doctors are faced with a seriously ill patient who defies all traditional treatment, a *consilium* is called. This is a meeting of physicians to clarify the diagnosis, current condition of the patient, and required treatment to cure the patient. The conclusion of the *consilium*, if successful, provides the doctor with moral backing and informed advice on how the patient should be treated. In much the same way, a *consilium* of ICS professionals needs to be called to address the international cyber dimension of CIs. This community needs to be mobilized to inform the policy makers of the international security community that cyber threats to ICSs are real and have serious implications for the future health of our national security, economies, and well-being of society. Some may indicate that the scientific community does not have that kind of attention-getting power, in terms of getting politicians to deal with the issues discussed in this chapter. However, the scientific community does have that kind of power if it wants to use it. For example, in 1939, two years before the United States entered World War II, the esteemed physicist Albert Einstein wrote a letter (Einstein 1939)† to President Franklin D. Roosevelt warning that malicious states were engaged in developing new weapons of mass destruction. This letter is credited with Roosevelt's decision to begin development of a nuclear weapon, today known as the Manhattan Project. The example is worth looking at again in terms of dealing with today's cyber threats. There may be no living scientist with the attention-getting capacity of an Einstein living today, but a letter signed by a *consilium* of leading opinion leaders in ICSs (perhaps together with a few enlightened IT professionals) and directed at world leaders is worth trying. The stakes are indeed high and an action like this could tip the scales in the right direction in terms of breaking through the veils of ignorance and denial regarding serious threats to ICSs emanating from cyber space. It would be most refreshing, at a future NATO, OSCE, EU, or UN meeting on cyber security policy, to see an ICS cyber security engineer and industry opinion leader make a presentation followed by his/her active participation in the discussion; not as a subject-matter expert, but as one of the representatives of "the nation."

Conclusion

World War I started 100 years ago. Technology then was applied in new and surprising ways to kill a lot of people and cripple the economies of the combatants for decades. Many historians look back and wonder how such a war could have happened. Today, we are possibly in a situation similar to what was prevalent in May 1914. Tensions are rising among nations and some feel confident in their abilities to quickly dominate the "battlefield" and win (using "Plan 17" and the "von Schlieffen Plan"). The terms "cyber-Pearl Harbor" and "cyber-Armageddon" are perhaps overused and overexaggerate what could happen. However, we should not let this time pass without at least trying to address the issues discussed in this article. There is a lot of work for our State Departments and Ministries of Foreign Affairs to undertake, in partnership with the technical community. We need to help the people who are worried about defending critical systems, and those involved in offense need to be told of the implications of their activities. Most importantly, politicians need to start caring about these issues. Many Department of State and Ministry of Foreign Affairs (MFA) people who go to meetings about confidence-building measures and codes

---

* Tarptautinių žodžių žodynas (International Words Dictionary), © Vyriausioji enciklopedijų redakcija, 1985.
† "Certain aspects of the situation which has arisen seem to call for watchfulness and, if necessary, quick action on the part of the administration."

of conduct for nations to follow in cyber space have no idea what control systems are. They think it is just about cyber crime, hacktivists, and denial of access to websites. They also do not like to discuss Stuxnet and the implications of Mr. Snowden, that is, that governments have impressive intelligence gathering capabilities that could be easily applied to executing other Stuxnets and have the capability (if they choose) to identify the attacker. The technical community needs to find a way to acquire an equal place at the table and give policy makers some understanding about what is actually at stake. Maximum effort should be directed to keep this a MFA problem and not become an issue for the Ministry of Defense. Unfortunately, in terms of dealing with increased risks from cyber space for the health of our national economies and well-being of society, that is exactly where the main effort toward addressing these threats is shifting.

I think, again, of the character Professor Barnhardt in the 1951 film *The Day the Earth Stood Still* with Michael Rennie who tried to call an international gathering of scientists to draw attention to a common danger. Unfortunately, the politicians would not agree to come to such a meeting. This chapter has tried to raise the importance of ICSs to our modern way of life. They are vulnerable to a variety of cyber based threats, both intentional and unintentional, ranging from the exploits of hackers to those executed or supported by states. It is the latter that needs to be brought up higher on the list of priorities to be dealt with in the international security policy-making arena. Local policies of government and industry fall short in meeting what is truly an international security issue. So far, nothing catastrophic has happened to our CIs, yet states are aware of the danger and a cyber arms race is underway. Attacking CIs with cyber weapons is an attractive (perhaps too good not to use) way of achieving a frustrated foreign policy objective. Cyber weapons offer the illusion of being a cost-effective "best bang for the buck" way of neutralizing a target. We should use the time available to point out what is at stake and say the right words before we are left face to face with living through a cyber-caused event disruptive to our economy and to the wellbeing of society. Quoting the final words of Klaatu at Barnhardt's meeting: "the decision rests with you" (us).

References

AL Arabiya News. (2012). Saudi Aramco says cyber-attack targeted kingdom's economy. *Al Arabiya News,* 09 December. http://english.alarabiya.net/articles/2012/12/09/254162.html.

Alert. (2014). ICS-ALERT-14-176-02A ICS Focused Malware (Update A) https://ics-cert.us-cert.gov/alerts/ICS-ALERT-14-176-02A, Last revised: July 01.

Bowden, M. (2011). *Worm: The First Digital War,* p. 221. New York: Atlantic Monthly Press.

Butrimas, V. and Bruzga, A. (2012). The cybersecurity dimension of critical energy infrastructure, per Concordiam, George C. Marshall European Center for Security Studies, 3(4), pp. 12–17. http://www.marshallcenter.org/mcpublicweb/MCDocs/files/College/F_Publications/perConcordiam/pC_V3N4_en.pdf.

Camilleri, S. (2014). *The Current State of Cyber Security Readiness in the Aviation Industry,* p. 9. Floriana: Durasee Services. http://nebula.wsimg.com/cfcfade61f01b17cb0dd794218accf24?AccessKeyId=8E0A7E654AC170A0FBBD&disposition=0&alloworigin=1.

Chris, J., Lee, B., and David, W. (2014). *Guide to Cyber Threat 6 Information Sharing (Draft).* NIST. http://csrc.nist.gov/publications/drafts/800-150/sp800_150_draft.pdf, p.4.

Clarke, R.A. (2010). *Cyber War: The Next Threat to National Security and What to Do About It,* pp. 268–271. New York: HarperCollins.

Daily Kos. (2014). The astonishing story of the federal reserve on 9–11. http://www.dailykos.com/story/2014/09/10/1328813/-The-Astonishing-Story-of-the-Federal-Reserve-on-9-11.

Demchak, C. and Dombrowski, P. (2011). Rise of a cybered westphalian age. *Strategic Studies Quarterly* 5(1), 54–57. http://www.au.af.mil/au/ssq/2011/spring/spring11.pdf.

Digital Dao. (2015). Evolving hostilities in the global cyber commons. http://jeffreycarr.blogspot. com/2012/11/osces-cyber-security-confidence.html.

Einstein, A. (1939). Letter from Albert Einstein to FDR, 8/2/39. *American Experience.* http://www.pbs. org/wgbh/americanexperience/features/primary-resources/truman-ein39/.

Elinor, M. (2010). Joe Weiss, crusader for critical infrastructure security (Q&A). http://news.cnet. com/8301-27080_3-20004505-245.html.

Estonian Chamber of Commerce in Lithuania. (2014). Traditional and Renewable Energy Forum.

Eugene Kaspersky Press Club. (2013). A speech by Eugene Kaspersky at the Press Club in Canberra, Australia. http://www.youtube.com/watch?v=6tlUvb26DzI.

Federal Power Commission. (1965). Report to the president by the federal power commission on the power failure in the Northeastern United States and the province of Ontario on November 9–10. Washington DC. http://blackout.gmu.edu/archive/pdf/fpc_65.pdf.

Gallagher, R. (2014). Operation Socialist: The inside story of how British spies hacked Belgium's largest telco. *The Intercept_,* December 13. https://theintercept.com/2014/12/13/belgacom-hack-gchq-inside-story/.

Gewirtz, D. (2012). Take action before the UN, Russia, and China hijack the Internet. *ZDNET.* http://www.zdnet.com/take-action-before-the-un-russia-and-china-hijack-the-internet7000008003/?s_cid=e539#postComment.

Ghena, B. and Beyer W. (2014). Green lights forever: Analyzing the security of traffic infrastructure, *Proceedings of the 8th USENIX Workshop on Offensive Technologies (WOOT '14).* https://jhalderm. com/pub/papers/traffic-woot14.pdf.

Hamodia (2013). Cyber attack shuts down Carmel Tunnels toll road. *Hamodia,* Sunday, October 27, http://hamodia.com/2013/10/27/cyber-attack-shuts-down-carmel-tunnels-toll-road/.

Healey, J. (2013). *A Fierce Domain: Conflict in Cyberspace, 1986–2012.* Vienna, VA: Cyber Conflicts Studies Association.

Heartbleed Bug. (2014). http://heartbleed.com/.

Homeland Security. (2014). *Vulnerability Notes Database.* Software Engineering Institute: Carnegie Mellon University. http://www.kb.cert.org/vuls/id/720951.

Hultquist, J. (2014). *Sandworm Team Targeting SCADA Systems.* http://www.isightpartners. com/2014/10/sandworm-team-targeting-scada-systems/, iSIGHT Partners.

Industrial Control Systems Cyber Emergency Response Team (ICS-CERT) (2015). https://ics-cert. us-cert.gov/.

Innovative Energy Solutions for Military Applications (IESMA). (2014). DELTA. Lithuania: Vilnius. http://www.iesma.info/homepage.

Integrated Management System Policy. (2014). http://www.sepsas.sk/seps/Dokumenty/ ISM/2014/05/07/Politika_ISM_EN.pdf; http://www.sepsas.sk/seps/en_index.asp.

ISA99 Committee. (2015). Industrial automation and control systems (IACS) security. http://isa99. isa.org/ISA99%20Wiki/Home.aspx.

Ito, Y. (2011). *Making the Internet Clean, Safe and Reliable: Asia Pacific Regional Collaboration Activities.* The Tokyo, Japan: Institute of Electrical and Electronics Engineers. http://ieeexplore.ieee.org/ stamp/stamp.jsp?tp=&arnumber=5978796.

Jacob, A., Judith, H., and Christian, S. (2013). Shopping for spy gear: Catalog advertises NSA tool-box. Spiegel online International, 29 December http://www.spiegel.de/international/world/ catalog-reveals-nsa-has-back-doors-for-numerous-devices-a-940994.html.

Klimburg, A. (2013). The Internet Yalta. *Center for a New American Security,* p. 2. http://www.cnas. org/theinternetyalta.

Koot, M. R. (2013). Belgacom on the brink of catastrophe (translation), September 23. http://blog. cyberwar.nl/2013/09/belgacom-on-brink-of-catastrophe.html.

Langner, R. (2011). Cracking Stuxnet, a 21st-century cyber weapon. Ted Talk at http://www.ted. com/talks/ralph_langner_cracking_stuxnet_a_21st_century_cyberweapon.

Langner, R. (2012). *Robust Control System Networks: Securing Control System Networks after Stuxnet,* Chapter 2, p. 9 (e-bookversion). New York: Momentum Press.

Langner, R. (2013). For technical analysis, I refer the reader to the works of Ralph Langner. *To Kill a Centrifuge: A Technical Analysis of What Stuxnet's Creators Tried to Achieve.* http://www.langner. com/en/wp-content/uploads/2013/11/To-kill-a-centrifuge.pdf.

Ministry of Foreign Affairs of the People's Republic of China. (2011). China, Russia and other countries submit the document of international code of conduct for information security to the United Nations. *Ministry of Foreign Affairs of the People's Republic of China*. http://www.fmprc.gov.cn/eng/wjdt/wshd/t858978.htm.

Müller-Maguhn, A. (2014). The NSA breach of Telekom and other German firms http://ml.spiegel.de/article.do?id=991503.

NATO Energy Security Centre of Excellence. (2014). NATO energy security centre of excellence. http://www.enseccoe.org/en/news/nato-ici-table-tc6a.html.

Organisation for the Prohibition of Chemical Weapons (OPCW). (1997). Chemical weapons convention. The Hague, Netherlands. http://www.opcw.org/chemical-weapons-convention/.

Organization for Security and Co-Operation in Europe (OSCE). (2011). A comprehensive approach to cyber security: Exploring the future OSCE role. http://www.osce.org/event/cyber_sec2011.

Organization for Security and Co-Operation in Europe (OSCE). (2012). Development of confidence-building measures to reduce the risks of conflict stemming from the use of information and communication technologies. http://www.delegfrance-osce.org/IMG/pdf/pcdec1039_reduce_risk_of_conflicts_from_use_of_ICT.pdf.

Organization for Security and Co-operation in Europe. (2013a). *Guide on Non-Nuclear Critical Energy Infrastructure Protection from Terrorist Attacks Focusing on Threats Emanating from Cyberspace*. http://www.osce.org/atu/103500.

Organization for Security and Co-operation in Europe. (2013b). *Guide on Non-Nuclear Critical Energy Infrastructure Protection from Terrorist Attacks Focusing on Threats Emanating from Cyberspace*, p. 64. http://www.osce.org/atu/103500.

Organization for Security and Co-Operation in Europe (OSCE). (2015). http://www.osce.org/who.

Parker, T. (2014). Attacking, defending and building SCADA systems. http://www.blackhat.com/asia-14/training/index.html.

Perlroth, N. (2012) In cyberattack on Saudi firm, U.S. sees Iran firing back. *New York Times*, 03 October. http://www.nytimes.com/2012/10/24/business/global/cyberattack-on-saudi-oil-firm-disquiets-us.html.

Perlroth, N. (2014). Russian hackers targeting oil and gas companies, 30 June. http://www.nytimes.com/2014/07/01/technology/energy-sector-faces-attacks-from-hackers-in-russia.html?_r=2.

Rafako. (2015). Road show 2015 w Rafako S.A. http://www.rafako.com.pl/centrum-prasowe/komunikaty-prasowe/-/16947.

Russell, A. (2004). CIA plot led to huge blast in Siberian gas pipeline. The daily telegraph, February. http://www.telegraph.co.uk/news/worldnews/northamerica/usa/1455559/CIA-plot-led-to-huge-blast-in-Siberian-gas-pipeline.html.

Saarinen, J. (2014a). *Siemens Industrial Products Shellshocked*. http://www.itnews.com.au/News/396628,siemens-industrial-products-shellshocked.aspx?eid=65&edate=20141014&utm_source=20141014&utm_medium=newsletter&utm_campaign=sc_weekly.

Saarinen, J. (2014b). Largest microsoft patch wednesday coming this week. http://www.itnews.com.au/News/397676,largest-microsoft-patch-wednesday-coming-this-week.aspx?eid=1&edate=20141110&utm_source=20141110_AM&utm_medium=newsletter&utm_campaign=daily_newsletter.

Selena, F. (2012). *New Exploits Targeting Critical Infrastructure Added to Metasploit*. http://www.techrepublic.com/blog/security/new-exploits-targeting-critical-infrastructure-added-to-metasploit/7660?tag=nl.e036.

Simonite, T. (2012). Stuxnet tricks copied by computer criminals, *MIT Technology Review*, http://www.technologyreview.com/news/429173/stuxnet-tricks-copied-by-computer-criminals/.

Symantec Security Response. (2014). Dragonfly: Cyber espionage attacks against energy suppliers, p. 3. http://www.symantec.com/content/en/us/enterprise/media/security_response/whitepapers/Dragonfly_Threat_Against_Western_Energy_Suppliers.pdf.

Target Hackers Broke in Via HVAC Company. (2014). *KrebsOnSecurity.com*, February 14. http://krebsonsecurity.com/2014/02/target-hackers-broke-in-via-hvac-company/.

UN General Assembly. (2013). Report of the group of governmental experts on developments in the field of information and telecommunications in the context of international security, 24 June A/68/98*. http://www.mofa.go.jp/files/000016407.pdf.

chapter six

Aurora generator test

Joe Weiss

Contents

This chapter provides a fundamental overview of the *Aurora effect,* and more importantly, the *Aurora generator test.* The project was conducted to determine if a cyber-related event could cause physical damage to critical hardware. As there has been much discussion and controversy regarding this event, this chapter will only provide what is publicly disclosed and known, rather than speculate on issues that are much more difficult to substantiate and verify.

Overview

The safe and reliable supply of electric power is vital to national security, as well as economic and social stability. A significant cross-sector vulnerability exists that could impact the availability and safety of electric power, along with the safety and reliability of AC-induction motors, generators, and transformers connected to affected electric substations.

The vulnerability, designated as *Aurora,* is an example in which a series of unintended consequences exist as a result of advances in materials and digital technology modernization. The trend is further amplified by continued failure to properly evaluate and address security issues before deployment of newer technologies. Thus, such implementations may create new and asymmetric opportunities to disrupt, damage, or destroy critical assets used by critical infrastructures, further adding gaps in the ability to protect such environments. Although originally thought to be primarily a physical-related issue, Aurora defines a narrower, yet significant, exploitable gap within electrical protection that currently exists in many electrical grids worldwide, where a physical gap can be exploited by cybermeans.

The fundamental principle behind this condition is known by experienced and practicing utility engineers and operators. The Institute of Electrical and Electronics Engineers (IEEE) Power Systems Relay Committee (PSRC) published a tutorial on generator protection tutorial history in 1995 that addressed the *out-of-phase* condition (IEEE, 2011). Rotating equipment such as motors and generators operate (spin) in synchronization with the electric grid. Electric utility personnel have known for years that, if rotating equipment that is not within synchronization (referred to as an out-of-phase* condition) is brought on to or reconnected to the electric grid, this can potentially damage shaft and winding torques, and will result in the equipment being instantaneously forced back into a synchronized state by the electric grid.

Basic physics principles govern such out-of-phase consequences, and the resulting torque may exceed equipment design limitations, thus severely damaging, if not destroying, rotating equipment, as well as any of their connected loads (e.g., pumps, gear boxes, relays, etc.).

Over several years, the likelihood of damage resulting from an out-of-phase synchronization event has led to the development and refinement of complex electrical grid protection and control mechanisms such as synchronization check relays specifically designed to prevent such an occurrence. Historical incidents of accidental malfunction or operations have demonstrated that an inadvertent out-of-phase operation can occur with devastating consequences.

Out-of-phase events can occur either accidentally or intentionally. An Aurora event is a deliberate attempt to damage or destroy susceptible equipment by cybermeans; facilities may implement traditional physical or cybersecurity controls to protect their environments, yet may still remain vulnerable to such an attack. The concern resulting from an Aurora-based event is that such an event can severely impact equipment that is important in sustaining an electric grid as well as the equipment that is connected to the affected substation; large motors and generators are of particular concern, as they are very expensive, and can have repair or replacement time frames ranging from several months to several years.

Reasons of concern specific to the Aurora event include

- Existing relay protection may not be fast enough to protect against an Aurora event—a physical gap in the protection of the electric grid.
- Digital devices permitting breaker control may exist in most transmission and distribution substations.
- Substation digital devices (e.g., breakers and other substation devices) may be susceptible to cyberattacks leading to an Aurora condition.
- Successful exploitation of the Aurora vulnerability may result in physical damage to rotating equipment and transformers connected to the electric grid.
- Synchronous rotating equipment, such as generators and AC induction motors that drive devices in other industries (such as water and oil pumps), may be susceptible to damage from the Aurora vulnerability.
- Damage to rotating equipment with long fabrication or procurement time frames is of concern; the vulnerability is not simply a short-term power disruption (estimated outage of 1 year or greater).
- Modeling predictions have been supported by both small- and full-scale testing.
- An Aurora event is not attributable, and is considered vendor agnostic (nonspecific).

---

* Phase difference is the difference, generally expressed in degrees or time, between two sinusoidal waves having the same frequency and referenced to the same point in time. When two oscillators have the same frequency, and have no phase difference, are said to be "in phase" with each other; however, when two oscillators have the same frequency, yet have a phase difference, the two oscillators are said to be "out of phase" with each other.

Impacted critical infrastructure sectors resulting from an Aurora effect would include:

- Oil and gas
- Manufacturing (and critical manufacturing)
- Nuclear and nonnuclear energy
- Water and wastewater
- Oil and petrochemical refining
- Transportation

Aurora generator test

Under the direction of the Department of Homeland Security (DHS), the Idaho National Laboratory (INL) conducted an experiment in March 2007, designated as the Aurora generator test, to determine if a cyber-related attack could physically damage, if not destroy, components of the electric grid. The test used a computer program to rapidly open and close electrical circuit breakers in and out of phase from the remainder of a local grid, causing a catastrophic failure.

The test was conducted to ascertain if the vulnerability could cause physical damage to rotating equipment; in this case, a 3.8 MVA diesel-powered generator (rated at 3.4 MW, but operated at 2.3 MW during the test) was configured to operate a local 13.8 kV distribution system,* costing approximately US$3 million to implement.† The objective of the test was to

- Perform a test that demonstrated the potential vulnerability of equipment connected to the electric grid
- Confirm any vulnerabilities or impacts resulting from the test using real-world scenarios and conditions
- Utilize industry best practices (as confirmed by participants prior to the test's execution) such that the system under which the test was configured in an acceptable method
- Generate data from the test to validate modeling and simulation results, while demonstrating and cataloging any physical consequences resulting from the test, and then provide a baseline for future tests
- Provide a common forum for representatives from various stakeholder groups including industry representatives, DHS, U.S. Nuclear Regulatory Commission (NRC), Federal Energy Regulatory Commission (FERC), North American Electric Reliability Corporation (NERC), Tennessee Valley Authority (TVA), as well as representatives from several foreign countries (such as the United Kingdom and Canada), to discuss results from the test

Industrial control systems' representatives were included in the vulnerability and evaluation efforts, which included both validation test planning and its preparations. DHS distributed information to Australia, Canada, New Zealand, and the United Kingdom to provide insight into risk assessment and mitigation planning.

---

* https://muckrock.s3.amazonaws.com/foia_files/14f00304-Documents.pdf, p. 50.
† https://muckrock.s3.amazonaws.com/foia_files/14f00304-Documents.pdf, p. 57.

Mitigation of an Aurora effect

Following the INL generator test, DHS assisted sector-specific technical groups in drafting mitigation plans that took a multi-tiered approach allowing for near-, medium-, and long-term solutions. The DHS then reached out to several protective relay vendors to develop mitigation-based approaches, such as improved access controls and modification of relay functionality. Additionally, DHS directly engaged the electric industry under the auspices of the Critical Infrastructure Partnership Advisory Committee (CIPAC), as well as briefing members of Congress through their respective Homeland Security Committees, along with other interagency stakeholders.

One possible mitigation solution is to add Aurora-specific synchronization-checking functionalities to all protective relays that potentially connect two (or more) systems together. Defined as *hardware mitigation devices* (HMDs), HMDs were developed to provide an interim solution until either a more suitable solution is developed, or overall power grid security controls mature sufficiently enough to negate the Aurora vulnerability. An HMD is a protective relay that is designed to provide electric facilities protection against damage from accidental out-of-phase or intentional Aurora events. To be effective with its protection, the device's function must isolate the equipment from the substation when the voltage and frequency are within a predefined range and not be sensitive to cyberthreats.

Although further implemented enhancements of security controls may improve the postures of supporting better and more reliable electrical grids, having appropriate relay protection, along with enhanced security controls, will improve its overall effectiveness.

The vulnerability mitigation efforts may be thought of in the following areas:*

- Increase requirements (skills, tools, and knowledge) needed to protect exploitation of platforms:
  - Strengthen access controls to critical relays that may be impacted by the Aurora event
  - Set alarms for remote access to relays
  - Separate functionality of configuration and read/control
- Vary environments limiting scalability of an Aurora event (diverse defense in depth):
  - Implement a timing sequence to prevent some breakers reclosing such that the hardwired breaker timing sequence will prevent the reclosing of some breakers
  - Devices would be simple in design, not connected to any external communications
  - Other technical options, depending on system topology, would further reduce the scalability or to protect specific point targets
- Provide high-assurance technical mitigation for high-consequence facilities:
  - Deploy devices capable of detecting a possible Aurora event and isolate rotating machinery
  - Deploy other technologies that can provide device-specific protection

Suggested mitigation efforts were aimed at enabling greater preventative measures such that it would take significantly more effort to access substation equipment remotely (security solutions, procedure changes, limited access, etc.), varying the exploitability of the vulnerability to reduce potential scalability of an event or potential attack (larger utility systems having one vulnerable path to exploit multiple substation devices). At the core of these efforts is a device, installed within an asset owner's fence on-site, such that the

---

* https://muckrock.s3.amazonaws.com/foia_files/14f00304-Documents.pdf, p. 38.

device can sense an out-of-phase condition or attack and open supply-side breakers to isolate rotating equipment prior to it being damaged.

As of June 2015, only two relay protection suppliers provide Aurora mitigation capabilities:

- Cooper Power Systems iGR-933 rotating equipment isolation device (REID)
- Schweitzer Engineering Laboratories SEL 751A feeder protection relay (Swearingen et al. 2013)

Controversy surrounding the disclosure of the Aurora generator test

On July 3, 2014, DHS released an 840-page redacted document pertaining to the INL generator test as part of a Freedom of Information Act (FOIA) request.* The FOIA request was made through a website called *Muckrock,*† which allows individuals to make requests, analyze, and share government documents through the FOIA process.

The FOIA request was made specific to *Operation Aurora*, which was a cyber-related attack against Google sometime in 2010. Many have speculated that the publicly disclosed 840-page redacted document was unintentional (Fisher 2014; Prince 2014), whereas DHS has publicly recorded that it was intentionally released (Department of Homeland Security 2014).

Images of the test site

Figures 6.1 through 6.7 are from the documents released by DHS. These images have been approved for general distribution by DHS.

Figure 6.1 Idaho Nuclear Technology and Engineering Complex (INTEC). (https://muckrock. s3.amazonaws.com/foia_files/14f00304-Documents.pdf, p. 85.)

---

* https://www.muckrock.com/foi/united-states-of-america-10/operation-Aurora-11765.
† http://www.muckrock.com.

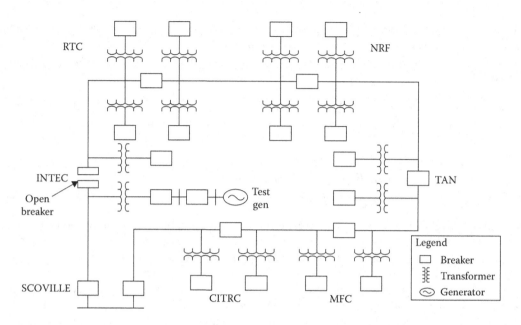

Figure 6.2 13.8 kV loop configured minimizing power disturbances to the remainder of INL. (https://muckrock.s3.amazonaws.com/foia_files/14f00304-Documents.pdf, p. 99.)

Figure 6.3 Preparation of the site. (https://muckrock.s3.amazonaws.com/foia_files/14f00304-Documents.pdf, p. 100.)

Figure 6.4 Generator used for the Aurora generator test. (https://muckrock.s3.amazonaws.com/ foia_files/14f00304-Documents.pdf, p. 103.)

Figure 6.5 Setup and configuration of the site. (https://muckrock.s3.amazonaws.com/foia_ files/14f00304-Documents.pdf, p. 105.)

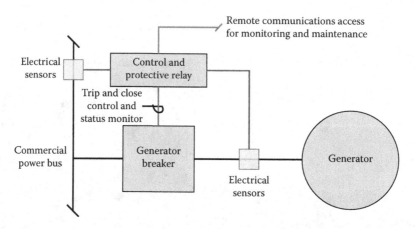

Figure 6.6 Simplified control diagram. (https://muckrock.s3.amazonaws.com/foia_files/14f00304-Documents.pdf, p. 106.)

Figure 6.7 Image snapshot from the video from the generator test. (https://muckrock.s3.amazonaws.com/foia_files/Aurora_high_res.wmv.)

References

Department of Homeland Security (DHS). 2014. http://www.dhs.gov/sites/default/files/publica-tions/priv-foia-log-july-2014.pdf,%20Page%204,%20Section%202014%20HQFO-00638.

Fisher, D., 2014. DHS releases hundreds of documents on wrong Aurora project, Threat Post, July 2014. https://threatpost.com/dhs-releases-hundreds-of-documents-on-wrong-aurora-project.

IEEE. 2011. Tutorial on the protection of synchronous generators, special publications of the IEEE power system relay committee. John Wiley.

Prince, B. 2014. DHS mistakenly releases 840-pages of critical infrastructure documents via mishandled FOIA request, Security Week, July 2014. http://www.securityweek.com/dhs-mistakenly-releases-840-pages-critical-infrastructure-documents-mishandled-fioa-request.

Swearingen, M., Brunasso, S., Weiss, J., and Huber, D. 2013. What you need to know (and don't) about the Aurora vulnerability, Power, September 2013, pp. 52–56. http://www.powermag.com/what-you-need-to-know-and-dont-about-the-Aurora-vulnerability/?pagenum=3.

section two

Governance and management

chapter seven

Disaster recovery and business continuity of SCADA

Steven Young

Contents

Business continuity process for SCADA

When addressing the problem of risk in supervisory control and data acquisition (SCADA) systems, it is important to review business continuity planning and disaster recovery (DR). A large portion of America's power grid and water-processing facilities is privately owned. These privately owned providers and users of SCADA systems need to have a continuity plan to survive threats to infrastructure. Business continuity planning addresses the overall issue of maintaining or reestablishing production in the case of an interruption. These interruptions may take the form of a natural disaster (e.g., hurricane, tornado, earthquake, and flood), an unintentional man-made event (e.g., accidental equipment damage, fire or explosion, and operator error), an intentional man-made event (e.g., attack by bomb, firearm or vandalism, and attacker), or an equipment failure. From a potential outage perspective, it may require typical time spans of days, weeks, or months to recover from a natural disaster; or minutes or hours to recover from a malware infection or a mechanical/electrical failure. Since there is often a separate discipline that deals with reliability and electrical or mechanical maintenance, some organizations choose to define business continuity in a way that excludes these sources of failure. Since business continuity also deals primarily with the long-term implications of production outages, some organizations also choose to place a minimum interruption limit on the risks to be considered. For the purposes of SCADA cybersecurity, it is recommended that neither of these constraints be made. Long-term outages (DR) and short-term outages (operational recovery) should both be considered. Because some of these potential interruptions involve man-made events, it is also important to work collaboratively with the physical security organization to understand the relative risks of these events and the physical security countermeasures that are in place to prevent them. It is also important for the physical security organization to understand which areas of a production site house data acquisition and control systems that might have higher-level risks (Falco 2006).

It is important to get a few key differentiators in place to discuss business continuity and DR in reference to SCADA systems. A business continuity plan (BCP) is a document containing the recovery timeline methodology, test-validated documentation, procedures, and instructions developed specifically for use in restoring organization operations in the event of a declared disaster. To be effective, the BCP also requires testing, skilled personnel, access to vital records, and alternate recovery resources, including facilities. Business continuity means working out how to stay in operation in the event of a disaster. In terms of DR planning for SCADA systems, it refers to the planning and preparation for disaster and the creation of a plan (paper or electronic) for response to disaster. Typically, these plans are information technology focused. A government entity or public utilities need both BC and DR to survive. DR replaces the loss of SCADA technology and the back-end IT infrastructure.

Types of plans

Information system contingency planning represents a broad scope of activities designed to sustain and recover critical system services following an emergency event. Information-system contingency planning fits into a much broader security and emergency management effort that includes organizational and business process continuity, DR planning, and incident management. Ultimately, an organization involved in SCADA technology would use a suite of plans to properly prepare response, recovery, and continuity activities for disruptions affecting the organization's information systems, mission processes, personnel, and the facility. Because there is an inherent relationship between an information system and the mission/business process it supports, there must be coordination between each plan during development and updates to ensure that recovery strategies and supporting resources neither negate each other nor duplicate efforts.

Continuity and contingency planning are critical components of emergency management and organizational resilience but are often confused in their use. Continuity planning normally applies to the mission/business itself; it concerns the ability to continue critical functions and processes during and after an emergency event. Contingency planning normally applies to information systems and provides the steps needed to recover the operation of all or part of designated information systems at an existing or new location in an emergency. Incident response planning is a type of plan that normally focuses on detection, response, and recovery to a computer security incident or event.

In general, universally accepted definitions for information system contingency planning and the related planning areas have not been available. Occasionally, this leads to confusion regarding the actual scope and purpose of various types of plans. To provide a common basis of understanding regarding information system contingency planning, this section identifies several other types of plans and describes their purpose and scope relative to information system contingency planning. Because of the lack of standard definitions for these types of plans, the scope of actual plans developed by organizations may vary. Each organization should plan according to their mission needs.

Business continuity plan

The BCP focuses on sustaining an organization's mission/business processes during and after a disruption. While recovery from a SCADA disaster is technologically significant, it is equally important to have the private business and/or agency recover from the incident. The link is that a system may be highly available; however, a company or agency may not be able to recover. When the agency or business cannot recover, the SCADA system/process may not be able to sustain itself due to a lack of funding or maintenance. A BCP may be written for mission/business processes within a single business unit or may address the entire organization's processes. The BCP may also be scoped to address only the functions deemed to be priorities. A BCP may be used for long-term recovery in conjunction with the continuity of operations (COOP) plan, allowing for additional functions to come online as resources or time allow. Because mission/business processes use information systems (ISs), the business continuity planner must coordinate with information system owners to ensure that the BCP expectations and IS capabilities are matched.

Continuity of operations plan

A COOP focuses on restoring an organization's mission-essential functions (MEF) at an alternate site and performing those functions for up to 30 days before returning to normal operations. Additional functions, or those at a field-office level, may be addressed by a BCP. Minor threats or disruptions that do not require relocation to an alternate site are typically not addressed in a COOP plan. A key assumption is that a SCADA process operated by a government agency (state, county, and local) is an essential function. For example, the ability to provide power or water is a key public health and safety function.

Standard elements of a COOP plan include

- Procedures
- Public communications in the event of a SCADA disaster
- Risk management
- Vital records
- Orders of succession (e.g., who will operate the system in the event of a terrorist event or pandemic)
- Devolution
- Delegation of authority
- Emergency operations center(s)

Crisis communications plan

Organizations should document standard procedures for internal and external communications in the event of a disruption using a crisis communications plan. A crisis communications plan is often developed by the organization responsible for public outreach, for example, "instructions to boil" orders if a water treatment plan is affected. Another example would be instructions for sheltering or evacuation in the event of a nuclear power disaster. The plan provides various formats for communications appropriate to the incident. The crisis communications plan typically designates specific individuals as the only authority for answering questions from or providing information to the public regarding emergency response. It may also include procedures for disseminating reports to personnel on the status of the incident and templates for public press releases. The crisis communication plan procedures should be communicated to the organization's COOP and BCP planners to ensure that the plans include clear direction that only approved statements are released to the public by authorized officials.

Critical infrastructure protection plan

Critical infrastructure and key resources (CIKR) are those components of the national infrastructure that are deemed so vital that their loss would have a debilitating effect of the safety, security, economy, and/or health of the United States. A critical infrastructure protection (CIP) plan is a set of policies and procedures that serve to protect and recover these national assets and mitigate risks and vulnerabilities. CIP plans define the roles and responsibilities for protection, develop partnerships and information-sharing relationships, implement the risk management framework defined in the National Infrastructure Protection Plan (NIPP) and Homeland Security Presidential Directive (HSPD7) for CIKR assets, and integrate federal, state, and local emergency preparedness, protection, and resiliency of critical infrastructure. Typically, SCADA continuity and DR plans are tactical interfaces to CIP plans.

Incident response plan

Incident response plans establish procedures to address cyberattacks against an organization's information system(s). These procedures are designed to enable security personnel to identify, mitigate, and recover from malicious computer incidents, such as unauthorized access to a system or data, denial of service, or unauthorized changes to system hardware, software, or data (e.g., malicious logic, such as a virus, worm, or Trojan horse). This plan may be included as an appendix of the BCP.

Disaster recovery plan

The disaster recovery plan (DRP) applies to major, usually physical disruptions to service that deny access to the primary facility infrastructure for an extended period. A DRP is an information system–focused plan designed to restore the operability of the target system, application, or computer facility infrastructure at an alternate site after an emergency. The DRP may be supported by multiple information system contingency plans to address recovery of impacted individual systems once the alternate facility has been established. A DRP may support a BCP or COOP plan by recovering supporting systems for mission/business processes or MEF at an alternate location. The DRP only addresses information-system disruptions that require relocation.

Plan objectives and differentiation

The core objectives of a BCP plan are to ensure the safety of staff and the public. When a water treatment facility is attacked, the public is particularly at risk of public health hazards. For example, SCADA systems could be attacked to initiate a spill of wastewater into the environment. They could also be attacked to prevent clean water from going to a needy location. BCP and DR plans also ensure the production and delivery of safe water as well as the delivery of clean power. DR plans and strategies should be maintained to ensure the integrity of critical data. Federal directives distinguish COOP plans as a specific type of plan that should not be confused with information system contingency plans, DRPs, or BCPs. Nongovernment organizations typically use BCPs rather than COOP plans to address mission/business processes.

Examples of SCADA systems at risk

There are several specific examples of risk in the water industry that illustrate the need for BCP and DR. For instance, a SCADA system uninterruptible power supply (UPS) could be impacted from a power circuit failure if a member of housekeeping staff plugs an industrial floor polisher into the UPS. A failure of a high-availability SCADA server could happen if two or more power supplies are plugged into same UPS circuit. The circuit could fail and the server may not recover properly. Hardware failures of programmable logic controllers (PLCs) are possible, and not enough onsite spares may be available. A core network switch or router could have a failure. Both power supplies from these types of appliances could fail with no spares being available for immediate installation. Viruses and malware are also possible concerns on any IT-related hardware.

SCADA contingency planning process

The process for developing a SCADA continuity plan is universal to most recovery plans. The seven steps in the process are

1. Developing the contingency planning policy
2. Conducting the business impact analysis (BIA)
3. Identifying preventive controls
4. Creating contingency strategies
5. Developing an information system contingency plan
6. Ensuring plan testing, training, and exercises
7. Ensuring plan maintenance

Ultimately, a recovery coordinator and continuity planner needs to be appointed with the authority to initiate recovery when the plans are developed. The continuity planner needs to be included in each phase of the planning to ensure understanding of the recovery actions.

Developing the contingency planning policy statement

To be effective and to ensure that personnel fully understand the organization's contingency planning requirements, the contingency plan must be based on a clearly defined policy. The contingency planning policy statement should define the organization's overall contingency objectives and establish the organizational framework and responsibilities for system contingency planning. To be successful, senior management, most likely the operating agency's chief information officer (CIO), must support a contingency program and be included in the process of developing the program policy. The policy should reflect the FIPS 199 impact levels and the contingency controls that each impact level establishes. Other key standards are applicable such as loss ratios established by the insurance industry. Key policy elements are as follows:

- Roles and responsibilities
- Scope as applies to common platform types and organization functions (i.e., telecommunications, legal, media relations) subject to contingency planning
- Resource requirements
- Training requirements

- Exercise and testing schedules
- Plan maintenance schedule
- Minimum frequency of backups and storage of backup media

Information system contingency activities should be compatible with program requirements for these areas, and recovery personnel should coordinate with representatives from each area to remain aware of new or evolving policies, programs, or capabilities. The policy must be written in coordination with other plans associated with each target system as part of organization-wide resilience strategy.

Business impact analysis

Before creating a BCP to deal with potential outages to SCADA systems, it is important to specify the recovery objectives for the various systems and subsystems involved based on typical business needs. Typically, this process is called business impact analysis (BIA). Three steps are typically involved in accomplishing the BIA:

1. *Determine mission/business processes and recovery criticality*: Mission/business processes supported by the system are identified, and the impact of a system disruption to those processes is determined along with outage impacts and estimated downtime. The downtime should reflect the maximum time that an organization can tolerate while still maintaining the mission.
2. *Identify resource requirements*: Realistic recovery efforts require a thorough evaluation of the resources required to resume mission/business processes and related interdependencies as quickly as possible. Examples of resources that should be identified include facilities, personnel, equipment, software, data files, system components, and vital records.
3. *Identify recovery priorities for system resources*: Based on the results from the previous activities, system resources can be linked more clearly to critical mission/business processes and functions. Priority levels can be established for sequencing recovery activities and resources.

There are two distinct types of objectives: system recovery and data recovery. System recovery involves the recovery of all communication links and processing capabilities, and it is usually specified in terms of a recovery-time objective (RTO). This is defined as the time required to recover all communication links and processing capabilities. Data recovery involves the recovery of data describing production or product conditions in the past and is usually specified in terms of a recovery-point objective (RPO). This is defined as the longest period of time for which an absence of data can be tolerated.

Once the recovery objectives are defined, a list of potential interruptions should be created and the recovery procedure developed and described. For most of the smaller scale interruptions, repair and replace activities based on a critical spares inventory will prove adequate to meet the recovery objectives. When this is not the case, contingency plans need to be developed. Due to the potential cost and importance of these contingency plans, they should be reviewed with the managers responsible for business continuity planning to verify that they are justified. Once the recovery procedures are documented, a schedule should be developed to test part or all of the recovery procedures. Particular attention must be paid to the verification of backups of system configuration data and product or production data. Not only should these be tested when they are produced, but the procedures that are followed for their storage should also be reviewed periodically to verify that the backups are kept in environmental conditions that will not render them unusable and that they are kept in a secure location, so they can be quickly obtained by authorized individuals when needed.

Determining business processes and recovery criticality

SCADA systems can be very complex and often support multiple mission/business processes, resulting in different perspectives on the importance of system services or capabilities. To accomplish the BIA and better understand the impacts a system outage or disruption can have on the organization, the continuity planner should work with management and internal and external points of contact (POC) to identify and validate mission/business processes and processes that depend on or support the information system. The identified processes' impacts are then further analyzed in terms of availability, integrity, confidentiality, and the established impact level for the information system. Adding information types to address this uniqueness will enhance the prioritization of system component impacts. Unique processes and impacts can be expressed in values or units of measurement that are meaningful to the organization. Values can be identified using a scale and should be characterized as an indication of impact severity to the organization if the process could not be performed. For example, an impact category such as "Costs" can be created with impact values expressed in terms of staffing, overtime, or fee-related costs (Swanson 2006). The continuity planner should next analyze the supported mission/business processes and, along with the process owners, leadership, and business managers, should determine the acceptable downtime if a given process or specific system data were disrupted or otherwise unavailable. Downtime can be identified in several ways:

- *Maximum tolerable downtime (MTD)*: The MTD represents the total amount of time the system owner/authorizing official is willing to accept for a mission/business process outage or disruption and includes all impact considerations. Determining the MTD is important because it could leave contingency planners with imprecise direction on (1) selection of an appropriate recovery method, and (2) the depth of detail that will be required when developing recovery procedures, including their scope and content.
- *Recovery-time objective (RTO)*: The RTO defines the maximum amount of time that a system resource can remain unavailable before there is an unacceptable impact on other system resources, supported mission/business processes, and the MTD. Determining the information system resource RTO is important for selecting appropriate technologies that are best suited for meeting the MTD. When it is not feasible to immediately meet the RTO and the MTD is inflexible, a plan of action and milestone should be initiated to document the situation and plan for its mitigation.
- *Recovery-point objective (RPO)*: The RPO represents the point in time, prior to a disruption or system outage, to which mission/business process data can be recovered (given the most recent backup copy of the data) after an outage. Unlike the RTO, the RPO is not considered as part of the MTD. Rather, it is a factor of how much data loss the mission/business process can tolerate during the recovery process. Because the RTO must ensure that the MTD is not exceeded, the RTO must normally be shorter than the MTD. For example, a system outage may prevent a particular process from being completed, and because it takes time to reprocess the data, that additional processing time must be added to the RTO to stay within the time limit established

by the MTD. Because of federal requirements, critical processes such as water and power must be recovered within 12 h (or less) and sustained for up to 30 days from an alternate site.

Identification of resource requirements

Realistic recovery efforts require a thorough evaluation of the resources required to resume mission/business processes as quickly as possible. Working with management and internal and external POCs associated with the system, the continuity planner should ensure that the complete information system resources are identified.

Identification of system resource recovery priorities

Developing recovery priorities is the last step of the BIA process. Recovery priorities can be effectively established by taking into consideration mission/business process criticality, outage impacts, tolerable downtime, and system resources. The result is an information-system recovery priority hierarchy. The continuity planner should consider system recovery measures and technologies to meet the recovery priorities.

Identification of preventive controls

In some cases, the outage impacts identified in the BIA may be mitigated or eliminated through preventive measures that deter, detect, and/or reduce impacts to the system. Where feasible and cost-effective, preventive methods are preferable to actions that may be necessary to recover the system after a disruption. A variety of preventive controls are available to SCADA systems. Depending on system type and configuration, some common measures are listed as follows:

- Appropriately sized UPSs to provide short-term backup power to all system components (including environmental and safety controls)
- Gasoline- or diesel-powered generators to provide long-term backup power
- Air-conditioning systems with adequate excess capacity to prevent failure of certain components, such as a compressor
- Fire suppression systems
- Fire and smoke detectors
- Water sensors in the computer room ceiling and floor
- Heat-resistant and waterproof containers for backup media and vital nonelectronic records
- Emergency master system shutdown switch
- Off-site storage of backup media, nonelectronic records, and system documentation
- Technical security controls, such as cryptographic key management
- Frequent scheduled backups including where the backups are stored (on-site or off-site) and how often they are re-circulated and moved to storage

Creation of contingency strategies

Organizations operating and maintaining SCADA systems for water and power are required to adequately mitigate the risk arising from the use of information and information systems in the execution of mission/business processes. The challenge for organizations is to implement the right set of security controls. Contingency strategies are created to mitigate the risks for the contingency planning family of controls and cover the full range of backup, recovery, contingency planning, testing, and ongoing maintenance.

Backup and recovery

Backup and recovery methods and strategies are a means to restore system operations quickly and effectively following a service disruption. The methods and strategies should address disruption impacts and allowable downtimes identified in the BIA and should be integrated into the SCADA system architecture. Specific recovery methods should be considered and may include commercial contracts with alternate site vendors, reciprocal agreements with internal or external organizations, and service-level agreements (SLAs) with equipment vendors. In addition, technologies such as redundant arrays of independent disks (RAID), automatic failover, UPS, server clustering, and mirrored systems should be considered when developing a system recovery strategy. Several alternative approaches should be considered when developing and comparing strategies, including cost, maximum downtimes, security, recovery priorities, and integration with larger, organization-level contingency plans (Sheffi 2005).

Backup methods and off-site storage

System data should be backed up regularly. Policies should specify the minimum frequency and scope of backups (e.g., daily or weekly, incremental or full) based on data criticality and the frequency with which new information is introduced. Data backup policies should designate the location of stored data, file-naming conventions, media rotation frequency, and the method for transporting data off-site. Data may be backed up on magnetic disk, tape, or optical disks, such as compact disks (CDs). The specific method chosen for conducting backups should be based on system and data availability and integrity requirements. These methods may include electronic vaulting, network storage, and tape library systems.

It is good business practice to store backed-up data off-site. Commercial data storage facilities are specially designed to archive media and protect data from threatening elements. If off-site storage is being used, data are backed up at the organization's facility and then labeled, packed, and transported to the storage facility. If the data are required for recovery or testing purposes, the organization contacts the storage facility requesting specific data to be transported to the organization or to an alternate facility. Commercial storage facilities often offer media transportation and response and recovery services. When selecting an off-site storage facility and vendor, the following criteria should be considered:

- *Geographic area*: Distance from the organization and the probability of the storage site being affected by the same disaster as the organization's primary site
- *Accessibility*: Length of time necessary to retrieve the data from storage and the storage facility's operating hours
- *Security*: Security capabilities of the shipping method, storage facility, and personnel; all must meet the data's security requirements
- *Environment*: Structural and environmental conditions of the storage facility (i.e., temperature, humidity, fire-prevention measures, and power-management controls)
- *Cost*: Cost of shipping, operational fees, and disaster response/recovery services

Alternate sites

Although major disruptions with long-term effects may be rare, they should be accounted for in the contingency plan. Thus, for all high-impact SCADA systems (water/power), the plan should include a strategy to recover and perform system operations at an alternate facility for an extended period. Organizations may consider low-impact systems for alternate site processing, but that is an organizational decision and not required. In general, three types of alternate sites are available:

1. Dedicated site owned or operated by the organization/agency
2. Reciprocal agreement or memorandum of agreement with an internal or external entity
3. Commercially leased facility

Regardless of the type of alternate site chosen, the facility must be able to support system operations as defined in the contingency plan. The three alternate site types commonly categorized in terms of their operational readiness are cold sites, warm sites, or hot sites. Other variations or combinations of these can be found, but generally all the variations retain similar core features found in one of these three site types. Progressing from basic to advanced, the sites are described as follows:

1. *Cold sites* are typically facilities with adequate space and infrastructure (electric power, telecommunications connections, and environmental controls) to support information system recovery activities.
2. *Warm sites* are partially equipped office spaces that contain some or all of the system hardware, software, telecommunications, and power sources.
3. *Hot sites* are facilities that are appropriately sized to support system requirements and are configured with the necessary system hardware, supporting infrastructure, and support personnel.

As discussed earlier, these three alternate site types are the most common. There are also variations, and hybrid mixtures of features from any one of the three. Each organization should evaluate its core requirements in order to establish the most effective solution. Two examples of variations to the site types are the following:

1. *Mobile sites* are self-contained, transportable shells custom-fitted with specific telecommunications and system equipment necessary to meet system requirements.
2. *Mirrored sites* are fully redundant facilities with automated real-time information mirroring. Mirrored sites are identical to the primary site in all technical respects.

There are obvious cost and ready-time differences among the options. In these examples, the mirrored site is the most expensive choice, but it ensures virtually 100% availability. Cold sites are the least expensive to maintain, although substantial time may be needed to acquire and install necessary equipment. Partially equipped sites, such as warm sites, fall in the middle of the spectrum. In many cases, mobile sites may be delivered to the desired location within 24 h, but the time necessary for equipment installation and setup can increase this response time. The selection of fixed site locations should account for the time and mode of transportation necessary to move personnel and/or equipment there. In addition, the fixed site should be in a geographic area that is unlikely to be negatively affected by the same hazard as the organization's primary site.

Sites should be analyzed further by the organization, including giving consideration to business impacts and downtime defined in the BIA. As sites are evaluated, the continuity or disaster planner should ensure that the system's security, management, operational, and technical controls are compatible with the prospective site. Such controls may include firewalls, physical access controls, and the personnel security requirements of the staff supporting the site.

Alternate sites may be owned and operated by the organization (internal recovery), or commercial sites may be available under contract. If the organization is contracting for the site with a commercial vendor, adequate testing time, work space, security requirements, hardware requirements, telecommunications requirements, support services, and recovery days (how long the organization can occupy the space during the recovery period) must be negotiated and clearly stated in the contract. Customers should be aware that multiple organizations may contract with a vendor for the same alternate site; as a result, the site may be unable to accommodate all of the customers if a disaster affects enough of those customers simultaneously. The vendor's policy on how this situation should be addressed and how priority status is determined should be negotiated.

Two or more organizations with similar or identical system configurations and backup technologies may enter into a formal agreement to serve as alternate sites for each other or may enter into a joint contract for an alternate site. This type of site is set up via a reciprocal agreement or memorandum of understanding (MOU). A reciprocal agreement should be entered into carefully because each site must be able to support the other, in addition to its own workload, in the event of a disaster. This type of agreement requires the recovery sequence for the systems from both organizations to be prioritized from a joint perspective, favorable to both parties. Testing should be conducted at the partnering sites to evaluate the extra processing thresholds, compatible system and backup configurations, sufficient telecommunications connections, compatible security measures, and the sensitivity of data that might be accessible to other privileged users, in addition to functionality of the recovery strategy.

An MOU or an SLA for an alternate site should be developed specific to the organization's needs and the partner organization's capabilities (Corbin 2008). The legal department of each party must review and approve the agreement. In general, the agreement should address, at a minimum, each of the following elements:

- Contract/agreement duration
- Cost/fee structure for disaster declaration and occupancy (daily usage), administration, maintenance, testing, annual cost/fee increases, transportation support cost (receipt and return of off-site data/supplies, as applicable), cost/expense allocation (as applicable), and billing and payment schedules
- Disaster declaration (i.e., circumstances constituting a disaster, notification procedures)
- Site/facility priority access and/or use
- Site availability
- Site guarantee
- Other clients subscribing to same resources and site and the total number of site subscribers, as applicable
- Contract/agreement change or modification process
- Contract/agreement termination conditions
- Process to negotiate extension of service
- Guarantee of compatibility

- Information system requirements (including data and telecommunication requirements) for hardware, software, and any special system needs (hardware and software)
- Change management and notification requirements, including hardware, software, and infrastructure
- Security requirements, including special security needs
- Staff support provided/not provided
- Facility services provided/not provided (use of on-site office equipment, cafeteria, etc.)
- Testing, including scheduling, availability, test time duration, and -additional testing, if required
- Records management (on-site and off-site), including electronic media and hard copy
- Service-level management (performance measures and management of quality of information system services provided)
- Work-space requirements (e.g., chairs, desks, telephones, personal computers)
- Supplies provided/not provided (e.g., office supplies)
- Additional costs not covered elsewhere
- Other contractual issues, as applicable
- Other technical requirements, as applicable

Equipment replacement

If the information system is damaged or destroyed or the primary site is unavailable, the necessary hardware and software will need to be activated or procured quickly and delivered to the alternate location. Three basic strategies exist to prepare for equipment replacement:

1. *Vendor agreements*: As the contingency plan is being developed, SLAs with hardware, software, and support vendors may be made for emergency maintenance service. The SLA should specify how quickly the vendor must respond after being notified. The agreement should also give the organization priority status for the shipment of replacement equipment over equipment being purchased for normal operations. SLAs should further discuss what priority status the organization will receive in the event of a catastrophic disaster involving multiple vendor clients. In such cases, organizations with health- and safety-dependent processes will often receive the highest priority for shipment. The details of these negotiations should be documented in the SLA, which should be maintained with the contingency plan (Gregory 2008).
2. *Equipment inventory*: Required equipment may be purchased in advance and stored at a secure off-site location, such as an alternate site where recovery operations will take place (warm or mobile site) or at another location where they will be stored and then shipped to the alternate site. This solution has certain drawbacks. An organization must commit financial resources in order to purchase this equipment in advance, and the equipment could become obsolete or unsuitable for use over time because system technologies and requirements change.
3. *Existing compatible equipment*: Equipment currently housed and used by the contracted hot site or by another organization within the organization may be used. Agreements made with hot sites and reciprocal internal sites stipulate that similar and compatible equipment will be available for contingency use by the organization.

When evaluating the choices, the continuity/disaster planner should consider that purchasing equipment when needed is cost-effective but can add significant overhead time to recovery while waiting for shipment and setup; conversely, storing unused equipment is costly but allows recovery operations to begin more quickly. When selecting the most appropriate strategy, note that the availability of transportation may be limited or temporarily halted in the event of a catastrophic disaster. Based on impacts discovered through the BIA, consideration should be given to the possibility of a widespread disaster entailing mass equipment replacement and transportation delays that would extend the recovery period. Regardless of the strategy selected, detailed lists of equipment needs and specifications should be maintained within the contingency plan.

Cost considerations

The continuity/disaster planner should ensure that the strategy chosen can be implemented effectively with available personnel and financial resources. The cost of each type of alternate site, equipment replacement, and storage option under consideration should be weighed against budget limitations. The coordinator should determine known contingency planning expenses, such as alternate site contract fees; and those that are less obvious, such as the cost of implementing an agency-wide contingency awareness program and contractor support. The budget must be sufficient to encompass software, hardware, travel and shipping, testing, plan training programs, awareness programs, labor hours, other contracted services, and any other applicable resources (e.g., desks, telephones, fax machines, pens, and paper). The organization should perform a cost–benefit analysis to identify the optimum contingency strategy.

Roles and responsibilities

Having selected and implemented the backup and system recovery strategies, the continuity/disaster planner must designate appropriate teams to implement the strategy. Each team should be trained and ready to respond in the event of a disruptive situation requiring plan activation. Recovery personnel should be assigned to one of several specific teams that will respond to the event, recover capabilities, and return the system to normal operations. To do so, recovery team members need to clearly understand the team's recovery-effort goal, the individual procedures the team will execute, and how interdependencies between recovery teams may affect overall strategies. The size of each team, team titles, and hierarchy designs depend on the organization. In addition to a single authoritative role for overall decision-making responsibility, including plan activation, a capable strategy will require some or all of the following groups:

- Management team (including the continuity/disaster planner)
- Outage assessment team
- Operating system administration team
- Server-recovery team (e.g., client server, Web server)
- Local area network/wide area network (LAN/WAN) recovery team
- Database recovery team
- Network operations recovery team
- Application recovery team(s)
- Telecommunications team
- Test team
- Transportation and relocation team
- Media relations team

- Legal affairs team
- Physical/personnel security team
- Procurement team (equipment and supplies)

Personnel should be chosen to staff these teams based on their skills and knowledge. Ideally, teams are staffed with personnel responsible for the same or similar functions under normal conditions. For example, server-recovery team members should include the server administrators. Team members must understand not only the contingency plan purpose, but also the procedures necessary for executing the recovery strategy. Teams should be sufficient in size to remain viable if some members are unavailable to respond, or alternate team members may be designated. Similarly, team members should be familiar with the goals and procedures of other teams to facilitate cross-team coordination. The continuity/disaster planner should also consider that a disruption could render some personnel unavailable to respond. In this situation, executing the plan may be possible only by using personnel from another geographic area of the organization or by hiring contractors or vendors. Such personnel may be coordinated and trained as an alternate team.

Each team is led by a team leader who directs overall team operations, acts as the team's representative to management, and liaises with other team leaders. The team leader disseminates information to team members and approves any decisions that must be made within the team. Team leaders should have a designated alternate to act as the leader if the primary leader is unavailable.

For most systems, a management team is necessary for providing overall guidance following a major system disruption or emergency. The team is responsible for activating the contingency plan and supervising the execution of contingency operations. The management team also facilitates communications among other teams and supervises information system contingency plan tests and exercises. Some or all of the management team may lead specialized recovery teams. A senior management official, such as the CIO, has the ultimate authority to activate the plan and to make decisions regarding spending levels, acceptable risk, and interagency coordination. The senior management official typically leads the management team.

Exercise and testing program

With all continuity programs, the process of conducting training, testing, and exercises (TT&E) is key to a successful recovery. Organizations should conduct TT&E events periodically, following organizational or system changes, or the issuance of new TT&E guidance, or as otherwise needed. Execution of TT&E events assists organizations in determining the plan's effectiveness and ensuring that all personnel know what their roles are in the conduct of each information system plan. TT&E event schedules are often dictated in part by organizational requirements.

For each TT&E activity conducted, results are documented in an after-action report, and lessons-learned corrective actions are captured for updating information in the plan. Testing is a critical element of a viable contingency capability. Testing enables plan deficiencies to be identified and addressed by validating one or more of the system components and the operability of the plan.

Testing can take on several forms and accomplish several objectives but should be conducted in as close to an operating environment as possible. Each information system component should be tested to confirm the accuracy of individual recovery procedures. The following areas should be addressed in a contingency plan test, as applicable:

- Notification procedures
- System recovery on an alternate platform from backup media
- Internal and external connectivity
- System performance using alternate equipment
- Restoration of normal operations

Table 7.1 offers insight into the process of selecting the appropriate exercise based on the maturity of the organization.

Table 7.2 provides a useful guide to the degree of resources required to actually complete a test when implementing a continuity exercise program.

A continuity exercise program has a variety of complexities that need preparation. Table 7.3 is a useful guide to preparing for the SCADA exercise.

Exercises

The following types of exercises are widely used in information system TT&E programs by single organizations:

- *Tabletop exercises:* Tabletop exercises are discussion-based exercises wherein personnel meet in a classroom setting or in breakout groups to discuss their roles during an emergency and their responses to a particular emergency situation. A facilitator presents a scenario and asks the exercise participants questions related to the scenario, which initiates a discussion among the participants of roles, responsibilities, coordination, and decision making. A tabletop exercise is discussion based only and does not involve deploying equipment or other resources.

Table 7.1 SCADA exercise types

Orientation	Drill	Tabletop	Functional	Full-scale
No previous exercise	Equipment capabilities	Practice group problem solving	Evaluate any function	Information analysis
No recent operations	Response time	Executive familiarity	Observe physical	Interbusiness cooperation
New plan	Personnel training	Specific case study	facilities use	Policy formulation
New procedure	Intrabusiness cooperation	Examine	Reinforce established	Negotiation
New staff, leadership	Resource and manpower	manpower contingencies	policies and procedures	Resource and manpower allocation
New facility	capabilities	Test group message	Test seldom-used resources	Media attention
New industrial risk		interpretation	Measure resource	Equipment capabilities
New mutual aid agreement with vendor, neighboring business, or outside business segment		Observe information sharing	adequacy	Personnel and equipment locations
		Assess interagency coordination	Interbusiness relations	Interbusiness relations
		Training personnel in negotiation		

Table 7.2 SCADA exercise test scopes

Scope characteristic	Orientation	Drill	Tabletop	Functional	Full-scale
Hazards	High profile	Any priority	Any priority	To highlight function	Highest priority
Agencies	Less active; less involved	Active and involved	Less and medium active and involved	Active and involved	Active and involved
Number of ongoing activities	Single functions	Single procedure or functions	One or two functions	Few to several disparate functions	Few to several disparate functions
Personnel involved	Coordination operations	Coordination operations	Policy, coordination, operations	Policy, coordination	Policy, coordination, operations
Types of activity	Walk through; identify roles and responsibility	Field command post; decision making	Problem solving; brainstorming; resource allocation task coordination	Decision-making policy making; negotiation; coordination; communication	Field operations; field command post; coordination; negotiation
Degree of realism	None	Live transmission of simulated messages	Scene setting with scenario narrative and low-key messages	Intense, fully simulated messages	Intense, live transmission of simulated messages

Table 7.3 SCADA exercise resource allocation requirements

Requirement	Orientation seminar	Drill	Tabletop	Functional	Full-scale
Experience	None	Orientation	Orientation	Series of progressively complex tabletops	Functional exercises and many drills
Staff	Minimal	Some experience understanding of the function of agency being tested	Minimal with little experience	Team with one or two leaders and considerable experience	Functional, tabletop drill experience
Time	2 weeks	1 month	1 month	3 months	More than 3 months
Skills	Leadership planning	Good understanding of single component being tested	Group process materials development	Promotions; logistics simulation	Writing, simulation, development
Materials	Proper plan	BC procedures are exercised	Narrative, problems, and low-key messages	Charts, displays, maps and messages	Victim tags, field simulation equipment
Methods	Lecturer, facilitator	Actual message transmission plus written	Problems; messages; low key, no transmission	Written message, some simulated transmission	Actual message transmission plus written
Facilities	Conference room	Field scene or EOC	Player room and minimal simulation facility	Player room, simulation room, communication (option)	EOC plus field scene and communication
Communication	None	Radio, e-mail, phone, website if appropriate	None	Telephone, e-mail, website, and selected radio	Radio, phone, e-mail, website
Support necessary	Good among coordination personnel	Involvement of business segment or function being exercised	Good among coordination personnel	Excellent chief executive and service chiefs	Chief executive, service chiefs, media

- *Functional exercises*: Functional exercises allow personnel to validate their operational readiness for emergencies by performing their duties in a simulated operational environment. Functional exercises are designed to exercise the roles and responsibilities of specific team members, procedures, and assets involved in one or more functional aspects of a plan (e.g., communications, emergency notifications, system equipment setup). Functional exercises vary in complexity and scope, ranging from validating specific aspects of a plan to full-scale exercises that address all plan elements. Functional exercises allow staff to execute their roles and responsibilities as they would in an actual emergency situation but in a simulated manner.

Training

Training for personnel with contingency plan responsibilities should focus on familiarizing them with roles and teaching the skills necessary to accomplish those roles. This approach helps ensure that staff are prepared to participate in tests and exercises as well as actual outage events. Training should be provided at least annually. Personnel newly appointed to roles should receive training shortly thereafter. Ultimately, personnel should be trained to the extent that that they are able to execute their respective recovery roles and responsibilities without the aid of the actual document. This is an important goal in the event that paper or electronic versions of the plan are unavailable for the first few hours as a result of the disruption. Recovery personnel should be trained on the following plan elements:

- Purpose of the plan
- Cross-team coordination and communication
- Reporting procedures
- Security requirements
- Team-specific processes (activation and notification, recovery, and reconstitution phases)
- Individual responsibilities (activation and notification, recovery, and reconstitution phases)

Plan maintenance

To be effective, the plan must be maintained in a ready state that accurately reflects system requirements, procedures, organizational structure, and policies. Information systems undergo frequent changes because of shifting business needs, technology upgrades, or new internal or external policies. Therefore, it is essential that continuity plans be reviewed and updated regularly as part of the organization's change management process to ensure that new information is documented and contingency measures are revised if required. A continuous monitoring process can provide organizations with an effective tool for plan maintenance, producing ongoing updates to security plans, security assessment reports, and plans of action and milestone documents.

As a general rule, the plan should be reviewed for accuracy and completeness at an organization-defined frequency or whenever significant changes occur to any element of the plan. Certain elements, such as contact lists, will require more frequent reviews. The plans for moderate- or high-impact systems should be reviewed more often. At a minimum, plan reviews should focus on the following elements:

- Operational requirements
- Security requirements

- Technical procedures
- Hardware, software, and other equipment (types, specifications, and amount)
- Names and contact information of team members
- Names and contact information of vendors, including alternate and off-site vendor POCs
- Alternate and off-site facility requirements
- Vital records (electronic and hardcopy)

Because DR and continuity plans contain potentially sensitive operational and personnel information, its distribution should be marked accordingly and controlled. Typically, copies of the plan are provided to recovery personnel for storage. A copy should also be stored at the alternate site and with the backup media. Storing a copy of the plan at the alternate site ensures its availability and good condition in the event that local plan copies cannot be accessed because of disaster. The continuity/disaster planner should maintain a record of the copies of the plan and to whom they were distributed. Other information that should be stored with the plan includes contracts with vendors (SLAs and other contracts), software licenses, system user manuals, security manuals, and operating procedures. Changes made to the plan, strategies, and policies should be coordinated through the continuity/disaster planner, who should communicate changes to the representatives of associated plans or programs as necessary. The continuity/disaster planner should record plan modifications using a record of changes, which lists the page number, change comment, and date of change.

SCADA system contingency plan development

The plan contains detailed roles, responsibilities, teams, and procedures associated with restoring an information system following a disruption. The plan should document technical capabilities designed to support contingency operations and should be tailored to the organization and its requirements. Plans need to balance detail with flexibility; usually, the more detailed the plan, the less scalable and versatile the approach. The information presented here is meant to be a guide; nevertheless, the plan format in this document may be modified as needed to better meet the user's specific system, operational, and organization requirements.

Plans should be formatted to provide quick and clear directions in the event that personnel unfamiliar with the plan or the systems are called on to perform recovery operations. Plans should be clear, concise, and easy to implement in an emergency. Where possible, checklists and step-by-step procedures should be used. A concise and well-formatted plan reduces the likelihood of creating an overly complex or confusing plan.

Supporting information

The supporting information component includes an introduction and concept-of-operations section providing essential background or contextual information that makes the contingency plan easier to understand, implement, and maintain. These details aid in understanding the applicability of the guidance, in making decisions on how to use the plan, and in providing information on where associated plans and information outside the scope of the plan may be found. The introduction section orients the reader to the type and location of information contained in the plan. Generally, the section includes the background, scope, and assumptions. These sections are described as follows:

- *Background*: This section establishes the reason for developing the plan and defines the plan objectives.
- *Scope*: The scope identifies the business impact and associated RTOs as well as the alternate site and data storage capabilities (as applicable).
- *Assumptions*: This section includes the list of assumptions that were used in developing the plan as well as a list of situations that are not applicable. The concept-of-operations section provides additional details about the information system, the three phases of the contingency plan (activation and notification, recovery, and reconstitution), and a description of the information system contingency plan roles and responsibilities. This section may include the following elements:
- *System description*: It is necessary to include a general description of the information system addressed by the contingency plan. The description should include the information system architecture, location(s), and any other important technical considerations. An input/output (I/O) diagram and system architecture diagram, including security devices (e.g., firewalls, internal and external connections) are useful. The content for the system description can usually be taken from the system security plan.
- *Overview of three phases*: The recovery plan is implemented in three phases: (1) activation and notification, (2) recovery, and (3) reconstitution.
- *Roles and responsibilities*: The roles and responsibilities section presents the overall structure of contingency teams, including the hierarchy and coordination mechanisms and requirements among the teams. The section also provides an overview of team member roles and responsibilities in a contingency situation. Teams and team members should be designated for specific response and recovery roles during contingency plan activation.

Activation and notification phase

The activation and notification phase defines initial actions taken once a system disruption or outage has been detected or appears to be imminent. This phase includes activities to notify recovery personnel, conduct an outage assessment, and activate the plan. At the completion of the activation and notification phase, planning staff will be prepared to perform recovery measures to restore system functions.

Activation criteria and procedure

The plan should be activated if one or more of the activation criteria for that system are met. If an activation criterion is met, the designated authority should activate the plan. Activation criteria for system outages or disruptions are unique for each organization and should be stated in the contingency planning policy. Criteria may be based on the following:

- Extent of any damage to the system (e.g., physical, operational, or cost)
- Criticality of the system to the organization's mission (e.g., CIP asset)
- Expected duration of the outage lasting longer than the RTO

The appropriate recovery teams may be notified once the system outage or disruption has been identified and the continuity/disaster planner has determined that activation criteria have been met.

Notification procedures

An outage or disruption may occur with or without prior notice. For example, advance notice is often given that a hurricane is predicted to affect an area or that a computer virus is expected on a certain date. However, there may be no notice of equipment failure or a criminal act. Notification procedures should be documented in the plan for both types of situation. The procedures should describe the methods used to notify recovery personnel during business and nonbusiness hours. Prompt notification is important for reducing the effects of a disruption on the system; in some cases, it may provide enough time to allow system personnel to shut down the system gracefully to avoid a hard crash. Following the outage or disruption, notification should be sent to the outage assessment team so that it may determine the status of the situation and appropriate next steps. When outage assessment is complete, the appropriate recovery and system support personnel should be notified.

Notifications can be accomplished through a variety of methods, which are either automated or manual and include telephone, pager, electronic mail (e-mail), cell phone, and messaging. Automated notification systems follow established protocols and criteria and can include rapid authentication and acceptance and secure messaging. Automated notification systems require up-front investment and a learning curve but may be an effective way for some organizations to ensure prompt and accurate delivery.

Notifications sent via e-mail should be done with caution because there is no way to ensure receipt and acknowledgment. Although e-mail has potential as an effective method of disseminating notifications to work or personal accounts, there is no way to guarantee that the message will be read. If using an e-mail notification method, recovery personnel should be informed of the necessity to frequently and regularly check their accounts. Notifications sent during business hours should be sent to the work address, whereas personal e-mail messaging may be useful in the event that the LAN is down.

The notification strategy should define procedures to be followed in the event that specific personnel cannot be contacted. Notification procedures should be documented clearly in the contingency plan. Copies of the procedures can be made and located securely at alternate locations. A common manual notification method is a call tree. This technique involves assigning notification duties to specific individuals who in turn are responsible for notifying other recovery personnel. The call tree should account for primary and alternate contact methods, and procedures to be followed if an individual cannot be contacted should be discussed.

Notifications also should be sent to POCs of external organizations or interconnected system partners that may be adversely affected if they are unaware of the situation. Depending on the type of outage or disruption, the POC may have recovery responsibilities. For each system interconnection with an external organization, a POC should be identified. These POCs should be listed in an appendix to the plan.

The type of information to be relayed to those being notified should be documented in the plan. The amount and detail of information relayed may depend on the specific team being notified. As necessary, notification information may include the following:

- Nature of the outage or disruption that has occurred or is impending
- Any known outage estimates
- Response and recovery details
- Where and when to convene for briefing or further response instructions
- Instructions to prepare for relocation for estimated time period (if applicable)
- Instructions to complete notifications using the call tree (if applicable)

Outage assessment

To determine how the plan will be implemented following a system disruption or outage, it is essential to assess the nature and extent of the disruption. The outage assessment should be completed as quickly as the given conditions permit with personnel safety remaining the highest priority. When possible, the outage assessment team is the first team notified of the disruption. Outage assessment procedures may be unique for the particular system, but the following minimum areas should be addressed:

- Cause of the outage or disruption
- Potential for additional disruptions or damage
- Status of physical infrastructure (e.g., structural integrity of computer room, condition of electric power, telecommunications, and heating, ventilation, and air conditioning [HVAC])
- Inventory and functional status of system equipment (e.g., fully functional, partially functional, nonfunctional)
- Type of damage to system equipment or data (e.g., water, fire and heat, physical impact, electrical surge)
- Items to be replaced (e.g., hardware, software, firmware, supporting materials)
- Estimated time to restore normal services

Personnel with outage assessment responsibilities should understand and be able to perform these procedures in the event the plan is inaccessible during the situation. Once impact to the system has been determined, the appropriate teams should be notified of updated information and the planned response to the situation.

Recovery phase

Formal recovery operations begin after the plan has been activated, outage assessments have been completed (if possible), personnel have been notified, and appropriate teams have been mobilized. Recovery phase activities focus on implementing recovery strategies to restore system capabilities, repair damage, and resume operational capabilities at the original or new alternate location. At the completion of the recovery phase, the information system will be functional and capable of performing the functions identified in the plan. Depending on the recovery strategies defined in the plan, these functions could include temporary manual processing, recovery and operation at an alternate system, or relocation and recovery at an alternate site. It is feasible that only system resources identified as high priority in the BIA will be recovered at this stage.

Sequence of recovery activities

When recovering a complex system, such as a WAN or virtual local area network (VLAN) involving multiple independent components, recovery procedures should reflect system priorities identified in the BIA. The sequence of activities should reflect the system's MTD to avoid significant impacts to related systems. Procedures should be written in a stepwise, sequential format so system components may be restored in a logical manner. For example, if a LAN is being recovered after a disruption, then the most critical servers should be recovered before other less critical devices, such as printers. Similarly, to recover an application server, procedures should first address operating system restoration and verification before the application and its data are recovered. The procedures should also include escalation steps and instructions to coordinate with other teams where relevant when certain situations occur, such as when

- An action is not completed within the expected time frame.
- A key step has been completed.
- Item(s) must be procured.
- Other system-specific concerns exist.

If conditions require the system to be recovered at an alternate site, certain materials will need to be transferred or procured. These items may include shipment of data backup media from off-site storage, hardware, copies of the recovery plan, and software programs. Procedures should designate the appropriate team or team members to coordinate the shipment of equipment, data, and vital records. References to applicable appendices, such as equipment lists or vendor contact information, should be made in the plan where necessary. Procedures should clearly describe requirements to package, transport, and purchase the materials required to recover the system.

Recovery procedures

To facilitate recovery phase operations, the plan should provide detailed procedures to restore the information system or components to a known state. Given the extensive variety of system types, configurations, and applications, this planning guide does not provide specific recovery procedures.

Procedures should be assigned to the appropriate recovery team and typically address the following actions:

- Obtaining authorization to access damaged facilities and/or geographic area
- Notifying internal and external business partners associated with the system
- Obtaining necessary office supplies and work space
- Obtaining and installing necessary hardware components
- Obtaining and loading backup media
- Restoring critical operating system and application software
- Restoring system data to a known state
- Testing system functionality including security controls
- Connecting system to network or other external systems
- Operating alternate equipment successfully

Recovery procedures should be written in a straightforward, step-by-step style. To prevent difficulty or confusion in an emergency, no procedural steps should be assumed or omitted. A checklist format is useful for documenting the sequential recovery procedures and for troubleshooting problems if the system cannot be recovered properly.

Recovery escalation and notification

As identified as part of the BIA, system components, infrastructure, and associated facilities are critical components supporting daily mission/business processes. The systems, applications, and infrastructure that connect users to these processes are subject to events causing service interruptions and outages. Including an escalation and notification component within the recovery phase helps to ensure that overall, a repeatable, structured, consistent, and measurable recovery process is followed. Effective escalation and notification procedures should define and describe the events, thresholds, or other types of triggers that are necessary for additional action. Actions would include additional notifications for more recovery staff, messages and status updates to leadership, and notices for additional resources. Procedures should be included to establish a clear set of events, actions, and results and should be documented for teams or individuals as appropriate.

Reconstitution phase

The reconstitution phase is the third and final phase of plan implementation and defines the actions taken to test and validate system capability and functionality. During reconstitution, recovery activities are completed and normal system operations are resumed. If the original facility is unrecoverable, the activities in this phase can also be applied to preparing a new permanent location to support system processing requirements. This phase consists of two major activities: validating successful recovery and deactivation of the plan. Validation of recovery typically includes several steps:

- *Concurrent processing*: Concurrent processing is the process of running a system at two separate locations concurrently until there is a level of assurance that the recovered system is operating correctly and securely.
- *Validation data testing*: Data testing is the process of testing and validating recovered data to ensure that data files or databases have been recovered completely and are current to the last available backup.
- *Validation functionality testing*: Functionality testing is a process for verifying that all system functionality has been tested and that the system is ready to return to normal operations.

At the successful completion of the validation testing, personnel will be prepared to declare that reconstitution efforts are complete and that the system is operating normally. This declaration may be made in a recovery/reconstitution log or other documentation of reconstitution activities. The continuity/disaster planner, in coordination with the information system owner or information system security officer and with the concurrence of the authorizing official, must determine if the system has undergone significant change and will require reassessment and reauthorization. The utilization of a continuous monitoring strategy/program can guide the scope of the reauthorization to focus on those environment/facility controls and any other controls that would be impacted by the reconstitution efforts. Deactivation of the plan is the process of returning the system to normal operations and finalizing reconstitution activities to protect the system against another outage or disruption. These activities include the following:

- *Notifications*: Upon return to normal operations, users should be notified by the continuity/disaster planner (or designee) using predefined notification procedures.
- *Cleanup*: Cleanup is the process of cleaning up work space or dismantling any temporary recovery locations, restocking supplies, returning manuals or other documentation to their original locations, and readying the system for another contingency event.
- *Off-site data storage:* If off-site data storage is used, procedures should be documented for returning retrieved backup or installation media to its off-site data storage location.

- *Data backup*: As soon as reasonable following reconstitution, the system should be fully backed up and a new copy of the current operational system stored for future recovery efforts. This full backup should be stored with other system backups and should comply with applicable security controls.
- *Event documentation*: All recovery and reconstitution events should be well documented, including actions taken and problems encountered during the recovery and reconstitution efforts. An after-action report with lessons learned should be documented and included for updating your information system contingency plan (ISCP).

Once all the activities and steps have been completed and documentation has been updated, the plan can be formally deactivated. An announcement with the declaration should be sent to all business and technical contacts.

Plan appendices

Contingency plan appendices provide key details not contained in the main body of the plan. Common contingency plan appendices include the following:

- Contact information for contingency planning team personnel
- Vendor contact information, including off-site storage and alternate site POCs
- Business impact analysis (BIA)
- Detailed recovery procedures and checklists
- Detailed validation testing procedures and checklists
- Equipment and system requirements lists of the hardware, software, firmware, and other resources required to support system operations. Details should be provided for each entry, including model or version number, specifications, and quantity.
- Alternate mission/business processing procedures that may occur while recovery efforts are being done to the system
- Testing and maintenance procedures
- System interconnections (systems that directly interconnect or exchange information)
- Vendor SLAs, reciprocal agreements with other organizations, and other vital records

Technical contingency planning considerations

This chapter complements the process and framework guidelines presented in earlier sections by discussing technical contingency planning considerations for specific types of information systems. The information presented in this section will assist the reader in selecting, developing, and implementing specific technical contingency strategies based on the type of information system. Because each system is unique, considerations are provided at a level that may be used by the widest audience. The list of platforms is not comprehensive but is representative of commonly found systems in production or development. Not all of the information presented may apply to a specific information system; the continuity/disaster planner should draw on the considerations as appropriate and customize them to meet a system's particular contingency requirements. The following representative platform types are addressed in this section:

- Client/server systems
- Telecommunications systems

Common considerations

When developing solutions for technical contingency plans, there are several areas that should be considered regardless of the platform or type of system in use. These considerations provide a common foundation for any type of contingency planning effort. Several of these contingency measures are common to all information systems. Common considerations include the following:

- Use of information gathered from the BIA process.
- Development of data security, integrity, and backup policies and procedures.
- Protection of equipment and system resources.
- Adherence and compliance with security controls in NIST SP 800-53.
- Development of primary and alternate sites with appropriately sized and configured power-management systems and environmental controls.
- Use of high-availability (HA) processes to provide for online real-time resilient access to alternate system resources. HA denotes systems that can achieve an uptime of 99.999% or better.

Use of the BIA

The BIA is the first source for determining resiliency and contingency planning strategies. BIA results determine how critical the system is to the supported mission/business processes, what impact the loss of the system could have on the organization, and the system RTO (Maiwald 2002). The BIA results can help determine the type and frequency of backup, the need for redundancy or mirroring of data, and the type of alternate site needed to meet system recovery objectives. Each of these strategy decisions have cost versus availability or recovery implications. Availability and recovery implications are discussed throughout the rest of this chapter.

Maintenance of data security, integrity, and backup

Maintaining the integrity and security of system data and software is a key component in contingency planning. Data integrity involves keeping data safe and accurate on the system's primary storage devices. There are several methods available for maintaining the integrity of stored data. These methods use redundancy and fault-tolerance processes to store data on more than one drive and eliminate loss of data from single drive failures. Data security involves protecting data both on-site and off-site from unauthorized access or use. Encryption is a common method for securing stored system data. Encryption is most effective when applied to both the primary data storage device and on backup media going to an off-site location. If using encryption for off-site data storage, it is important that media readers (e.g., tape drives and CD or DVD readers) are available at the alternate site location to correctly read the encrypted data during recovery efforts. A solid key management process must be established so encrypted data are available as needed. Keying material, which is the data used to establish and maintain the keys, needs to be managed, ideally at a central location in the organization. These keys should be stored separate from, but accessible to, the primary encrypted backup data. Keeping backups of data in a secure off-site location allows for a ready access to backups during a contingency event. An effective data backup process is crucial to a continuity/disaster planner's overall recovery strategy. Data backups are done primarily for recovery purposes. Backups can be done through many different methods and techniques. MTD determinations and security requirements from the BIA help dictate the best method for backing up a particular system for recovery.

Data backups should be conducted on all systems on a regular basis (Barker 2005). Systems can be backed up for individual computers or on a centralized storage device, such as network attached storage (NAS) or storage area network (SAN). There are three common methods for performing system backups:

1. *Full*: A full backup captures all files on the disk or within the folder selected for backup. Because all backed-up files are recorded to a single media or media set, locating a particular file or group of files is simple. However, the time required to perform a full backup can be lengthy. In addition, maintaining multiple iterations of full backups of files that do not change frequently (such as system files) could lead to excessive and unnecessary media storage requirements.
2. *Incremental*: An incremental backup captures files that were created or changed since the last backup, regardless of backup type. Incremental backups afford more efficient use of storage media, and backup times are reduced. However, to recover a system from an incremental backup, media from different backup operations may be required. For example, consider a case in which a directory needs to be recovered. If the last full backup was performed 3 days prior and one file had changed each day, then the media for the full backup and for each day's incremental backups would be needed to restore the entire directory.
3. *Differential*: A differential backup stores files that have been created or modified since the last full backup. Therefore, if a file is changed after the previous full backup, a differential backup will save the file each time until the next full backup is completed. A differential backup takes less time to complete than a full backup. Restoring from a differential backup may require fewer media than an incremental backup because only the full backup media and the last differential media would be needed. One disadvantage is that differential backups take longer to complete than incremental backups because the amount of data since the last full backup increases each day until the next full backup is executed.

A combination of backup operations can be used depending on system configuration and recovery requirements. For example, a full backup can be conducted on the weekend with differential backups conducted each evening. In developing a system backup policy, the following questions should be considered:

- Where and how will media be stored?
- What data should be backed up and how often should it be backed up?
- How quickly are the backups to be retrieved in the event of an emergency?
- Who is authorized to retrieve the media?
- Where will the media be delivered, and what is the rotation schedule of backup media?
- Who will restore the data from the media?
- What is the media-labeling scheme?
- How long will the backup media be retained?
- When the media are stored on-site, what environmental controls are provided to preserve the media?
- What is the appropriate backup medium for the types of backups to be performed?

Certain factors should be considered when choosing the appropriate backup solution:

- *Equipment interoperability:* To facilitate recovery, the backup device must be compatible with the platform operating system and applications and should be easy to install onto different models or types of systems.
- *Storage volume:* To ensure adequate storage, the amount of data to be backed up should determine the appropriate backup solution.
- *Media life:* Each type of medium has a different use and storage life beyond which the media cannot be relied on for effective data recovery.
- *Backup software:* When choosing the appropriate backup solution, the software or method used to back up data should be considered. In some cases, the backup solution can be as simple as a file copy using the operating system file manager; in cases involving larger data transfers, a third-party application may be needed to automate and schedule the file backup.

Protection of resources

Part of a successful contingency planning policy is making a system resilient to environmental and component-level failures that would otherwise cause system disruptions. There are several methods for making valuable hardware and software resilient. Determination of the appropriate methods should be based on risk-informed decisions. Depending on the results of the risk management process, these methods may or may not be applicable for a particular system.

The system and its data can become corrupt as a result of a power failure. Critical hardware, such as servers, can be configured with dual power supplies to prevent corruption. The two power supplies should be used simultaneously so that if the main power supply becomes overheated or unusable, the second unit will become the main power source, avoiding any system disruption.

The second power supply will protect against hardware failure, but not power failure. However, a UPS can protect the system if power is lost. A UPS usually provides 30–60 min of temporary backup power to permit a graceful shutdown. A UPS can also protect against power fluctuations by filtering incoming power and providing a steady power source. If HA is required, a gas- or diesel-powered generator may be needed. The generator can be wired directly into the site's power system and configured to start automatically when a power interruption is detected. A combination UPS/generator system can provide clean, secure power for a system as long as fuel is available for the generator. Fuel availability should be considered for those who opt for a UPS/generator to support their system environment. In addition to backing up data, organizations should also back up system software and drivers. Organizations should store software and software licenses in an alternate location. This includes original installation media, license terms and conditions, and license keys, if required. Image loads for client systems (such as desktops and portable systems) should also be backed up and stored at an alternate location along with complete documentation of the software included in the image load, any configuration information for the type of computer for which the image is intended, and installation instructions.

Organizations may use third-party vendors to recover data from failed storage devices. Organizations should consider the security risk of having their data handled by an outside company and ensure that proper security vetting of the service provider is conducted before turning over equipment. The service provider and employees should sign nondisclosure agreements, be properly bonded, and adhere to organization-specific security policies.

Identification of alternate storage and processing facilities

Backup media should be stored off-site in a secure, environmentally controlled location. When selecting the off-site location, the hours of the premises, the ease of accessibility to backup media, the physical storage limitations, and the contract terms should be taken into account. The continuity/disaster planner should reference the organization's resilience policy and the BIA to assist in determining how often backup media should be tested. Each backup tape, cartridge, or disk should be uniquely labeled to ensure that the required data can be identified quickly in an emergency. This requires that the organization develop an effective media marking and tracking strategy. Alternate processing facilities provide a location for an organization to resume system operations in the event of a catastrophic event that disables or destroys the system's primary facility. There are three primary types of alternate processing facilities corresponding to the level of readiness to function as a system's operations facility:

1. *Cold sites*: Cold sites are locations that have the basic infrastructure and environmental controls available (such as electrical and HVAC) but no equipment or telecommunications established or in place. There is sufficient room to house needed equipment to sustain a system's critical functions. Examples of cold sites include unused areas of a data center and unused office space (if specialized data center environments are not required). Cold sites are normally the least expensive alternate processing site solution, as the primary costs are only the lease or maintenance of the required square footage for recovery purposes. However, the recovery time is the longest, as all system equipment (including telecommunications) will need to be acquired or purchased, installed, tested, and have backup software and data loaded and tested before the system can be operational. Depending on the size and complexity of a system, recovery could take several days to weeks to complete.

2. *Warm sites*: Warm sites are locations that have the basic infrastructure of cold sites but also have sufficient computer and telecommunications equipment installed and available to operate the system at the site. However, the equipment is not loaded with the software or data required to operate the system. Warm sites should have backup media readers that are compatible with the system's backup strategy. Warm sites may not have equipment to run all systems or all components of a system but rather only enough to operate critical mission/business processes. An example of a warm site is a test or development site that is geographically separate from the production system. Equipment may be in place to operate the system but this would require reverting to the current production level of the software, loading the data from backup media, and establishing communications to users. Another example is equipment available at an alternate facility that is running noncritical systems and that could be transitioned to run a critical system during a contingency event. A warm site is more expensive than a cold site, as equipment is purchased and maintained at the warm site with telecommunications in place. Some costs may be offset by using equipment for noncritical functions or for testing. Recovery to a warm site can take several hours to several days, depending on system complexity and the amount of data to be restored.

3. *Hot sites*: Hot sites are locations with fully operational equipment and the capacity to quickly take over system operations after loss of the primary system facility. A hot site has sufficient equipment and the most current version of production software installed as well as adequate storage for the production system data. Hot sites should have the most recent version of backed-up data loaded, requiring only updating with data produced since the last backup. In many cases, hot-site data and databases are updated concurrently with or soon after the primary data and databases are updated. Hot sites also need a way to quickly move system users' connectivity from the primary site. One example of a hot site is two identical systems at alternate locations that are in production, serving different geographical locations or load balancing production workload. Each location is built to handle the full workload, and data are continuously synchronized between the systems. This is the most expensive option, requiring full operation of a system at an alternate location and full telecommunications capacity with the ability to maintain or quickly update the operational data and databases. Hot sites also require operational support that is nearly equal to the production.

In order to establish what type of recovery site is needed, the continuity/disaster planner should look at information provided in the BIA to determine what critical mission/business processes a system supports, the MTD, and the impact the loss of the system would have on the business. An information system recovery strategy may incorporate one or more of these types of alternate processing facilities. For example, some functionality of a system may be highly critical and require a hot site to minimize the downtime and impact on mission/business processes. However, other functionality of the same system, such as a reporting or batch-printing process, may be able to be down for several days with little impact and would just need extra space in the alternate facility to place additional equipment after it is purchased.

Use of HA processes

HA is a process wherein redundancy and failover processes are built into a system to maximize its uptime and availability (Marcus 2005). The concept of HA is to achieve an uptime of 99.999% or higher, which equates to just a few minutes per year of downtime. Several vendors offer HA products and services designed to minimize downtime by building redundancy and resiliency into the architecture.

HA can be an expensive option for systems, involving duplicate hardware and special failover software to eliminate any single point of failure. Normally, there are higher-cost maintenance and support requirements associated with HA systems. Therefore, HA is not a viable option for many systems and should be considered only for those systems that cannot tolerate downtime. Examples of this may be air traffic systems and financial systems. Also, HA systems cannot be a replacement for a solid backup strategy, as a corruption of data on a system may propagate through an HA system, making the system unusable. Without a backup of the system separate from the system itself, recovery may not be possible. HA can be implemented at a single site with all system redundancy residents at that site. This will keep the system running at an HA level as long as there is no interruption of the facility housing the system. However, when implementing HA products or services in a system, the continuity/disaster planner should have HA processes extended to an alternate location. Mechanisms such as block mirroring to an alternate site should be considered to provide redundancy and backup of system data outside of the system facility. Whenever a write is made to a block on a primary storage device, the same write is made to an alternate storage device, either within the same storage system or between separate storage systems at different locations.

Client/server systems

Client/server systems can have processing and data at both the server and client workstation levels. Client workstations are normally desktop computers, although portable devices may be connected to servers as clients. Portable devices include laptops, notebook computers, and handheld devices (e.g., smart phones and specialized equipment such as inventory collection bar-code readers). Advances in wireless and smartphone technology have allowed users access to key server functionality and services such as e-mail from their mobile phones. This is normally done by using proprietary third-party software that establishes the communications and data transfer to and from the phone via the network provided by mobile cell carriers (Gimes 2005). Servers support file sharing and storage, data processing, central application hosting (such as e-mail or a central database), printing, access control, user authentication, remote access connectivity, and other shared system services. Local users log in to the server through networked client machines to access resources that the server provides.

Client/server systems contingency considerations

Contingency considerations for client/server systems should emphasize data availability, confidentiality, and integrity at both the server system level and the client level. To address these requirements, regular and frequent backups of data should be stored off-site. Specifically, the system manager should consider each of the following practices for client/server systems:

- *Store backups off-site or at an alternate site*: Backup media should be stored off-site or at an alternate site in a secure, environmentally controlled facility.
- *Standardize hardware, software, and peripherals*: System recovery is faster if hardware, software, and peripherals are standardized throughout the organization. Additionally, critical hardware components that need to be recovered immediately in the event of a disaster should be compatible with off-the-shelf computer components. This compatibility will avoid delays incurred in ordering custom-built equipment from a vendor.
- *Document system configurations and vendor information*: Well-documented system configurations ease recovery. Similarly, vendor names and emergency contact information for vendors that supply essential hardware, software, and other components should be listed in the contingency plan so that replacement components may be purchased quickly.
- *Coordinate with security policies and system security controls*: Client/server contingency solutions should be coordinated with security policies and system security controls. In choosing the appropriate technical contingency solution, similar security controls and security-related activities (e.g., risk assessment, vulnerability scanning) applied in the production system should be implemented in the contingency solution to ensure that executing the system contingency solution does not compromise or disclose sensitive data during a system disruption or emergency.

- *Use results from the BIA*: The impacts and priorities of associated information systems discovered through the BIA should be reviewed to determine related requirements.
- *Minimize the amount of data stored on a client computer*: Critical user data should be stored on central servers that are backed up as part of an organization's enterprise backup strategy rather than on the client computer hard drive.
- *Automate backup of data*: Client/server systems should have software installed that automatically schedules data backups to a central data backup location. Data for backup should be stored at a common directory name (such as C:My Documents) to ease in automated backup and to make sure that only pertinent data are backed up. If the client system backup process is not automated from the network, users should be encouraged to back up data on a regular basis. Automated backup schedulers should be set up for stand-alone desktops and portable devices whenever possible.
- *Provide guidance on saving data on client computers*: Instructing users to save data to a particular folder on the computer eases the IT department's client-support requirements. If a machine must be rebuilt, the technician will know which folders to copy and preserve during recovery.
- *Store backup information at an alternate site*: If users back up data on a stand-alone system rather than saving data to the network, a means should be provided for storing the media at an alternate site. Software licenses and original system software, vendor SLAs and contracts, and other important documents relevant to the stand-alone system should be stored with the backup media. The storage facility should be located far enough away from the original site to reduce the likelihood that both sites would be affected by the same contingency event. Contingency considerations for servers in a client/server system rely extensively on LAN and WAN connectivity to communicate with their clients. Because of this, server components must consider system contingency measures similar to those for LANs and WANs.
- *Standardize hardware, software, and peripherals*: Recovery may be expedited if hardware, software, and peripherals are standardized throughout the client/server system. Recovery costs may be reduced because standard configurations may be designated and resources may be shared. Standardized components also reduce system maintenance across the organization.
- *Document systems configurations and vendors*: The server architecture and the configurations of its various components should be documented. In addition, the contingency plan should identify vendors and model specifications to facilitate rapid equipment replacement after a disruption.
- *Coordinate with security policies and security controls*: Server contingency solution(s) should be coordinated with network security policies; similar security controls and security-related activities (e.g., risk assessment, vulnerability scanning) in the production environment should be implemented in the contingency solution(s) to ensure that, during a system disruption, executing the technical contingency solution(s) does not compromise or disclose sensitive data. Security of data within a client/server system is key as most systems are multi-tenancy, having multiple users and applications residing on the same system, with different security requirements and controls.
- *Coordinate contingency solutions with cyberincident response procedures*: Because many application servers use web services to provide an image of the organization to the public, the organization's public image could be damaged if the application server were defaced or taken down by a cyberattack. To reduce the consequences of such an attack, contingency solutions should be coordinated closely with cyberincident response procedures designed to limit the impacts of a cyberattack.

- *Use results from the BIA*: Impacts and priorities discovered through the BIA of associated LANs and/or WANs should be reviewed to determine recovery requirements and priorities.

Client/server systems contingency solutions

Encryption is a popular security tool used on client devices. With the increased use of digital signatures for nonrepudiation and the use of encryption for confidentiality and/or integrity, organizations should consider including encryption in their backup strategy. Encryption should also be considered for backup media that goes off-site for storage so as to secure data should it be lost or stolen en route or at the alternate site. If encrypted data are sent off-site for storage, there should be a cryptographic key management system in place to make sure the data are readable if they need to be recovered onto a new or replaced system. The cryptographic key and the encryption software both need to be on the new system along with the keying material. Keying material is the data, such as the keys and initialization points for encryption, used to establish and maintain the encryption parameters. The keying material can be stored at a central location (such as an enterprise key management and encryption system) or on removable media separate from the backup media itself. Client/server system data backups can be accomplished in various ways, including those listed as follows:

- *Digital video disk (DVD)*: DVD read-only memory (DVD-ROM) drives come standard in most desktop computers; however, not all computers are equipped with writable DVD-ROM drives. DVDs are low-cost storage media and have a higher storage capacity of around 4.7 gigabytes (GB). To read from a DVD-ROM, the operating system's file manager is sufficient; to write to a DVD-ROM, a rewritable DVD (DVD-RW) drive and the appropriate software are required.
- *Network storage*: Data stored on networked client/server systems can be backed up to a networked disk. The amount of data that can be backed up from a client/server system is limited by the network disk storage capacity or disk allocation to the particular user. If users are instructed to save files to a networked disk, the networked disk itself should be backed up through the network or server backup program. Common types of network storage architecture include NAS and SAN. These storage systems incorporate resiliency and redundancy within their design and can be configured to maintain redundancy across several locations.
- *External hard drives*: Data replication or synchronization to an external hard drive is a common backup method for portable computers and stand-alone devices. Handheld devices or laptops may be connected to an external hard drive and the desired data is replicated from the portable device to the external hard drive. Many external hard drives have backup software included for use in backing up primary drives.
- *Internet backup*: Internet backup, or online backup, is a commercial service that allows users of desktop and portable devices to back up data to a remote location over the Internet for a fee. A utility is installed onto the desktop or portable device that allows the user to schedule backups, select files and folders to be backed up, and establish an archiving scheme to prevent files from being overwritten. Data can be encrypted for transmission; however, this will impede the data transfer. The advantage of Internet backup is that the user is not required to purchase data.

Servers normally have much larger amounts of data that need to be maintained and secured. It is recommended in environments with multiple servers that storage not be dedicated to each server but rather centralized for use by multiple servers. SAN and NAS are common multiserver storage systems. Centralizing the data of multiple servers allows for a common backup of data for off-site storage. Given the large amount of data that must be backed up, it is recommended that a separate and dedicated network be used just for the data transfers required for backing up data. This will enable the primary network to be dedicated to production traffic and not impact the backup process.

Contingency solutions may be built into the client/server system during design and implementation. For example, a client/server system may be constructed so that all data resides in one location (such as the organization's headquarters) and is replicated to the local sites. Changes at local sites could be replicated back to headquarters. If data are replicated to the local sites as read only, the data in the client/server system are backed up at each local site. This means that if the headquarters server were to fail, data could still be accessed at the local sites over the WAN. Conversely, if data were uploaded hourly from local sites to the headquarters' site, then the headquarters' server would act as a backup for the local servers.

As the aforementioned example illustrates, the client/server system typically provides some inherent level of redundancy that can be incorporated in the contingency strategy. For example, consider a critical system that is distributed between an organization's headquarters and a small office. Assuming data are replicated at both sites, a cost-effective recovery strategy may be to establish a reciprocal agreement between the two sites. Under this agreement, in the event of a disruption at one office, essential personnel would relocate to the other office to continue to process system functions. This strategy could save significant contingency costs by avoiding the need to procure and equip alternate sites. If considering the use of remote sites for system backups or the use of Internet or other means of backup, the continuity/disaster planner should ensure that the remotely hosted storage services can provide the same level of protection of data as the original site. This can be done through SLAs and periodic reviews and assessments of the remote-storage facility and processes.

Telecommunications systems

There are two primary classes of telecommunications systems: LANs and WANs. Wireless connectivity, prevalent for use with portable devices, can be used in either LAN or WAN environments. A LAN is located within an office or campus environment. It can be as small as two PCs attached to a single network switch, or it may support hundreds of users and multiple servers. LANs can be developed using any of several topologies. Each connection on a LAN is considered a node. A WAN is a data-communications network that consists of connecting two or more systems that are dispersed over a wide geographical area. Communications links, usually provided by a public carrier, provide the connection to enable one system to interact with other systems. WANs can connect LANs together, can connect to mainframe systems, and can connect client computers to servers. WANs provide much of the communications requirements of geographically dispersed environments. Types of WAN communications links include the following methods:

- *T-1*: T-1 is a dedicated phone connection supporting data rates of 1.544 megabits per second (Mbps). A T-1 line consists of 24 individual 64-kbps channels, and each channel can be configured to carry voice or data signals. Fractional T-1 communications links also can be provided when multiples of 64-kbps lines are required.
- *T-3*: T-3 is a dedicated phone connection supporting data rates of about 45 Mbps. A T-3 line consists of 672 individual channels, each of which -supports 64 kbps. T-3 is also referred to as a digital signal (DS) 3.

- *Frame relay*: Frame relay is a packet-switching protocol for connecting devices on a WAN. In frame relay, data are routed over virtual circuits. Frame relay networks support data transfer rates at T-1 and T-3 speeds.
- *Asynchronous transfer mode (ATM)*: ATM is a network technology that transfers data at high speeds using packets of fixed size. Implementations of ATM support data transfer rates of from 25 to 622 Mbps and provide guaranteed throughput.
- *Synchronous optical network (SONET)*: SONET is the standard for -synchronous data transmission on optical media. SONET supports gigabit transmission rates.

Telecommunications contingency considerations

When developing the telecommunications recovery strategy, the continuity/disaster planner should apply the following considerations:

- *Telecommunications documentation:* Physical and logical telecommunications diagrams should be up to date. The physical diagram should display the physical layout of the facility that houses the LAN and/or WAN, and cable jack numbers should be documented on the physical diagram. Diagrams should also identify network-connecting devices, IP addresses, domain name system (DNS) names, and types of communications links and vendors. The logical diagram should present the telecommunications infrastructure and its nodes. Network discovery software can provide an accurate picture of the telecommunications environment. Both diagrams help recovery personnel to identify where problems have occurred and to restore telecommunications services more quickly.
- *System configuration and vendor information documentation*: Configurations of network connective devices that facilitate telecommunication (e.g., circuits, switches, bridges, and hubs) should be documented to ease recovery. Vendors and their contact information should be documented in the contingency plan to provide for prompt hardware and software repair or replacement. The plan also should document the communications providers, including POC and contractual or SLA information.
- *Coordinate with security policies and security controls*: Telecommunications contingency solution(s) should be coordinated with network security policies to protect against threats that could disrupt the network. Therefore, in choosing the appropriate technical telecommunications contingency solution(s), similar security controls and security-related activities (e.g., risk assessment, vulnerability scanning) in the production systems should be implemented in the contingency solution(s) to ensure that, during a network disruption, executing the technical contingency solution(s) does not compromise or disclose sensitive data.
- *Use results from the BIA*: Impacts and priorities discovered through the BIA of associated systems should be reviewed to determine telecommunications recovery priorities. The BIA should identify the high-availability FIPS 199 impact levels for any data networks and e-mail that support COOP-mission, primary, or national essential functions.

Telecommunications contingency solutions

While similar contingencies exist for both LAN and WAN telecommunications systems, there are different strategies and solutions the continuity/disaster planner should consider when determining an overall telecommunications recovery strategy. Differences in solutions primarily exist due to geographic and connectivity ownership. While LANs are typically in small areas (offices or campuses) and the routing and wiring is owned or managed by the organization, WANs typically rely on network service providers (NSPs) for both routing and wiring.

When developing a recovery plan for a SCADA system, the continuity/disaster planner should identify single points of failure that affect critical systems or processes outlined in the BIA. This analysis could include threats to the cabling system, such as cable cuts, electromagnetic and radio frequency interference, and damage resulting from fire, water, and other hazards. As a solution, redundant cables may be installed when appropriate. For example, it might not be cost-effective to install duplicate cables to desktops. However, it might be cost-effective to install a gigabit cable between floors so that hosts on both floors could be reconnected if the primary cable were cut.

Contingency planning also should consider network-connecting devices, such as hubs, switches, routers, and bridges. The BIA should characterize the roles that each device serves in the network, and a contingency solution should be developed for each device based on its BIA criticality. As an example of a contingency strategy for network-connecting devices, redundant intelligent network routers may be installed in a network, enabling a router to assume the full traffic workload if the other router fails.

Remote access is a service provided by servers and devices on the LAN. Remote access provides a convenience for users working off-site or allows servers and devices to communicate between sites. Remote access can be conducted through various methods, primarily through a virtual private network (VPN). If an emergency or serious system disruption occurs, remote access may serve as an important contingency capability by providing access to organization-wide data for recovery teams or users from another location. If remote access is established as a contingency strategy, data bandwidth requirements should be identified and used to scale the remote access solution. Remote access will work only if the remote access server and the network are both functioning at either the primary or the alternate location.

Wireless (or WiFi) LANs can serve as an effective contingency solution to restore network services following a wired LAN disruption. Wireless networks do not require the cabling infrastructure of conventional LANs; therefore, they may be installed quickly as an interim or permanent solution. However, wireless networks broadcast data over a radio signal, enabling the data to be intercepted. When implementing a wireless network, security controls such as data encryption should be employed if the communications traffic contains confidential information. Wireless LANs allow for quick temporary access of portable devices, which typically have wireless antennas built into them. Wireless routers commonly provide password authentication and transmission encryption as standard features.

WAN contingency solutions include all of the measures discussed for client/server systems and LANs. In addition, WAN contingency planning must consider the communications links that connect the disparate systems. WAN contingency strategies are influenced by the type of data routed on the network. A WAN that hosts a mission-critical system may require a more robust recovery strategy than a WAN that connects multiple LANs for simple resource-sharing purposes. Organizations should consider the following contingency solutions for ensuring WAN availability:

- *Redundant communications links:* Redundant communications links are usually necessary when the network processes critical data. The redundant links could be the same type, such as two T-1 connections; or the backup link could provide reduced bandwidth to accommodate only critical transmissions in a contingency situation. For example, an integrated services digital network (ISDN) line with a bandwidth of 128 Kbps could be used as a contingency communications link for a primary T-1 connection. If redundant links are used, the continuity/disaster planner should ensure that the links have physical separation and do not follow the same path; otherwise, a single incident, such as a cable cut, could disrupt both links.

- *Redundant network service providers*: If near-100% connectivity is required, redundant communications links can be provided through multiple NSPs. If this solution is chosen, the continuity/disaster planner should ensure that the NSPs do not share common facilities at any point, including building entries or demarcations (places where the WAN connection ends within a facility).
- *Redundant network-connecting devices*: Duplicate network-connecting devices, such as routers, switches, and firewalls, can create HA at the LAN interfaces and provide redundancy if one device fails. Duplicate devices also provide load balancing in routing traffic.
- *Redundancy from NSP or internet service provider (ISP)*: The continuity/disaster planner should consult with the selected NSP or ISP to assess the robustness and reliability within their core networks (e.g., redundant network-connecting devices and power protection).

To reduce the effects of a telecommunications disruption through prompt detection, monitoring software can be installed. The monitoring software issues an alert if a node or connection begins to fail or is not responding. The monitoring software can facilitate troubleshooting and often provides the administrator with a warning before users and other nodes notice problems. Many types of monitoring software may be configured to send an electronic page or e-mail to a designated individual(s) automatically when a system parameter falls out of its specification range.

Conclusion

While addressing the problem of risk in most SCADA and control systems is vitally necessary today, as a whole, it is important to consider and review the business continuity planning and DR processes. As a large portion of infrastructure operations (and their facilities) are privately owned worldwide, infrastructure services providers, as well as users of SCADA and control systems, need to have a continuity plan to survive threats to their infrastructure. As such, having a good, solid BCP will address the overall issue of maintaining or reestablishing production in the case of an interruption.

References

Barker, R., *Storage Area Network Essentials*. Indianapolis: Wiley Press, 2005.

Corbin, A., *Corbin on Contracts*. St. Paul: West Publishing, 2008.

Falco, J., *Guide to Supervisory Control and Data Acquisition (SCADA) and Industrial Control Systems Security*. Gaithersburg: National Institute for Standards and Technology, 2006.

Gimes, R. A., *Windows Desktop and Server Hardening*. Indianapolis: Wiley Press, 2005.

Gregory, W. A., *Law of Agency and Partnership*. St. Paul: West Publishing, 2008.

Maiwald, E., *Security Planning and Disaster Recovery*. Chicago: McGraw-Hill, 2002.

Marcus, E., *Blueprints for High Availability*. Indianapolis: Wiley Press, 2005.

Sheffi, Y., *The Resilient Enterprise*. Cambridge: MIT Press, 2005.

Swanson, M., NIST special publication 800-34 Rev. 1 contingency planning guide for federal information systems. Gaithersburg: National Institute for Standards and Technology, 2006.

chapter eight

Incident response and SCADA

Steven Young

Contents

Difficulties with SCADA and incident response

Supervisory control and data acquisition (SCADA) systems and their reliance on proprietary networks and hardware have long been considered immune to the network attacks that have wreaked so much havoc on corporate information systems. Many of these systems were boasted by various water and power corporations as closed systems. To many agencies, companies, and individuals, "closed systems" meant that they were not vulnerable to attacks or exploitation. Research indicates that this confidence is misplaced. The move to more open standards such as Ethernet, transmission control protocol/Internet protocol (TCP/IP), and web technologies enables hackers to take advantage of the control industry's lack of preparedness and sense of security. Much of the available information about cyberincidents represents a characterization as opposed to an analysis of events. Another clear problem is the lack of a clear incident response protocol to SCADA events (Turk 2005). Most companies prefer not to share cyberattack incident data and their incident response capabilities because of potential financial repercussions. The following discussion does not set out to delineate SCADA threats or controls as many publications delineate them. Instead, the discussion will focus on how to respond to SCADA threats after controls have failed or have been circumvented.

Incident analysis

Incident detection and analysis would be easy if every precursor or indication were guaranteed to be accurate; unfortunately, this is not the case. For example, user-provided indications, such as a complaint of a server being unavailable, are often incorrect. Intrusion detection systems are notorious for producing large numbers of false positives—incorrect indications. These examples demonstrate what makes incident detection and analysis so difficult; each indication should ideally be evaluated to determine if it is legitimate. Making matters worse, the total number of indications from human and automated sources may be thousands or millions a day (Grance 2008). Finding the few real security incidents that occur out of all the indications is a difficult task.

Even if an indication is accurate, it does not necessarily mean that an incident has occurred. Some indications, such as modification of critical files, could happen for several reasons other than a security incident, including human error. Given the occurrence of indications, however, it is reasonable to suspect that an incident might be occurring and to act accordingly. In general, SCADA incident handlers should assume that an incident is occurring until they have determined that it is not (U.S. Department of Energy 2008). Determining whether a particular event is actually an incident is sometimes a matter of technical judgment.

Some incidents are easy to detect, such as a physically damaged SCADA sensor. However, many incidents are not associated with such clear symptoms. Small signs, such as one change in one system configuration file may be the only indications that an incident has occurred. In SCADA incident handling, detection may be the most difficult task. Incident handlers are responsible for analyzing ambiguous, contradictory, and incomplete symptoms to determine what has happened. Although technical solutions exist that can make detection somewhat easier, the best remedy is to build a team of highly experienced and proficient staff members who can analyze the precursors and indications effectively and efficiently and take appropriate actions. Without a well-trained and capable incident response staff, incident detection and analysis will be conducted inefficiently, and costly mistakes will be made (Falco 2011). Such mistakes may take on additional meaning with loss of life and secondary effects of loss of power or clean water.

The incident response team should work quickly to analyze and validate each incident, documenting each step taken. When the team believes that an incident has occurred, it should rapidly perform an initial analysis to determine the incident's scope, such as which networks, control systems, automated laboratories, or applications are affected. Teams need to determine who or what originated the incident and how the incident is occurring (e.g., what tools or attack methods are being used, what vulnerabilities are being exploited). The initial analysis should provide enough information for the team to prioritize subsequent activities, such as containment of the incident and deeper analysis of the effects of the incident. When in doubt, incident handlers should assume the worst until additional analysis indicates otherwise. In general, it is important to profile all SCADA systems, and understand what normal behavior is for their operation. Profiling is measuring the characteristics of expected activity so that changes to it can be identified (Cooper 2001).

While it is expensive for multiple facilities, it is also recommended to establish a centralized logging server that monitors all SCADA devices on the network, and perform event correlation.

Incident prioritization

Prioritizing the handling of the incident is perhaps the most critical decision point in the incident handling process. Incidents should not be handled on a first-come, first-served basis because of resource limitations. Instead, handling should be prioritized based on two factors:

1. *Current and potential technical effect of the incident:* Incident handlers should consider not only the current negative technical effect of the incident (e.g., unauthorized user-level access to data) but also the likely future technical effect of the incident if it is not immediately contained (e.g., root compromise). For example, a worm spreading among workstations may currently cause a minor effect on the agency, but within a few hours, the worm traffic may cause a major network outage.
2. *Criticality of the affected resources:* Resources affected by an incident (e.g., firewalls, web servers, Internet connectivity, user workstations, and applications) have different significance to the organization. The criticality of a resource is based primarily on its data or services, users, trust relationships and interdependencies with other resources, and visibility.

Incident notification

When a SCADA incident is analyzed and prioritized, the incident response team needs to notify the appropriate individuals within the organization and, occasionally, other organizations. Given the magnitude and complexity of today's information security threats, cooperative incident response is likely the most effective approach. Incident response policies should include provisions concerning incident reporting—at a minimum, what must be reported to whom and at what times (e.g., initial notification, regular status updates). The exact reporting requirements vary among agencies, but parties that are typically notified include

- Municipal or agency chief information officer (CIO) operating the plant
- Chief information security officer (CISO)
- Business continuity or continuity of operations officer
- IT disaster recovery coordinator
- Other incident response teams within the organization
- System owner
- Public affairs (for incidents that may generate publicity)
- Legal department (for incidents with potential legal ramifications)

Choosing a containment strategy

When an incident has been detected and analyzed, it is important to contain it before the spread of the incident overwhelms resources or the damage increases. Most incidents require containment, so it is important to consider that early in the course of handling each incident. An essential part of containment is decision making (e.g., shutting down a system, disconnecting it from a wired or wireless network, disconnecting its modem cable, or disabling certain functions). Such decisions are much easier to make if strategies and procedures for containing the incident have been predetermined. Organizations should define acceptable risks in dealing with incidents and develop strategies accordingly.

Containment strategies vary based on the type of incident. For example, the overall strategy for containing a virus infection is quite different from that of a network-based distributed denial of service attack. It is highly recommended that organizations create separate containment strategies for each major type of incident. The criteria should be documented clearly to facilitate quick and effective decision making. Criteria for determining the appropriate strategy include

- Potential damage to and theft of resources
- Need for evidence preservation
- Service availability (e.g., network connectivity, services provided to external parties)
- Time and resources needed to implement the strategy
- Effectiveness of the strategy (e.g., partially contains the incident, fully contains the incident)
- Duration of the solution (e.g., emergency workaround to be removed in 4 h, temporary workaround to be removed in 2 weeks, permanent solution)

In certain cases, some organizations delay the containment of an incident so that they can monitor the attacker's activity, usually to gather additional evidence. The incident response team should discuss delayed containment with its legal department to determine if it is feasible. If an organization knows that a system has been compromised and allows the compromise to continue, it may be liable if the attacker uses the compromised system to attack other systems. The delayed containment strategy is dangerous because an attacker could escalate unauthorized access or compromise other systems in a fraction of a second. Only a highly experienced incident response team that can monitor all of the attacker's actions and disconnect the attacker in a matter of seconds should attempt this strategy. Even then, the value of delayed containment is usually not worth the high risk that it poses.

Another potential issue regarding containment is that some attacks may cause additional damage when they are contained. For example, a compromised host may run a malicious process that pings another host periodically. When the incident handler attempts to contain the incident by disconnecting the compromised host from the network, the subsequent pings will fail. Because of the failure, the malicious process may overwrite all the data on the host's hard drive. Handlers should not assume that, just because a host has been disconnected from the network, further damage to the host has been prevented.

Evidence gathering and handling

Although the primary reason for gathering evidence during an incident is to resolve the incident, it may also be needed for legal proceedings. In such cases, it is important to clearly document how all pieces of evidence, including compromised systems, have been preserved. Evidence should be collected according to procedures that meet all applicable laws and regulations, developed from previous discussions with legal staff and appropriate law enforcement agencies, so that it should be admissible in court. In addition, evidence should be accounted for at all times; whenever evidence is transferred from person to person, chain of custody forms should detail the transfer and include each party's signature (Kent 2006). A detailed log should be kept for all evidence, including the following:

- Identifying information (e.g., the location, serial number, model number, hostname, media access control (MAC) address, and IP address of a computer)
- Name, title, and phone number of each individual who collected or handled the evidence during the investigation
- Time and date (including time zone) of each occurrence of evidence handling
- Locations where the evidence was stored

Collecting evidence from computing resources presents some challenges. It is generally desirable to acquire evidence from a system of interest as soon as one suspects that an incident may have occurred (Kerr 2006). Many incidents cause a dynamic chain of events to occur; an initial system snapshot may do more good in identifying the problem and its source than most other actions that can be taken at this stage. From an evidentiary standpoint, it is much better to get a snapshot of the system "as is" rather than doing so after incident handlers, system administrators, and others have inadvertently altered the state of the machine during the investigation. Users and system administrators should be made aware of the steps that they should take to preserve evidence.

Basic forensics for standard computers

Before copying the files from the affected host, it is often desirable to capture volatile information that may not be recorded in a file system or image backup, such as current network connections, processes, login sessions, open files, network interface configurations, and the contents of memory. These data may hold clues as to the attacker's identity or the attack methods that were used. It is also valuable to document how far the local clock deviates from the actual time.

However, risks are associated with acquiring information from the live system. Any action performed on the host itself will alter the state of the machine to some extent. In addition, the attacker may still be on the system and notice the handler's activity, which could have disastrous consequences.

An incident handler should be able to issue only the minimum commands needed to acquire the dynamic evidence without inadvertently altering other evidence. A single poorly chosen command can irrevocably destroy evidence; for example, simply displaying the directory contents can alter the last access time on each listed file. Furthermore, running commands from the affected host is dangerous, because they may have been altered or replaced (e.g., Trojan horses, rootkits) to conceal information or cause additional damage. Incident handlers should use write-protected removable media that contain trusted commands and all dependent files, so that all necessary commands can be run without using the affected host's commands (Steele 2010). Incident handlers can also use write blocker programs that prevent the host from writing to its hard drives.

After acquiring volatile data, an incident handler with computer forensics training should immediately make a full disk image to sanitized write-protectable or write-once media. A disk image preserves all data on the disk, including deleted files and file fragments. If it is possible that evidence will be needed for prosecution or internal disciplinary actions, the handlers should make at least two full images, label them properly, and securely store one of the images to be used strictly as evidence. (All evidence, not just disk images, should be tagged and stored in a secure location.) Occasionally, handlers may acquire and secure the original disk as evidence; the second image can then be restored to another disk as part of system recovery.

Obtaining a disk image is superior to a standard file system backup for computer forensic purposes because it records more data. Imaging is also preferable because it is much safer to analyze an image than it is to perform analysis on the original resource—the analysis may inadvertently alter or damage the original. If the business impact of taking down the system outweighs the risk of keeping the system operational, disk imaging may not be possible. A standard file system backup can capture information on existing files, which may be sufficient for handling many incidents, particularly those that are not expected to lead to prosecution.

Both disk imaging and file system backups are valuable, regardless of whether the attacker will be prosecuted, because they permit the target to be restored while the investigation continues using the image or backup.

Computer forensic software is valuable, not only for acquiring disk images, but also automating much of the analysis process, such as

- Identifying and recovering file fragments and hidden and deleted files and directories from any location (e.g., used space, free space, slack space)
- Examining file structures, headers, and other characteristics to determine what type of data each file contains, instead of relying on file extensions
- Displaying the contents of all graphics files
- Performing complex searches
- Graphically displaying the acquired drive's directory structure
- Generating reports

During evidence acquisition, it is often prudent to acquire copies of supporting log files from other resources—for example, firewall logs that show what IP address an attacker used. As with hard drive and other media acquisition, logs should be copied to sanitized write-protectable or write-once media. One copy of the logs should be stored as evidence, whereas a second copy could be restored to another system for further analysis. Many incident handlers create a message digest for log files and other pieces of digital evidence; this refers to generating a cryptographic checksum for a file. If the file is modified and the checksum is recalculated, there is only an infinitesimal chance that the checksums will be the same. (Message digests are also useful for other computer forensic purposes—for example, when acquiring media, handlers can generate checksums of the original media and the duplicates to show that integrity was maintained during imaging.) Incident handlers should also document the local clock time on each logging host and what deviation, if any, there is from the actual time.

To assist in incident analysis, handlers may want to duplicate an aspect of an incident that was not adequately recorded. For example, a user may have visited a malicious website, which then compromised the workstation. The workstation contains no record of the attack. A handler may be able to determine what happened by setting up another workstation and contacting the same website, while using packet sniffers and host-based security software to record and analyze the activity. Handlers should be very careful when duplicating such attacks so that they do not inadvertently cause another incident to occur.

Another example in which incident duplication may occur is when an internal user is suspected of downloading inappropriate files. If the firewall has recorded which file transfer protocol (FTP) servers the user visited, an incident handler may decide to access the same FTP servers to determine the types of materials they contain and whether the filenames on the user's workstation correspond to filenames on the FTP servers. Handlers should only consider accessing external services if they are available to the public (e.g., an FTP server that permits anonymous logons). Although it may be acceptable to monitor network traffic to determine what FTP account and password a user provided, it is usually not acceptable to reuse that information to gain access to the FTP server.

Identifying the attacker

During incident handling, system owners and others typically want to identify the attacker. Although this information can be important, particularly if the organization wants to prosecute the attacker, incident handlers should stay focused on containment, eradication, and recovery. Identifying the attacker can be a time-consuming and futile process that can prevent a team from achieving its primary goal—minimizing the business impact. The following items describe the most commonly performed activities for attacker identification:

- *Validating the attacker's network address:* New incident handlers often focus on the attacker's IP address. The handler may attempt to verify that the address was not spoofed by using pings, traceroutes, or other methods of verifying connectivity. However, this is not helpful, because at best it indicates that a host at that address responds to the requests. A failure to respond does not mean the address is not real—for example, a host may be configured to ignore pings and traceroutes. The attacker may have received a dynamic address (e.g., from a dial-up modem pool) that has already been reassigned to someone else. More importantly, if the IP address is real and the team pings it, the attacker may be tipped off that the organization has detected the activity. If this occurs before the incident has been fully contained, the attacker could cause additional damage, such as wiping out hard drives with evidence of the attack. The team should consider acquiring and using IP addresses from another organization (e.g., an Internet service provider [ISP]) when performing actions such as address validation, so that the true origin of the activity is concealed from the attacker.
- *Scanning the attacker's system:* Some incident handlers do more than perform pings and traceroutes to check an attacking IP address—they may run port scanners, vulnerability scanners, and other tools to attempt to gather more information on the attacker. For example, the scans may indicate that Trojan horses are listening on the system, implying that the attacking host itself has been compromised. Incident handlers should discuss this issue with legal representatives before performing such scans, because the scans may violate organization policies or even break the law.
- *Researching the attacker through search engines:* In most attacks, incident handlers will have at least a few pieces of data regarding the possible identity of the attacker, such as a source IP address, an e-mail address, or an Internet relay chat (IRC) nickname. Performing an Internet search using this data may lead to more information on the attacker—for example, a mailing list message regarding a similar attack, or even the attacker's website. Research such as this generally does not need to be performed before the incident has been fully contained.
- *Using incident databases:* Several groups collect and consolidate intrusion detection and firewall log data from various organizations into incident databases. Some of these databases allow people to search for records corresponding to a particular IP address. Incident handlers could use the databases to see if other organizations are reporting suspicious activity from the same source. The organization can also check its own incident tracking system or database for related activity.
- *Monitoring possible attacker communication channels:* Another method that some incident handlers use to identify an attacker is to monitor communication channels that may be used by an attacker. For example, many bots use IRC as their primary means of communication. Another example is that attackers may congregate on certain IRC

channels to brag about their compromises and share information; however, incident handlers should treat any such information that they acquire only as a potential lead to be further investigated and verified, not as fact.

Eradication and recovery

After an incident has been contained, eradication may be necessary to eliminate components of the incident, such as deleting malicious code and disabling breached user accounts. For some incidents, eradication is either not necessary or is performed during recovery. In recovery, administrators restore systems to normal operation and, if applicable, harden systems to prevent similar incidents. Recovery may involve such actions as restoring systems from clean backups, rebuilding systems from scratch, replacing compromised files with clean versions, installing patches, changing passwords, and tightening network perimeter security (e.g., firewall rule sets, boundary router access control lists). It is also often desirable to employ higher levels of system logging or network monitoring as part of the recovery process. Once a resource is successfully attacked, it is often attacked again, or other resources within the organization are attacked in a similar manner. Because eradication and recovery actions are typically operating system (OS) or application specific, detailed recommendations and advice regarding them are outside the scope of this discussion. The author recommends reviewing specific SCADA system manufacturer documentation for recovery actions.

Lessons learned

One of the most important parts of incident response is also the most often omitted: learning and improving. Each incident response team should evolve to reflect new threats, improved technology, and lessons learned.

Many organizations have found that holding a "lessons learned" meeting with all involved parties after a major incident, and periodically after lesser incidents, is extremely helpful in improving security measures and the incident handling process itself. This meeting provides a chance to achieve closure with respect to an incident by reviewing what occurred, what was done to intervene, and how well intervention worked. The meeting should be held within several days of the end of the incident. Questions to be answered in the lessons learned meeting include

- What exactly happened, and at what times?
- How well did staff and management perform in dealing with the incident?
- Were the documented procedures followed? Were they adequate?
- What information was needed sooner?
- Were any steps or actions taken that might have inhibited the recovery?
- What would the staff and management do differently the next time a similar incident occurs?
- What corrective actions can prevent similar incidents in the future?
- What additional tools or resources are needed to detect, analyze, and mitigate future incidents?

Small incidents need limited postincident analysis, with the exception of incidents performed through new attack methods that are of widespread concern and interest. After serious attacks have occurred, it is usually worthwhile to hold postmortem meetings that cross team and organizational boundaries to provide a mechanism for sharing information. The primary consideration in holding such meetings is to ensure that the right people are involved. Not only is it important to invite people who have been involved in the incident that is being analyzed, but it is also wise to consider who should be invited to facilitate future cooperation.

The success of such meetings also depends on the agenda. Collecting input about expectations and needs (including suggested topics to cover) from participants before the meeting increases the likelihood that the participants' needs will be met. In addition, establishing rules of order before or at the start of a meeting can minimize confusion and discord. Having one or more moderators who are skilled in group facilitation can yield a high payoff. Finally, it is also important to document the major points of agreement and action items and to communicate them to parties who could not attend the meeting.

Lessons learned meetings provide other benefits. Reports from these meetings are good material for training new team members by showing them how more experienced team members respond to incidents. Updating incident response policies and procedures is another important part of the lessons learned process. Postmortem analysis of the way an incident was handled will often reveal a missing step or an inaccuracy in a procedure, providing impetus for change. Because of the changing nature of information technology and changes in personnel, the incident response team should review all related documentation and procedures for handling incidents at designated intervals.

Another important postincident activity is to create a follow-up report for each incident, which can be quite valuable for future use. First, the report provides a reference that can be used to assist in handling similar incidents. Creating a formal chronology of events (including time-stamped information such as systems log data) is important for legal reasons, as is creating a monetary estimate of the amount of damage the incident caused in terms of any loss of software and files, hardware damage, and staffing costs (including restoring services). This estimate may become the basis for subsequent prosecution activity by entities such as the U.S. Attorney General's office. Follow-up reports should be kept for a period as specified in record retention policies.

Incident response framework

The U.S. Department of Homeland Security (DHS) is responsible for helping federal departments and agencies secure their unclassified networks and also work with owners and operators of critical infrastructure and key resources (CIKR) organizations—whether privately owned, state, or municipality-owned—to encourage and bolster their cybersecurity readiness, risk assessment and mitigation, and, most importantly, incident response capabilities (U.S. Department of Homeland Security 2010).

Activities are currently underway to implement recommendations outlined from the cyberspace policy review built using the Comprehensive National Cybersecurity Initiative (CNCI) (Executive Office of the President of the United States, n.d.) launched by President George W. Bush through National Security Presidential Directive 54/Homeland Security Presidential Directive 23 (NSPD-54/HSPD-23) in January 2008. NSPD 54/HSPD 23, along with critical infrastructure protection authorities under the Homeland Security Act of 2002, empowers DHS to coordinate national efforts in the prevention of damage to, protection of, and restoration of computers, electronic communications systems, electronic communication services, wire communication, and electronic communication, including information contained therein, to ensure availability, integrity, authenticity, confidentiality, and nonrepudiation is maintained across cyberspace. President Obama determined that the CNCI (and its associated activities) should evolve further, (The Whitehouse, n.d.), becoming key elements of a broader, more up-to-date national U.S. cybersecurity strategy. These initiatives play a key role in supporting the achievement of many of the key recommendations of President Obama's cyberspace policy review (The Whitehouse 2009).

DHS has made significant efforts to enhance the security of the nation's critical infrastructure, as well as its cyberinfrastructure and networks. Current tools include the national cybersecurity protection system, of which the Einstein cyberintrusion detection system is a key component; the National Cybersecurity and Communications Integration Center (NCCIC), which serves as the nation's principal hub for organizing cyberresponse efforts; and an agreement between DHS and the U.S. Department of Defense, enhancing the United States' capabilities to protect against threats to critical civilian and military computer systems and networks.

President Obama's cybersecurity policy review called for *a comprehensive framework to facilitate coordinated responses by government, the private sector, and allies to a significant cyberincident.* Thus, DHS coordinated the interagency, state and local government, and private-sector working group that (eventually) developed the National Cyber Incident Response Plan (NCIRP).

This plan enables DHS to coordinate responses of multiple federal agencies, state and local governments, international partners, and private industry to incidents at all levels. It is designed to be flexible, as well as adaptable, allowing synchronization of response activities across jurisdictional lines. Essentially, the NCIRP committee's objective is to partner with volunteers from the 18 CIKR sectors, state, and federal agencies (including those within DHS) to develop an NCIRP.

In September 2010, the NCIRP was tested during the CyberStorm III national exercise (DHS, n.d.), which simulated a large-scale attack on the nation's critical information infrastructure. Seven Cabinet agencies, 11 states, 12 international partners, and 60 private-sector companies participated in the CyberStorm III exercise. In addition to the CyberStorm III participation, several sector partners participated in several other exercises to test and implement network-level and protective strategies, which included the NCIRP tabletop exercise, which was designed to assist sector partners to detect threats and rapidly restore outages caused by those with malicious intent (e.g., cyberattacks), as well as any events caused through natural disasters.

Evidence retention

Organizations should establish policy for how long evidence from an incident should be retained. Most organizations choose to retain all evidence for months or years after the incident ends.

The following factors should be considered during policy creation:

- *Prosecution:* If it is possible that the attacker can be prosecuted, evidence may need to be retained until all legal actions have been completed. In some cases, this may take several years. Furthermore, evidence that seems insignificant now may become more important in the future. For example, if an attacker is able to use knowledge gathered in one attack to perform a more severe attack later, evidence from the first attack may be key to explaining how the second attack was accomplished.

- *Data retention:* Most organizations have data retention policies that state how long certain types of data may be kept. For example, an organization may state that e-mail messages should be retained for only 180 days. If a disk image contains thousands of e-mails, the organization may not want the image to be kept for more than 180 days unless it is necessary. In a civil case, some recommended best practices in an active SCADA breach are as follows: (1) suspend related automated corporate and agency document destruction policies, (2) notify opponents, litigants, and third parties of the obligation to preserve data, and (3) form a preservation response team and begin formulation of a plan for responding to the new litigation. While these actions do not appear to be particularly ominous, proper execution requires an investment of significant time and effort by an IT support team. An organization will typically "recycle" backup tapes containing files created by employees and systems. Examples of these files include laboratory data, maintenance, and purchase records. The data on those tapes, once overwritten (i.e., "recycled"), can only be recovered for use in litigation under very limited circumstances. This makes acting quickly to suspend the destruction of that data crucial very early on in the litigation process. By suspending document destruction broadly across the organization, counsel can determine what geographic locations, servers, networks, databases, and removable media (e.g., backup tapes, CDs, DVDs) contain potentially responsive information. All other sources can then continue under the normal nonlitigation mode of document retention. This approach to preservation will help counsel and litigants avoid the sometimes disastrous results of an aggressive requesting party who intends to create a damaging spoliation problem rather than merely obtaining and reviewing discoverable information.
- *Cost:* Original hardware (e.g., hard drives, compromised systems) that is stored as evidence, as well as hard drives and other devices that are used to hold disk images, are individually inexpensive for most organizations. However, if an organization stores many such components for years, the cost can be substantial. The organization also must retain functional computers that can use the stored hardware (e.g., hard drives) and media (e.g., backup tapes). Cost also impacts an organization from a litigation standpoint. E-discovery requests from a SCADA systems breach can quickly consume the majority of a power or water provider's litigation budget. Such requests also have a crippling effect on municipalities operating their own wastewater systems.

In some cases, the cost of and methods of employing electronic discovery (e-discovery) have overshadowed the merits of the outlined issues outlined thus far. One very important reason to educate municipalities and utilities about adhering to defensible e-discovery processes is to avoid the potential for sanctions, which have been on the rise as judges learn more about electronic data document retention and recovery. One thing that should be explained is that judges have been known to issue sanctions against the client (and not singularly the firm representing them) for egregious failures in the methodologies applied to the e-discovery process. Therefore, explaining clearly what e-discovery is and the importance of providing adequate discovery of those electronic documents, if requested, is crucial to reducing litigation costs. Rules relating to e-discovery are still in the stages of infancy, but the courts are making an effort to address problems in common law as they arise. As SCADA breaches become more sophisticated, it will be essential to develop strict procedures to support litigation against attackers of systems and their facilities.

References

Cooper, M. *Intrusion Signatures and Analysis*. Indianapolis: New Riders, 2001.

Executive Office of the President of the United States. (n.d.). The comprehensive national cybersecurity initiative. http://www.fas.org/irp/eprint/cnci.pdf.

Falco, J. *Guide to Industrial Control Systems Security*. Gaithersburg: National Institute for Standards and Technology, 2011.

Grance, T. *Computer Security Incident Handling Guide*. Gaithersburg: National Institute for Standards and Technology, 2008.

Kent, K. *Guide to Integrating Forensic Techniques into Incident Response*. Gaithersburg: National Institute for Standards and Technology, 2006.

Kerr, O. S. *Computer Crime Law*, 2nd Edn. St. Paul: West Publishing, 2006.

Steele, J. *Digital Forensics for Network, Internet, and Cloud Computing*. New York: Syngress, 2010.

The Whitehouse. Cyberspace policy review. http://www.whitehouse.gov/assets/documents/Cyberspace_Policy_Review_final.pdf, 2009.

The Whitehouse. (n.d.). Foreign policy. https://www.whitehouse.gov/issues/foreign-policy/cybersecurity/national-initiative.

Turk, R. J. *Cyber Incidents Involving Control Systems*. Idaho Falls: Idaho National Labs, 2005.

U.S. Department of Energy. *21 Steps to Improve Cyber Security of SCADA Networks*. Washington, DC: U.S. Government Printing Office, 2008.

U.S. Department of Homeland Security. Communications sector-specific plan. http://www.dhs.gov/xlibrary/assets/nipp-ssp-communications-2010.pdf, 2010.

chapter nine

Forensics management

Craig Wright

Contents

The forensic process with regard to a supervisory control and data acquisition (SCADA)-based investigation has a few minor differences from many common forensic engagements. Systems are usually shut down for analysis, but SCADA systems are generally required to remain available. Remember, there is a large amount of volatile evidence that may be collected on a live system (Decker et al., 2011), and many SCADA systems cannot be shut down to be imaged and analyzed. The topics addressed in this chapter include

- Locating and gathering volatile evidence on a SCADA host
- Investigating log files for evidence
- Interpreting the memory state and memory dump information
- Investigating the system backups
- Analyzing Internet trace data and events

The term *evidence location* refers to the process of investigating and gathering information of a forensic nature and particularly of legal importance (Cardwell, 2011). This evidence aids in the investigation of both criminal investigations and civil suits. As many SCADA* systems are connected to networks, an Internet worm could have the impact of affecting the physical world. Worse, many SCADA systems are connected to the world without people officially knowing.

SCADA systems, essential utilities, and telecommunications now rely heavily on information technology for the management of their everyday operations, with greater volumes of susceptible economic and commercial information being exchanged electronically over potentially insecure channels all the time. The massive increase in complexity and interconnectivity coupled with simple point-and-click attack tools (such as Metasploit) has appreciably amplified the necessity to ensure the privacy, security, and availability of information systems. It has also led to an increase in the numbers of attacks against these systems and hence the need to have a forensic and incident response process in place (Weiss and Solomon, 2011).

Many SCADA systems are evidence poor when compared to modern operating systems. That stated they still manage to leave hidden files that can be extremely helpful to any investigation. More importantly, the logs and network traces that they produce are extremely valuable to an investigator in analyzing an attack or compromise against a SCADA system. Even file attributes and time stamps are valuable. Often, a perpetrator may attempt to change a file's attributes in order to either cover their tracks or hide important data that may be present in the system. Collating time stamps, for instance, can aid in reconstructing the actions taken by the suspect. The files are often more difficult to obtain, and the richest source of forensic data (if recorded) is most frequently incorporated in network captures.

Some of the more important sources of electronic evidence on a SCADA host include the following:

- Files
- Memory dumps
- Network trace files

The threats

The threat agents acting against SCADA systems exist in several general categories. Any of the following may be a source of threat that can lead to an incident:

- Accidental antagonists who cause you harm through ignorance or by negligence.
- Incidental antagonists who seek another target but attack because you are there and obtainable.
- Insiders. They may compromise or steal information assets because of motivations ranging from dissatisfaction to economic gain.
- Competitors may attack to gain a benefit or to achieve market dominance.
- Cybervandals, who could attack because you are there or you have a product they do not like.
- Hackers and crackers who attack in an attempt to obtain information concerning everything that is denied to them or who might be offering their technical proficiency to another with motives of their own.
- Thieves that may attack to further their own financial well-being.

---

* These are systems that are used by many critical services, including power and emergency services.

- Terrorists can attack in order to disrupt the connection linking the general public and critical infrastructure.
- The military involved in information warfare actions.

In particular, the threats may be summarized as

- Third-world countries
- Organized crime
- Hackers
- Terrorist organizations
- Internal competitors (within a nation)
- Foreign competitors
- Foreign intelligence agencies

Hostile nations such as China, North Korea, Cuba, and Iran are only one source of remote threat. Friendly nations have been known (and caught) in these activities in the past. SCADA systems are critical and as a result are becoming more and more targeted each week.

Initial steps

Like any forensic investigation, the first step involves planning. When investigating a router, there are two primary considerations that will affect the course of action that you will take. The first questions to ask are

- Do you need to track and monitor an active network connection?
- Is it more important to stop any damage or loss of valuable information?

It is more common that the investigator will want to minimize the likelihood of continuing data loss. In this situation, it is necessary to disconnect the router from the primary network. When doing this, it is necessary to maintain the state of the interfaces. In disconnecting the router from the network, it is best to disconnect the devices they connect to. The reason for this is that a disconnected interface can result in lost evidence.

In the event that an active network connection needs to be monitored (such as an ongoing attack), always seek authorization from management. It is also necessary to take any additional steps that are required to minimize the chance of further loss. There will be times when the risk of monitoring an ongoing situation will be outweighed by the added benefit obtained from monitoring and recording the activities and network traffic associated with an incident. It is essential that the determination and planning for this type of response has occurred prior to an incident occurring. When an incident occurs, it is too late to decide to track the network connection.

Make a record

As with any forensic investigation, it is essential to keep detailed notes. Ensure that you maintain a record of the time, date, and other information. This information should include the name of the person who discovered the problem and how you were made aware of the issue. Each time any change is made or any activity is undertaken, make a note describing the actions, the results, and the place and time at which they occurred.

Interview the point of contact

Before accessing any SCADA device or system component, find out as much information about the device as possible. To do this, you will need to interview the point of contact (POC) for the device. This person is likely to be a network administrator or other such person within the organization. Interviewing this person is important as they should have valuable information about the device. At a minimum, you should attempt to obtain the following information:

- Network diagrams
- Configuration details
- Change logs if available
- Authentication credentials

The configuration of SCADA systems, control servers, and even network routers can vary significantly even across similar devices (Hull et al., 2012). Logging information, for instance, can be maintained locally on the device or sent to a secure logging server. With access to this information, you can start to plan which services and functions on the router are likely to be the most volatile and likely to change.

Preinvestigation tasks

Before accessing the device, there are a few preliminary tasks that will ensure success. Many organizations will not have all of the documents listed here, but they will generally have many of these. Starting this process will allow you to see what you have and what is missing. These are as follows:

1. Determine the scope. What is it that you are planning to investigate?
2. Determine the risk. What information is the most crucial and what will be lost first?
3. Detail what your requirements are. Why are you conducting the investigation?
4. Collect the system and network design documentation. This can be broken down into the following components:
   a. System logical/infrastructure diagram. This is a diagram showing the components of the system in enough detail to support the concept-of-operations document.
   b. Concept-of-operations document for systems. This document details the purpose of each system (what is the purpose of the system; what does it do/provide?):
      i. How it fulfills that purpose—how does it tick?
      ii. Component dependencies on other components—what parts of the system rely on the external systems and interdependencies?
      iii. Other parts of the system; what do they rely on them for and how?
5. List of mandatory requirements
   a. This component should detail exactly what mandatory requirements the organization is required by legislation to meet. Attach copies of the relevant parts of the legislation.
   b. This should also show, in a matrix, how you have met each regulation in enough detail so that there is no doubt that all the requirements have been met or about how this has been done.

6. Risk-based requirements
   a. This should be a map of the prioritized countermeasures mapped out to the risks identified in the risk assessment, with specific reference to those countermeasures designed to counter the specific risks.
   b. Evidence is required that illustrates why the countermeasures are considered effective.
7. List of critical configurations
   a. These are the critical configurations that should be checked or changed on a regular basis so as to ensure integrity of the system. The list may include the following:
      i. Device configuration (rule sets, object definitions, filter lists).
      ii. System passwords and access methods.
      iii. Logging and monitoring systems.
      iv. The designers should also specify how these configurations/settings can be most efficiently checked on a regular basis.
8. Detailed configuration documentation
   a. This document should cover the detailed configurations of each component of the system. For non-security-enforcing devices, it should cover at least the following information for each component:
      i. Host name
      ii. Network address
      iii. Function
      iv. O/S version and patch level
      v. Application configuration settings
      vi. User accounts (including enable/privileged accounts)
      vii. Integrity testing settings
      viii. Interface details
9. Detailed network diagrams, clearly indicating the following:
   a. Host names of all components.
   b. Network addresses of all components.
   c. Function of all components.
   d. Network addresses of all network segments.
   e. Netmasks of all network segments.
   f. Any virtual local area networks (VLANs) and virtual private networks (VPNs).
   g. Policy documents, any related policy. This is likely to include an access policy.
   h. The access policy should contain at least those services that are allowed to be
      i. Externally accessible by anyone
      ii. Externally accessible by customers
      iii. Externally accessible by external support providers
      iv. Available to all internally connected clients
   i. Access between internal networks, especially those networks that have different requirements for different levels of security. This should detail those services that are allowed between internal-network segments:
      i. Those services to be allowed on an individual basis
      ii. Those services available only from the system management segment
      iii. Those services available only from the systems console
10. Procedures and plans
    a. Change-implementation procedures
    b. Operational support procedures
    c. Contingency plans (something could go wrong during the test)

This process should provide information that will allow you to understand your organization in a more complete manner. This includes

- Whether the information provided is required for services used to conduct business
- What level of security is needed to validly conduct business, including that which is permitted, denied, and logged
- Defining from where and by whom are connections and services needed

In testing services and systems over the network, the end result is an increased understanding of what is running. Any interaction with a device will change the volatile evidence it contains. Do not waste this. Use this to create an understanding of what and why. Most crucially, document each and every step you make.

It is generally best to make a direct connection to a SCADA hardware component via the console port rather than accessing it through a network connection. Where a direct connection to the console port is not possible, the use of the encrypted protocol secure shell (SSH) to remotely access the device is warranted if enabled.

Document your steps

One of the most important links to remember is to record what you do. When using a number of interactive tools, it will be possible to save the commands issued and the output from these. In addition, screenshots and general notes add value to your investigation.

Volatile data collection procedures

There are a number of key points to remember when collecting volatile evidence from a hardware component of a SCADA system. These points are listed later. Depending on the situation, it may be necessary to disconnect selected interfaces or attached devices, but always attempt to minimize any changes to the device.

Do
- Access the device through the console where possible
- Record your entire console session—starting *before* connecting to the device
- Run show commands from a script
- Record the actual time and the router's time—take screenshots
- Record the volatile information

Do not
- *Reboot*
- Access the device through the network unless it is isolated
- Run configuration commands
- Rely only on persistent information

Documentation

Always maintain a log of all commands you have run. Take screenshots and, where possible, script the commands that you will issue on the device and log the output from these commands.

You can never document too much!

Once the functionality of the system is captured, the use of software functional flows through tools, including unified modeling language (UML) activity diagrams, can be completed or updated (frequently, this process is completed for the first time). Following this, system integration points and dependencies are determined, and the system security can be analyzed in order to determine the source of an initial compromise.

SCADA forensics means collecting volatile evidence

One of the most crucial aspects of digital forensics is one of the most often overlooked. This is the gathering of volatile data as evidence. When investigating a SCADA system for possible evidence or information and facts relevant to the case, it is important to ensure that you have collected all relevant volatile data. In fact, if network logging is enabled, it may be the prime source of information for analysis. Volatile data maintain current information about the system, the registry, cache, and memory. Network captures are volatile until a recording regime is implemented, at which point they can become long-term storage that may be used to posthumously review what has occurred with respect to a system. They allow us to step back in time and see what occurred as well as to analyze a system after the event.

If an attacker has modified the password or the organization has forgotten it, it may be necessary to gather as much information as possible by using network scanning techniques. This process can be used to obtain limited amounts of nonvolatile information even when no access to the device is available.

In all events, if the system is powered down, valuable information is lost and may not be recovered. Worse, many SCADA systems cannot be powered down even if a known compromise exists. With nonvolatile memory, however, the data are not lost when the power is cycled. As such, network and memory traces should be maintained off-line for future analysis.

Some of the most crucial areas to check for evidence within volatile data include registers, cache, physical and virtual memory, network connections, running processes, and disk (for instance, the cache file). Any external device associated with the system should also be considered and checked for evidence (floppy, tape, CD/ROM, and printers). Captured data must then be gathered and saved in external devices so that it may be safely removed and kept off-line at another location.

RFC 3227 lists the order of volatility in a computer system as

- Registers, cache
- Routing table, address resolution protocol (ARP) cache, process table, kernel statistics
- Memory
- Temporary file systems
- Disk
- Remote logging and monitoring data that are relevant to the system in question
- Physical configuration, network topology
- Archival media

Where possible, this order of collection should be followed with SCADA systems with the exception that selected evidence should be captured prior to an event as a routine function.

Deploying SCADA forensic tools

When you are conducting a forensic investigation on a desktop computer or standard server, there is no shortage of tools available; however, the standard forensics tools do not cover the majority of SCADA hardware available. In either case, there are far fewer tools available for the analysis of a SCADA system than there are for a typical digital forensic investigation. An analysis of a standard system or network remains promising and, where possible, a hex dump of the system can be the most important thing to obtain. With this information, a standard forensic analysis may be conducted, and in many cases the file system can be checked for known malware signatures and may also be compared to the flashed software that should be installed.

Hex dumps of the file system

A hex dump of the system is a physical acquisition of the systems memory. In the majority of systems available, this will necessitate the use of a "flasher" system. This is a specialist support tool that is designed for the repair and servicing of SCADA hardware and control systems (including remote terminal units [RTUs] and programmable logic controllers [PLCs]). The benefit to the auditor is that these systems allow for the dumping of the systems memory. These are called "flashers" as they enable the manipulation of the flash memory on the system.

Note that the forensic process is highly dependent on the make and model of the system.

Where possible, a hex dump of the system is the most important thing to obtain if the logic card, PLC, or other hardware-based system is suspected and network traces have not been maintained. With this information, a standard forensic analysis may be conducted, and in many cases the file system can be checked for known malware signatures and compared against the expected file signatures to determine changes to the file system.

Operating systems

There are too many SCADA systems to cover in a single chapter, but luckily, most of the systems will either run one of the common ones, or the operating system (OS) will not be of great consequence to the analysis process. The main operating systems that the SCADA forensic analyst needs to have some knowledge of are included next.

Microsoft Windows CE, 95, and 98 (embedded)

Microsoft Windows is becoming more common in embedded SCADA. The WinCE operating system is in effect the same as that used by many early Windows PDAs. There are numerous emulation products that can be used to both mount the captured file system and to emulate the effects of malicious code that has been captured from one of these systems.

Linux variants

Linux has been implemented both by a number of SCADA system vendors as well as being used as a loader for other systems.

The analysis process for Linux-based systems is essentially the same as the imaging process for any other SCADA system. The benefit is that when an image has been captured, it can be mounted for analysis within a UNIX-based system or any common forensic tool.

Malicious code and the SCADA system

There are just as many reasons why an attacker would want to take over a SCADA system as a standard desktop computer or server, and the list of these reasons is growing. In fact, there are all the reasons to attack a standard computer system and many more. In general, an attacker will be looking for any of the data that one would generally expect to find on any other system. This can include system configurations, control lists, and personal information. In addition, there are specific targeted reasons to attack individual SCADA systems that present further security issues.

Managing the environment

- Network captures and analysis
- Logs and data stores
- The hosting environment
- Software

As much of the SCADA environment will be outside the reach of a forensic investigation (for instance, it is generally rare to be able to remove and flash an RTU), it is important to obtain as many sources of information as possible. Network logs, traffic captures, and other sources of evidence can be maintained without great cost due to the low cost of storage.

In many SCADA environments, a complete dump of all traffic passing the network (maintained for all time) can generally be created and stored in perpetuity for under $10,000. In the event of an incident, this allows the investigator to analyze traffic to and from the various components in the SCADA system post event—in effect, to look back in time and see what occurred.

As any attack will generally propagate across the network, a complete capture can be used to determine attacks, to carve out malicious code, and to create a timeline of events that have occurred.

It is important to manage logs and the security of the captures as it is likely that these will contain a wealth of information (including user names and passwords) that could aid an attacker. For this reason, logs should be maintained in an isolated system where access is restricted and information is not transmitted to less secure networks.

Volatility

When analyzing any hardware device, it is essential to comprehend and take into consideration the volatility of data. The analyst must consider

- Understanding forensic data spoilage and decay
- Understanding volatility in SCADA systems
- How to minimize data loss while maintaining evidence and system availability

SCADA cards (such as PLCs and RTUs) commonly store evidential data in volatile memory. These data are commonly destroyed on power-cycling the system. The protocols utilized by the SCADA system vendor need to be adhered to when accessing information in a forensically sound manner. Assuming that the operating system of a SCADA system has not been modified, either by the user or through the introduction of malicious code, represents a flawed approach to the forensic process. Attackers have been known to replace the operating system (such as with Linux variants), and shellcode attacks are becoming more common.

Determining the event

- Assessing an event
- Data recovery and collection
- Examination of live systems
- Tracing, filtering, and extraction of data
- Analysis

Intrusion detection

To effectively implement any intrusion detection, the system being used to control access to data must be able to identify and authenticate users. This also implements the simplest form of intrusion prevention (users must log on), and is the foundation of auditing. Both network intrusion detections systems (NIDS) and host intrusion detections systems (HIDS) can be implemented.

The initial step in implementing a successful intrusion detection system (IDS) is to create a baseline of normal traffic. This reduces the likelihood of false positives. An IDS that is designed to detect anomalous behavior is known as a behavior-based IDS. An IDS that works by using a library of signatures (similar to how the majority of antivirus software functions) is categorized as a knowledge-based IDS.

The design and architecture of the network is critical to the successful implementation of an IDS due to the effects of collision domains across the network. Host-based IDSs can be used to identify attacks that are derived from the host itself (HIDS management can be an issue due to a combination of factors such as cost and correlation management).

Snort

Snort is the *de facto* standard for intrusion detection/prevention. It is an open-source network intrusion prevention and detection system utilizing a rule-driven language, which combines the benefits of signature, protocol, and anomaly based inspection methods (see http://www.snort.org/ for more details).

Incident handling

The term *incident* is defined as any irregular or adverse event that occurs to any part of the organization. Some examples of possible incidents include

- Compromise of system integrity
- Denial of system resources
- Illegal access to a system (either a penetration or an intrusion)
- Malicious use of system resources
- Any kind of damage to a system

Some possible scenarios for security incidents are

1. Any strange process running and accumulating a lot of central processing unit time
2. Discovering an intruder logged into a system
3. Discovering malware has infected the system
4. Being alerted to a remote site as it is attempting to penetrate the system

The steps involved in handling a security incident are categorized into six stages:

1. Protection of the system
2. Identification of the problem
3. Containment of the problem
4. Eradication of the problem
5. Recovering from the incident
6. The follow-up analysis

The actions taken in some of these stages are common to all types of security incidents.

Attackers are not terribly considerate, and attacks may occur at any time of the day or night in our permanently connected Internet world. In the case of targeted attacks, an attacker is more likely to attack the site during the organization's off hours (including weekends and public holidays).

It is important to know how long it will take the staff to respond. Earlier in the book, we covered time-based security. If it takes a system administrator 24 hours to respond on a weekend, it is unlikely that they will stop an attack. It is also likely that the attacker will have sufficient time to be able to destroy evidence or cover up their attack.

Both time and distance are important considerations when considering incident response. Where it is unlikely that the primary contact will be able to respond within a reasonable time frame, a secondary contact must be called in addition to the initial person. It is the responsibility of the employees on the incident call list to establish whether they are able to respond to the incident within an acceptable time frame.

Another important consideration is the press. If a member of the press obtains information concerning a security incident, it is likely that an attempt to gather further information concerning the incident will be made. Worse, they will attempt to obtain this information from personnel on site. These personnel are likely to be involved in responding to the incident when the press calls. Not only does this interrupt the incident process, but providing information to the wrong individuals can have detrimental side effects.

Keeping a log book

Logging of information is critical in any situation that could end up in court. Any incident has the potential to end up in a criminal trial. At the beginning of an incident, the implications remain unknown and may only be discovered during the course of the investigation (if at all). A written log should be maintained for all security incidents that are being investigated. This notebook should be kept in a location that is not generally accessible to others and in a format that is not easily altered (i.e., do not take notes using a pencil). The log book should be maintained at least for the minimum statutory period.

The types of information that should be logged are

- Dates and times of incident-related phone calls
- Dates and times when incident-related events were discovered or occurred

- Amount of time spent working on incident-related tasks
- People you have contacted or have contacted you
- Names of systems, programs, or networks that have been affected

Informing the appropriate people

It is important that the appropriate people are informed as soon as an incident is determined. What is more important, though, is to have a list of these people prior to the incident. Preparation is important.

It is also important to be able to contact people quickly. This means keeping the phone numbers and contact details of key contacts and ensuring that alternate contacts are defined.

Follow-up analysis

Postincident response is just as important as the procedures used to determine and respond to the incident. Once the incident has been dealt with and systems have been restored to a satisfactory condition (ideally being in a normal mode of operation), a postmortem analysis can occur in order to discover what went wrong.

All involved parties (or a delegate from each group) should be present at a meeting to discuss the actions that were taken during the incident. This should culminate in the creation of a lessons-learned document. Where necessary, existing procedures should be evaluated and modified.

The outcome of this process should include a set of recommendations that should be presented to the suitable management representatives. The security incident report needs to be written and distributed to the appropriate parties.

The forensic process

- The methodology in SCADA environments
- Live forensics
- Network forensics

SCADA systems are collations of standard Windows systems, network devices, and specialized control systems (such as those based on programmable logic controllers [PLCs]). They are in effect a collection of integrated devices that incorporate the features of personal computers with hardware-based control units. This makes the analysis of these devices a composite exercise based on many systems, some of which are mission critical and cannot be removed from service.

The concept of SCADA forensics is very similar to the procedures and methodologies that are used with any form of forensics. When we discuss SCADA forensics, there are investigative methods that you should use when performing a forensic investigation of such a device that are the same as those used in a normal computer, and there are also some that differ. In some cases, the SCADA device or controller is effectively a small UNIX computing platform or an embedded system (including WinCE). In others, such as those running the Windows operating system, they are analogous to a standard Windows host or server (the control and management systems are generally deployed using Windows or Unix hosts with all the standard issues).

Components of a SCADA system

The SCADA system has several components. Our intent here is to discuss some of the more common ones. The other components include the following:

- The first component is the human–machine interface (HMI). This is the control or management system that allows the operator to interact with the system. This component of the SCADA system includes some form of input device, such as a keypad or touch screen.
- RTUs (remote terminal units). These convert sensor signals, allowing them to be transmitted digitally.
- Supervisory systems to process signals and send commands to the units.
- PLC (programmable logic controllers). These are small integrated systems and can be single-chip devices. A PLC is similar to any other microprocessor except that there generally is a restriction on its size and it is limited through its power consumption.
- Networking systems. Often overlooked in the description of a SCADA system, the network is the backbone passing all traffic to and from the various components within the system.
- Databases and reporting systems. These include logging and historical collation.

Investigative methods of SCADA forensics

There are four main steps when it comes to performing a forensic investigation of any device:

1. Examination
2. Identification
3. Collection
4. Documentation

We start off by securing the evidence. It is essential that you follow a process that has been approved by legal counsel to secure the evidence collected from the SCADA system. The examiner can rarely if ever seize a SCADA device, so this should not be a consideration. This is probably one of the most difficult aspects of a SCADA environment. The best means to analyze attacks and incidents is to have a complete set of network traces if these are available. This is seldom the case, however, and the limited amount of data collected in many sites makes a complete analysis difficult.

Investigative methods: Step 1—Examination

In the examination step of forensics, you first need to understand the potential sources of the evidence, which can be the systems, the network, the office systems, and any other peripherals or media that the system being examined has come into contact with or can connect to. In addition to these sources, you should also investigate any system that has a relationship to the SCADA system being examined. These include

- Access terminals
- Logging servers
- Routers

Investigative methods: Step 2—Identification

In the identification step of forensics, you start the process by identifying the type of system you are investigating. Once you have identified the system, you then have to identify the operating system that the system is using, the types and manufacture of the PLCs, and the network design and implementation.* It is critical to the investigative process that you determine the operating system and manufacture of each device in the system (including those you may not consider, such as the routers and switches). Furthermore, once you have identified the operating systems, it is important to note that it is possible that the system could be running two operating systems (such as a Linux variant). Many SCADA systems run a child system over a base OS. During the identification process, there are several sources that can assist you, including the manufacturer's documentation, the design specifications, network diagrams, and the HMI itself. Always collect the manufacturer serial number, the PLC type, and the supervisory system itself.

The Internet is a good place to research different manufacturer specifications.

Investigative methods: Step 3—Collection

During this part of the forensic investigation, it is imperative that you collect data and potential evidence from the memory systems that are part of, or are suspected to be part of, the SCADA system being investigated. There are over 1000 types of SCADA systems available today and many types of control and management systems that work with them. All of these connect using networks, and all network traffic over these links can be captured. It is important to understand the limitations of the system being analyzed and when a drive can be copied.

It is imperative that you collect all of the types of information consisting of both volatile and dynamic information and across the various cards and controller units. Consequently, it is imperative that you give the volatile information priority while you collect evidence. The reason for giving this information priority is because anything that is classified as volatile information will not survive over time and as the system is utilized.

Many believe that a SCADA system can be air-gapped or isolated. With wireless, 3G, and other forms of connectivity, it is rarely the case that SCADA networks are isolated. Network traffic analysis should also aim to capture any "rogue" and misplaced traffic that does not "fit" the network.

Investigative methods: Step 4—Documentation

As with any stage of the forensic process, it is critical to maintain comprehensive documentation and ensure the "chain of custody." In collecting information and potential evidence, always record all visible data. The records you have created need to include the case number and the date and the time when the evidence was collected. Many investigators will also photograph the entire investigation process, including any systems that could be connected to the SCADA system or that are at present connected to it. This also helps in determining where the examiner may need to connect to later.

---

* Many older SCADA systems do not use TCP-/IP-based networks. These can still be captured and analyzed at the layer two level and can be dissected as with any other network packet.

One element of this process of documenting the scene includes the generation of a report. This document consists of the detailed information that describes the entire forensic process being performed. This report will include the state and status of the captured system throughout the collection process. The last stage in the collection process consists of gathering all of the information together and storing it in a secure and safe location.

SCADA investigative tips

When it comes to the SCADA system, there are several things you need to consider while carrying out an investigation. SCADA systems can be managed and maintained at all times. A further complication is the fact that unknown backdoors into SCADA systems can provide a suspect or attacker with immediate access 24 hours a day, 7 days a week from a remote location. With GPRS, 3G, and other network technologies being incorporated into SCADA systems, the likelihood of a remote command being executed is constantly increasing. These backdoors include authorized networks designed to connect remote users to the system by design or as a means for engineers to work remotely.

The National Institute of Standards and Technology (NIST) document *Guide to Supervisory Control and Data Acquisition (SCADA) and Industrial Control System Security* (800–82) is an excellent source of detailed information for those who want to learn more on SCADA security concerns and practices.

Some points to remember in conducting an investigation include the following:

- If the system is "ON," do *not* turn it "OFF," as turning the system "OFF" could result in physical system damage.
- Write down all information on display and, where possible, photograph it.
- If the system is "OFF," leave it "OFF" as, like a desktop computer, turning it on could change or destroy evidence.
- Attempt to get hold of the instruction manuals that pertain to the system.
- Interaction with the SCADA system can result in the destruction of evidence. It is essential not to interrogate the control system without following set procedures.

Available hardware

Access to a range of hardware is an issue that impacts SCADA system forensics. The combination of proprietary hardware and a lack of support from the existing forensic tool suites make acquisition difficult. Moreover, accessing the systems can be difficult in itself with the requirements to limit downtime. The difficulty is that existing forensic tools (excluding forensic analysis against the Windows and Linux systems in the SCADA network) do not generally support these systems, with many producers creating SCADA systems that are only accessible using proprietary computer software.

Forensically acquiring such systems is difficult if not impossible. The ease with which an error can overwrite evidence compounds this issue. With over 1000 separate system types, the level of complexity is only increasing. For the most part, the increasing domination of selected market leaders is making this process more streamlined for the majority of systems. The difficulty is with the less common makes.

Generally, all SCADA units will comprise a combination of common categories of hardware components:

- Microprocessor
- Visual display unit (this may be solely a function of the HMI)
- Read-only memory (ROM)
- Random-access memory (RAM)
- Main board
- Measurement devices and sensors
- Radio module and antenna
- Battery and charging unit
- Digital signal processor (DSP)
- Audio components (microphone and speaker)
- Human input interface (such as a keypad, keyboard, or touch screen)

The ROM will usually contain the OS. This is commonly loaded into RAM on boot, and in some cases access to the ROM is restricted. The RAM is most commonly a flash system that both stores the user data and databases as well as acting as memory to run programs on the system. Updating the operating system and programs frequently requires that the system is reflashed. For this reason, SCADA systems are commonly left running old and insecure versions of software/firmware and frequently contain backdoors and other vulnerabilities. Many vendors provide utilities that can be used to load updated ROM images to the system.

Generally, most models of SCADA system have cables and flashing equipment available that can be used by the auditor (although it is not common to find these in a standard jump bag). In many cases, this equipment is in fact designed for use by system service and repair personnel. This means that such equipment may be difficult to obtain for the less common models. Forensically sound access to the RAM and ROM contained on the SCADA units is also difficult to achieve. For this reason, a combination of approaches is necessary.

The techniques used to analyze data in computer forensics should be deployed following the capture of the image from the SCADA system. This makes SCADA system forensics a multiphase process with capture and examination commonly being done using separate tools. The amalgamation of hardware and software together in the acquisition of flash RAM from SCADA systems with some level of integrity is being challenged by advances in attack methodologies. The ability to execute malicious code using shellcode through the means of a buffer overflow allows the attacker to have code to run in memory while not being installed. As this code does not touch any storage systems (even flash), it adds an additional layer of complexity to the forensic process.

New techniques to extract data

Many systems do not allow users to readily access the protected areas of the system. In this case, the process of fault injection and differential fault analysis may be needed.

The following equipment is necessary to conduct fault analysis on a SCADA unit:

- Signal reader
- Digital oscilloscope
- Acquisition and analysis equipment and hardware and software programs
- Cables and other peripheral systems
- High-power microscope
- Laser

Fault testing involves a process of

1. *Identifying when to inject fault*: This is where the digital signal reader and oscilloscope come into use. The EM and voltage readings of a system will vary significantly when running different algorithms.
2. *Identify where to inject fault*: The differences noted in step (1) can be detected and marked as "break points" to inject faults.
3. *Fault injection*: There exist a limited number of research and commercial toolsets that can be used to inject faults into the SCADA system.
4. *Differential fault analysis to extract keys*: These methods have been used to extract keys from flash-based systems and cable networks for years.

Router and switch forensics

When viewed as a whole, SCADA systems incorporate a large amount of network systems. Routers, switches, and transmission equipment form the backbone of any SCADA system, yet most investigators do not understand how they work and how they fit into the bigger picture of security and functionality. Moreover, these devices form a core set of controls and monitoring systems that can be used to capture attacks that have occurred against a SCADA network or system.

With the extensive use of clear-text authentication protocols still in use on many SCADA systems, network controls and access are critical. Any attacker with the ability to compromise a network device has the ability to capture and intercept traffic going to and from the control stations and to change the responses and commands.

At its simplest, a router is designed to transmit packets between different networks. In addition, it can also act as a control point, filtering unwanted protocols, networks, and other security concerns. Routers also act as a gateway between local and wide area networks. Routers are often used as a relay for network attacks. Privileged access to the router may be used to reconfigure it or cause a denial of service (DoS). Controlling interactive logins to the router helps prevent these and other conditions from occurring.

The examples stated in this chapter use Cisco, which has the greatest market share of Internet-based routers. That stated, any router or switch can be substituted for the examples presented.

The role of SCADA systems during an investigation

Routers and switches are the most common product that the forensic investigator needs to become familiar with in a SCADA investigation. Although when working in a SCADA environment, the forensic investigator needs to become familiar with a wide range of products, network devices form the backbone of an analysis and allow for capture without impacting the SCADA equipment directly. The differences in the various brands and the volatile nature of the information stored within a router or switch make this field of forensics difficult for the novice. The main secret is to take the time to plan the investigation prior to accessing the device.

Attacks against routers are becoming more common due to their position in the network and their criticality for the continued operation of interconnected systems. The primary reasons that routers are attacked include that they

- Allow denial of service (DoS) attacks against the network
- Provide a platform to compromise other systems
- Offer the ability to bypass firewalls, IDSs, and other security devices through route changes
- Offer the ability to act as a sniffer on network monitor
- Offer the ability to intercept and modify traffic

The evidence available on the vast majority of routers is volatile in nature. This means that evidence will be lost if any number of events occur. These can be anything from a loss of power through to timeouts and natural system purges. Information contained in the active physical memory of the router will be lost on a power down. Additionally, static memory sources (such as flash memory) may be overwritten if an orderly shutdown is allowed to occur. Much of the information contained within a router that is related to a forensic investigation is volatile in nature. This can include dynamic route updates, ARP information, dynamic name caching, and even logs.

Routers are often used as a relay for network attacks. Privileged access to the router may be used to reconfigure it or cause a DoS attack. Controlling interactive logins to the router helps prevent these and other conditions from occurring.

Data capture

In switches and routers, flash memory is considered as being persistent and holds the start-up and configuration files and other files and information. This information is generally considered nonvolatile. The primary concern in the investigation of volatile router information is capturing information contained within the device's RAM. This will include the running configuration and any dynamic tables. These tables include data such as

- ARP
- Routing tables
- Network address translation (NAT) information
- Access control list (ACL) violations
- Interface statistics
- Protocol statistics
- Local logging

For the most part, an investigation of volatile information on the router will consist of an analysis of the device's dynamic random-access memory (DRAM) and static random-access memory (SRAM) states. For the most part, router intrusions will occur at the network perimeter. Intrusions are usually conducted in order to gain unauthorized access to other systems or to conduct eavesdropping attacks where the router is used as a network sniffer. An investigation into the volatile information of a router or switch is commonly conducted in order to find evidence of

- A direct compromise of the network device
- An analysis of the routing tables to detect manipulation
- An analysis of the ARP tables to detect manipulation
- Uncovering evidence of data theft

- Conducting an analysis of DoS attacks
- Investigating intermittent device reboots and network performance degradation

It is important to respond as soon as possible to a network attack if volatile data are to be collected successfully. Routers and switches generally save the stored configuration of the router in the nonvolatile RAM (NVRAM). The current configuration may not match the stored configuration. The current configuration is volatile data and is maintained within the device's RAM. If an intruder deletes the configuration or somebody power cycles the Cisco router, any information stored within the device's RAM will be lost.

Code reviews and testing third-party software

An in-depth study of a software audit is beyond the scope of this book; it is, however, necessary to touch on the subject. Testing methodologies that relate to software are described, as many SCADA systems are legacy based and poorly documented. As a result, a number of software testing methodologies may need to be deployed in analyzing these systems. These range from the black-box test commonly used when code is unavailable (such as in the case of third-party software reviews and reviews of package software) through to white-box and crystal-box assessments. In the latter, all code is available and tested.

It is not essential that the auditor understands the intricacies of coding. Rather, it is sufficient to understand how the various testing approaches function and to have sufficient understanding to be able to work with the test engineer who has designed the test cases associated with software in order to be able to understand their work. In particular, the auditor should be able to understand the reports produced by the test engineer.

We shall quickly rehash the types of software audit before going further. At the extremes, these are the following:

Black-box testing

Black-box software testing does not require any understanding of internal behavior. No access to code is available, but rather the response to input is validated. UML diagrams may be available in some instances, and in this case a test of functionality will be matched to the functional requirements in the specification. In any event, input will be matched to output to test for expected or unexpected behavior. Some of the various testing methods include

- Equivalence partitioning
- Boundary value analysis
- All-pairs testing
- Fuzzing
- Model-based testing
- Traceability matrix

White-box testing

This type of testing includes access to the internal data structures. At the extreme (crystal-box tests), the tester has access to all code, algorithms, and design notes. White-box testing will include tests to ensure predefined criteria have been met. Some examples of this form and testing include

- Static code testing
- Mutation testing
- Completeness testing
- Fault injection testing
- Lexical code analysis

Testing in combination

The most effective means of testing software comes from a combination of methods being deployed together. Unfortunately, access to code is not always available. In cases of packaged software and many third-party products, access to the code is restricted. Access to code is also effective in increasing the capabilities of the traditional black-box test (commonly called a gray-box test when code is available to conduct the test using black-box test methods).

Correcting a software problem after the event is far more expensive than stopping it before it goes into production release. It is often stated that postrelease fixes are in the order of hundreds of times more expensive to fix than correcting the issue in code and requirements reviews.

When auditing software, it is necessary to consider the following aspects of development associated with the code:

- Software quality
- Correctness
- Completeness
- Integrity
- Capability
- Reliability
- Efficiency
- Portability
- Maintainability
- Compatibility
- Usability

Test engineers will generally develop metrics to report on each of these aspects of software development.

Various levels of testing

Unit testing

Unit testing focuses on individual software modules (the components of the software). Each module is tested individually in order to validate the software implementation component by component. An example would be the testing of individual classes associated within an object-oriented development environment.

Integration testing

Integration testing is designed to uncover defects in the interfaces and interaction amid the integrated software modules. This form of testing starts with individual modules and joins them to form progressively larger associative groups. Each phase works on larger groupings until the software architecture is tested as an entire system.

Acceptance testing

Acceptance testing is conducted by the end user. The goal is to decide whether or not to accept the final software product. Acceptance testing may be conducted between development phases.

Regression testing

Regression testing is a process whereby a previously conducted test is rerun on the software. This type of testing is conducted in order to ensure that prior defects have not been reintroduced or regressed into the code. This type of testing is frequently automated.

Some specific types of regression testing include sanity testing (this is a check for unexpected and unforeseen behavior) and smoke testing (which is a test to ensure that the product provides basic functionality).

Testing cycles

There are many ways of engineering software. Each of these comes with its own test methodologies. One of the more common ones is the software development life cycle (SDLC). Some of the common foes involved with testing include the many phases of the project that are analogous to many other audit processes.

Requirements analysis

The first stage of testing generally starts with the creation of a document detailing what is necessary. In this phase, both developers and testers will work together to determine what tests may be conducted.

Test planning

This phase includes the creation of a strategy and the scope of the testing. Like an audit, system testing should be conducted as a project. Some areas to consider include

1. The creation of a test strategy
2. The formulation of a test plan
3. The creation of a test bed or other testing system

Test development

The development phase of testing involves the creation of a number of test procedures based on the requirements derived in the preceding stages. Some of the steps involved with this phase of testing include

1. The development of test procedures
2. The creation of test scenarios

3. Creating test cases and populating simulated data
4. The creation of test programs and scripts and possibly the sourcing of third-party testing software (such as the static analysis platforms by Fortify)

Test execution

The test execution phase involves the actual testing of the software based on the processors decided earlier. Any errors or defects in the code would then be reported to the development team.

Test reporting

In test reporting, test metrics that were developed in the preceding stages are coupled with data concerning errors and defects and possibly recommendations for improvement. This will also include recommendations as to whether the software needs further testing before being released.

Retesting the defects

Defects may be the result of either errors in the code or in the test process itself. It is necessary to ensure that any defects that are a result of the testing process are rectified. Defects may or may not be corrected. Many defects do not have a security-related consequence and could be left for future software versions.

UML and mapping processes

This book is not the place to delve into the intricacies of UML. To this end, a number of resources have been provided for those wishing to learn more. UML is a visual representation language designed for the purpose of modeling and communicating the information contained within systems. To do this, it uses a series of diagrams and supporting text.

It can provide details of many process fields such as the following:

- Actors; examples could include a manager leading a team executing a project and staff members on the project team
- The various processes that occur
- Relationships between actors and entities

Unified

In UML, "unified" refers to the Object Management Group (OMG) and Rational Software Corporation coming together to create an industry standard for engineering practices. This was a desire to create a common language.

Model

A model is a depiction of a subject. A model is used to encapsulate a set of ideas (called abstractions) concerning a subject. A model provides a simple means to create a common understanding among different team members and other individuals. This helps to create an understanding of the requirements of the system and to communicate the impact of changes that will occur to the system through development and use.

The creation of a model should be done in stages. An attempt to create a model all in one go is likely to become overwhelming. This may be possible with small systems, but large systems with many thousands of tables are beyond the human capacity to comprehend all at once.

When modeling, good practice dictates that the auditor will capture the relevant information that is required to gain an understanding of the problem at hand. This information may then be used to solve problems and issues that have arisen and will aid in the recommendation of a solution. It is also necessary to exclude information that is not relevant to the task at hand. It is easy to be waylaid by immaterial facts that can in no way lead to a change in the system or are not related to the scope of an audit.

In order to effectively manage the overall complexity involved within the audit of complex systems such as mainframes, models are an effective tool to achieve our goal. This process is best completed through the following:

- Managing the abstractions that make up the model
- Including enough detail to understand the abstraction but not so much as to sidetrack the audit
- Excluding irrelevant information
- Working with multiple teams to ensure that the model is relevant

Language

A language enables both people and systems to communicate about a subject. The subject incorporates the requirements and the system with respect to system development and audit. Language simplifies the process of communicating between individual team members and allows for the successful completion of the project.

Languages are not always composed of words. In fact, complex abstractions such as mathematics are languages.

UML is formally defined by its creators as a language for specifying, visualizing, constructing, and documenting the artifacts of a system-intensive process. This is a system-intensive process used as an approach that centers on a system. It includes the various stages used to both produce and maintain a system. This is based on the requirements of the system. The specification includes the creation of a model describing the system. This model simplifies the analysis of the system and allows even complex systems to be audited within a reasonable timeframe and scope.

This process involves visualization through the use of diagrams designed to render the model into a simple form so that it can be communicated. This diagram is then an expression of the system. It could be likened to a blueprint for a building. Ideally, this blueprint is designed before the building, but like many system-design projects, development of a model or blueprint has either been excluded or lost. The subsequent creation of this model through audit captures a baseline that can be used not only to understand the process at hand but can also be used in future reviews and assessments. Documenting these systems captures the knowledge and requirements associated with the system.

UML and processes

UML is not a process; it is a tool to capture processes and system design. A process relates a series of stages that are illustrated through the use of a methodology in order to decipher

an issue. It then enables the development of a system that is designed to satisfy the requirements of a system owner or users. UML can aid the forensic analyst in determining the
source and consequences of an attack against a SCADA system.

The use of the UML method addresses the following stages of the development process:

- Requirements or information gathering
- Analysis
- Design

This methodology addresses the entire development process, from the requirements
or information gathering through to the final analysis.

The distinct means of collecting and using requirements, analyzing requirements, and
finally designing a system are the techniques utilized. Artifacts are the "work products"
produced and used within a process. These include the documentation and the actual
system.

Each classification of UML diagram is known as a modeling technique.

The use of a UML diagram (as depicted in Figure 9.1) can greatly simplify the forensic
audit process for complex systems (such as SCADA networks).

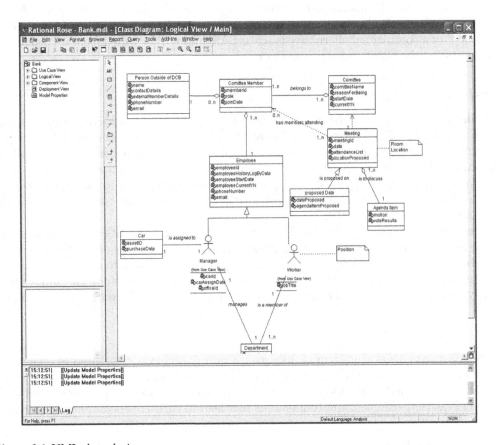

Figure 9.1 UML class designs.

Further information about UML

The following sites are the principal sources for information about the UML standard:

- The Object Management Group (OMG): http://www.omg.org and http://www.omg.org/uml
- Rational Software Corporation (IBM): http://www.rational.com and http://www.rational.com/uml

The subsequent sites present information concerning the next major change to the UML (the OCL) and a variety of other information on the subject:

- The object constraint language (OCL): http://www.klasse.nl/ocl/index.html
- The UML Forum is a virtual community concerning the UML: http://www.uml-forum.com
- The Cetus Team provides UML tools, methodologies, and processes: http://www.cetus-links.org

Analyzing logs, traffic, and unstructured data

The data stored in logs and other captures in a well-secured and monitored SCADA system can be analyzed by the forensic examiner for defined classifications and labels. A random forest (Ho, 1995) classification algorithm will be implemented using the R statistical language* or a commercial alternative (such as SAS) and will be called from unstructured data sent from the client and server systems.

Unstructured data

Log files are text based for the most part, and text is generally considered to be unstructured (Cherkassky and Mulier, 1998). However, nearly all documents demonstrate a rich amount of semantic and syntactical structure that may be used to form a framework in structuring data. Typographical elements such as punctuation, capitalization, white space, and carriage returns, for instance, can provide a rich source of information that will be used in the creation of data grammars for use in analyzing forensic events in a SCADA system (Berry and Linoff, 1997).

The use of these elements can aid in determining paragraphs, titles, dates, and so on. These in turn may be used to formulate structure in the data. This of course returns to the field of computational linguistics in an attempt to give meaning to groups of words or phrases and layout. With this, the SCADA analyst can make sense of the vast amounts of data collected in the course of logging and collecting what could be years' worth of data.

Characters, words, terms, and concepts

At the most basic level, this form of document mining system is structured to take input from raw documents in order to create output in the form of patterns, trends, and other useful output formats. The result is a system designed to be an iterative process through a loop of queries, searches, and refinements that lead to further sets of queries, searches,

---

* R is available from http://cran.r-project.org/.

and refinements (Fieldman and Sanger, 2007). For each of these iterative phases, the output should move closer to the desired result, which will be algorithmically determined and stored.

In the creation of this system, the general model of classic data mining is roughly followed (Fieldman and Sanger, 2007):

1. Preprocessing tasks
   a. Document fetching/crawling techniques
   b. Categorization
   c. Feature/term extraction
2. Core mining operations
   a. Distributions
   b. Frequent and near frequent sets
   c. Associations
   d. Isolating interesting patterns
   e. Analyzing document collections over time
3. Presentation and browsing functionality
   a. Pattern identification
   b. Trend analysis
   c. Browsing functionality
      i. Simple filters
      ii. Query interpreter
      iii. Search interpreter
      iv. Visualization tools
      v. Graphical user interface (GUI)
      vi. Graphing
4. Refinement
   a. Suppression
   b. Ordering
   c. Pruning
   d. Generalization
   e. Clustering

Preprocessing includes the routines, processes, and methods required to prepare data for a text-mining systems core knowledge-discovery operation and will generally take original data and apply extraction methods to categorize a new set of documents represented by concepts.

Core mining operations include pattern discovery trend analysis and incremental knowledge-discovery algorithms, and they form the backbone of the text-mining process. Together, preprocessing and core mining are the most critical areas for any text-mining system. These stages will be carefully monitored to ensure that they are correctly implemented. This is important, as a failure to implement this stage could produce data with little value (Fieldman and Sanger, 2007), and the storage of complete files (in place of hash values) could even result in negative consequences.

When analyzing data, common patterns include distributions concept sets, and associations may include comparisons. The goal of this process is to ascertain relationships and hence discover any "nuggets" of valuable information from undiscovered relationships. This will extend the e-Discovery function of the database into alerting the analyst to anomalies and unexpected events that can be used for future pattern discovery.

Cluster dendrogram

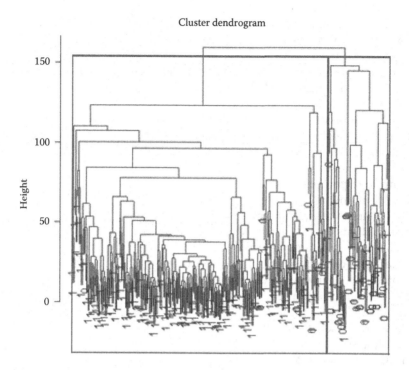

Figure 9.2 RF algorithms will sort grammars into the classification database.

Presentation layer components include GUI and pattern-browsing functionality and may include access to character and language editors and optimizers. This stage includes the creation of concept clusters and also the formulation of annotated profiles for specific concepts of patterns.

Refinement (which is also called postprocessing) techniques include methods that filter redundant information and cluster closely related data. This stage may include suppression ordering pruning generalization and clustering approaches aimed at discovery optimization (Figure 9.2).

Algorithmic classification

Random forests tend to be very stable in model building. Their relative insensitivity to the noise that breaks down single decision-tree induction models makes them compare favorably to boosting approaches, while they are generally more robust against the effects of noise in the training dataset. This makes them a favorable alternative to nonlinear classifiers like artificial neural nets and support vector machines.

Each decision tree in the forest is constructed using a random subset of the training dataset using the techniques of bagging (replacement). A number of entities will thus be included more than once in the sample, and others will be left out. This generally lies in the ratios of two-thirds to one-third for inclusion/exclusion.

In the construction of each decision-tree model, an individual random subset of the training dataset uses a random subset of the presented variables in order to decide where to partition the dataset at each node. No pruning is performed as all decision trees are assembled to their maximum magnitude. The process of building each decision tree to

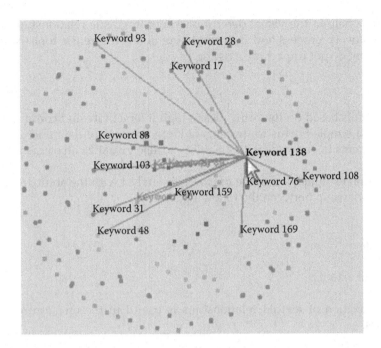

Figure 9.3 Keyword network views and association maps.

its maximal depth results in a less biased model. The entirety of the decision-tree models taken together form the forest. In this, the forest characterizes the final ensemble model. Each decision tree in this model effectively casts a vote, with the majority outcome being classified as the outcome. In the case of regression models, the average value over the ensemble of regression trees is averaged to produce the assessment (Figure 9.3).

The use of and implementation of a random forest model is favored in analyzing SCADA logs and captures for a number of reasons:

1. The amount of preprocessing that needs to be performed on the data is minimal at most.
2. The data do not need to be normalized and the approach is resilient to outliers.
3. Variable selection is generally not necessary in the event that numerous input variables are present prior to model building.
4. All of the individual decision trees are in effect independent models. When taken with the multiple levels of randomness that exists within random forests, these models tend not to overfit to the training dataset.

This approach will allow for an automated implementation of the defined classification scheme.

Keyword network view

Keyword network views display relationships between keywords. In these, the most frequent keywords appear in the center of the view, with the less frequent keywords appearing on the outskirts of the circle. When a specific keyword is selected, lines are drawn from that keyword to all relating keywords.

These maps help in the visual determination of linguistic relationships and will aid both the e-Discovery process and in formulating detailed forensic tools for the SCADA environment that do not impact the existing devices.

Visualization

Visualization tools based on the principles of high interactivity and coordinated multiple views provide a simple means to investigate large volumes of data and allow the highlighting of elements in one view with an ability to also visualize an element differently in another view.

Visualization techniques provide the forensic analyst with the ability to create a comprehensive relationship between the following:

- Accounts
- Keywords
- Time
- Patterns of activity

The visualization of textual relationships is useful in the creation of classification methodologies.

Summary

The chapter started with an introduction to SCADA system forensics. We continued the discussion with a look at the concept of SCADA network forensics and how many of the same things must be considered in forensics on normal systems. We also discussed some of the differences that must be considered when performing forensics on SCADA systems. We then discussed the methods of investigating a SCADA system and detailed a number of issues with the components in that system. We talked about securing the evidence and how the SCADA system should be seized. The next method we discussed was the acquiring of the evidence. We covered the need to create an exact image of the evidence, and once the evidence is secured and acquired, the need to go on and examine the evidence that was acquired.

It needs to be noted that security exclusions within SCADA systems often leave the most critical systems in many environments vulnerable to attack. In some cases, the organization is aware of this vulnerability, maintaining an unfounded perception that nothing can ever be done. This is far from the truth. It is essential to take a risk-based approach that truly ascertains the risk associated with all systems, even those forgotten ugly sisters. The techniques involved with testing mainframes (such as documentation using UML) also work well with other types of testing. For instance, network and firewall tests map well to functionality analysis using UML. Having these tests can aid and simplify the inevitable forensic incident that will one day occur.

References

Berry, M. and Linoff, G. (1997). *Data Mining Techniques (For Marketing, Sales, and Customer Support)*. Indianapolis: John Wiley.

Cardwell, G. S. (2011). Residual network data structures in android devices. Masters thesis, Computer Science Department. Naval Postgraduate School. California, Retrieved from http://faculty.nps.edu/cdprince/mwc/docs/THESIS/2011-08_thesisCardwell.pdf.

Cherkassky, V. and Mulier, F. M. (1998). *Learning from Data: Concepts, Theory, and Methods.* New York: Wiley.

Decker, M., Kruse, W., Long, B., and Kelley, G. (2011). Dispelling common myths of "Live Digital Forensics." *DFCB.* Retrieved from www.dfcb.org/docs/LiveDigitalForensics-MythVersusReality.pdf.

Feldman, R. and Sanger, J. (2007). *The Text Mining Handbook, Advanced Approaches in Analysing Unstructured Data.* Cambridge: Cambridge University Press.

Ho, T. K. (1995). *Random Decision Forest.* Proceedings of the 3rd International Conference on Document Analysis and Recognition, Montréal, Canada.

Hull, J., Khurana, H., Markham, T., and Staggs, K. (2012). Staying in control: Cybersecurity and the modern electric grid. *IEEE Power & Energy.* pp. 41–48. IEEE. Retrieved from http://magazine.ieee-pes.org/january-february-2012/staying-in-control/ and http://magazine.ieee-pes.org/files/2011/12/10mpe01-hull.pdf.

Weiss, M. and Solomon, M. G. (2011). *Auditing IT Infrastructures for Compliance.* Sudbury, MA: Jones & Bartlett Learning.

chapter ten

Governance and compliance

Wayne Boone (revised by Allan McDougall)

Contents

General

The protection and assurance* of supervisory control and data acquisition (SCADA) systems throughout all phases of operations falls under the purview of asset protection and security (AP&S) specialists as part of an integrated security program. Unlike a project, which has a start and end date, separately dedicated resources, and, most importantly, a set of deliverables to hand over to business line managers, a program is ongoing and supports the business objectives of the enterprise both routinely and after a major interruption. An integrated program features all AP&S functions under the line or functional[†] control of a senior security official within the organization.

---

* Assurance in this case refers to the continued provision of availability, integrity, and confidentiality (in that order) of information and services provided by a SCADA system.

† A line relationship refers to a superior–subordinate relationship in which the superior has the authority to assign and commit the subordinate's activities, resources, and time. The superior can essentially command the subordinate to perform legitimate tasks. A functional replacement exerts control, not through command or direction, but through setting the parameters that are considered to be acceptable within an organization. One way to look at this is to see line authority as the ability to require work to be done, while functional authority defines how that work is to be done to satisfy management's requirements.

Given their relative lack of integration within an enterprise, their distributed architecture, their often dated technology and lack of built-in security (Nicholson et al. 2012), and their nexus to national objectives,* SCADA systems require especially effective governance and oversight. The lack of technical uniformity in legacy SCADA systems (Mahoney and Gandhi 2011), the relative ease of connectivity among information systems (ISs), the traditional reliance on physical security safeguards to protect ISs (Markulec 2008), and the focus on availability or "uptime" of ISs (sometimes to the detriment of integrity and confidentiality) all result in potential risks that must be identified, analyzed, assessed, and then managed. Risk management has been discussed in detail in Chapter 4. This chapter discusses the role of governance and oversight in support of enterprise risk management. As a contextual statement:

Governance + Safeguards + Oversight + Continual Risk Assessment = Risk Management

Risk management is an ongoing activity, meaning that it requires a *program*. It requires dedicated resources (personnel, material, information, and processes) that are focused on the production of measurable results; in this case, the protection of the availability, integrity, and confidentiality (AIC) of valued assets such as SCADA systems. Risk can be described in terms of the probability that the organization will suffer some negative effect or condition and has been discussed in other chapters of this book. Risk management deals with the measures and controls that are put in place to ensure that the level of risk to which the organization is exposed does not reach unacceptable levels. This is a constant balancing act that requires management to plan, implement, monitor, and adjust various different kinds of controls.

These controls are often communicated as requirements within the organization. Generally, they are defined to address vulnerabilities (the most controllable of the factors contributing to risk) by reducing the means or opportunity associated with some form of attack. These controls, however, are fluid (they can degrade or evolve) and operate within a fluid environment (climate, demand, etc.). Within any effective risk management program is a process for continually reviewing changes to the accepted risk posture, based on changes to the mission, supporting assets, threats to those assets, or emerging vulnerabilities of those assets. Once the risk level becomes significant, changes are made to implemented safeguards or additional safeguards are introduced to mitigate the risk to a level acceptable to senior management.

Before proceeding further, the difference between governance and oversight should be made clear. *Governance* provides the structural *framework* for the risk management program to operate effectively. It consists of a suite of requirements (legal, regulatory, policy) as well as roles and responsibilities. *Oversight* provides the *processes* for ensuring that the risk management program continues to work effectively, is compliant with external and internal direction, and provides useful information to senior management for informed decision making.

Within the governance framework for managing and leading the AP&S program, oversight provides the data on which governance decisions can be made. The first set of data is communicated by management and expresses the residual risk for which the organization is aiming. The second set of data involves the assessed risk of the business lines of the organization before (real risk) and after (residual risk) decisions are taken. This is gathered

---

* These are typically considered to include sovereignty, national security, economic prosperity, and the health and safety of citizens.

through a range of reports, both direct (visits, inspections, assessments, audits, etc.) and indirect (security incident reporting, etc.). Based on the levels of risk identified and senior management's communicated threshold, the senior security official can develop his or her corporate security program, integrating all AP&S functions for efficiency and effectiveness to protect valued corporate assets.

At the tactical level, the SCADA security practitioner can implement appropriate technical and nontechnical safeguards within the governance framework to meet the agreed residual risk. These have to be appropriately described in terms of their functionality and then monitored with respect to their performance. All these activities have to take place in the context of an approved structure. Governance and oversight are, therefore, inextricably linked. In the subsequent sections, both will be described and explained, after which their integration and dynamics will be illustrated.

Governance explained

As noted, governance provides the framework, which includes structures and processes for collective decision making (Nye and Donahue 2000, cited in Masera et al. 2006). Implicit in this is a proactive nature of governance, or Van der Vlueten's (2010) "precautionary measures" (p. 2056) that project "soft power" (p. 2058) of systematic and deterministic *influence* applied to critical infrastructures, as opposed to the traditional and perhaps outdated strict *control* measures. This framework for influence must be legitimate, with a solid "legal basis" (Masera 2010, p. 112). The governance structure must integrate all factors affecting operations, including, for example, geography, regulations, treaties, risks, norms, culture, markets, and criticality of service, and provide salient information where and when it is needed in support of decision making to meet the same objectives, based on clearly expressed requirements. Finally, the governance frame must reconcile often conflicting regulatory direction, typically by utilizing appropriate legal cross-reference taxonomies to promote mutual understanding among engineers, developers, risk analysts, business line owners, and senior management (Maxwell et al. 2012). This is part of the challenge of governance, and of due diligence, as a demonstration of compliance where warranted.

Essential to effective and informed decision making is trusted information; a governance framework aids in ensuring such trust. For example, the governance structure of any organization (which could include a national critical infrastructure [NCI] in total) must exist at all levels of business, including local, regional, state/provincial, national, and international; this will ensure consistent, understandable information from all levels that is more easily assimilated at the center. Given the extensive reach of most NCIs, governance needs to consider "transnational, interpretative and historical analysis" (Van der Vleuten and Lagendijk 2010, p. 2053) so that decisions are truly enterprise centric.

Governance must extend over all stakeholders, all infrastructures, and all processes. The "golden rule is that all concerned parties need to work together" (Bakvis and Juillet 2004, p. 117). Since most NCIs are distributed, the governance process becomes more of a network or system of systems (Lewis 2006; Masera et al. 2006). This network can cross all boundaries and is only constrained by the influences of the NCI and its relevant supply chains. Conceptually, the value of this governance network lies in the resultant reconfiguration into one big, level playing field, as opposed to personal or individual turfs which are managed differently. Such a governance structure, enforced by effective oversight, should result in continuously improving operations and protection from sanctions for noncompliance.

The extended reach of governance through all geographical, organizational, and cultural* distances depends on a clear message, delivered by strong leadership. This is the top-down aspect of governance. Distributed line managers who receive this direction and operate within its boundaries, thereafter reporting progress within governance templates, represent the bottom-up aspect. Both are necessary. Confirmation of compliance from the bottom up is assisted by AP&S specialists who conduct periodic oversight activities, which will be discussed in detail later.

Explicit in governance is accountability for actions taken, another concept that permeates the full organization and NCI. It may include an individual's accountability for his or her actions. It may include a senior executive's accountability for the performance and management of the personnel, resources, and operations within a specific mandate. The governance structure lays out these accountabilities in roles and responsibilities, especially those of senior management. Nash (2009, p. 75) refers to addressing an "accountability conundrum" in the health-care sector by focusing on operational or functional accountability while "promoting a 'no-blame' culture for innocent slips." Accountability by the executive suite is that much greater due in part to the Gramm–Leach–Bliley Act, the Sarbanes–Oxley Act, and the Health Information Portability and Protection Act (Berghel 2005), all of which identify executives individually and collectively as accountable for displaying due diligence in the protection of valued information and financial assets. This is regulation driven, as will be discussed further later, but since it is mandatory and directive, it belongs as part of governance.

Governance and vision

There is little question that an organization requires vision as a precursor to goal-setting and mission assignment. According to Frisina and Frisina (2011), vision defines leadership's focus and is a measurable indicator of success. A clear vision contributes to an appropriate governance structure, not only for success, but for very survival (Landau et al. 2006). Vision provides a "futuristic [proactive] orientation ... and ... references to a tangible course of immediate action" that focuses on improvement through an integration of ideas from all levels. The governance structure facilitates this information flow. So, while a vision statement may be abstract, it remains salient to the ethos or "core values" of the organization and its intent to achieve mission success, however expressed or measured. Vision, and by extension governance, reflects the "genetic code" (Landau et al. 2006, p. 146) of the organization and is always sensed in the background of operations.

Consider an organization that lacks a clear vision as compared to one that has a clear vision. Those working within the organization lacking the vision are essentially within a rudderless ship. They are able to respond to commands and direction, but are not able to take those extra or intangible steps that go beyond those instructions because they lack the understanding of the organization's desired end state. While this effect is understood, the lack of vision can also harm the resilience of the organization. This is because the lack of a desired end state makes it a matter of guesswork when the employees are forced to bring their work back into line after unforeseen circumstances. Where an organization has a clear vision, those working under management have a far better understanding of what is important institutionally and, should they need to exercise their initiative, have a much greater chance of pushing the organization in the right direction.

---

* "Cultural" here refers to the way that individual managers "do things."

Vision, expressed in the governance structure, mobilizes and focuses all efforts, strengthens the self-image of all, and illustrates what a desirable future will look like (Landau et al. 2006; O'Connell et al. 2011). Whether the vision is developed by the leader, by the leader and top managers, by the leader and followers, or by the organization as a whole (O'Connell et al. 2011), it nonetheless "create[s] the spark that lifts organizations beyond the mundane" (Senge 1990, cited in O'Connell et al. 2011). Implemented within the governance framework, the vision becomes the "road map [or] trail blazer" (Landau et al. 2006, p. 148) or the "blueprint" (O'Connell et al. 2011, p. 105) to legitimize and encourage change; but it must be connected to the mandated mission of the organization, otherwise, it will fail to provide the required rationale to stakeholders at all levels. Although vision is considered to represent only 10% of the driver for change, with the other 90% being implementation (Jick 2001, cited in O'Connell et al. 2011, p. 107), it is, nonetheless, key to setting the desired direction that will be managed by the governance framework. Vision is not intended to result in "institutional conformity"; nor is it intended to be a threat to the established identity or culture of an organization, both of which are possible if the vision and the governance framework is not implemented carefully.

Setting the framework: policy suite* as a governance component

The policy suite, as a contributor to the governance framework, also represents the foundation on which the entire security program is built. It is the mechanism by which organizations can integrate external requirements (such as those demanded by regulations) into its internal processes. In systems that are well designed, those who perform work have a clear understanding of what is to be done, their capabilities and limits in accomplishing those tasks, and how to resolve challenges that may arise as a result of unforeseen conditions. At the very end, they are able to identify the positions or accountable positions from which they would need to seek guidance. One of the clearest indications of a good governance structure is that all employees understand the reach and limits of authority that can be exercised in meeting service delivery mandates. A poorly governed system, on the other hand, may be characterized by an organization that does not have clear goals, where the personalities of line managers and supervisors drive the treatment of employees, and problems do not get resolved because of bickering or conflict between departments. In short, the governance function, expressed in policy, is vital to the organization meeting its goals and maintaining a positive work environment.

Policies are designated as either internal or external, depending on the intended audience. External policies may direct how the organization acts with respect to entities outside of its structure and operations (such as sales). Internal policies may guide the actions of day-to-day operations and how suborganizations interact. At the most basic level, they express the will of senior management, including the importance of the goods or services provided by the organization, the importance of protecting and using assets appropriately, and encouragement to apply industry-standard best practices. Policy suites with a commitment to maximizing performance of the organization should address "Senior leadership commitment ... Constancy and clarity of purpose ... Performance improvement ... across the organization ... Transparency ... [and] Strategies" (Noonan 2009). They should also make a clear statement on the importance of the organization's success, however defined or measured.

---

* A policy suite includes the policy along with its supporting standards, directives, guidelines, and procedures.

Policy is mandatory, for the most part, since it is key to governance and the definition of what is considered to be acceptable or not. Degrees of requirement for compliance are typically set out in policy in the use of the words "must," "shall," "will," "should," may," and the like. The implications of these words are important; it is a challenge to expect deterministic performance or results if there is little compulsion in the policy. While, for the most part, all governance relies on influencing others to comply, the wording should nonetheless be as unambiguous as possible at the outset. At the same time, it is important that policies leave adequate flexibility so that tactical-level managers can respond to changes in their environment without constantly having to return to the executive table. Because it is intended to be mandatory, policy should be free of any influence that is not mapped directly to mission success. In researching the relationship between academic and support staff in major universities, Small (2008, p. 182) noted the prevailing opinion of support staff that "Policies that result from overt academic politics, are overly complex, generate inconsistent results, or are perceived … as inaccurate or grossly unfair all present significant problems for … services staff." He also noted "considerable annoyance [by support staff] at the absence of useful feedback mechanisms on policy issues, and disappointment when … feedback … is ignored." The latter is both a governance and an oversight process; without feedback, the governance models cannot be validated and it is not possible to exert effective oversight.

One of the key components of an effective policy suite is consistency* in its rationale, expectations, and direction. This includes internal and external consistency. The former refers to the supporting standards flowing logically from the policy, and the procedures representing an efficient implementation of standards. The latter refers to implementation up, down, and across the organization (without exceptions, since they introduce vulnerabilities). For the individuals of an organization, the policy suite should provide clear guidance, flexibility for changing environments, and should be constantly responding to the needs of the organization, taking into account both tactical- and executive-level issues. The supporting documents to the policy suite will be addressed later in the chapter.

Drivers for governance

To understand governance fully, one must understand the various external requirements that are placed on an organization. These pressures may be internal or external in nature. Some of the external pressures include the following:

- *Laws* that define criminal activity and set punishments for those who are convicted of crimes
- *Regulations* that set down the obligations, constraints,† and restraints‡ that governments expect of certain kinds of industries
- *Standards* that are developed by regulators, professional associations, or interest groups, and which are considered essential for measuring the activities of the organization (including the deployment of its infrastructure) and in relationship to compliance with industry best practices

---

* Cronin and Motluk (2011, p. 235) discuss the negative results of the Ontario Energy Board and the provincial government's "pronouncements, proposals and policies [as] inconsistent, misguided and counterproductive."
† That which *must* be done.
‡ That which *may not* be done.

- *Measures* and, in some nations, decrees that place temporary restrictions or requirements on organizations
- *Trade or industry associations* that present consensus-driven opinions of various organizations in the same business or performing the same activity
- *Social norms* that are driven by the public's reception of the organization's brand and how it responds to the public's concerns of the day

These external pressures are important because they limit, to varying degrees and using various consequences, what decisions management can make with respect to the operations of the company.

As previously suggested, there may also be conflicting pressures, which Kiyavitskaya et al. (2007, p. 429) refer to as "a 'regulation compliance' problem" applied to software development, which requires methods and tools for automating regulatory analysis and analyzing several policy documents. Mahoney and Gandhi (2011, p. 44) note overlaps in regulatory standards and best practices, which require human intervention to reconcile "top-down regulations with bottom-up evidence of compliance."

In delving into the realm of laws and regulations, one encounters terms whose meaning are highly contextual in nature, and therefore open to misinterpretation. Take, for example, the word "policy." For those involved in regulatory affairs, the policy may actually precede the formation of a law—it describes the general direction of government with respect to a program, topic, or issue. To those involved in business management, it may refer to the high-level, overarching decision of management with respect to how a company should address a certain business or operational requirement. Or, the policy may result from the requirement to have some measure, process, control, or safeguard in place because of a law or regulation. For those working in information technology (IT) security or technical security, a standard may even be misrepresented as a policy, as it directs a specific measure to be implemented to protect a network. Understanding context is essential for effective governance to be implemented and a failure in this respect is one of the major contributing factors to organizational confusion and disharmony.

Governance may be considered in layers for understanding. The first layer of governance may be described as legal and may be divided into two categories:

1. *Criminal law*: further subdivided into *male prohibita* (prohibited by laws but not necessarily evil in and of itself—such as public intoxication) and *male in se* (prohibited because the act is considered to be evil in and of itself—such as rape or murder). In both cases, the injury is considered to be against society or the state, and while the response may include an element of compensation for the victim, it could also include punishment against the offender in terms of loss of life (via the death penalty), liberty (incarceration), or property (forfeiture of proceeds of crime).
2. *Administrative law*: where the focus is on regulations that prescribe or prohibit certain kinds of conduct. Regulations generally apply to conduct (personal or business) and, while society is still considered to be the aggrieved party, the penalties are generally in terms of fines.

Neither of these two categories is open to significant debate. Companies, including the various levels of employees within the company, are expected to adhere to the law. Another consideration, when considering the legal layer, involves to whom the law would actually apply when work is being performed on behalf of the company. Following company policy does not excuse an individual with respect to the commission of a criminal act—which applies always at a personal level (as does accountability). However, the concept of *respondeat superior* may apply; this can be described (in the context of common law) as the employer of an individual taking on legal accountability for the actions of a subordinate when that subordinate performs an act within the scope of his or her employment. This means that the executive management of a company may become more legally liable for injuries associated with the work that they designed, if their processes are deemed not to be in line with the requirements of the law. This, however, does not excuse the employee who commits an act that is contrary to the law.

After criminal laws come regulations. While criminal law focuses on and applies sanctions against the individual, regulations tend to deal more with the organization, although the individual is not immune. These may also include mechanisms such as measures, rules, and directives that have the force of regulations. While criminal acts require that both *mens rea* and *actus reus* must be proven beyond a reasonable doubt, regulatory compliance only requires a favorable weight in terms of the balancing of probabilities. Under prescriptive regimes, the inspector simply needs to show that a declared control is not present or not functioning as described. In performance-based regulations, this means that the controls can be counted on to perform up to a certain level of risk control (effective risk management).

From a governance perspective, criminal law and regulations are also somewhat different. Criminal law will certainly form part of the requirements to which a company must adhere at all times. This is the result of two factors. First, adhering to the laws of the country in which the company is operating is often part of the conditions of being allowed to open the company in the first place and, as a result, a breach of those conditions could lead to the enterprise simply being shut down. The second is that senior management, who may be held at least partially liable (as identified earlier) will not likely risk penalties that can range from significant fines through incarceration or even execution on behalf of an organization or the performance of its employees, depending on the country in which the company is operating. Regulations, however, are somewhat different because, as noted, the penalties are often financial in nature. As a result, regulations require a certain balance in how they affect a company's conduct of the cost–benefit analysis at the enterprise level. Regulations that do not carry adequate penalties for single acts or that fail to take into account repeated and willful failures to comply run a significant risk of simply being considered a cost of doing business, if the alternative (compliance) is relatively more costly. This approach is, of course, inappropriate from a legal and ethical perspective, and it is for these reasons that many regulations have increased penalties over time.

There are other mechanisms that government entities can use to communicate the state's requirements to companies. Most of these are specific to a single process or service, or else are constrained in terms of their duration; they nonetheless carry the weight of law or regulation. In countries such as Canada and the United States, government departments or agencies may issue processes or procedures that would have the full weight of law when operating under the authority of an elected official or its delegated representative. For example, under the Canadian Marine Transportation Security Act (Minister of Justice 1994), inspectors "may direct vessels to proceed to, or remain outside of certain areas. Areas covered by security measures could include ports, terminals, piers, marine facilities and vessels" (Transport Canada 2010).

Outside of the authority of the state, companies are also legally influenced by civil law. This follows closely with companies and their personnel being declared liable for some form of injury (including elevated levels of risk). Consider the three following scenarios:

1. A pipeline fails to detect a leak and releases a significant amount of material into an environmentally sensitive area and causes significant damage to property.
2. A nuclear reactor releases radiation into the environment, leading to persons being exposed to levels that are known to be a significant factor in the formation of cancerous growths.
3. A traffic system directs two vehicles in such a way that they collide, unaware that their traffic control system had flaws leading to a failure to communicate the need to wait to one vehicle.

In each of these scenarios, companies may well be subject to some form of civil action if those affected seek compensation for their injuries. Depending on the results of the civil action, the company could face simple shortfalls (leading to a loss of consumer confidence), or could be put out of business entirely. This is in addition to any personal liability that may be assigned to the directors of the company in a manner similar to the *respondeat superior* considerations discussed above. Where management believes that it could run into these kinds of situations, it is unlikely that they will be willing to assume such a risk. Consequently, they will ensure that steps are taken within the organization to keep them (as well as the organization and its employees) protected from prosecution.

To summarize, the formation of a company's governance structure begins outside the company with the legal requirements that are placed on it. These vary from very specific requirements that influence the behavior of persons or legal entities (criminal law) to those that influence industries and organizations through regulations. These requirements generally become the upper layer of requirements that are communicated in terms of "must," "shall," or "will" within the company's policy suite.

Governance and professional associations

In many cases, the state does not have the sole external voice with respect to governance. Many organizations participate in what can be described as *industry* or *trade associations*. These associations operate in a kind of balance between businesses, on the one hand, and practitioners, academics, and analysts, on the other. Participants and members are expected to conduct their businesses in compliance with the decisions of the respective association, as well as promoting its agenda and ethos. The association provides oversight over the actions of its members, clearly communicating (through values and ethics) what constitutes correct behavior and dealings, sanctioning those that fail to adhere to them. This oversight often provides the organization with an air of credibility through membership and access to information generated by the association, often in terms of best practices, standards, and so on. If the organization does not maintain its membership in good standing, then it may lose the competitive, reputational, and professional development advantages that come with membership.

Membership in a trade or industry association may be voluntary or mandatory under regulations. This is similar to the way in which doctors, lawyers, and engineers must belong to professional associations to conduct business legitimately. This can manifest itself a number of different ways. The state could have set a requirement that all organizations that deliver a certain service or provide a certain good must be overseen by a professional association that has the necessary expertise to determine what constitutes negligence or inappropriate conduct. In this manner, the state could be said to be shifting the responsibility for setting and maintaining standards back to the industry where that specialized knowledge is required. Also, factors associated with the ability to compete effectively within the market may be extant. In some cases, a group of organizations will establish control over enough of a market to effectively limit new competition, in spite of *trust* and *antitrust* laws. In those cases, the association is seen as a "regulator" between the market and the associations, which hopefully are able to realize competitive advantages from having control over such a large part of that market. This can be particularly prevalent in emerging industries where new businesses are fragile and, in some cases, will form alliances similar to medieval guilds to seize and stabilize market share. Finally, membership in associations is associated with *branding*, or the ability to convince customers that the organization adheres to certain principles and practices. In these cases, membership in the association is held up as a reference check to show the market that the organization acts responsibly, professionally, and ethically in the conduct of business. What is being communicated is that the organization must adopt the principles and practices demanded by the trade or industry association and incorporate them into its own culture, governance framework, and practices.

With several external requirements having been identified and incorporated into the governance framework, governance may next be addressed as a management tool within risk management. To manage risk at acceptable levels, management requires certain conditions to be maintained. These may be associated with quality management, AP&S best practices, or a host of other efforts. As suggested earlier, from a governance perspective, risk management begins at the inception of the organization and continues thereafter as a program requirement.

Governance and the mission

Having established the value of mission in support of governance framework development, the next layer of internal governance addresses the *mission* statement of the organization. The mission statement explains what the organization actually does, or why it is there in the first place and where it wants to go; that is, the leader's intent. Lawler (2006, p. 549) notes that a mission statement is "neither a strategic plan nor a method of controlling the organization … Instead, it provides a broad sense of what the organization does and wants to be." The mission statement becomes meaningful when it includes the value of the organization's products and the "strategic intent" (Prahalad and Hamel 1990; Lawler 2006, p. 550) of the organization, which includes, among other things, the indicators of its success. For example, the mission of the Masters in Infrastructure Protection and International Security (MIPIS) program at Carleton University, Ottawa, Canada, is to produce graduates who are

> effective, competent, knowledgeable and articulate specialists in CIP who can collaborate in multi-disciplinary and multi-jurisdictional teams to provide reasoned asset protection and security (AP&S) leadership, program implementation and advice to industry and governments at all levels in support of national objectives. (MIPIS 2012)

In meeting this mission statement, all faculty, staff, and students are clear on the expected outcome (in this case "employable graduates") and all efforts taken in class, in assignments, and in applied activities should contribute to it. From a governance perspective, program directors and external university staff will be able to validate all courses taught and all curricula provided to confirm the extent to which they contribute to meeting the stated mission.

When the goals are articulated and clear, it is much easier to communicate, to train, and to motivate all stakeholders. Shared understanding leads to shared action and shared rewards when all are moving in the same direction. It is a senior management responsibility to keep the mission statement current and at the forefront of communications. In this manner, it provides focus for the organization's activities, which are also kept in line with the commander's or leader's intent. All actions thereafter can reflect initiative and confidence that they will be appropriate to meeting all missions and service delivery mandates.

This is important for three reasons:

1. The mission statement, by clearly defining "why" the organization does what it does, *allows workflows and efforts within the organization to be prioritized* based on the ability to achieve the outcomes expressed by the mission statement.
2. It also *establishes the general focus of effort* within the company—essentially keeping the organization's energy and efforts focused (a primary element in reduction of waste and in efficient management).
3. The mission statement also serves to *help identify and quantify unacceptable efforts and activities.* Where energy and activity run contrary to the mission statement of an organization, then the efforts or energy expended may be seen as being hostile or undesirable—leading to consequences ranging from orders to cease doing something to the dismissal of personnel.

Governance and goal-setting

From both an operational and a governance perspective, the organization is really a system of systems. Each system culminates in some goal being met. Each system is built on the coordinated efforts of a number of personnel, plus material, infrastructure, information, and processes under a governance framework, that achieve, at an individual level, a contributing subgoal. Taken in aggregate, they become goals, objectives, and benchmarks with the following characteristics:

1. The ultimate goal (mission) of the organization should be clearly defined and articulated so that it is understandable by all and so that it can be determined if it was met.
2. The first level of system is organized in such a way that the ultimate goal is realized by meeting all specified requirements (effectiveness as a primary goal) with the best possible use of resources (efficiency as a secondary goal).
3. Each subsystem is organized so that its own outcome is clearly defined, first individually and then as a component of or contributor to the overall goals, objectives, and benchmarks, and its own work is as efficient as possible.
4. Each process that comprises the system is clearly designed, implemented, monitored, and maintained under a governance framework in such a way that it continuously offers the best probability of success for each outcome that is used to support the system (or goals), ultimately contributing to meeting the overall mission.

Where any single process supporting goal achievement fails to deliver the intended or designed outcome, the overall quality of service is affected. At some point, the combination of failures will reach a point where the overall outcome may be that the company fails to meet its mission (or the expectations of its clients) and the overall effort will have been wasteful and counterproductive. From an NCI perspective, including SCADA systems, such failures can have a deleterious impact on the meeting of national objectives.

Governance and the supporting policy suite

The next source of authority for governance requirements comes from internal management decisions. These focus on ensuring that the company's processes are effective and efficient. Management determines—often based on the advice of technical personnel in the company—how rigorously to apply certain standards, guidelines, and procedures that are intended to ensure that the company has the best chance of succeeding and generating wealth for its shareholders, or meeting all service delivery mandates.

Internal requirements, captured in the supporting policy suite, also need to be communicated in a manner that is clearly understood by the all stakeholders to the company. If the requirements are not clearly communicated, then how can senior management expect individuals to adhere to them clearly? This can become a problem in organizations in which middle or line management is not well governed, and therefore fails to understand the balance between policy direction and the realities of dynamic operations. This may pose a situation where workers are confused about what they are expected to accomplish, and the organization as a whole remains uncertain as to the expected quality of outcomes from its processes. This ineffective communication is indicative of a lapse in governance.

When establishing requirements, management has useful tools at its disposal in the supporting policy suite. Policies are a major contributor to, and recipient of, governance, but they are effective only through the implementation of their supporting *standards, guidelines,* and *procedures.* This is important for three key reasons:

1. Each one has its own level of authority (external/internal; line/staff officers; practitioners, etc.) but is also written for specific audiences, meaning that the language used to communicate each can become relevant to the potential of successful outcomes. For example, technical direction for rebuilding a server may be too complex for a manager or non-IT staff member. Or, security-related procedures may be of apparently sufficient inconvenience that the employee many choose not to follow them.
2. Each one is developed through different processes (technical/nontechnical; taking a standard at face value/customizing standards from industry best practices, etc.), meaning that their approval can be bogged down if submitted to an inappropriate level of management or can cause a detrimental effect on the company, as the time of key personnel is inconvenienced by them or if compliance is irrelevant to them.
3. The organization may require flexibility as to how each one is applied at different operational or business levels, and misaligning these may result in the organization not being able to respond as needed to changes in conditions.

Standards

Having defined through vision and policy *what the intent is,* the company must refine how it intends to determine if that intent is being met. This is the role of standards, which are defined by the National Standards Policy Advisory Committee (NSPAC) as "A prescribed set of rules, conditions, or requirements concerning definitions of terms; classification of components; specification of materials, performance, or operations; delineation of procedures; or measurement of quantity and quality in describing materials, products, systems, services, or practices" (NSPAC 1978). Standards are typically developed by volunteer practitioners and professionals in an area of specialization and reflect industry best practices applied to specific situations. Changes from standards are decided based on threat risk assessment. Even standards development is governed by a framework, often the American National Standards Institute (ANSI), as it attempts to accrue benefits such as efficiency, safety, quality, or consistency.

There are two levels to standards that work together—one more general than the other. Consider measuring how far you intend to travel on a highway. First, you use a *system of measurement* that aligns well with how things are measured within the same kind of activity. If you are traveling on the highway in the United States, you may measure using the U.S. system of miles per hour. If you are traveling in Canada, you would likely use kilometers per hour. Either way, you are selecting a system that is used commonly within your environment so that you can compare the performance of your organization within cooperative and competitive communities. The second part of this exercise describes how the organization sets an *expected level of performance* that is based on a number of different factors, including the following:

1. Minimum levels of performance required by law or regulation that the company cannot operate below (i.e., minimum mandated service levels).
2. Minimum levels of performance that are required to maintain the viability of the company in terms of operations and financial returns (i.e., minimum operational levels).
3. Minimum levels of performance that are needed to maintain the financial break-even point of the company (i.e., minimum financial levels).
4. Minimum levels of performance that are needed to meet forecasted (communicated) results of the company (i.e., expectations of board of directors).
5. Minimum levels of performance needed to support the plans and priorities of the organization (i.e., expectations of senior management).

Establishing and communicating the need for a common measuring system and the means for conducting that measurement, both of which are expressed in a standard, is a key decision to be made within an organization.

A standard provides the target or expected indicator of success for how work is to be conducted within the organization—although not to the level of detail associated with specific procedures. For example, in the case of conduct of a background check, one might identify the standards in terms of the following:

1. With respect to an individual proving his or her identity, the standard shall specify the requirement to present two pieces of government-issued photo identification (or equivalent).
2. With respect to the gathering of informed consent, the documentation must clearly indicate the checks being conducted and the individual required to sign/initial beside each individual check, acknowledging that he or she understands the checks to be conducted and consents to them being conducted.
3. With respect to the verification of education or training, certified true copies of degrees, diplomas, or certificates from accredited programs that are recognized by the government licensing body shall suffice.
4. With respect to reliability, a certain kind of scoring shall be calculated based on positive, neutral, and negative information regarding the individual, gained typically through the conduct of past reference checks or subject interviews. Individuals must earn a threshold number or else they will not be granted a clearance.

Based on these standards, the security clearance analyst can perform the work and provide clear, unambiguous guidance to the clearance applicant. Receipt of the required evidence will always result in the granting of a clearance if there are no adverse findings. Senior management will be displaying due diligence in granting clearances, since the standards are demanding enough that employees meeting the standard should be trusted to perform their duties appropriately. Senior management's intent will have been met.

In considering technical standards, they may describe very clear and specific conditions and settings for equipment, sensors, and so on, including clipping levels.* There are two factors that should be taken into account when considering technical standards. First, adherence to a technical standard means simply that a certain measurable implementation is achieved, but it should never be construed as achieving an acceptable level of security, however calculated. An acceptable state of security or protection is achieved only when key risks are identified and analyzed, and residual risks[†] assessed. Standard implementation contributes to risk assessment, but can be considered "rules-based" security; this is neither adequate nor cost effective. Any additional safeguards to be implemented will not come from standards, but from threat risk assessment of the difference between the risks mitigated by implementation of baseline or standards-based safeguards and those risks remaining to be mitigated by additional safeguards. Threat risk-based security sits on top of rules-based security to provide the most appropriate protection. Each technical standard was written taking into account a typical operating and threat environment, and therefore cannot be relied on to provide the requisite security in any specific environment. To claim a level of security, the individual making the assessment must first verify that the operating environments (the exemplar of the standard and the actual operating environment) are sufficiently similar to assess the value of implementing the standard to mitigate risk to an acceptable level. If senior management accepts this residual risk, then the standard will have been adequate; unfortunately, this seldom occurs, and additional analysis is required. The fear is that implementation of standards by unknowledgeable AP&S practitioners, who do not advise on additional threat risk assessments to be conducted, may be considered "enough" by senior management, when, in fact, key unmitigated risks may remain. Standards, as all components of the policy suite, are only as useful as the practitioner who implements them and the security official who conducts governance over their implementation.

There is an inherent danger in the use of standards, particularly in organizations that have been driven by IT security pattern activities. This is where compliance with the standard replaces risk management. The standard (how to perform the task) and the goal defined in the standard are based on a certain risk environment. While networks may provide a reasonably stable platform, this is not the case in all aspects of security. In physical security, for example, the operating environment may change significantly (temperature, humidity, hurricanes, etc.), the threat environment may change or shift, and vulnerabilities may become far more accessible as infrastructure or systems deteriorate. What is needed is for management to be very clear that there is still a need for risk assessments as part of the routine activities. These may confirm compliance with a baseline requirement as being appropriate, or not. Either way, making the assumption that compliance with a standard will result in security is, at the very best, guesswork.

---

* Clipping levels are settings in a computer system that would delineate "normal" operation; actions outside of these clipping levels may be considered anomalous and an alarm should be raised so that an investigation can be launched.
† This is the risk remaining after safeguards are implemented. It is the residual risk that is assumed by senior management under a functioning risk management program.

Procedures and guidelines

Below the level of standards are procedures and guidelines. Procedures are used to define the specific mandatory steps that are taken to best assure a desirable, deterministic, and consistent outcome. While the policy states the ultimate management intent and the standard describes the clear targets or objectives that need to be reached to demonstrate the extent to which that intent is being met, the procedure provides a "road map" to complete a task as efficiently* and effectively as possible. Procedures are also used as a basis for quality assurance activities by assisting analysts or auditors in determining if the outcome was arrived at through a sound, proven, and approved process.

Guidelines are used to provide some level of advice to those performing the tasks. They are a "recommended practice that allows some discretion or leeway in its interpretation, implementation, or use" (BusinessDictionary.com 2012). They may involve what can be described as "tricks of the trade" or alternative methods to use if the first method does not lead to an anticipated result. Guidelines are intended to be considered, customized, and employed by trained, knowledgeable practitioners. The shortcoming of guidelines rests in the fact that they are not mandatory; experienced practitioners can use them as inputs in making an informed decision, while those without experience or ethics can justify inappropriate action by implementing some or none of recommended guidelines, regardless of the operational requirement. In this manner, guidelines may actually introduce new vulnerabilities into a system.

Another aspect of guidelines is that there may be more than one per activity, depending on the operating environment. While this will be rare in the IT and networked environment, the less stable physical and personnel security domains could, in fact, have several. What is important is that the guideline adheres to the standard, achieves the appropriate and relevant goals, and contributes toward the success of the organization.

Challenges to implementing a policy suite

There are various challenges faced by organizations when discussing policies, standards, procedures, and guidelines. *Policies* need to be signed off by the appropriate level of accountable management, typically the executive. This means that they need to be developed at a strategic level, taking into account a larger corporate picture (operational, legal, social, financial, etc.) and then be signed off at senior levels—often a time-consuming process as that approval process will likely involve several checks and balances and also be subject to senior management's schedule. Standards, on the other hand, can be drawn from a narrower "technical" community (usually with expertise in that area) and are then endorsed by senior management based on the assessment of that expert or community of experts that the standard contributes directly to policy fulfillment. This process should be much less onerous than that of policy development, the main effort being to demonstrate how the standard supports management's intent. Procedures and guidelines are even more focused and straightforward and can, therefore, be signed off locally, since that is the level at which they will be implemented and since they are generally already derived from existing doctrine, policy, or standards.

---

* Note that efficiency is primary in the case of procedures. Given that procedures will have been formally promulgated, practiced, and refined, the efficiencies gained in prompt, deterministic, and appropriate actioning of the procedure will result in both efficiency and effectiveness.

The other core difference lies in the intended audience of each—policies are intended for management: the strategic level of governance; standards are intended for the management of specific objectives or areas of responsibility: the operational level of governance; and procedures are intended for supervisors and those performing the tasks: the tactical level of governance.

In summary, the policy suite ensures that those working within the organization have a clear understanding of the requirements of their positions. There is a reasonable expectation that if management wants something to be done, it has to be clear in communicating its intent and its expectations. This is the beginning, or "front end" of governance. Ensuring that all stakeholders comply (hopefully willingly) with management's intent is a separate process, called oversight, which is management's exercising of due care (for assets) and due diligence (for meeting mission objectives) in ensuring that the company is well managed. At this point, all external requirements should have been incorporated appropriately and managed in accordance with the overall intent and it is now a matter of making sure that those requirements continue to be met.

Spheres of governance

Before addressing the "how" of governance (oversight activities), it is useful to discuss briefly the "where" of governance. Conceptually, there are different areas in which governance takes place; this is important because the governance process and methods will change with the area. These areas are both physical and figurative. Figure 10.1 depicts three areas.

At the outermost sphere lies the area of interest for senior management, who are interested in market forces, competitors, consumer trends, industry best practices, and strategic influences. Analysis of these factors is compared to the interests of the board of governors, senior executives, employees, and customers, all assisting in the development of strategic plans. Senior management cannot affect the area of interest, but can draw information and intelligence from it.

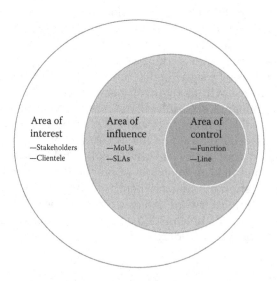

Figure 10.1 Spheres of governance. (From Boone and Moore. Illustrating asset protection and security concepts. Ottawa, ON: Carleton University. 2012.)

The area of influence represents a space where management can actually bring to bear their own resources or exert their intent. This area may be house-related organizations, capabilities, or other resources that management may use, if the proper negotiations and approvals have been sought. These could include memoranda of understanding (MoUs) or service-level agreements (SLAs), or more informal agreements based on political, economic, cultural, historical, ethnic, religious, or personal relationships. The use of negotiation, relationship building, quid pro quo arrangements and other implementations of "soft power" are the most appropriate. Management gains synergy through exploiting this area, and also gains operational or tactical information that can assist in short-term decision making. The area of influence is where the concept of *staff* or *functional* management takes place, as will be discussed later. This area is important from an AP&S governance perspective, since this is the sphere wherein most of this type of governance takes place.

The area of control exists where management "owns" the resources, and can utilize them as they wish, to complete all tasks and achieve all objectives in support of the mission. The area of control can be equated to the concept of *line* management, where employees report directly and formally to a "boss," as will be discussed later as a key governance concept.

Lines of governance

Operating concurrently with the spheres of governance are the so-called lines of governance. These lines map conceptually to traditional organization charts under the area of control sphere, wherein direct reporting relationships are established. This is perhaps the most straightforward iteration of governance. But, a key form of governance takes place in the area of influence sphere; this is staff or functional governance. Both are illustrated in Figure 10.2 (AP&S reporting relationships). Given the major themes of this book, security-related examples are offered.

The senior corporate officer represents the executives and is accountable to the shareholders, and could be appointed as the chief executive officer, president, and so on. He or she has a series of direct reports, as shown earlier by the chief operations officer, the human resources officer, the enterprise risk officer, the chief financial officer, and the chief information officer, all comprising the "C-suite." These are typical line reporting relationships. The corporate security officer may report to the enterprise risk officer in a line relationship, and may have several AP&S specialists reporting directly to him or her in a line relationship. Superimposed on line relationships are staff or functional reporting relationships, illustrated with the dotted lines. For example, the operational security manager is functionally responsible to the chief operator for providing advice, guidance, assessment, and any other assistance required to support operations. The chief operator cannot task the operational security manager, who already has a direct reporting relationship to the corporate security officer, with any tasks other than those related directly to the provision of advice and guidance. But, the operational security manager can *influence* the chief operations officer to take the security-related advice. If unsuccessful at the tactical level (i.e., the chief operator does not agree to implement the recommendations), then the operational security managers have additional recourse. They can report to their line supervisor, who is also the corporate security officer. The corporate security officer has at least three choices: he can escalate the noncompliance to his line supervisor, the enterprise risk officer, for resolution with the chief operations officer on a peer-to-peer basis; he can use his *functional* authority as a representative of the senior corporate officer to escalate the noncompliance to the highest level for resolution down to the chief operations officer; or

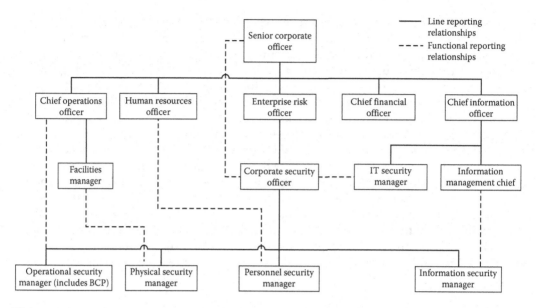

Figure 10.2 AP&S reporting relationships. (From Boone and Moore. Illustrating asset protection and security concepts. Ottawa, ON: Carleton University. 2012.)

he can attempt to influence the chief operations officer, working at a higher level (but still not a peer) than his subordinate operational security manager.

There is a myth that an individual must "stand to" for any corporate officer of higher position that directs him or her. This is patently not the case. In fact, if the higher position is using his or her authority to direct work which would be outside of the corporate interest or in a manner that is harmful to the other individual, they may be guilty of an abuse of authority.

There are several other examples in Figure 10.2 that illustrate the flow of information, guidance, advice, and tasking between line and staff/functional reporting relationships. The physical security manager influences the facility manager toward compliance with AP&S policy, who in turn carries out all manner of non-security-related tasks for the chief operations officer. The personnel security officer provides recommendations on the granting of security clearances and access to valued assets to both his colleague in physical and information security, and he also assists the human resources officer in hiring matters, clearances, and administrative investigations. The information security manager, responsible for providing advice on the protection of information in all forms, assists his physical security colleague regarding security containers, his IT security colleague in the protection of information in digital form, and his information management colleague regarding proper designation and classification of sensitive information. The IT security manager typically reports directly to the chief information officer, but has a functional reporting responsibility to the corporate security officer (in the latter's appointment as the senior security adviser to the senior corporate officer). Neither has control or "hard power" over the other; rather, both rely on the governance framework, professionalism, goodwill, and a strategic focus to work collaboratively.

While there are many other combinations and permutations of line and functional reporting relationships, the key point to remember with respect to governance is that each of the functional authorities is operating *on behalf* of the senior corporate officer, and all advice or recommendations from AP&S staff (at any level or specialty) have the full weight of that position.

Much has been written about this so-called "horizontal" governance structure in both government and private industry. Several key lessons emerge that demonstrate the benefits of flatter structures that venture out from the area of control to the areas of influence and interest. There is a change in mindset from the closed silo mentality ("this is mine, do not encroach") to a more open, willing, and collective attitude toward mission success (Bakvis and Juillet 2004). Information is shared more freely, aided by technology to shorten the distances between collaborators. Since more tools, thinking, expertise, and experience are brought to bear across traditional reporting lines, the results are synergy and maximum exploitation of resources; employees are empowered and regain the initiative to be proactive within the clear parameters of the leader's intent. Accountability is accepted freely, without fear of reprisal for taking incorrect action, since the desired end state is well known.

There are downsides to functional governance and horizontal reporting relationships. They take considerably more time to establish and maintain understanding, trust, and willing assistance. There are hard and soft costs associated with having meetings, changing the culture from one of "I" to one of "we," preparing and disseminating hard copies of records of decisions, and the lost opportunity costs associated with the impact on other projects that are not getting their due attention. And, in many cases, there is the requirement for compromise in solutions, which may be difficult for some managers to accept if they have traditionally gotten their way.

Within many communities, potential confusion arises when considering the difference between functional authorities and line managers. This confusion is based on a misinterpretation of a concept referred to as the "primacy of operations." In organizations that do not have a mature grasp of the relationship between line managers and functional authorities, this is sometimes interpreted to mean that the organization called "operations" is the most prominent administrative division within the organization, and is not to be deterred by "staff" positions or functional authorities, who, in their minds, wish only to impede operations (a rather narrow interpretation by some line managers and certainly not indicative of a corporate view). This is a poor or incomplete interpretation on two fronts. First, any organization is a team effort, each with its role to play. Second, this interpretation is often used by line managers within the operations domain to attempt to prioritize their efforts over other parts of the organization—potentially putting the organization at risk from failing to perform tasks appropriately in the absence of a corporate view. A more appropriate interpretation of the concept would be that the organization's focus is on the activities that lead to the best possible outcomes with respect to the quantity and quality of services delivered or goods produced.

As fiscal restraint continues to be the norm, the above vulnerability is becoming all too present in our systems. The problem is that the "sexy" frontline forces do not exist for long without the rather "unsexy" backfield personnel. Consider frontline IT personnel. While these personnel may be instrumental in the detection of and response to an incident, a lack of payroll will quickly take its toll, as those persons who have not been paid become increasingly unsettled, aggravated, angered, and ultimately motivated to leave the organization. As noted above, what needs to be clear is that decisions must be made that best support the organization's probability for success. That means all work units and individuals must be pushing the wheel in the same direction.

One mechanism that is used to reduce an organization's exposure to ineffective governance is called a *delegation mechanism*. The delegation mechanism is used as both a basis for exercising authority (in terms of committing resources) and as a means of reducing potential conflicts within the organization. To accomplish this, the delegation mechanism includes the following:

- The specific source of the authority making the delegation (thereby identifying the levels of accountability impacted).
- The specific accountability of the individual being delegated (described in terms of desired outcomes).
- The authority to assign resources from those assigned to him or her for the purpose of achieving and maintaining that accountability for results.
- The resources that are considered necessary for there to be a reasonable expectation that the work needed to maintain the accountability can be carried out successfully.
- Any restraints or constraints (limitations from inside or outside the organization) that management imposes on the individual.
- A limitation in terms of conditions to be met to maintain the delegation, as well as the potential consequences for failing to maintain them.

As you can well imagine, there is a significant difference between the description of a functional authority and a line manager.

The relationship between the functional authority and those involved in the "line" management is not an equal balance. While the functional authority may hold a lower position administratively and may not appear to command the same level of resources as does a line manager, it should be clear that the functional authority is speaking in response to a corporate priority that has already been established by senior management. In short, the functional manager is speaking with the authority of the highest levels of the organization as described by his or her delegation mechanism. The functional authority must remain cognizant that his or her authority extends only within the bounds of the unique expertise for which he or she is functionally responsible, and only on behalf of the delegation from the senior corporate officer. As a result, a relatively tenuous balance must be achieved. This balance is achieved by having the line manager integrate the requirements of the functional authority into the day-to-day operations, as opposed to having the functional authority attempt to impose new systems onto the line management. This is the essence of the horizontal governance framework previously discussed.

For those line managers operating in technical environments, this relationship has additional connotations. It must not be forgotten that the control systems, networks, infrastructure, and everything else exist to serve the corporate interest, and that the corporate interest's accountability lies with the senior corporate officer. It is up to the various functional authorities to advise and guide (influence) the senior corporate officer, not dictate conditions. In short, functional authorities define the extent to which decisions can be made appropriately, but do not dictate the specific decisions to be made. At the same time, it is important for the senior corporate officer to understand that the functional authority, if discharging his or her duties appropriately, is expected to provide honest and impartial guidance and advice, perhaps at odds with corporate vision, but nonetheless required to meet legal, regulatory, or policy requirements. Finally, it is incumbent on the various functional authorities within the same organization to understand that the organization has to maintain an outward-facing view (toward the client who pays the bills) and that unhealthy internal competition between groups that should be working on the same team is, in fact, less than appropriate from a corporate perspective. Ultimately, the senior corporate officer, acting as the face of the corporate entity, needs to be assured that all of his (and hence the organization's) accountabilities are being maintained appropriately by both his line officers and his functional authorities. A good governance structure will go a long way to ensure this.

Oversight

With the various requirements integrated into the line management of the organization, the next step involves monitoring the application of those requirements. This is a particularly delicate issue for many organizations and may require significant senior management support, because it involves balancing the line and functional accountabilities to the point where the right balance is struck. The monitoring of the application of requirements is its own cycle. This cycle can be described as the following:

1. Identification and approval of the requirement so that it is endorsed by senior management (the functional authorities provide this input based on their unique expertise in a certain specialty).
2. Communication of the requirement to ensure that personnel are aware of the requirement and their responsibility to embrace it.
3. Familiarization and training that focuses on the requirement and how it is integrated into day-to-day operations (this is typically achieved by the functional authority through training and awareness sessions).
4. Phased implementation of the requirement into operations (fully appreciating that the imposition of seemingly additional requirements to line operations detracts from those operations, and must therefore be implemented slowly, iteratively, and sagely).
5. Confirmation that those with positions that involve meeting the requirement understand their accountability, their responsibility to senior management to meet the requirement, and the potential consequences associated with failing to do so.
6. Conduct of site visits that begin with a focus on education and that gradually add elements associated with enforcement.
7. Integration of the requirements into reporting mechanisms, with the functional authority informing both senior management and line management.
8. Depending on the results of the oversight activities, the adjustment of the system through any of the addition of new criteria, the removal of criteria, the broadening of criteria, or the clarification of criteria.

This is also a cyclical process, meaning that part of the functional authority's oversight activities will involve keeping track of each requirement and where it falls in the cycle.

This cyclical process is also fraught with a simple danger—that of the human ego. Those working in organizations are often intensely proud of their efforts and any outside comment that could detract from their value may be seen as a personal attack. Line managers must be able to keep the activity in perspective. It is simply an assessment or evaluation of how the organization is progressing. On the other hand, functional managers must be able to maintain a level of composure. This does not just apply to arguments with persons, but also in terms of being able to approach a situation clinically and from a technical perspective. It means being able to evaluate the situation in front of him or her on its own merits and not to become so involved in ensuring compliance with standards as to become inflexible or institutionally brittle.

Oversight of any activity involves management ensuring that its requirements are appropriately arrived at, implemented, and maintained so that the organization functions appropriately and within an acceptable level of risk. As a result, oversight in support of governance can be broken down into two major components. The governance structure was established in the first part of this chapter; oversight activities take place within this structure. Properly executed, these two result in effective governance.

One of the first steps in implementing oversight is determining who will do it. Typically, AP&S oversight falls on the corporate security officer as part of his advisory role on the state of security in the organization. This individual faces a daunting burden, in that he or she is the gateway between all external entities (and their requirements) and the organization itself (with all its internal requirements). As the focus for all requirements affecting the organization, this appointment bears the ultimate corporate accountability with respect to the protection of the organization's valued assets and, by default, the achievement of goals that utilize those assets.

Having established who will conduct oversight activities, the governance staff must then determine exactly what will be proven or confirmed. One key confirmation is accountability, or giving a reason why direction was or was not followed. A basic principle with accountability is that each individual who must achieve requirements or meet accountabilities must be provided with the authority and resources to achieve objectives. The level of authority and resources granted are commensurate with the level of accountability borne by the individual and, of course, directly linked to the work needed to be done to achieve those requirements. An individual who is not accountable for anything but his or her own tasks (e.g., in a traditional line relationship) may likely have very limited authority and resources. On the other hand, the senior corporate officer (the focal point for all accountabilities) will act as the font of all authority and allocation of resources within the organization.

The corporate security officer requires help to conduct oversight activities. It is unrealistic to expect the senior corporate officer to understand (and be able to keep track of) each nuance of the requirements for which he or she is accountable. The organization will likely be subject to several requirements of a technical nature—ranging from the handling of dangerous goods to the protection of personal data on networks—that require the full attention of persons with special knowledge, skills, abilities, and experience. As suggested in the section on lines of governance, these persons are delegated under the authority of the senior corporate officer as *functional authorities*, who, in matters of their corporate specialty, become accountable not to their line manager, but to the senior corporate officer, to ensure that the programs that support these technical requirements remain up to date and relevant to the efforts of the organization. As a result, the functional authority's power does not come from an authoritative base (such as pay grade or rank) or position in a line organizational chart, but from a reference base of unique expertise. This can become confusing in larger organizations that have established a culture of strict hierarchies or similar structures. The following should be absolutely clear, however, regarding the role of the functional authority in exerting influence within a governance structure:

- The functional authority bears a significantly greater burden than most line managers, in that his or her efforts can have an impact at an enterprise-wide level and not simply with respect to the performance of subelements within the group. This is regardless of the classification level of the relative individuals; it is up to the line manager to get over any ego trip that would prevent him or her from taking advice from, or even listening to, someone of a "lower rank."

- The functional authority may be delegated as a line manager with respect to organizing his or her own resources (as illustrated in Figure 10.2), but is also delegated by the senior corporate officer directly to act on that senior official's behalf with respect to meeting the requirements in a certain field (in this case, the protection of all valued assets in the organization).

- The functional authority, when speaking from his or her unique specialty, is not speaking as a line manager, but as a functional authority and, therefore, on behalf of the senior corporate officer.

- Those line managers or employees who decide to disregard the legitimate efforts of the functional authority are not disobeying the individual based on his or her line position (which may be of a lower rank than that of the disregarding manager) but, rather, are disregarding direction issued under the delegated authority of the senior corporate officer. This can also be considered disloyalty to the senior authority.

- The functional authority, due to this additional delegation, is often also assessed with greater regard to features of character, as he or she will be holding a position of elevated responsibility and trust within the organization. Essentially, since more authority and positional "soft power" is vested in this functional authority over more senior personnel, more scrutiny is undertaken in holding functional authorities often to a higher standard of accountability.

Appointment as a functional authority is based on the individual's ability to demonstrate that he or she possesses wider and more comprehensive training, education, knowledge, skills, abilities, and experience to address the potentially significant body of technical elements needing to be addressed for the organization to show that it has actually met the requirements placed on it. The typical line manager, on the other hand, faces a much narrower set of accountabilities, due to his or her more focused and less diverse range of responsibilities. While the functional authorities are accountable and responsible for ensuring that the requirements (and how they are to be met) are clearly communicated to those with line authority, the line manager is accountable to his or her superior only to ensure that he or she accomplishes a certain volume of work as assigned by his supervisor. Given that the corporate security officer lacks hierarchical control over line managers, he or she must rely on influence, with the veiled threat of repercussions from senior corporate officers.

This has become a significant challenge in a compliance-driven culture. Given that functional positions are often seen as little more than administrative or corporate support, they run the risk of being staffed with technically incapable persons. They also run the risk of becoming stale as training costs and similar activities are not maintained. It should be clear to an organization's management that the senior functional authorities must be knowledgeable and technically capable.

Another key difference between the line manager and the functional authority lies in the impacts associated with each position's responsibilities. The work of the line manager falls under accountabilities that are generally limited in scope, in that they are derived from his or her immediate supervisor, and, as a result, the impact of the decision is largely limited to the nature of the processes supported by that work. The functional authority, as noted earlier, works in a domain that is corporate wide; any lapses of judgment or deliberate, inappropriate acts could impact the whole organization.

Oversight activities

There are many activities that comprise oversight, all of which provide evidence of the degree of compliance with the policy suite, which is the expression of senior management's intent. They could include the following:

- *Audits:* This entails taking a snapshot of an operation and comparing it to the applicable standards, best practices, and procedures.
- *Assessments:* These are less constrained than audits, and use the complete policy suite and industry best practices to determine how appropriately controls are implemented. Where audits are often compliance related, assessments are more risk related.
- *Monitoring:* This is real- or near-real-time reporting of performance, typically conducted at the tactical or system level, to confirm correct functioning.
- *Modeling and simulation:* This confirms correct functioning without risk to operational systems.
- *Testing:* This also confirms correct functioning without risk to operational systems, with the added benefit of putting some additional "not business as usual" pressure on the system (personnel, equipment, facilities, infrastructure).
- *Technical vulnerability assessment (TVA) and penetration testing (PenTest):* These specialized oversight activities are applied to IT systems (including SCADA). TVAs are typically passive, while PenTests are typically more active, sanctioned "attacks" on the protective posture of an IT system.
- *Training and awareness:* As noted, this goes a long way to confirm correct performance, as well as the insight to identify an anomaly and report it to the appropriate authority (typically a functional authority with the requisite expertise to take action).

No one oversight activity is either adequate or preferred. Each requires special skill sets on the part of functional authorities to acquire the salient information; this is the easy part. The challenge is to collate the information among perhaps previously siloed functional authorities, regardless of their individual support toward mission success. Once this challenge is met, it remains only to analyze the results and prepare consolidated reports for senior management. Once this information is passed, one can conclude that oversight, contributing to governance, has been achieved. Governance will have truly contributed to informed decision making. Details on this follow.

Taking action from oversight

The final element of oversight involves the response to what is found during monitoring activities. While the requirements themselves may have some impact within the organization, the way that the organization responds to the extent to which those requirements are met will have an operational effect throughout the organization—for good or ill. Again, the interests of the corporation must be paramount in the minds of those making recommendations, and this begins with the functional authorities providing sound, relevant guidance from within their areas of expertise. The following approach may prove to be useful as a guide:

- Where the line unit exceeds the requirement but has a detrimental effect on other programs, then controls should be eased (while still within acceptable risk levels), thereby establishing a more appropriate balance.

- Where the line unit exceeds the requirements or meets the requirements in a particularly innovative way that is either neutral in terms of its impact or leads to improvement in the organization's overall performance, positive reinforcement (recognition and awards) may be considered and lessons learned applied more broadly in the organization.
- Where the line unit meets its requirements but does not exceed them or apply any innovative practices, then that compliance should be applauded as a matter of fact but not necessarily rewarded.
- Where the line unit fails to meet its requirements, but does so because of the impact on other critical processes or systems and can express this clearly in risk management terms (this is accountability in play), then the functional authority and line management should determine how to change the requirement or recommend an exemption for senior management authorization. Additional training and education should be considered as a supplementary measure.
- Where the administrative unit fails to meet its requirements and can offer no legitimate basis for not adhering to them, then graduated disciplinary measures may be warranted.

These actions will require a coordinated effort among senior management (as the assumer of risks associated with each case), the functional authority (in terms of program management, but also with potential impacts on the ability to maintain the requirements across the organization), and the line management of the area or unit involved. The decision arrived at by these three groups provides a clear direction for change within the organization. Once the adjustments have been made, the functional authority must rebalance his or her own program to adjust the control posture of the rest of the organization.

Conclusion

In the short term, changing the mindset of stakeholders toward a more horizontal, influencing governance framework will take strong will, strong communication, and, above all, strong leadership, including the use of rewards and sanctions. Writing in regard to governance, Frisina and Frisina (2011, p. 28) noted that "individual leader behavior is singularly the most important predictor to organizational performance." But, from a corporate perspective, it will be worth it if managers at all levels appreciate the value of AP&S specialists providing influence, as opposed to direction (or even bullying), and accept their advice willingly. The results will surpass the cost–benefit threshold (Berghel 2005), and since "effectiveness, not efficiency, is the prime driver" (Bakvis and Juillet 2004), overall improvement in the ability of the organization to meet all goals will be both positive and readily measurable.

The concept of oversight has often simply referred to checklists and other mechanisms by which something is checked as being present or not. As argued above, this is but one small aspect of oversight and governance. In reality, oversight is much more in line with the identification and management of requirements, accountability, responsibility, and delegation within the organization. Each of these is intended to support the organization's ability to meet its own requirements, not the requirements of any individual program. As a final note, it is clear that oversight is truly a team-level effort. Those involved in the management of organizations must become deeply aware of the relationship between line and functional authority and how they influence each other; within their own company in the areas of control, and also outward into the areas of influence and interest. It will be through that understanding and reinforcement of mission success as a key measurement tool that oversight within an organization under an effective governance framework becomes both clearer and more relevant to its activities.

References

Bakvis, H. and Juillet, L. (2004). *The Horizontal Challenge: Line Departments, Central Agencies and Leadership*. Canada: Canada School of Public Service.

Berghel, H. (2005). The two sides of ROI. *Communications of the ACM*, 48(4), 15–20.

Boone, W. and Moore, P. (2012). Illustrating asset protection and security concepts. Ottawa, ON: Carleton University. (unpublished manuscript, Master of Infrastructure Protection and International Security program).

BusinessDictionary.com. (2012). Guideline [definition]. http://www.businessdictionary.com/definition/guideline.html.

Minister of Justice. (1994). Canadian Marine Transport Security Act (c. 40). The Department of Justice Canada. http://laws-lois.justice.gc.ca/PDF/M-0.8.pdf.

Cronin, F. J. and Motluk, S. (2011). Ten years after restructuring: Degraded distribution reliability and regulatory failure in Ontario. *Utilities Policy*, 19(4), 235–243.

Frisina, M. E. and Frisina, R. W. (2011). Correcting your leadership "zero": Aligning your behavior with your mission, vision, and values. *Employment Relations Today*, 38(1), 27–33.

Jick, T. D. (2001). Vision is 10 percent, implementation is the rest. *Business Strategy Review*, 12(4), 36–38.

Kiyavitskaya, N., Zeni, N., Mich, L., Breaux, T. D., Antón, A. I., and Mylopoulos, J. (2007). Extracting rights and obligations from regulations: Towards a tool-supported process. In *Proceedings of the IEEE/ACM 22nd International Conference on Automated Software Engineering*, 429–432, Atlanta, GA, IEEE Computer Society.

Landau, D., Drori, I., and Porras, J. (2006). Vision change in a governmental R&D organization. *The Journal of Applied Behavioral Science*, 42(2), 145–171.

Lawler, E. (2006). Business strategy: Creating the winning formula. In Gallos, J. (Ed.), *Organization Development: A Jossey-Bass Reader*, Chapter 27. San Francisco, CA: Jossey-Bass.

Lewis, T. G. (2006). *Critical Infrastructure Protection in Homeland Security: Defending a Networked Nation*. Hoboken, NJ: Wiley-Interscience.

Mahoney, W. and Gandhi, R. A. (2011). An integrated framework for control system simulation and regulatory compliance monitoring. *International Journal of Critical Infrastructure Protection*, 4(1), 41–53.

Markulec, M. (2008). SCADA systems: Unknown connections could spell trouble. *Power Engineering*, 112(11), 188–244.

Masera, M. (2010). Governance: How to deal with ICT security in the power infrastructure? In Lukszo Z., et al. (Eds), *Securing Electricity Supply in the Cyber Age*, 111–127. Dordrecht, The Netherlands: Springer.

Masera, M., Wijnia, Y., de Vries, L., Kuenzi, C., Sajeva, M., and Weijnen, M. (2006). Governing risks in the European critical electricity infrastructure. In Gheorghe, A. V., et al. (Eds), *Critical Infrastructures at Risk Securing the European Electric Power System*. Dordrecht, The Netherlands: Springer.

Masters of Infrastructure Protection and International Security (MIPIS). (2012). Vision statement: Infrastructure protection and international security program. Ottawa, ON: Carleton University. http://www1.carleton.ca/ipis/.

Maxwell, J., Antón, A., Swire, P., Riaz, M., and McCraw, C. (2012). A legal cross-references taxonomy for reasoning about compliance requirements. *Requirements Engineering*, 17(2), 99–115.

Nash, D. (2009). The accountability conundrum: Staying focused, delivering results. *American Journal of Medical Quality*, 24(2), 5S–43S.

National Standards Policy Advisory Committee (NSPAC). (1978). *National Policy on Standards for the United States and a Recommended Implementation Plan*. Washington, DC: NSPAC.

Nicholson, A., Webber, S., Dyer, S., Patel, T., and Janicke, H. (2012). SCADA security in the light of cyber-warfare. *Computers & Security*, 31(4), 418–436.

Noonan, A. (2009). Report on the university health system consortium (UHC), presented at 2008 quality and safety fall forum. *American Journal of Medical Quality*, 24(2 Suppl.), 16.

Nye, J. S. and Donahue, J. D. (2000). *Governance in a Globalising World*. Washington, DC: Brookings Institution.

O'Connell, D., Hickerson, K., and Pillutla, A. (2011). Organizational visioning: An integrative review. *Group & Organization Management*, 36(1), 103–125.

Prahalad, C. K. and Hamel, G. (1990). The core competence of the corporation. *Harvard Business Review*, 68(3), 79–91.

Senge, P. M. (1990). *The Fifth Discipline: The Art and Practice of the Learning Organization* (1st edn). New York: Doubleday/Currency.

Small, K. (2008). Relationships and reciprocality in student and academic services. *Journal of Higher Education Policy and Management*, 30(2), 175–185.

Transport Canada. (2010). Security measures. Canada: Transport Canada. http://www.tc.gc.ca/eng/marinesecurity/regulations-361.htm.

Van der Vleuten, E., and Lagendijk, V. (2010). Interpreting transnational infrastructure vulnerability: European blackout and the historical dynamics of transnational electricity governance. *Energy Policy*, 38(4), 2053–2062.

chapter eleven

Project management for SCADA systems

Darrell G. Vydra

Contents

Introduction

Information technology (IT) in critical infrastructure protection (CIP) and supervisory control and data acquisition (SCADA) systems has grown exponentially over the past 40 years. New hardware, software, automated platforms, and integrated systems have forced and challenged utility and energy firms to constantly evaluate and access how to either maintain current systems or upgrade to newer ones, often resulting in a "forklift" change. Along these lines, the utility and energy firms face other challenges such as budget decisions, training the workforce or hiring new staff, life-cycle management decisions such as end-of-life and midlife upgrades, (software) licensing, and interoperability.

In order to keep pace with new information technology (IT) innovations and upgrades, utility and energy firms are continuously implementing these solutions and upgrades through the project management discipline identified by the Project Management Institute* or PMI®. While this chapter will not teach one how to become a Project Management Professional† or PMP®, it will review and reveal some of the basic project management building blocks for reference and relate them to SCADA projects in support of CIP. Experienced project managers need to have not only a solid foundation of IT principles, but now must have a fundamental understanding of SCADA and control systems by ensuring that these system are less vulnerable to the myriad of escalating threats discussed throughout this book.

---

* The Project Management Institute is located in Newtown, PA. Address is 14 Campus Boulevard Newtown Square, PA 19073-3299, USA.
† Professional certification awarded to those individuals who meet a series of rigorous requirements including passing the PMP® exam.

Table 11.1 Listing of project manager objectives for securing SCADA systems

Knowledge area	Focus
Project integration management	Multifunctional directing and controlling
Project scope management	Technical objective(s) to achieve
Project time management	Schedule for on-time delivery
Project cost management	Funding for at-cost delivery
Project quality management	Level of technical precision and accuracy
Project human-resource management	Staffing for accomplishing tasks
Project communications management	Information distribution to team members and stakeholders
Project risk management	Preparing for obstacles and events jeopardizing progress
Project procurement management	Acquiring products and services enabling task accomplishment
Project stakeholder management	Proactive handling of decision makers and influencers

Areas of knowledge needed

According to the Project Management Body of Knowledge or PMBOK®, a project is "A temporary endeavor undertaken to create a unique product, service, or result" (PMI, 2013, p. 553). Furthermore, there are ten knowledge areas (PMI, 2013, p. 61) that serve as functional guides in accounting for and applying sound holistic project management discipline (Table 11.1).

A project manager (PM) begins his or her work up front as soon as the sponsor (the authorizing agent who provides the legal and fiscal "go-ahead") approves the project charter, which is "A document issued by the project initiator or sponsor that formally authorizes the existence of a project and provides the project manager with the authority to apply organizational resources to project activities" (PMI, 2013, p. 559). In addition to these ten knowledge areas, the "traditional" way of project management has five distinct process groups. These traditional process groups are phases of the project from its birth through its death. They are shown in Table 11.2.

However, since around 1990, there has been a deviation from the traditional five process groups. A more modern or new system/product development calls for the process groups shown in Table 11.3.

Table 11.2 Identified traditional activity of processes with descriptions

Process group (traditional)	Description
Initiation	Starting the project out from the top level view
Planning	Outlining the detailed tasks to accomplish the mission and identifying and gathering the resources to enable task accomplishment
Execution	Implementing the tasks
Monitoring and controlling	Supervising and ensuring task quality metrics and making corrections thereof
Closing	Ending the project by verifying the successful delivery of the tasks and documenting them

Table 11.3 Identified modified/current activity of processes with descriptions

Process group (modern)	Description
Requirements	Deriving what the product or system functionality must do
Analysis	Assessing candidate systems for optimization and selecting the best one
Design	Blueprinting the optimal candidate for production
Build and test	Developing the final system and conducting interim testing along the path
Accept and produce	User approval and fielding of the system

There are variations of the modern process groups, but in SCADA CIP projects, it is critical for the PM to ensure that all requirements are considered before going into the analysis and design phases as SCADA CIP projects are normally compliance and regulatory driven either by public or private/industry.

All projects have a life of their own, and the vast majority of these projects add value to the organization after they are completed. For example, a large professional sports team may take on the construction of a new stadium which may take a year to build and cost $1 million, but will also derive over $1 billion in revenue of the course of its life time or life cycle. Therefore, the value of the new stadium is not simply as a better state-of-the-art venue for its athletes and fans but a money-making product that justifies its cost and rationalizes it business case. PMs need to understand the project's contribution to the organization and the impact of successfully delivering the project to completion.

Like military officers, PMs are responsible for everything that happens and does not happen on their projects. While they do not need to be the subject matter expert (SME) on any given technical area, PMs need to recognize what the "end-state" of their projects is and to be able to extract the technical details from their SME or SMEs in order to provide leadership, management, and support to their technical project staff. For example, in a project in which water engineers are constructing and implementing several hundred miles of new water-pipeline infrastructure in an urban environment, the PM would want to know what technical requirements are needed by whom and how long it would take both conservatively (pessimistically) and aggressively (optimistically). Moreover, asking experienced engineers for this information before the project begins will initiate a process of validating all of the technical details required to build the project management plan.

Similarities and differences with the SCADA community

The SCADA industry arena is in many ways very similar to other industries that have been becoming more reliant on IT for automation, customer transactions, monitoring and controlling, supply-chain management, financial controls, other critical business functions. According to the International Information Systems Security Certification Consortium (ISC2, 2015), there is a triad of three elements in security: confidentiality, integrity, and availability (CIA). In reality, any organization that implements a high level of confidentiality (providing information only to those who need it) with safeguarding integrity (providing unalterable data checks) will succeed in allowing its approved internal users, partners, and customers with an unmatched level of availability (enjoying the use of the asset when demanded).

The utilities and energy industry (which employs SCADA) is unique from other industries in a few ways; namely, its delivery of services must be in real time, and its products must be constantly monitored to guarantee a high level of quality. Also, the core business of these firms is heavily dependent on operational engineers whose main role is to maintain their products (and production thereof) 24/7. Thus, engineers at these firms often are the line and organizational managers and leaders for their businesses and expect IT to ensure and enable the availability of these product-supporting systems. Finally, in the utilities and energy industry, there may be several thousand daily quality checks between dispersed monitoring systems (programmable logic controllers [PLCs] or remote terminal units [RTUs]) to not only ensure the availability of natural gas, water, or electricity but also to maintain the safety level of those products. For example, a metropolitan water firm that supplies clean water for a city hospital must closely check the chlorine level to prevent serious injuries to patients.

The nature of the majority of the IT security projects involving SCADA is to improve or enhance the "C" and the "I" of the CIA triad: confidentiality and integrity. In addressing the aspect of confidentiality, the key principle is to only allow access to those individuals who need access to critical systems through a multilayer authentication process, often incorporating biometric factors, which are the most difficult to break. The need-to-know guideline is emphasized here. Additionally, blocking access to all Internet sites and/or databases is another form of confidentiality in that organizations now find it easier to allow selected users to navigate to approved "places" by "white-listing" them. In other words, it is easier for organizations to establish a limited number of safe destinations for staff to work without fear of compromise versus attempting to limit ("black-listing") the growing number of potential harmful sites. Enabling sound integrity safeguards is also a challenging task for utilities and energy firms because there may be countless PLCs and RTUs that are automated and periodically send and receive a variety of data values for several critical measurements so as to maintain levels of water, electricity, gas, and other deliverable products. Preventing a malicious attack that may change the digital level of a key reading from 1000 units to 100 units may cause a human operator to take action from a "false positive" reading and actually lower the real 100-unit level to a 10-unit level, thus causing an actual serious condition in the system. Conversely, a passive hacker may simply spy on utilities transmissions over a long period of time as an "unauthorized" entity (confidentiality violation) and, when a vulnerable situation occurs, send unauthorized requests or commands to operators to severely alter safe levels of gas, water, or electricity.

Managing stakeholders and projects

Managing the stakeholders of energy and utility organizations is a critical task for PMs during a SCADA project. Stakeholder management is the newest addition to the family of knowledge areas found in the PMBOK. Although most people may recognize the term stakeholder and what it means, the official PMBOK definition is "An individual, group, or organization who may affect, be affected by, or perceive itself to be affected by a decision, activity, or outcome of a project" (PMI, 2013, p. 563). PMs, therefore, must be very cognizant of who their project stakeholders are and how to effectively manage them. One of the most important responsibilities for PM is keeping stakeholders informed. Setting up a stakeholder register for SCADA projects is an effective tool for accomplishing a consistent and accurate communications plan to keep stakeholders informed. Table 11.4 illustrates a sample stakeholder register.

When a stakeholder's influence (power) is high, his or her ability to affect the project is great. That is not to say that he or she would try to micromanage the project or to change the scope, but a powerful stakeholder can help assist the PM by marshalling resources,

Table 11.4 Sample table of identified roles and tasks based on a given project

Name	Position	Influence	Interest	Method	Frequency
Robert Sans	Chief technical officer (CTO)	High	Moderate	Dashboard	Weekly 5 min con call
Jane Hoe	Sponsor	Moderate	High	Phone, e-mail, face-to-face	Ad hoc as per important events; Mondays at 2 pm
Dan Gump	Network engineer	Low	Moderate	Project meetings	Thursdays at 10 am

resolving impasses, and expediting contracts if he or she thinks that the project has strategic value to the organization. It is imperative for the PM to provide a precise summary for higher ranking officials via a "milestone briefing" or a quick read like a dashboard, which captures essential information and displays it neatly for the reader. In short, an influential stakeholder does not possess a great deal of time but has the ability to assess facts quickly and ask specific questions for edification. On the other hand, if a stakeholder has a great interest in the project but is only moderately powerful, it is best to allow this stakeholder to "consume" project information frequently and in as much volume as much as he or she wants. Although these types of stakeholders may not exert a great deal of power, they could persuade a more influential stakeholder at some point in the project because he or she may be considered a very informed and knowledgeable player of whom senior staff may ask opinions.

Delivering high-quality products and/or services is one of the most important things that a PM must execute in his or her project. According to the PMBOK, project quality management "Includes the processes and activities of the performing organization that determine quality policies, objectives, and responsibilities so that the project will satisfy the needs for which it was undertaken" (PMI, 2013, p. 562). Quality is the degree to which the PM realizes his or her scope or the technical deliverable or deliverables. In other words, the product or service that the PM presents to the customer (whether internal or external) must be measured to the customer's satisfaction. During the early stages of the project, the PM must work with stakeholders on the exact measurable quality standards that guarantee the success of the project and document them for agreement. Scope, which is "the sum of products, services, and results to be provided as a project" (PMI, 2013, p. 560), is paramount to the project's success because it level sets what technical objective must be accomplished within the schedule and budget. However, the PM must constantly check the quality of those delivered objectives throughout the project to avoid rework of nonconformance.

How to be successful with SCADA implementations

Most successful PMs spend a great deal of time in planning out their phased tasks, not only in order to understand how tasks are sequenced and resourced but also to identify potential risks along the project path. Risks are not always negative, but PMs normally look for those negative risks first. According to the PMBOK, "risk is an uncertain event or condition that, if occurs, has a positive or negative effect on one or more project objectives" (PMI, 2013, p. 556). By identifying risks of all kinds up front, PMs can then plan out various ways to deal with and minimize risk. The four strategies that deal with threats or risks that may have negative effects on a project are: (1) risk avoidance, (2) risk transfer, (3) risk mitigation, and (4) risk acceptance. Risk on a project is not necessarily a "show-stopper" for that project, but not planning to take precautionary or preventative action or not having a plan to address a risk if it should occur can have disastrous consequences on a project. Therefore, during the planning phase of a project, PMs need to include all identified risks in a risk register (Siemens, 2015) and systematically collaborate with appropriate team members on how best to tackle these individually to prevent negative impacts on the project.

How are SCADA implementations unique?

SCADA projects are unique in that PMs need to consider how these projects will enhance the CIP of the organization. The PM needs to design various solutions or courses of action by which to evaluate potential solutions that best solve the problems that the project is intended to fix. One way to accomplish this task is to build a prototype (s) in a lab and test these working models against real-world situations. In today's marketplace, several vendors offer design and test software for building prototypes with which to evaluate and judge different solutions. For example, SIEMENS builds a number of SCADA human–machine interfaces (one called SIMATIC WinCC) (Siemens, 2015) that help PMs and potential operators to visualize and test tasks. Testing solutions is critical for the PM so that he or she can obtain an independent objective analysis of a solution rather than receiving biased recommendations from self-interested third parties. In summary, PMs need to verify that their candidate SCADA solutions will afford the maximum protection for CIP assets.

The traditional SCADA arena is being challenged by IT in that now operators (several physical miles away) have the ability to traverse series of networks to "see" into numerous remote devices that directly monitor energy and utility operations. Often, in design-related projects, PMs get involved in the initial discussions about how to safeguard and protect data access from would-be threats while enabling those legitimate users to perform their daily jobs. Traditional SCADA and ICS devices communicated with a centralized operating station via a simple serial connection, which was a closed network. However, with Internet protocol (IP) addressing on digital devices that connect via physical lines or radio frequency (RF) and the demand by business back-end offices for support information (i.e., billing), allowing only authorized users to gain access to critical systems, and only when they need to, becomes problematic. Therefore, the PM must ensure that adequate testing of the data's confidentiality and integrity occurs in a preproduction environment during the build and test phase. If this effort does not occur, an unsecure system may be built and fielded.

Conclusion

PMs managing CIP in SCADA environments need to leverage many skills and abilities in their intellectual tool bag. Finalizing scope, dividing projects into manageable phases, applying a disciplined approach to defining requirements and designing solutions, testing unit or piece components and holistic systems throughout the project, and ensuring that a smooth transition takes place from the project to operations are just a few of the duties and responsibilities of the SCADA PM. He or she must communicate regularly with several stakeholders and inform them on project progress while guiding team members in the delivery of successful products and services. In this environment, there is no room for error or rework. Once completed, CIP projects normally affect thousands of people in urban and suburban communities. Therefore, SCADA PMs should remind themselves what is at stake and drive their projects to success to meet the highest quality standards.

References

International Information Systems Security Certification Consortium (ISC2). (2015). Confidentiality, integrity, and availability (CIA triad). TechTarget. http://whatis.techtarget.com/definition/Confidentiality-integrity-and-availability-CIA.

Project Management Institute (PMI). (2013). *Project Management Body of Knowledge (PMBOK®)*, 5th edn. Project Management Institute.

Siemens. (2015). SIMATIC WinCC: Maximum plant transparency and productivity. http://w3.siemens.com/mcms/human-machine-interface/en/visualization-software/scada/simatic-wincc/pages/default.aspx.

section three

Architecture and modeling

chapter twelve

Communications and engineering systems

Jacob Brodsky

Contents

Where security fits in processes

This chapter describes the concept of designing for process integrity. Too often, supervisory control and data acquisition (SCADA) and control systems are discussed in isolation from everything that they monitor and control. Yet, the processes these systems control are the very reason for their existence. It is as if one were fascinated with the knobs, displays, and buttons of an autopilot to the exclusion of the rest of the aircraft. This chapter describes engineering tips and analysis that can be used to secure a process at the very lowest levels. This chapter will also discuss dependencies of the control system on infrastructure such as virtual private networks (VPN), satellite networks, and wireless radio networks. It will also discuss policies that can be used to secure (or abused to violate) process integrity.

Describing a process

Consider a coal-fired electric power generation plant. It exists to produce electricity for the grid on a large scale at an economical rate, with reasonable pollution controls. Note the last part of that sentence. The license for the plant's operation is dependent on proper documentation of stack emissions and that there should not be excess heavy metals, sulfur, or ash coming out of that process.

The plant and all of its systems have standard process behaviors for both routine and exceptional situations. It is the job of a control engineer to specify control elements, instruments, and strategies to effect nominal behavior and responses to common upsets and emergencies. When the design is complete, there should be two formal documents handed over to the operations staff: (1) the process description document and (2) the control narrative document.

The broad outline and summary specifications of how this plant works are described in a document called the *process description*. In that document, one will find an outline of how things are supposed to work in nominal conditions. This document does not discuss failure modes, contingency planning, safety, or anything of that sort. The process description contains the ultimate and nominal performance expectations of the infrastructure. The process description remains unchanged as long as the infrastructure designs also remain unchanged.

In the case of the coal-fired power plant, the process description document describes the broad specifications such as maximum blower air volume, maximum coal feed rate, maximum boiler temperature; nominal steam generation rates, water flows, turbine inlet and outlet temperatures, stack emissions, and so on. It is essentially a document of the design goals.

In another example, a process description of a simple wastewater pumping station would indicate what areas feed to that pumping station, where the pumped flow goes, what the overall design flows are, how many wet wells there are, and how large each wet well and pump is. It is not expected that either of these examples would have information concerning safety trip reactions, reaction to alarm conditions, or security violation procedures.

There is a second document called the *control narrative*. This document is excruciatingly detailed. It is intended to list every automated contingency. The purpose is for tactical operational reference. It is intended to describe exactly what an operator should expect to happen, given conditions X, Y, and Z, at some stage of the automated process. The ultimate goals process methods and routines are presumed to be known by the reader.

To do this, the control narrative breaks the overall process into atomic components called control loops. A control loop has one or more sensors, and actuators to control valves, pumps, mixers, heaters, or something of that sort, and it does so to maintain or reach some set-point parameter. For example, a control loop might keep water supply for a reservoir that feeds a boiler at some particular level. If the level drops, the rate at which the water is pumped into the reservoir increases. If the level rises, the rate at which water is pumped drops.

These elemental control loops are then described in terms of what they each do, and then where they fit into the process as a whole. There are also descriptions of what process reactions to safety or alarm condition trips are effected into the process.

For example, a dewatering belt filter press typically has a safety trip wire to shut down everything should someone fall onto the moving belt from a nearby catwalk. If that safety trip wire is pulled, the press will stop immediately, but the rest of the process will also need to react, including the material being dewatered, metered coagulant feed pumps, and downstream systems such as a lime slaker, screw conveyer, and mixer. If the latter safety system shutdowns do not occur, this is unlikely to hurt anyone, but would leave a prodigious and possibly hazardous mess to clean up, and would probably slow down first responders.

Another example: If a wastewater pumping station fails to see a pump run for some configurable time period, this is cause for an alarm. Either the station is not receiving sufficient flow, or the pump is not starting for some reason (perhaps a fuse burned out on one of the three phases of the motor).

As process security systems mature, there will need to be a control narrative written to respond to security stimuli. For example, if someone connects an unrecognized device to a data switch in the field, a controller might be configured to discover this and to place the process immediately into a safer state that can only be disabled by a physical key switch held by an operator. If the fraction of bandwidth in use on a network doubles, a controller might send commands to the input/output (I/O) to place valves in some nominal default position where things will continue to run safely, even though they may not be optimal.

Writing and maintaining a control narrative document is painstaking work, yet it is one of the most important centerpiece documents of understanding between operations, engineering, and IT. It describes what the process is supposed to do and how it is supposed to happen. It is supposed to be a living document. It should be negotiated and modified with annotations of who signed off on them and why, and when these changes were incorporated; and who did the testing of the changes, and when. Ideally, it would be cited in annotations on a source code control system of each of the proportional integral derivative (PID) controllers/variable frequency drive (VFD)/programmable logic controller (PLC)/remote terminal unit (RTU)/human–machine interface (HMI) changes. Some are considering the use of a wiki to handle control narrative documents and changes.

Network integrity monitoring

It is essential to understand that modern control systems will need to manage their own integrity through the monitoring of process networks. Note that this goes beyond just Ethernet networks. It should include monitoring for spread-spectrum wireless gear, narrowband radio, serial RS-485 and RS-485-type networks such as FieldBus, CANBus, DeviceNet, ControlNet, ProfiBus, and the like. Some PLC manufacturers have the ability to explore and upload/download programs or even firmware through these various networks, and one can connect to devices reachable only through several kinds of media and protocols. For example, the parameters for a VFD might be downloaded from DeviceNet, via a PLC that speaks DF1 on a serial cable attached to a port on another PLC via ControlNet, which in turn has an EthernetIP interface to an Ethernet switch that also has a virtual local area network (VLAN) port that can be accessed from the PC in your office. In other words, there is a significant possibility that these specialized networks may not be as stubby (dead end) as one might first think.

This integrity monitoring should include, as a minimum, some method of monitoring bandwidth and port states. If something drops off-line, knowing where and what ports or trunks are dead is crucial for rapid response. Given complex networks such as the example cited earlier, one could be wandering across acres of plant campus before finding where a DC power supply attached to a media converter failed. The display of this data is something that IT network security staff should be heavily involved with.

Looking toward the future, many PLC manufacturers have the ability to respond to a simple network management protocol (SNMP). A custom management information base (MIB), or perhaps even a standard MIB that covers typical network behavior such as this, would be a fairly straightforward thing to incorporate into a control systems network data-gathering center. It is doubtful that operators would use a network data-gathering center, but it is very likely that engineers and IT would use it for forensic and diagnostic purposes.

One example of data that might have dual use for both engineering purposes and alarms is the PLC cycle time. Most PLC gear has some way of reporting how long it took to calculate the relay ladder logic, or to cycle back to the beginning of the main* routine. The PLC cycle time can indicate that things are nominal, or that something peculiar is going on. Note that the infamous Stuxnet attack against the uranium enrichment plant in Natanz, Iran, was very careful to edit a routine that would have alerted engineers that there was some extra code in the PLC. That routine was the routine that reported cycle time overruns.

PLC cycle time can vary, depending on what the PLC is doing. There may be threads of code that do not normally execute as part of a routine scan cycle. For example, if a filter goes into backwash mode, the PLC scan time may change. However, if one sees the PLC scan time change without any indication of what triggered the change, that would be cause to go looking for potential problems.

Control validation

Designing a process for better security seems daunting. Some hazards are simply unavoidable. Nevertheless, there are things one can do; for example, hardwire a normally open timer contact to a motor start line. The timer is started when the status of the motor changes from running to stopped. Until that timer expires, it will block any further attempts to restart the motor. Most processes have very little need to start and stop large motors frequently. This simple restart–disable timer can help prevent abuse of large assets even if someone or something were to take direct control of the I/O.

Other protective features could include more aggressive set-point validation efforts. If sudden large excursions of set points are not expected to be part of the process, include input validation on the PLC or RTU that would do something reasonable with that set point (e.g., accept it, but not allow any further large excursions for some time-out, or reject it outright, or perhaps slowly slew the set point to that excursion). This validation is something that would be discussed in the control system narrative document.

Sometimes, bandwidth restrictions are a good thing. For example, if it takes half an hour to download new firmware into a device on a slow network, it is less likely to go unnoticed. Control systems, particularly PLC systems and distributed control systems (DCSs), tend to have very regular polled I/O with very predictable bandwidth characteristics. Setting a bandwidth limitation for some slightly higher rate than nominal would make excess traffic or excess latency noticeable. Thus, if someone inserts some new gear in the middle, it would be noticed.

Another way to validate a process is to include diverse and orthogonal instrumentation. For example, if a wastewater plant has influent flow at a certain temperature, one would then expect certain bacteria to be active, which then would mandate certain return activated sludge and aeration rates. However, if the dissolved oxygen meters do not indicate the expected results, it could mean that the bacteria are dying, or that the wastewater is not being aerated properly. Quick sample checks can be conducted to see if the bacteria are present in significant numbers. If the numbers are low, one might look for toxic contaminants in the wastewater. If the numbers are nominal, then one might look for defective instruments. Often, the dissolved oxygen probes will need to be cleaned. However,

---

* Most controllers have a primary dispatch program, much like the main() function one finds in the C programming language. This main routine is the primary loop that either has the logic embedded in it or dispatches other routines to perform the logic required. The loops should complete in a short period of time, measured in milliseconds. This period of time is referred to as the cycle time of a controller. If the work is not completed within a certain limit, the controller is designed to go to a fault state.

the key to this discussion is that the process has multiple set points and inputs. If they do not agree, one can recognize that something is wrong.

Another way to know that something is wrong is to examine the turbidity of the flow from the aeration basin to the clarifiers. If the turbidity increases for no apparent reason, we know once again that something is not right.

Yet another cross-checking method is to use local and remote counters. Normally, one would not use the HMI counters because they are dependent on a properly functioning HMI and PLCs. However, a PLC event counter could be compared against an event counter on the HMI, and if the two of them disagree on a quiet and relatively quiescent system, it is time to investigate.

Managing process dependencies

An attacker interested in damaging many industrial processes can do surprisingly well by monkeying around with the electric grid that feeds a large industrial complex. Every process design must take into account what happens when the power flickers. Sequencing and staging process devices back online after a power failure is code that is often handwritten in relay ladder logic by an engineer.

Full review of the ladder logic code by both IT and engineering would be of significant help. Why have IT review it? Because, in the process of explaining it to them, and in the process of them asking questions, one may discover all sorts of situations that were not accounted for in the control system narrative. It also informs the IT staff what to expect in the field, and what areas are more sensitive to network surgery than others.

The same issue of power fluctuations is also present in telecommunications problems. Simulate the power failure to a switch and then discuss how things come back up, and how to improve the situation. Many switches are notoriously poor at properly negotiating speeds, VLANs, trunks, and so forth. In an office, this is no big deal. On the shop floor, it may well turn out that things do not return to service as smoothly as they otherwise might. An IT network expert can help configure the switch not to waste so much time after it comes up.

Conversely, sometimes there are services that need to be enabled for proper industrial protocol work. For example, Internet group management protocol (IGMP) snooping is essential for good performance when using EthernetIP. A resilient plant would include careful configuration management of all switches, routers, firewalls, and so forth. Another point: While SNMP monitoring with IT is helpful, do not forget about designing the process so that the controller is made aware of the following situations:

1. Degraded bandwidth
2. Unknown personnel access
3. Missing HMI stations
4. Full network emergency: go-safe mode

Clearly, the latter is dangerous and disruptive, but it is less dangerous than leaving things just as they are. To make a controller aware of these problems, it would be wise to purchase switches that communicate using industrial protocols as well as SNMP. If a port that is normally live goes dead, there may be options to build in to the control system narrative that can react to problems like this.

The use of transmission control protocol/Internet protocol (TCP/IP) networks has tended to make people sloppy about choosing appropriate media for the plant. In particular, there is a disturbing trend among many control systems vendors to use wireless Institute of Electrical and Electronics Engineers (IEEE) 802.11 and IEEE 802.15.4 devices for I/O. While wireless systems can be very reliable, they are not perfect. They do fail. They can also be jammed with many things that a first responder might bring, such as a wireless remote video camera.

One advantage of having a large plant campus is having control over the real estate where these radio frequency (RF) paths will be used. Physical control of the premises is often a significant part of staying safe when using wireless I/O or wireless machine-to-machine communications. Nevertheless, do keep in mind that there are other users of the spectrum. The author recommends that engineers and IT staff in the United States read 47CFR15.5(b)* and carefully consider what the implication of unlicensed wireless use can be. Those of you whose operations are not in the United States, take heed: This paradigm is nearly the same in every country on the planet.

The basic premise is this: If you choose not to license your operations, you forfeit the ability to complain to your country's legal system if someone else should either accidentally or legitimately interfere with your transmissions. Think long and hard whether you can live with losing that wireless link, because some day you will.

It is also very important to realize that the IEEE boilerplate for the 802.11 and 802.15.4 specifications has a feature called clear channel availability. This feature is used to implement what the networking community called carrier sense multiple access (CSMA)/collision avoidance (CA). To do this, because it is a direct-sequence spread-spectrum device, it can only detect background energy; and if it detects background energy of any sort, it inhibits transmission. That background energy detection is basically protocol independent. If the signal, after despreading, presents some very low level of energy to the detection circuitry, the device will assume that everyone else can hear that energy as well. Note that, in an industrial environment, this is not a good assumption.

Thus, it takes very little signal strength to inhibit an 802.11- or 802.15.4-based device. Many vendors sell mesh network devices. However, a mesh can be defeated very easily with a simple video transmitter on channel. Network routing techniques, no matter how sophisticated, will not help if the sensor device does not transmit while waiting for the channel to clear.

This is why, for security purposes and rapid diagnostics, it pays to monitor the radio spectrum of all wireless devices in the control system. The training and cost of test equipment is significant. However, the downtime and confusion from a jamming attack will be significant as well. Those who choose to use wireless I/O or machine-to-machine communications should be prepared to respond to RF problems. Also note that, if the problem comes from outside company property, there is no legal recourse. A video baby monitor could cause significant mayhem.

Even if equipment is licensed, do not rest easy. There have been inadvertent interference cases with narrowband SCADA systems. It is imperative that a SCADA system user know how to locate sources of interference and intermodulation. In this case, however, the system operator has a legal right to the channel. If on-channel interference is detected, whether deliberate or not, the SCADA system operator can go to law enforcement and judicial authorities to demand the user of the interfering energy cease and desist. Unfortunately, intermodulation distortion is not so easy to deal with, but it can be mitigated with attenuators, polarization changes, and better antennas with more directivity.

---

* 47 CFR 15.5(b) is the Electronic Code of Federal Regulations. Section 15.5 refers to the "general conditions of operation," which pertains to use of radio frequencies, including "(b) Operation of an intentional, unintentional, or incidental radiator is subject to the conditions that no harmful interference is caused and that interference must be accepted that may be caused by the operation of an authorized radio station, by another intentional or unintentional radiator, by industrial, scientific and medical (ISM) equipment, or by an incidental radiator." This law is enforced by the Federal Communications Commission. http://www.ecfr.gov/cgi-bin/text-idx?SID=bb7d157e1e996cfcf3bf45ddb4ef3ac7&mc=true&node=se47.1.15_15&rgn=div8.

Perhaps the utility or company has a right of way where one can pull fiber-optic cables. While it can avoid many of the pitfalls of wireless data, even fiber-optic cables can have problems. For example, an oil pipeline that uses a cable installed alongside the pipeline may not be able to issue commands if there is a break somewhere along that pipeline. If the break catches fire, the cable will be cut. Without alternate routes to get to an RTU, there may not be any way to issue commands that will shut down the source of the fuel. If security and integrity matter, the network should be organized into multiple rings, and these rings should have integrity signals sent both ways round, to be certain that, if needed, the ring will continue to handle traffic to as many stations as possible.

When designing a ring, or any other meshed or partially meshed wide area network (WAN), be sure to make estimates of full traffic across any one segment failure and the rerouted traffic volumes. If the office traffic is aggregated over that ring, it is important to negotiate a higher priority, or at least a reserved bandwidth for process traffic, with the IT network design staff.

Another point to consider is whether and how a WAN will react to a power outage. Are there batteries in place to handle the outage? If so, how long will they last? How much temperature control do these sites have and how sophisticated is the battery charger? Over the years, the author has learned many lessons about battery maintenance. Today, many vendors sell battery float systems that can actually test the battery charge/discharge curve periodically. This makes it possible to raise an alarm on loss of battery capacity.

If neither option is available, but one is still working in an urban area, one can always get an internet digital subscriber line (DSL), cable TV, or even a fiber-optic cable that attaches to an Internet service provider (ISP). This is one area where one should plan for outages and attacks. All equipment should be run through a highly secured VPN. The VPN keys should be kept within the company. There are very few reasons to use a public certificate authority.

Nevertheless, one should ask hard questions on what dependencies the ISP has to maintain your connection and how long it might take them to recover from an outage. The sad truth is that there are few standards for ISP reliability for infrastructure. If the application is for a power company, the chances are the ISP depends on that very same electric power company. Using their facilities to communicate back to the operations control center during an extended outage will make a recovery much messier and much more complicated than it would otherwise be with an independent infrastructure.

Many places choose to use uninterruptible power supply (UPS) gear. Some will make the mistake of placing the interface of the UPS on the wider area network. Since the UPS can interrupt flow of power to the devices, this becomes an often overlooked attack point. Cycling control power that originates from the UPS can make the process automation equipment do strange things. IT security experts should go looking for situations like this and make recommendations for alternative methods for UPS monitoring and control.

Every communications path will fail at some time or another. Redundancies can fail to function properly, or may themselves be dependent on the very thing that triggered the primary failure (e.g., a common UPS). At each step of the way, one should plan on what is supposed to happen when communications fail. Whether dealing with a three-node local area network (LAN), or a complex morass of telecommunications technologies, security depends on having a definitive plan in the control systems narrative that will take over when communications fail.

Cold (black) starts

If the control system is completely dead from an extended outage, how does one bootstrap it back in to operation? An effective control system security program should augment this situation and respect it, not get in the way.

For example, a black start for a power plant may be something that one might assign to an engineer or a senior operator role, not to a mechanic's helper. The control system should be started in a manner that ensures access by senior operations and engineering staff, but not necessarily a junior operator or contractor.

If none of the regular staff with routine access controls are available, there will need to be some emergency administrator passwords that would be made available to the C-level executives. Once those keys are used, one would immediately need to assign new keys and new passwords on the system.

Like starting a car, starting a plant should be reasonably automated. There are certain start-up presets that will need to be configured. These are bootstrap presets intended to get things moving until the rest of the plant can react and adjust these presets to a more moderate rate. However, such presets presume that there is control in all places. This is one condition that is not often seen but does require certain access requirements. A wise security posture would take such presets and start-up configurations into consideration. Again, this should be found in the control system narrative.

Version control

Most engineers with any experience know the mass confusion that can happen following the start-up of a new process. Control system narratives are read furiously and the controls go through their first trials to see where the glitches are. Most of them are probably known. However, there can be some unusual situations where memory leaks, integer overflows, and subtle bugs can creep into PLC and HMI code.

It is routine for one person to be on 24 h call while others go on vacation. So the question is, following a start-up, how does one know where the correct version of the code is? What were the recent edits? Unless you use a full source code control system, or a very regimented version control policy, there is no way of knowing. Many manufacturers offer source code tracking systems for situations like this.

Generally, these systems cause a great deal of griping and gnashing of teeth. Almost nobody likes them. Even when they clearly save the day, few realize their value until, one day, someone makes undocumented changes. That is when managers and 24 h call personnel realize that although these version control systems are a pain to use, they are invaluable for getting the last known good configuration back online, and also for forensic purposes. These systems are also useful for forensic purposes to determine who left behind a logic bomb.

Key servers

With source code control systems, encrypted VPNs, and secure authentication available in protocols, many IT security people may express a very strong desire to park all the keys and ID authentication on one central server of everything on the office side of the networks. This is almost always a bad idea. First, it makes the control system dependent on the availability of the office network. Second, there are many failure modes which the office network probably did not consider when discussing control systems needs.

A better solution is to take a subset of the office authentication servers and to distribute them on the control systems side, and to synchronize them periodically. There will be complaints from the office security people, but they also need to see the issue at hand. To bother securing something, there has to be something worth securing. If the key server and authentication systems get in the way of this effort or slow things down excessively, or include assets that are dependent on some of the very things one would need the control system to resolve, then it does no good to be secure. To wit: Steel safe doors and walls would make airliner cockpits very secure, but would weigh so much that the airliner would hardly get off the ground while empty, let alone with paying passengers or cargo.

Summary

Process engineering has become a significant user of IT resources. However, its policies are not aligned with office policies. Further, there is no way they can be aligned with office policies. Instead, one should write, review, and update a control system narrative, in conjunction with engineering, operations, and IT to build a cohesive system with some self-awareness.

chapter thirteen

Metrics framework for a SCADA system

Robert Radvanovsky

Contents

As there is neither an established nor an agreed on security framework model that currently exists for supervisory control and data acquisition (SCADA) and control systems environments, we felt that the document written by the U.S. Department of Homeland Security (DHS), titled "Primer control systems cyber security framework and technical metrics," dated June 2009, applied most significantly in outlining and describing how SCADA and control systems should be secured, and how their metrics are determined. It is with appreciation that our thanks goes to DHS for such a document (U.S. DHS, 2009).

Introduction

The SCADA and control systems cybersecurity framework consists of seven cybersecurity elements, providing a foundation for the establishment of usable metrics. Each of the seven elements provides and represents an important aspect of the posture of the control systems cybersecurity effort at any given moment in time. There is at least one recommended metric for each element. An ideal value associated with each metric indicates the best that could possibly be attained for that metric. The preferred values are provided as a work in progress; thus, these seven elements of cybersecurity for control systems are briefly defined later, along with an explanation of each element:

1. *Security group knowledge*: Aspects of the system or associated management processes that impact the security group's ability (i.e., the people who are directly responsible for the cybersecurity of the control systems) to know the system and manage changes, including:
   a. Aspects of the system and processes associated with configuration management.
   b. Tools (or in some cases, lack of tools) supporting the tracking of changes.
   c. The collection and analysis of system logs and forensics.
2. *Attack group knowledge*: Attributes of the system, processes, or actions that provide potential attackers with means to gain information about the system, including the following:
   a. Software defects or configuration settings that return information when the system is probed by an unauthenticated user.
   b. Any information about the system obtained through public sources.
   c. Designing or implementing weaknesses allowing users with little or no authenticated privileges to gain information by listening on communication paths.
3. *Access*: Attributes of the system design, configuration, or deployment that provide a potential attacker with the ability to send or receive data to/from a component of the control systems from the attacker's location, including the following:
   a. Physical access to control systems components.
   b. Access to control systems components through external/internal networks.
   c. Access from internal components that may have been compromised.
   d. Access does not address whether the communication channel can be used to gain any useful information or whether sending data can provide the attacker with any desired result.
4. *Vulnerabilities*: Defects or weaknesses in the control systems that can be exploited to gain unauthorized privilege. This excludes defects that allow information to be obtained once access is gained without also explicitly gaining privilege. If a single defect allows an attacker to gain information and also gain privilege, that defect is defined as a vulnerability.
5. *Damage potential*: The amount of loss that a malicious attacker has the power to cause once they have gained privilege on a control system. It does not include any weaknesses associated with the process of gaining malicious control. Although actual damage may be reduced by a quick response to an attack, this dimension does not include any effects associated with attack detection or control systems recovery.
6. *Detection*: The ability to detect attacks and provide timely notification. This includes
   a. Antivirus software
   b. Intrusion detection systems (IDSs)
   c. Intrusion prevention systems (IPSs)
   d. System logging
7. *Recovery*: The ability to restore control systems from a compromised state to an uncompromised state. It includes the reliability of the backup and restore facilities and the time required to recover from an attack.

Security group knowledge

The first control systems cybersecurity element is *security group knowledge*, which represents those people within an organization who are (generally) responsible for the cybersecurity efforts of the enterprise's SCADA and control systems. Security risk is tightly correlated with the security group's knowledge of any of the control systems environments. For most situations, the security group has knowledge of these systems, including hardware and software components, network topologies, communication paths, normal operational behavior, and perhaps its vulnerabilities. This type of knowledge is necessary for such a group to make any type of security-based decisions that protect the control systems environments from any potential attack vectors. Such changes occurring to these control systems without the security group's knowledge may inadvertently introduce newer vulnerabilities into the systems environments, possibly inhibiting the introduction of any mitigation efforts. Knowledge of the system implies a configuration management process, which may include the security group in the planning of all changes and provides a mechanism for alerting the security group to any unauthorized changes.

Attack group knowledge

The second control systems cybersecurity element is *attack group knowledge*, which represents any potential adversary who may have an interest in attacking the plant or facility through a cybermethod. The cybersecurity risk from specific targeted attacks is minimized when potential attackers are unable to obtain any information about the targeted control system's environment. Preferably, anyone who is not authorized to use a control system should be prevented from gaining knowledge of its design, its configuration, even its location within the plant or facility, as well as obtaining any information that would allow these would-be attackers to plan and execute such an attack vector. This includes information that an attacker might gain about a control system after they have compromised portions of it, as well as any information they may obtain from other sources before attacking (e.g., a vendor's website touting the targeted facility as a success story; this may also include additional external sources, such as through social media outlets).

Access

The third control systems cybersecurity element is *access*. Although the majority of most authentication mechanisms are designed to prevent unauthorized use of data access paths, the existence of every path, authenticated or not, negatively impacts cybersecurity risk. The preferred scenario is to disallow any and all (where possible) communication channels between the control system's environment and any location external to those control systems, in which there may be the potential of attack vectors. Even though achievement of this hypothesis is usually not practical for most circumstances, the element should include (again, where possible) the absence of any electronic connections between the Internet and the control systems environment(s).

Vulnerabilities

The fourth control systems cybersecurity element is *vulnerabilities*, which are defined as any weakness or defect in the system that provides a potential would-be attacker with the means to gain privileges otherwise intended for authorized users only. An exploit of kinds of vulnerability leads to the compromise of the systems being targeted for attack. An ideal system has no weaknesses, no defects, and is therefore safe from any vulnerability weaknesses. Unfortunately, most (if not all) real systems have one or more weaknesses, and if an attack group is targeting the plant or facility, these would-be attacks will be actively searching vulnerability disclosure sites and using those techniques, which include techniques such as reverse engineering, to find any weakness.

Damage potential

The fifth control systems cybersecurity element is *damage potential*, which represents the ideal control system's environment that prevents physical damage to itself, even if electronic networks are completely compromised by a would-be attacker. Since risk is the expected value of loss, the damage potential is directly proportional and tied to risk. Thus, the amount of damage that can be caused by a compromised control system is determined by the type of process that it controls and by the very nature of any engineered safety systems (e.g., physical safety mechanisms may be in place that prevent significant damage despite a successful attack on the electronic control systems).

Detection

The sixth control systems cybersecurity element is *detection*, in which an ideal control systems environment includes detection mechanisms that alert the security group whenever there is an unauthorized event in the control systems. Unauthorized events come in several forms, and include activities such as an unauthorized user attempting to gain access to control systems environments or a forged message from a control systems device.

Recovery

The seventh control systems cybersecurity element is *recovery*. Ideally, most control systems can be restored to an uncompromised, working state immediately after an attack has been detected. *Recovery time* is related to *damage potential* because the cost of a successful attack correlates with the length of time that the control system is in a compromised state. *Damage* will tend to be less severe if the time to recover is minimized; however, the relationship between recovery time and damage potential is highly nonlinear and system dependent.

Defining cybersecurity metrics

The measurement of how each system applies the seven elements is instrumental to the overall cybersecurity risk of each system. Ten technical security metrics correlate support efforts in establishing measures for each control systems environment, of which at least one technical security metric is defined for each environment.

Several documents were used to acquire some useful guidance for developing a cybersecurity metrics program, as they contained suggested metrics of varying types. The technical metrics identified are based on the framework outlined earlier. Each metric was selected through consideration of measurable system attributes that provided meaningful representation, as well as relationship to risk for each of the seven cybersecurity elements.

Each metric identified is associated with (at least) one control systems cybersecurity element, as there is at least one metric associated with each of the seven cybersecurity elements. The metric defined attempts to answer the question: *What can be measured objectively on a given control system that is reasonably representative of how each system approaches its ideal associated with the control systems cybersecurity element?* For this framework, the metrics chosen may be different, but there should be at least one metric for each of the seven control systems cybersecurity elements. The owners or operators of a given control systems environment should consider how the metrics framework may be applied to their own control systems environment in a manner that is consistent over time, allowing greater accuracy to track progress in the cybersecurity process.

The outlined metrics are as follows:

- Rogue change days
- Security evaluation deficiency count
- Data transmission exposure
- Reachability count
- Attack path depth
- Known vulnerability days
- Password crack time
- Worst-case loss
- Detection mechanism deficiency count
- Restoration time

Rogue change days

The metric *rogue change days* are the number of rogue changes multiplied by the number of days the changes were unknown to the security group. A *rogue change* is any change to the system configuration without prior notification to the security group. For example, if two modems were added to the control systems' environment without the knowledge of the security group, and this change was not discovered by the security group until 10 days later, this would add $2 \times 10 = 20$ rogue change days to the metric calculation. This is the first metric for the security group knowledge security element. The preferred value is zero.

Security evaluation deficiency count

The metric *security evaluation deficiency count* is the number of control systems network devices that have not undergone a cybersecurity evaluation. This metric emphasizes the need to measure and track system knowledge about the security attributes of those control systems. For example, if two remote telemetry units (RTUs) that have not undergone security evaluations and one programmable logic controller (PLC) that has undergone security evaluation have been added to the control systems, this would add a count of $3 - 1 = 2$ to this metric calculation. This is the second metric for the security group knowledge security element. The preferred value is zero.

Data transmission exposure

The metric *data transmission exposure* represents the unencrypted data transmission. A key allegation is that all and any data that can be monitored by a would-be attacker would increase the likelihood of security risk. Some data is more sensitive than other data; however, for sake of ease, it is simply a count of the number of clear-text channels used by the control systems environment. For example, if *telnet* is used to connect to the control systems environment from the Internet, and if it is the only channel used for external access, then the value of the metric is one. Telnet channels are included in this metric because telnet uses a clear-text protocol that attackers can tap into to obtain passwords as well as other sensitive data. This is the metric for the attack group knowledge security element. The preferred value is zero.

Reachability count

The metric *reachability count* is the number of referential locations in relation to a specific point of origin (e.g., the Internet). A key assertion is that a reduction in the number of the referential locations tends to reduce the cybersecurity risk. This metric represents the count of the incoming and outgoing network communication channels plus the number of physical access data channels. For example, the reachability count (from the Internet) for a control system that is protected by a firewall (or some deterministic device) may be calculated with the following example. Suppose the control systems environment consists of 10 machines with two open transmission control protocol/Internet protocol (TCP/IP) ports each, and suppose the firewall prevents access to one of the two ports on each machine, but has no outgoing restrictions. The metric value is 10 incoming channels (one for each machine) plus 10 outgoing channels (one for each machine): $10 + 10 = 20$. This is the first metric for the access security element. The preferred value is zero.

Attack path depth

The metric *attack path depth* is the minimum number of independent, single-machine compromises required for a successful attack from an external source. This metric emphasizes having multiple layers of defense (defense in depth). A system configuration that can be successfully attacked by a single exploit should be avoided (if and when possible). For example, the attack path depth metric has a value of one if there is a modem that provides remote access from the public telephone network to critical control systems' components, as a successful attack requires only the compromise of a single device. This is the second metric for the access security element. The preferred value is infinity (∞).

Known vulnerability days

The metric *known vulnerability days* represents the sum of known and unpatched vulnerabilities multiplied by their exposure time interval. A key assertion is that the longer a vulnerability is known, the greater the risk that it will be exploited. The value of the metric increases each day when there are known and unpatched vulnerabilities. For example, if there are exactly three known and unpatched vulnerabilities on a given system, and if those vulnerabilities were publicly announced 2 weeks ago today, the current value of the metric should be calculated as $3 \times 14 = 42$ known vulnerability days. This is the first metric for the vulnerabilities security element. The preferred value is zero.

Password crack time

The metric *password crack time* represents the shortest time (in days) needed to crack/break a single password for any account on a given system. This metric is a measure of the minimum amount of time a would-be attacker would need to compromise the system by password cracking. For example, suppose the encrypted password files have been copied from all of the computers in the control room, and the first of these passwords was cracked in 18 days while the second password was cracked in 30 days using the software tool John the Ripper.* If no other passwords were cracked in fewer days, the metric calculation would yield a value of minimum (18, 30) = 18 days. This is the second metric for the vulnerabilities security element. The preferred value is infinity (∞).

Worst-case loss

The metric *worst-case loss* represents the maximum dollar value of the damage (or loss) that could be inflicted by malicious personnel via a compromised control systems environment. A key assertion is that system risk is strongly related to worst-case loss. Although there may be successful attacks where the actual loss is much less than the worst case, a reduction in the worst-case loss reduces the potential for loss and, therefore, reduces risk. For an example calculation of this metric, consider a chemical plant in which a major explosion can be triggered by signals from a control system. The value of the metric is the estimated cost resulting from such an explosion in dollars. The estimated cost may include repairs, replacements, and lost revenues from plant downtime. This is the metric for the damage potential security element. The preferred value is zero.

Detection mechanism deficiency count

The metric *detection mechanism deficiency count* represents the number of externally accessible devices that *do not* have malware or attack detection mechanisms. A key assertion is that detection mechanisms reduce risk, especially when applied to devices that can be used as entry points for potential attacks. For an example calculation of this metric, suppose the control room has 15 computers, each with one or more currently enabled universal serial bus (USB) ports, and assume that 12 of the computers have antivirus protection installed, but three do not. This would add 15 − 12 = 3 to this metric calculation. This is the metric for the detection security element. The preferred value is zero.

Restoration time

The metric *restoration time* represents the worst-case elapsed time to restore the system to a known uncorrupted (sometimes called an unmodified) state. This metric can be determined by running a test to measure the actual time elapsed from a worst-case compromise to a fully restored and 100% operational system. If a test is not feasible, and there have been no cybersecurity events on the control systems where the restoration time was tracked, the metric may be estimated. For example, assume a situation where all 20 computers in the control room have been compromised by a virus. However, the effects of the virus are relatively benign, allowing the response team to address one computer at a time. For this scenario, individual computers are taken off the network, while the remainder of the system continues operating in a degraded mode. The team cleans the virus from each machine, and then reintroduces the computer to the network and restores the applications in an up-to-date status. If this activity for a single machine takes 1½ h, the restoration time would yield a metric value of 20 × 90 = 1800 min. This is the metric for the recovery security element. The preferred value for this metric is zero.

---

* John the Ripper may be found at http://www.openwall.com.

Conclusion

The control systems cybersecurity framework consists of seven control systems cybersecurity elements, each pertaining to risk. Reviews of control systems cybersecurity assessments have demonstrated the framework's ability to address control systems' risk exposure. As a result, the seven control systems cybersecurity elements represent a foundation for managing the cybersecurity of control systems environments and provide a framework for the 10 metrics.

The 10 metrics support assessment of cybersecurity risk exposure over time. These metrics have been applied to control systems environments and have been proven to be practical and useful. However, every system and facility is unique, so there may be a need to select tailored metrics or measurement technologies in line with particular circumstances. An organization's tailored technical metrics should have at least one metric for each of the seven cybersecurity dimensions.

An important use of these metrics is in tracking the improvement or degradation of control systems' cybersecurity posture along all seven elements representing cybersecurity. As the cybersecurity posture improves, the risk to control systems from a cyberattack diminishes. Diligent use of the control systems cybersecurity framework and application of the technical metrics will aid in making more effective cybersecurity decisions for control systems environments.

Reference

U.S. Department of Homeland Security (U.S. DHS). Primer control systems, cyber security framework and technical metrics. Control Systems Security Program, National Cyber Security Division, U.S. DHS. June 2009. https://ics-cert.us-cert.gov/sites/default/files/documents/Metrics_Primer_7-13-09_FINAL.pdf.

chapter fourteen

Networking topology and implementation

Jacob Brodsky

Contents

Introduction

Before discussing network security issues, it is important to give some context about how operational networks are designed and operated for those who are not familiar with them. It is hoped in this chapter to distinguish some of the differences between office-based IT networks and operational networks.

While from a superficial perspective, it appears that operations and office networks look very similar, they are not; operations network hardware tends to be smaller, simpler, and slower, and it has wider environmental parameters. Typically, it will have dual power supply systems, often with 48-V DC or +24-V DC supplies. Fans are avoided so that they do not suck in dirt, moisture, or a corrosive atmosphere, or cause the unit to overheat when they stop working (a very common failure mode).

Among office IT networking staff, there is usually a need to consolidate all network hardware into one big managed network with a few large switches. This is mostly due to performance and operational philosophy concerns and the comparatively low expense of wiring from the switch to a desk in the office. Office networks tend to be quite dynamic, with ports powering up and down all the time, offering many different services, and requiring connectivity to a very wide range of addresses.

In contrast, operational networks tend to be very static. A programmable logic controller (PLC), once configured and running, hardly changes at all. The device remains on the network for the duration of the process. Many processes, such as a blower system, stay online continuously. Likewise, the PLC is expected to run continuously. It is commonplace to see a PLC running without reboot, restart, or even a power cycle for stretches of time measured in years.

As such, it is quite reasonable and practical to set a static IP address. In fact, this removes a dependency (the domain name [DNS] server and the dynamic host configuration protocol [DHCP] server) that would otherwise slow down the recovery of communications. Operational networks usually do not change frequently enough that a DHCP and a DNS are worth the effort to set up and maintain.

In operational networks, one often manually configures switch/router ports so that there is no autonegotiation of any sort. This speeds up the reacquisition of the network following an outage.

Operations network topologies are different. Typically, in an office network, everything is brought back to a few core switches where one can easily manage and reconfigure everything. However, on a plant floor, particularly where there are machine-to-machine connections, one would tend to see smaller switches with rapid recovery routes in a distributed manner. Wiring home runs to a central switch on a plant floor is also significantly more expensive than it is in an office environment. Plant wiring distances are greater and may have issues such as chemical or moisture exposure, high heat, explosive atmospheres, and so on. This often runs costs orders of magnitude higher than they would be in an office. In operational networks, it is usually cheaper to install small industrialized switches that share trunking cables than it is to make home runs back to a large switch in the center of the plant.

Other differences are that in an office, one needs flexibility to access everything. As such, it is common to use methods such as address blacklists in a firewall. In operational networks, the connections are well known and well established. It is quite practical to white list the few addresses that are needed to communicate within the control systems.

This brings up the most important point: latency.

Operational networks, particularly I/O networks, cannot tolerate an interruption of as little as tens of milliseconds. They will fault. This is by design. A PLC or an RTU that cannot communicate with a remote device or controller in a timely fashion will have problems with deterministic expectations of the design. This goes to the very definition of real-time environments. To make this reliable, operational networks are usually segmented and firewalled very tightly so that the real-time devices can continue to operate in real time reliably. This is called the zone-and-conduit system.

To reiterate, operations networks typically use hardened media, applications, and embedded devices that, once installed, are not expected to change for a long time. These are often decentralized networks designed to break apart into various zones connected by conduits (the zone-and-conduit model). These zones and conduits are oriented around the process, not the data flow. This is done to continue providing some rudimentary functionality in the event the network is broken or compromised in some other part. Thus, if a conduit between zones fails, one may continue to operate that segment of the process by updating the set points and monitoring the alarm states from the operator interface terminal (OIT: a stand-alone, stripped-down human–machine interface) in that zone.

In the office, wireless networks are commonplace and even expected. Many are pushing for wireless networks for industrial applications. Wireless communications have some positive aspects: As described earlier, wiring in industrial environments can be very expensive to install and maintain. However, wireless networks are not a free lunch. In a wireless network, everything has access to the spectrum used by wireless devices. It is possible to jam such a spectrum with very inexpensive devices. It is also possible to join such networks and, even if one cannot get access, to use up bandwidth so that real-time functions are affected. Furthermore, many industrial processes use the same bands as WiFi and other wireless protocols for radar level measurement or heating materials.* Thus, given these concerns about availability and the lack of media control, conservative engineering and IT security practice suggest that such networks should not be used for safety or critical controls. It is also a good idea to monitor the condition of the network very carefully. There will be more about this later.

On the positive side, the very localized, limited traffic profile of an operational network means that one can also alarm the traffic rates at both low and high levels, and one can set up distributed firewalls with very limited addresses. Thus there are opportunities from a security perspective where one can alarm and firewall many features that would be impractical in an office network.

Staffing differences

There is this one crucial difference that makes shared network infrastructure very difficult—out-of-service maintenance on an office network is usually done after working hours when few people would be impacted. Conversely, in an operational network, out-of-service maintenance is usually done during working hours, perhaps even during a shift change, such that the maximum number of people are available to assist with running parts of the process manually. These are typically 24-hour operations with limited tolerance for downtime, especially when there are few on-site to deal with it.

The out-of-service maintenance issue is one of the primary reasons why operational networks and office networks should not be managed by the same staff or the same infrastructure. It is a matter of philosophy and performance expectations. Furthermore, while the knowledge, skills, and abilities involved in these networks are supposed to be very similar, often they are not. Most employees in routine jobs act according to force of habit.

The habits and expectations for operational networks are different from the habits and expectations for office networks. While senior staff may be able to comprehend the reasoning and technologies in use, the junior and journeymen staff often do not.

If a network operations center (NOC) is used to monitor the operations networks, they must be available 24/7 and coordinate very closely with other operator activities. In practice, this is rarely a practical thing to do. Again, due to philosophical differences between office and operational networks, such information is usually best displayed in front of the operators who need it. Equipping and training IT staff on issues like process safety, first aid, arc flash protection, confined spaces, climbing safety, and where to find the various cabinets, just so that they can do what an operator does most of the time, is usually impractical.

Types of operational networks

There are two broad types of operational network architectures:

- Real time
- Event based

---

* The bands used by unlicensed radio are known internationally as industrial, scientific, and medical or ISM bands. They were originally intended for applications that need RF for heating, sensing, and imaging purposes. Many industrial processes already use the ISM bands, complicating any efforts to manage unlicensed activities.

Common low-level programmable automation controllers (PAC) and programmable logic controllers (PLC) networks typically use real-time networking protocols. A device asks another device what a value or a state is, and it reports what it is "right now." This architecture is simple to implement. There are variations in this scheme. The oldest is a master–slave network where a master asks and the slave replies.

There is another a real-time method called the producer–subscriber model. In this variation, used by the EthernetIP,* a device multicasts to other devices the values that have been requested. Other devices will hear this multicast and will multicast the values or states that have been requested by the others.

The latter is considered good practice for handling resiliency and redundancy in a multicontroller machine-to-machine network. However, for it to work efficiently, it is almost essential for switches to be configured with a virtual local area network (VLAN) with just the producers and subscribers. It is also helpful for the switch/routers to have Internet group message protocol (IGMP) snooping enabled—particularly for places where trunking or routing is needed. This enables just those devices that produce or subscribe to these feeds to get the data they need. Otherwise, the multicast/broadcast traffic will be very significant, and it could saturate lower bandwidth trunks.

The problem with real-time protocols is that they do not scale well for use across a wide area network (WAN). They require very regular message patterns. For example, to find out if something has gone into alarm state and then gone back out of alarm state, it is necessary to check it at at least twice the rate it is expected to happen. For further discussion, look up the Nyquist theorem.

Thus, even if the alarm is not expected to change for years, one still has to ask for it every few milliseconds. This method works fine when bandwidth is plentiful, reliable, and easy to install, such as in the case of a very limited local area network (LAN).

For less reliable connections with irregular latency, it is commonplace to use event-based protocols. Older readers may perhaps be familiar with the NetDDE protocol. This protocol was used between applications on different computers to indicate an interest in a particular piece of information. It could request an advisory message whenever that data changed.

Thus, if the data point did not change after the connection was established, there would be no traffic other than a periodic "All is well" message every so often.

Most event-based protocols send periodic messages to confirm the connection is active so that one would know that the communications system integrity is good. While most TCP/IP connections have the facility to send and receive a keep-alive message, often the time period for such messages is ridiculously long (hours) and cannot reliably be changed by the application software due to security, operating system, or lower-layer application limitations. Thus, event-oriented protocols such as DNP3 (the distributed network protocol is published as IEEE-1815), will send a link status message of their own. In this particular example, it would be a message known as a link status request. If the reply failed to come back, then the DNP protocol software would close the TCP connection state and then attempt to reopen it.

The disadvantage with event-based protocols is that they can get significantly more complex than a real-time protocol. Typically, the events are queued. To conserve bandwidth, they may not get sent right away. Thus they would also need a time stamp of when the event occurred. This means that the device needs to have an accurate way to determine the time.

When the message gets to the other end, there are two considerations to make: (1) the time when the event was actually generated, and (2) the time when it arrived at the application. If communications are not reliable, there can be many minutes or even hours of

---

* Ethernet Industrial Protocol managed by http://odva.org.

difference between these two times. It would be foolish to use the field-time stamp of the event to prosecute an operator if the event only arrived seconds earlier.

Some event-oriented protocols send information in numbered I/O style. For example, DNP3 sends messages that often look like "RTU #234, digital input #62 state is now ON" with a chatter flag at some time stamp. Conversely, there are object-oriented protocols, such as the IEC-61850 model used in substations, that convey process-oriented objects, such as "a model xxx high voltage tie-breaker is opening at location yyy." They often are more verbose, but they are supposed to be easier to set up and integrate. These object models are used in the generic object-oriented substation event (GOOSE) protocol. It is commonly found in substations in Europe as well as a few in North America. However, as of the time of writing in mid-2015, the plug-and-work aspect of the GOOSE protocol, particularly between different vendors, is still a work in progress.

Test procedures for various protocols exist in various forms. Classic protocols such as Modbus have fairly straightforward and simple tests. In general, real-time protocols are not too difficult to test for compatibility.

However, event-oriented protocols typically have more states, more objects, and more commands to test. Object-oriented event protocols are even more complex with even more objects to validate and test.

From a security perspective, the more states, functions, and object types there are the more likely it is that someone will find a flaw to exploit as an attack vector. While protocol flaws are unlikely, software complexity increases as the statefulness of the object increases.

Security hints and tips

With these characteristics in mind, there are many things one can do to detect and protect a control system network. It should be noted that because traffic saturation is an issue, access to a control system network must be controlled very tightly. Thankfully, such control is much less onerous than it is with an office network. Unlike office networks, operational networks have very well defined traffic flows that rarely ever change.

Again, the zone-and-conduit systems of the network should have well defined meeting points where firewalls can be configured to help limit the spread of malware. The networks should be designed so that if a conduit fails, the process zone can continue to function at some reduced level of automation. For example, it may have control loops that still work, but the set point for that control loop may have to be updated manually instead of undergoing automatic updates from other zones.

In the case of organizations in which the control system network is frequently used by contractors and vendors, it may be useful to set up 802.1x authentication for all transient switch ports (e.g., a configuration port for a variable frequency drive). First, this ensures that nobody except those who have authorization to enter the network get access to it. Second, it attaches an identification and an audit trail to identify whose devices are being used.

Devices that have no need for outside network communications should not be given default routes. This makes external hacks into the network from outside the LAN more difficult.

One may also wish to install a firewall between the router and the plant operational networks, which can be configured to allow only certain ports/protocols between only certain devices.

Do not use "dumb" switches anywhere. Use only managed switches. Configure each port for all the common assignments such as enabling/disabling, traffic monitoring, VLAN assignment, access/trunk service, and so on.

Avoid using VLAN 1 (the common default VLAN). Disable it if possible. This prevents accidental connections from laptops with internal virtual switches, trunks from other switches, and the like.

Using simple network management protocol (SNMP), monitor and alarm all port state changes from normal. This is important because operators need to be made aware of locations where work is going on and where outages take place. This is a very important visibility issue with the operators. If they see a port light up when it is not supposed to, they need to investigate what is going on. Nobody should be working on the controls system without the knowledge and permission of the operators and plant engineering staff.

Profile and track the traffic levels. It may prove useful to alarm on unusual traffic rates, both high and low. As long as there are not frequent downloads of new programs or configurations, such alarms would not be onerous. It may prove useful to alarm on traffic at times when no changes to configurations are expected.

Watch all address resolution protocol (ARP) traffic. ARP cache poisoning is a well-known mode of attack. ARP cache problems can lead to very long delays for rediscovery when replacing devices such as serial port servers. Some devices, especially network equipment, are known to have ARP cache timeouts on the order of many hours. On lightly loaded and heavily segmented networks, the overhead from ARP cache timeouts set to 2 or 3 min is manageable. This means that one could replace a device and perhaps wait for up to a couple minutes instead of hours for it to be rediscovered by the network equipment.

Shut down all self-discovery protocols such as Cisco Discovery Protocol (CDP), universal plug and play (UPnP), and the like. Shut down all unnecessary router broadcasts such as open shortest path first (OSPF) messages on terminal LANs. Do not give potential attackers any more information than is absolutely essential.

To improve OSPF traffic control and flow, it would be very wise to configure the routers for strictly industrial WAN traffic and to set it up as a "totally stubby" network. This means that even if other routers are aware of that an area border router exists on two sides of a control system WAN, they will be unable to route through it. It is also advisable to avoid the use of unnumbered IP addresses in point-to-point network connections. This will yield specific diagnostics on what exactly went up or down and what failed where.

Again, it must be reiterated that office network outage scheduling and control system outage scheduling are polar opposites. Leveraging an office IT WAN for control system VPN use is virtually a guarantee that someone will get very upset and annoyed. It is best to keep these networks as independent as possible and to use as completely separate physical infrastructure as possible. The money and time lost to just one single event is enough to justify the extra hardware.

As an overall design issue, it is very unwise to rely on assets that depend on the control system. For example, if the SCADA system belongs to a power company and the ISP depends upon that power company for electricity, it would not be a good idea to use the ISP as a VPN conduit for SCADA assets. When designing communications networks for infrastructure, they should stand on their own.

Network forensics

For the sake of diagnostics and forensics, it is useful to offer the following services to those devices that can use it:

- Network time protocol (NTP) and/or IEEE 1588 servers
- SNMP trap receivers

- Syslog servers
- A stand-alone, nonforwarding post office protocol e-mail server (preferably *not* connected to office network)

The NTP server is nearly self-explanatory. Without it, forensic analysis is much more difficult. When the router logs something in syslog, it should have the same time stamp as the local plant DCS does so that cause and effect can be determined.

Many embedded devices, such as variable frequency drives or PLCs, can send e-mail messages, SNMP traps, or Syslog entries. However, they were not designed for the rough-and-tumble world of an office network, never mind the Internet. Patching a PLC that periodically sends e-mails of performance statistics is fraught with all sorts of validation and process-availability issues. It is best not to expose such devices to an unsecured environment of any sort.

Record keeping

Control systems, thanks to their static nature, should be very easy to document and inventory. The inventory should include each device, the address, a descriptive designation, the VLAN where it resides, and the location where it can be found.

There is also a need to keep track of switch configurations, especially VLANs and trunks. Trunks should be restrictive. Each switch should have a default VLAN that does not get trunked anywhere. All unused ports should have shut-down states, and preferably a plastic nontamper plug placed in the hole. While such plugs are hardly secure, they keep casual miscreants at bay. They also help to reduce confusion and accidents when switches are in close proximity to office network devices.

There is a tool available from the Industrial Control Systems Computer Emergency Response Team (ICS-CERT) website of the US Department of Homeland Security (DHS),[*] known as the control system evaluation tool or CSET (formerly known as CS2SAT: Control System Cyber Security Self Evaluation Tool). It is an excellent document intended to record and assist in identifying and evaluating risks in a control system network.

The CSET tool is a great way to document what the design of a control systems network is supposed to look like and to identify risks in the design. However, it does not show what is actually in the network.

To find out what is actually in an industrial control systems (ICS) network, one must resort to scanning tools. Scanning the network is recommended regularly with tools such as NMAP, with one very critical caveat: The default scan rates of this or any other scanning tool can be very disruptive to normal control system network operations. The tester must know what switches to use to slow down the scan to a tolerable level where it will not interfere with routine real-time traffic. This is particularly the case where older mixes of 10BASE-T network hardware are still present. There are documented cases where accidental exposure to office traffic has physically damaged control system hardware.[†]

It is also a good idea to set up monitoring ports for each VLAN to listen for any broadcasts or multicasts that do not belong. Most devices are quite chatty and will make all sorts of rude self-identifying traffic, even unprovoked. Regular documentation of what normal broadcast traffic looks like is essential.

---

[*] https://ics-cert.us-cert.gov.
[†] Browns Ferry Unit 3 (see U.S. NRC, 2007).

Another thing to consider is the physical limits of the power and cable routing. If there is a UPS or a DC battery system in the cabinet, consider what happens when the network devices lose power. This has process implications as much as anything. This is where the OT staff *must* talk to the engineering staff to coordinate power and failure modes. It is wise to set up and sign off on a document that details where the power and fuses are.

Many of these and other suggestions for configuring these switches were derived from a document by the National Security Agency in Report Number I33-010R-2004. It is an office oriented document, but many of the tips and tricks are quite valid.

Note for aggregation routers (MPLS)

Some organizations may use multiprotocol label switching (MPLS) to transport network traffic from place to place. If this is the case, it is important that the control system/SCADA traffic should be tagged voice level priority (6) or video priority (5) in the IEEE 802.1Q frames. Bandwidth can be limited quite significantly, but it deserves the highest priority below the network level because, fundamentally this is the infrastructure. If it fails, there will not be anything to conduct business over anyhow. Many office IT departments may be offended by this, but it is essential. Nobody should have to interrupt the SCADA system just so that they can send high-definition video of dancing kittens.

Wireless networks

Many organizations are moving toward using wireless infrastructure and even industrial control systems. However, there are several key risks that must be enumerated and for which there must be backup plans ready to execute before such techniques are applied.

Some operational and security factors to consider:

1. Wireless media is not controllable. Others can access and possibly even use it.
2. Everything must be encrypted. Do not rely on spread-spectrum sequences to effect security.
3. *Do not* put critical I/O on the network without a guaranteed backup plan of what will happen *when* the network fails.
4. *Do not put process safety on wireless!* Anyone can access the spectrum and interrupt traffic, even if they cannot get network access.
5. Monitor traffic on the air. Be ready to go signal hunting for rogue sources. If there is no in-house knowledge of how to do this, it would be best to reconsider whether wireless systems are a good fit.
6. Reliability is not the only issue with wireless. Failure modes and diagnostics matter.
7. Licensed wireless communications, although usually operating at slower speeds, are more reliable. It is possible to locate interference. There is also a legally enforceable remedy wherein, once presented with the license and the evidence, the police may arrest people to force owners of interference sources to vacate the spectrum.
8. Wireless networks can be silently monitored. Since there is no control of the media, one should ensure that all keys are kept off the air. Key update schemes should be applied with care. Paying careful consideration to what listeners might hear is critical.

Things to monitor on a control systems network

First, traffic on each point-to-point WAN connection or switch trunk should be recorded and monitored. If traffic reroutes, it is important to ensure that the link can handle the bandwidth. Remember that milliseconds matter.

Second, the devices on the networks often have features worth knowing, such as PLC cycle times, RTU traffic statistics (how many error messages or have happened in the last five-minute period, how many failed authentications have occurred, how many restarts have occurred, etc.).

Third, the physical infrastructure should be monitored for power, cabinet openings, internal temperatures, battery charge state, power supply statuses, I/O base statuses, remote port statuses, and so on.

Disaster recovery

In general, a disaster recovery plan is an essential planning part of all control systems networks. Network designs should have diverse, noninterdependent methods for communicating. The records for what configurations exist and how to restore them should be maintained in a safe for all duty engineering access. Each duty engineer will need to document each segment of the plant/distribution process systems.

Most of all, backups should be kept in a safe, and copies should be present in more than one location (example: the chief security officer's safe, the plant engineer's safe, and perhaps a safe in engineering).

After a hack, it is imperative to have version control software so that one can revert back to earlier versions made prior to the hack. The sad truth is that insiders have wreaked more dangerous hacks than outsiders. When disgruntled employees install a hack, it is important to go back in history to view what was done and when. A version control system has a reputation for being a royal pain to use—until the first hack happens. Then, lots of people are very happy that it exists.

Summary

This chapter outlines many tips and tricks to keep a system safe. It is meant as a smorgasbord of ideas, not all of which may be practical in any particular application. Every system is different, and everyone should discuss the specifics carefully and confidentially within the company before implementing a plan.

Reference

U.S. NRC (United States Nuclear Regulatory Commission). 2007. Effects of Ethernet-based, non-safety related controls on the safe and continued operation of nuclear power stations. NRC Information Notice 2007-15, Office of Nuclear Reaction Regulation, Washington, DC. April 17, 2007. Available onlined at http://www.nrc.gov/reading-rm/doc-collections/gen-comm/info-notices/2007/in200715.pdf.

chapter fifteen

Active defense in industrial control system networks

Robert M. Lee

Contents

Introduction

Advanced adversaries are dangerous because they have well-funded, focused, and determined personnel on their teams. They have the time and resources available to them to research a target and move past a mindset of single incidents and breaches into conducting full campaigns. These campaigns can take months or years to execute and, due to cultural and technical barriers within ICS organizations, they often go unnoticed. The adversary may have tools and tactics available to them, but their greatest strength is in their personnel. The only way to counter these human operators is with well-trained and empowered defenders. Defenders must also move past single intrusions to thinking about defense as a campaign as well—they must utilize a strategy. The concept of an active defense is taking the defenders' greatest strength, their personnel, and empowering them to break down barriers of communication and technology to identify, respond to, and learn from adversaries. It is a strategic approach to ensuring security.

To fully appreciate the concept of an active defense requires historical context. The term is not a trend of recent activity nor is it something that originated with the advent of the word *cyber*. Active defense is a military strategy that is applicable in the field of cybersecurity. Unfortunately, there is also confusion around the term. Popular news-media websites, security practitioners without any understanding of the original strategy, and academics with a lack of technical experience have tried to essentially copy and paste the terminology of an active defense into the digital domain. Thus the term has mistakenly come to mean hacking back or otherwise performing intelligence or offense-based actions against an adversary. With an appreciation of the history behind the strategy, however, it is revealed that this classification of the term is wholly wrong. Understanding the history behind the strategy helps identify how it can be used in industrial control system (ICS) networks and the value that can be obtained. But it is also crucial to understand that there are no easy fixes in security. Employing an active defense does not take the place of all of the hard work required to establish the proper foundation for the strategy to succeed. This chapter will focus on presenting the active defense strategy. To accomplish this, the chapter will start by highlighting the strengths of ICS networks and emphasizes that these networks are defensible. Then, a model will be presented to discuss the foundation required to achieve an active defense, and the historical context of the strategy will be presented. The last portion of the chapter will present a model that can be utilized to achieve an active defense.

Why it works in ICS

ICS networks are largely static. While diligence is required to maintain the process, address alarms, and keep the operations running, the networked infrastructure itself does not change that often. Consultants often half-heartedly joke that during assessments at various facilities there are always physical connections or pieces of infrastructure that they inquire about. The response is always the same: "I'm not sure what it does but it's been there forever—so don't touch it." Many components of the ICS have been around for a long time; they are designed with that longevity and ruggedness in mind. The network connections should also be relatively static. The number of users in the control network browsing the Internet to social media, streaming sites, and other locations should be minimal. Even in areas where Internet browsing is not governed well, it is easy to identify the normal communications internal and external to the ICS. Additionally, these environments also usually have smaller networks. There may be networks separated across a large geographical area, but there are usually only a few Internet protocol (IP)–connected devices at each location. Even larger ICS networks only have a few hundred or few thousand IP-connected devices. This provides an awesome opportunity for defenders.

Compare the relatively small and static networks of an ICS to that of an enterprise IT environment. In an enterprise IT environment, there are often hundreds of thousands or millions of IP-connected devices. Load balancers, proxy servers, and entire zones of infrastructure for health care, legal, finance, and public relations–type job functions are normal. Asset identification, including mapping data flows and connections, can take years to fully accomplish in these types of networks. Once assets are identified, though, they can be quickly changed. New technical refreshes and upgrades to infrastructure, software from the latest IT efficiency increasing trend, and every flavor of cloud deployment connected to the environment take place in relatively short amounts of time. Thousands of users are in these environments as well, communicating to all sectors of the organization, both internal and external to their network. Mapping out the data flows of the *typical* enterprise IT user is no small challenge. Simply put, an adversary can do nothing clever at all and still manage to hide within the daily noise of thousands of systems and thousands of users accessing every part of the network and the Internet at any point in the day. And if an adversary wants to guess what type of systems are going to be in an environment, what type of exploits they need, and what type of understanding of the systems will be required—it is largely similar between various enterprise networks.

Contrast this with an ICS. One facility running one process in one state within one organization can have an entirely different setup in terms of the mixture of IT and OT infrastructure than another facility in the same state and within the same organization. Vendors and systems such as the Windows operating system may be similar, but how those systems are configured to keep operations running is often different. An adversary that truly wants to understand how to impact the process of an ICS organization must start nearly from scratch in their reconnaissance and attack efforts if they want to have any real impact inside the organization. Stealing intellectual property or mapping systems is likely not difficult for them, but being able to execute any sort of physical damage, manipulation of the process, or large-scale impact would take a significant investment in their most sensitive resource—time. ICS networks present themselves as some of the weirdest, hardest to understand, and most foreign networks possible to adversaries. That puts the defender in a great position.

Defenders have largely static networks, less users and data flows, and a more defensible network than almost any enterprise IT network out there. The adversaries have to dedicate more time to learning these networks than enterprise facilities, and the stakes are higher. Bringing down operations in a critical site can have large-scale policy implications and political impact for any national-level adversary. Defenders often feel these adversaries are taking advantage of the Wild West–type nature of the Internet, but make no mistake about it—national-level adversaries who are most interested in impacting ICS live in governments full of bureaucracy and PowerPoint as well. ICS networks are vulnerable. The adversaries are targeting them. But defenders are in a great position to make a difference.

Building the foundation

If ICS networks are such a great place for defenders, then it begs the question why security is not significantly higher across the industry than it is currently. This usually comes down to people and processes—not technology. Security teams are often undertrained, underempowered, and overutilized. There are commonly barriers between IT and OT security teams, and silos of excellence form, the members of which only share among themselves. There is a lack of awareness around the value of security and the threats out there. And the hype surrounding ICS cyberattacks only makes it worse. Take, for example, the 2008 attack on the Baku-Tbilisi-Ceyhan (BTC) pipeline in Turkey. At the time, the Turkish government claimed the attack was a physical attack orchestrated by the Kurdistan Workers' Party (PKK) (Hurriyet 2008). The PKK members acknowledged this and took credit for the attack (Ismail 2008). Yet in 2014, the news-media organization Bloomberg published a story saying that both the victim and the adversary were wrong and that it was actually Russia launching a cyberattack (Robertson and Riley 2014).

The scenario was plausible—IP-connected cameras into the control center allowed attackers to move from the Internet into the control system networks. From there, they modified alarming conditions and IP-connected devices at a pump station to orchestrate an attack. The problem? It simply did not happen. When this story was released, I looked into it, found it to be ridiculous, and wrote a white paper at SANS Institute noting why it was probably not true (Lee et al. 2014). After that, other members of the community identified why it probably did not occur. Interestingly, a few months later, documents were uncovered that found the IP-connected cameras were installed after the attack as a result of the attack; they could not have been used by the adversaries to get into the network (Lee 2015a). This is a bold case study showing the level of hype and national media attention ICS cyberattacks can garner. What is most interesting about it, though, is that a significant portion of the ICS community still believes the case study to be true, having never read the rebuttal to its claims. Hype is harder to disprove than to generate. And that hype drives resource investments into a made-up problem instead of the real problems that exist. Resources may get allocated but not against the real threats faced. As an example, most ICS organizations need to build a strong foundation to achieve security—not to buy another over-the-top product that flashes brightly on the network. Tools and technologies are extremely useful, but they must be applied in the correct manner, and they are largely worthless without trained and empowered personnel operating in a culture that understands the value of security.

In an effort to discuss the value of building an appropriate framework for security inside an organization, I came up with a model to help guide organizations. The model helps users understand the resource investments made and to take a more nuanced approach toward security. Additionally, it sets the discussion for the introduction of a model for an active defense and what value an active defense actually has. The strategy is effective but only with the appropriate foundation.

The sliding scale of cybersecurity

The sliding scale of cybersecurity adds nuance to the discussion of cybersecurity by categorizing the actions, competencies, and investments of resources that organizations can make to defend against threats (Lee 2015b). The model serves as a framework for understanding what actions contribute to cybersecurity. In this way, it is useful in setting the appropriate foundation that must take place for an active defense to be a good return on investment in an organization.

The model is structured into five categories (Figure 15.1): Architecture, Passive Defense, Active Defense, Intelligence, and Offense. A short discussion of each category will be described below.

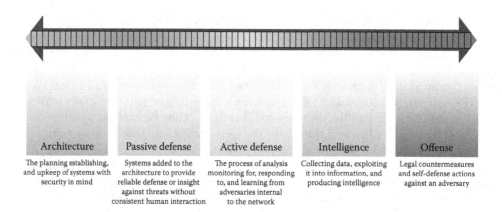

Architecture	Passive defense	Active defense	Intelligence	Offense
The planning establishing, and upkeep of systems with security in mind	Systems added to the architecture to provide reliable defense or insight against threats without consistent human interaction	The process of analysis monitoring for, responding to, and learning from adversaries internal to the network	Collecting data, exploiting it into information, and producing intelligence	Legal countermeasures and self-defense actions against an adversary

Figure 15.1 The sliding scale of cybersecurity. (From Lee, R.M., 2015, The sliding scale of cyber security: A SANS analyst whitepaper. https://www.sans.org/reading-room/whitepapers/analyst/sliding-scale-cyber-security-36240.)

The sliding scale aspect of the model illustrates that some actions in each category can be closely related to adjacent categories. For example, patching vulnerabilities in software would be in the Architecture category, but patching is farther right on the scale—still in Architecture but closer to the Passive Defense category—than engineering the system. Yet, no action in Architecture could reasonably be seen as an active defense, intelligence, or offense-based activity. Another example would be that of intelligence operations. An intelligence operation that is conducted in the adversary network would be closer to an offense action, and more quickly converted to one, than collecting and analyzing open-source information. Likewise, collecting, analyzing, and producing intelligence from incident-response data in the form of threat intelligence is closer to active defense, where analysts would consume the intelligence for the purpose of defense.

The weight of each category is not equal in its contributions towards security. The clearest example of this is the discussion of architecture compared to offense. Actions taken to engineer and implement systems with security in mind will drastically increase the defensive posture of those systems. The return on investment through those actions would be significantly higher than conducting offense for the same purposes of security. A sufficiently advanced and determined adversary will always find a means to bypass a well-established architecture. Thus, the focus of investments cannot be on the architecture alone. All the categories of the sliding scale are important, but the expected return on investment should guide how organizations implement security and when they focus on another category. As an example, an organization that has a poorly maintained architecture and passive defenses would find less value out of active defenses and should not pursue intelligence or offense without remedying the fundamental issues first.

The goal of achieving cybersecurity should be obtained through establishing a foundation and culture for security that expands over time. This allows defenders to better themselves and their defense posture in the face of threats and challenges. This reveals another potential use for the scale: a model for the progression of security maturity in an organization. Organizations should focus on achieving the appropriate foundation from the categories on the left-hand side of the scale before investing in the ones further to the right. Investing in architecture appropriately builds the foundation for effectively applying passive defenses on top of the architecture and achieves more benefit out of those investments. Likewise, active defense is more achievable and efficient when done in an environment with proper architecture and passive defenses. Conducting active defense actions, such as network security monitoring or incident response, is more difficult and costly without that foundation. The aspect of cost highlights the return on investment of the categories as well. As an example, executing offense-based actions in an effective way requires, at a minimum, the use of intelligence, which ultimately stems from understanding and appreciating the organization's active defense, passive defense, and architecture actions well enough to truly know and target the threat. Yet, offense-based actions return a significantly lower value to security than properly structuring and implementing the architecture. Thus, it is highly recommended that organizations focus primarily on the left-hand side of the scale, starting with architecture.

Architecture

Arguably, one of the most important aspects of security is ensuring the proper architecture of the systems, which includes the mapping of the organization's mission, funding, and manning.* Architecture refers to *the planning, establishing, and upkeep of systems with security in mind.* Ensuring that security is designed into the system provides a foundation upon which all other aspects of cybersecurity can build. Additionally, the establishment of a proper architecture aligned with the organization's needs causes the other categories to become more effective and less costly. For example, a network that is not properly segmented and maintained with software patches is wrought with more issues than the defenders can reasonably handle. Real threats that defenders should identify, such as adversaries inside the network, are lost in the noise of security issues, incidental malware, and network configuration problems that come with poorly implemented architecture.

The starting point for architecture is generally the planning, engineering, and design of the system to support the organization's needs. The term *architecture* here should not be confused with an IT term. It includes the cyberengineering of the ICS and the various components involved in the establishment and maintenance of the system. The organization should first identify the objectives supported by its systems, which might be different across companies and industries. Security measures for the systems should support these goals. Rather than aiming to defend against an adversary, the architecture should accommodate normal operating conditions and emergency operating circumstances. This could include accidental malware infections, peaks in network traffic from misconfigured systems, and systems that cause disruption to each other simply by being placed within the same network. All of these conditions and more are typical of normal environments in today's networked infrastructure. Designing systems with these scenarios in mind helps maintain the confidentiality, availability, and integrity of the system in support of the organization's business needs.

A secure production, acquisition, and implementation of the system is another key component to the architecture category. It is important to secure each element in this chain to help ensure quality controls are put into place. In combination with maintaining the system, such as applying security patches, these actions make it easier to defend the system. The applications of software and hardware patches are sometimes mistaken as an action of defense; instead, they are steps that contribute to security but are not themselves defensive actions.† These actions and others associated with good architecture also reduce the attack surface, to minimizing the opportunities adversaries have to gain access to a system and restricting their actions once access is gained.

Passive defense

Once an organization has established the proper foundation for security through the investment in the architecture category of this model, it is then necessary to invest in passive defenses. Passive defenses are added on top of a good architecture to secure systems in the presence of an adversary. Adversaries or threats that have the opportunity, intent, and capability to do harm will eventually bypass a good architecture; passive defenses are

---

* It is important to note that "systems" does not just refer to individual systems. Systems in this paper also refer to the system of systems whether they are networks or individual hardware or software components. This includes software such as applications and all the individual components of the broader system.
† The United States Department of Defense military services have on multiple occasions referred to the architecting and patching of systems as a defensive role. This has often been referred to as Defense Cyber Operations (DCO). However, the architecting and patching of systems is required as a basic aspect of security; the action contributes to the ability to be able to defend the system but its purpose is the maintenance and operation of the system besides just adversary-based scenarios.

required.* Before discussing the definition of a passive defense, it is important to understand the history of the term.

Traditionally there have been two forms of defense: passive and active. Many of the debates between the definitions of these two terms took place from the 1930s to the 1980s, well before the advent of the term *cyber*.† The U.S. Department of Defense settled on the following definition for passive defense: "measures taken to reduce the probability of and to minimize the effects of damage caused by hostile action without the intention of taking the initiative" (U.S. Department of Defense 2015). The translation of this definition to the field of cybersecurity has been a contention point for some academics, security practitioners, and military professionals. Although the definition itself may seem easy to understand, its application to the normal operating environment of the cyberlandscape requires more than a literal translation.

Understanding the intention, and not just the literal definition, helps the transition of the terms. First, the intent of passive defenses in the original debates was to provide a level of defense against an adversary without requiring the intervention of the military services themselves. An example would be the hardening of a bunker for protection against the dropping of a bomb. Although this may seem similar to applying a software patch to a system, it is more akin to hardening the structure than defending against an adversary. It is not an aspect of defense but just an understanding of the typical environments systems find themselves in—patching is a maintenance action. Similarly, constructing barriers against the elements around a military conference room would not be considered "passive defenses against the wind" but instead just a normal required action for the environment. Likewise, passive defenses would include the strengthening of those barriers and the addition to the building of decoys, camouflage, or other secondary aspects. Lastly, the physical world suffers from attrition. Adversaries' resources become depleted; for example, they have one less bomb after one is dropped. In the digital world, adversaries' resources do not become depleted in the same way; once a piece of malware is used, if it is not detected and countered, it can be reused in a number of other campaigns. One of the adversaries' resources that does become depleted, though, is time and the resources associated with it and their personnel. Depleting an adversary's resources, including their time to plan and achieve their objectives, is of critical importance to a defender. Passive defenses help achieve this.

In examining the history of passive defense terminology, it is possible to determine that there is a concept of add-ons to structures for the purpose of their protection. This concept of protecting against an adversary and not necessarily enhancing the purpose of the system itself helps develop a definition for a passive defense. Passive defenses in the physical world do not require constant intervention from personnel either. Therefore the definition of a passive defense is *systems added to the architecture to provide consistent protection against or insight into threats without constant human intervention.* Sample systems that are added to the architecture to add protection to assets, stop or limit well-known security gaps, reduce the probability of interaction with a threat, or give insight into encounters with threats would be firewalls, antimalware systems, intrusion prevention systems, antivirus systems, intrusion detection systems, and similar traditional security systems. These systems require maintenance, turning, and care over time but not constant human

---

* Adversaries that have the opportunity, intent, and capability to do harm are known as threats.
† A major reason for these debates was the advent of long-range bombers and intercontinental ballistic missiles. The RAND institute as well as early Air Force and Army publications and field manuals present a good look at this debate.

intervention to make the systems work. They are consistent but not necessarily always effective.

Active defense

Passive defense mechanisms will eventually fail in the face of determined and well-resourced adversaries. Countering advanced and determined adversaries requires an active approach to security built on the premise that highly trained security personnel are needed to neutralize highly trained adversaries. It is vital to empower these trained security personnel and to have them operate within a good architecture secured and monitored with well-placed passive defenses. However, active defense tends to be the subject of fierce debate and misuse in media and news outlets when discussed in the context of cybersecurity. Due to some of the misuse of the terminology, it is important to cover the historical context of the term in some depth.

In the 1970s, the term active defense was also heavily debated when used in context of land warfare by the U.S. Army. Army General William E. DePuy, the first commander of the Army Training and Doctrine Command, used the term in a 1974 paper discussing the 1973 Arab/Israeli war. In this context, he was discussing the ability for the defending forces to be able to move instead of fighting in a static position: "What that means is that the defending force must possess the ability to move. It must engage in an active defense of the sector (DePuy 1974)." He later expanded upon his use of the term when he wrote: "The concept of active defense is to wear down the attacker by confronting him successively and continuously with strong combined arms teams and task forces fighting from mutually supported battle positions in depth throughout the battle area (Depuy 1974)." He placed the term in the 1976 *Field Manual 100-5 Operations*. General DePuy noted later that the term active defense came under heavy criticism due to misunderstanding of the term in the field manual despite the fact that the document was credited with beginning a revolution in army doctrine post Vietnam. He stated "the term 'active defense' is mentioned only in passing in 100-5 as an adjective and seldom in 71-2. However in 71-1 'active defense' becomes the official descriptor of the defensive doctrine set forth in this family of manuals, although, as we shall see later, there is no consensus on the meaning of that term (DePuy 1980)."

Despite the heavy debates around the term, which mimic present-day debates on the term's use in cybersecurity, an official definition was adopted by the U.S. military for the purposes of military action not in the context of cybersecurity (U.S. Department of Defense 2015). The definition, relating to traditional warfare, is "the employment of limited offensive action and counterattacks to deny a contested area or position to the enemy." The use of counterattack here has been misused as a literal translation into cybersecurity for "hack-back." Unfortunately, this understanding does not accurately reflect the intention of the term. As it turns out, simply copying terms from the physical domains of warfare into cybersecurity does not accurately portray the meaning of the terms. The meaning of the term active defense was always centered on maneuverability; the ability to incorporate military intelligence and indicators to identify an attack; the ability to respond to the attack or against the capability within the defensive zone or contested area; and the ability to learn from the encounter. This was highlighted within a RAND study from 1965 and the discussion of the use of integrated air defenses to track and destroy intercontinental ballistic missiles (ICBM) before they struck their target (Latter and Martinelli 1965). It is important to note for the discussion of cybersecurity that the focus of the "counterattack" was only inside the defended area and against the capability, not the adversary; that is, a counterattack in cybersecurity would be more properly reflected in the concept of incident response wherein personnel "counterattack" by containing and remediating a threat. The incident responders or other personnel do not go on the offensive against adversaries in their networks or systems, just as the ICBM active defense mechanisms of integrated air defenses destroyed missiles—not people or their cities.

From this background and understanding of active defense a definition can be constructed for cyber security: *the process of analysts monitoring for, responding to, learning from, and applying their knowledge to threats internal to the network.* It is important to add the ending piece of "internal to the network" to further discourage misrepresentation of the definition as a hack-back strategy. Analysts that can fall into this category include incident responders, malware reverse engineers, threat analysts, network security monitoring analysts, and other security personnel who utilize their environment to hunt for the adversary and respond to them.

The focus on analysts instead of tools brings about a proactive approach to security that highlights the intention of the original strategy: maneuverability and adaptability. Systems themselves cannot provide an active defense; systems can only serve as tools for the active defender. Likewise, simply sitting in front of a tool such as a system information and event manager does not make an analyst an active defender—it is as much about the actions and process as it is about the placement of the person and their training. What makes advanced threats persistent and dangerous is the adaptive and intelligent adversary behind the keyboard. Countering these adversaries requires equally flexible and intelligent defenders.

Intelligence

One of the keys to effective active defense is the ability to consume intelligence about the adversary and have it drive security changes, processes, and actions in the environment. Consuming intelligence is part of an active defense, but generating intelligence falls within the category of intelligence. It is within this phase that analysts produce data, information, and intelligence about the adversary from a variety of sources and methods.

Intelligence is a commonly used word, yet the concept is often misunderstood. In the U.S. Department of Defense's definition of terms, the word appears 998 times (U.S. Department of Defense 2015). Military intelligence has made up the bulk of the field of study and has contributed largely to the understanding of the term in the field of cybersecurity. The U.S. military definition of intelligence is "the product resulting from the collection, processing, integration, evaluation, analysis, and interpretation of available information concerning foreign nationals, hostiles or potentially hostile forces or elements, or areas of actual or potential operations. The term is also applied to the activity which results in the product and to the organizations engaged in such activity (U.S. Department of Defense 2015)." In short, intelligence is defined as both a product and process. It is defined here, for the purposes of cybersecurity, as *the process of collecting data, exploiting it into information, and producing an assessment that satisfies a previously identified knowledge gap.* The intelligence process (Figure 15.2) has been documented thoroughly and is often presented as a continual cycle of collecting data, processing and exploiting that data into information, and analyzing and deriving information from various sources to produce intelligence.

The understanding of the relationship of data, information, and intelligence is where some of the abuses of the word intelligence in cybersecurity stem from Lee (2015c). A visual understanding of this process can be seen in Figure 15.2. Numerous security vendors have touted tools that produce intelligence. This has also led to the often abused term of "actionable intelligence." Tools do not create intelligence. Only analysts can create

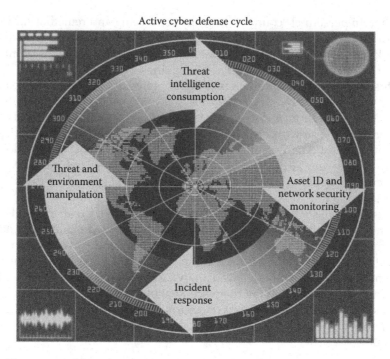

Figure 15.2 The active cyber defense cycle. (From The graphic is courtesy of the SANS ICS515—Active Defense and Incident Response course.)

intelligence. Tools and systems are useful for collecting data from the operational environment, whether they be an organization's networks or the adversary's systems. Tools and other systems created for the purpose of processing and exploiting data into useful information is also a worthwhile investment. However, the analysis and production of that information and other sources of information, as well as the execution of needed processes such as the analysis of competing hypotheses, can only be done by human analysts. These human analysts understand the internal decisions or actions that need to be made and analyze various sources of information to generate intelligence assessments. These assessments are needed to develop recommendations for internal decisions and courses of action. Tools alone cannot accomplish that process.

Intelligence in the field of cybersecurity can fall into a range of activities. For example, a group of persons accessing an adversary network to collect and analyze information would be conducting a cyberintelligence operation. Another example would be documents that "call home" after being stolen by an adversary. These documents are inside the adversary's network and are transmitting back information to the defenders about the true location of the adversary's environment. The information gathered would represent useful intelligence for national policy makers, the military, or others on the research, development, and plans to use adversary capabilities. Likewise, researchers standing up honeypots to analyze attacks against control systems are gathering information and analyzing this data to create intelligence about adversaries without engaging in an operation against the adversaries. Finally, another good example would be analysts collecting data and information from systems that have been compromised by adversaries in their networks or other networks to derive intelligence about threats they are facing. This last example has been identified as *threat intelligence* in the cybersecurity community.

Threat intelligence is a specific type of intelligence that seeks to give defenders knowledge of the adversary, their actions within the defender's environment, and their capabilities as well as their tactics, techniques, and procedures.* The goal is to learn from the adversary with the intent of better identifying and responding to them. Threat intelligence is extremely useful, but due to a lack of understanding in the field of intelligence, many organizations have not taken full advantage of it, which leads to cynicism regarding the term. Properly taking advantage of threat intelligence requires at least three things:

1. Defenders must know what qualifies as their threats (i.e., only those adversaries that have the opportunity, capability, and intent to do them harm).
2. Defenders must be able to use intelligence to drive actions in their environments.
3. Defenders must understand the difference between generating intelligence and consuming it.

Currently, most organizations do not accurately understand their threat landscape; that is, they cannot properly determine which adversaries and capabilities actually constitute a threat to them and which do not. For example, without a firm understanding of the architecture and passive defenses in an organization, it is not feasible to identify if an identified vulnerability exists within an organization's systems or if the vulnerabilities can be or have been fixed; thus, there also cannot be an accurate representation of risk. If defenders do not know their business processes, security status, network topologies, and architecture, it is impossible to effectively use threat intelligence. Likewise, many defenders do not have the internal organizational knowledge or empowerment from decision makers to take the actions required to protect their environment. There cannot be a failure of intelligence if the intelligence cannot be used anyway. Lastly, there is a significant difference in the analysts, processes, and tools required to generate intelligence and those required to consume it. Generating intelligence often requires a significant investment of resources, a wide availability of data collection opportunities, and a singular focus in terms of learning all there is to know about the target. Intelligence consumption, however, requires analysts to be familiar with the environment that the threat intelligence is meant for, to understand the business operations and technology that can be impacted by it, and to be able to put the intelligence into a form that is usable by the defenders. Generating intelligence is an action of intelligence, whereas consuming it is a role for active defense.

Stated simply, organizations must understand themselves, understand the threats, and empower personnel to use that information for defense to properly use threat intelligence. This basic concept is more difficult than it appears as it must build on all the other categories presented so far in the sliding scale of cybersecurity. It is this core foundation that makes threat intelligence extremely valuable to defenders, and being without it drastically reduces any value that can be obtained from intelligence.

Offense

With the proper foundations represented so far within the sliding scale of cybersecurity, including a heavy investment in intelligence, offense can contribute to cybersecurity. That being said, it is wholly discouraged that any private organization, especially those in the

---

* To learn more about cyber threat intelligence, consider taking SANS FOR578—Cyber Threat Intelligence for a deep dive into the material by Mike Cloppert, Chris Sperry, and the author of this paper. https://www.sans.org/course/cyber-threat-intelligence.

ICS community, use offense. Offense is the final phase of the sliding scale and represents direct action taken against the adversary outside friendly networks. Those practicing offensive operations require the understanding and skillsets found in the other phases and often require actions from those categories. For example, identifying a threat in the environment is often done in the active defense phase. To perform active defense correctly requires the foundation that passive defense and architecture establishes. Then, identifying information about the adversary, building the required knowledge to conduct an operation, and establishing markers for success are achieved in the intelligence phase. Offense is costly when considering the single action, but when the foundation required to be successful is taken into consideration, it reveals itself to be the most costly action that organizations can take.

The word offense was chosen for the sliding scale of cybersecurity over the terminology of a cyberattack due to the wide set of actions often covered by it. Often, organizations and news media describe cyberattacks with a variety of definitions including those actions of network breaches and espionage that would be better described as an adversary intelligence operation. The U.S. Department of Defense's joint publication for the definition of terms does not contain a definition for offensive cyberoperations; however the publication discusses offensive cyberoperations in the following way: "to project power by the application of force in or through cyberspace" (U.S. Department of Defense 2013). It is important to note here that the use of the word "force" aligns with the international use of the term, which is used to describe a set of unlawful actions outside of war. The U.S. military has unofficially and commonly used the actions of "deny, disrupt, deceive, degrade, and destroy" to describe a cyberattack (AFCYBER 2008).

A distinction needs to be made between the projection of power onto states by states and those actions organizations can take to increase their cybersecurity. Offensive actions must be discussed as an option that can increase cybersecurity, but the legality of these options for civilian organizations is highly contested. Offensive actions by states that would be deemed legal under international law are also highly debated, and the most complete document to address the debate to date is the Tallinn Manual (Schmitt 2009). Some interesting case studies concerning this debate have arisen recently, including the alleged North Korean attack on the civilian company Sony. Even without firm attribution, the United States likely had reason and legal impunity to apply countermeasures in the form of a cyberattack (Schmitt 2014). This discussion is outside the scope of this paper however.

Whatever the national and international laws evolve to, the actions by organizations, civilian or national, on the offensive must be legal in nature to be deemed an act of cybersecurity and not an act of an aggressor. Offense can be done for purposes other than cybersecurity such as national policy or conflict. However, to contribute to cybersecurity, the definition for these offensive actions is defined here as *legal countermeasures and counterstrike actions taken against an adversary outside of friendly systems for the purpose of self-defense.* It is in the opinion of the author that civilian organizations cannot currently participate in such actions and remain within the spirit of the law. While loopholes may be found, it is due to the law's inability to keep up with technical actions and not due to informed debate and discourse that would allow such actions. Additionally, with an appreciation of the return on investment for offense-based actions, it should be easily determined that organizations should have already achieved a hypothetical maximum return on investment from the other categories before seeing any value from offense in terms of security. Reasons based on vengeance or retaliation are not only illegal under international law but are also never seen as acts of self-defense.

The active cyber defense cycle

The sliding scale of cybersecurity establishes the appropriate terminology and foundation required to introduce one model for achieving an active defense. This model was created by the author and is based on lessons learned while working in the private industry, academia, and the government. It is in current use today by a number of organizations and is identified as the active cyber defense cycle (ACDC). The model consists of four continuous portions: threat-intelligence consumption, asset identification and network security monitoring, incident response, and threat and environment manipulation, as illustrated in Figure 15.2.

This conceptual framework allows for the articulation of a strategy specifically for an active defense. This strategy can be leveraged at an organizational level for the purposes of organizing, training, and equipping personnel as well as synchronizing otherwise disconnected teams. It can also be leveraged at the tactical level to guide activities within a team and provide an overall picture for the purpose of the active defense. Most commonly, it has been used as a guide for defenders and a model for security operations centers.

Without an understanding of the larger effort, interactions with the adversary are seen as singular events. Defenders then fail to identify the patterns of a larger campaign and generate appropriate responses and lessons learned. These network events often contribute to meaningless statistics such as "500,000 attacks" instead of identifying the campaign and actions related to it, which can be countered.* Additionally, when not guided by a strategy, individuals tend to focus their efforts on their specialities and interests instead of the organization's needs.

ACDC is a strategy for taking an active approach to identifying and countering adversaries for the purpose of achieving the security and reliability of systems. The premise of the strategy is to build on properly architected systems and passive defenses. This allows for the most scarce resources in an organization—trained security personnel and their time—to be effectively used on threats not mitigated by good architecture and passive defenses. When traditional threats and vulnerabilities are drastically reduced by good architecture and passive defenses, it is possible for active defenders to identify and focus efforts on countering advanced threats. Simply put, separating out the chaff allows defenders to focus on advanced and persistent adversaries.

ACDC is made up of four distinct phases of operations. These steps can sometimes overlap in terms of operators' skills and tool usage but they each represent a specific type of interaction with the adversary and contribution to the cycle. Successful use of the strategy depends on the defenders ability to sync the efforts of each phase and move quickly but accurately through the cycle. Training that takes place to hone efforts when no identified threat is present allows increased management and better organizational planning and processes. When a threat is identified, the accurate and timely repetition of the cycle works to detect, deny, and counter the adversary while extracting lessons learned for defense and training efforts internal to an organization. This information can also be used to share threat information with those external to the organization.

Threat-intelligence consumption

Threat-intelligence consumption focuses on identifying information sources specifically useful to the organization and putting them in the context of security operations. Threat

---

* Richard's TAO blog and Trollman's presentation.

intelligence is a specific form of intelligence focused on understanding threats. The term is best understood through the understanding of its two root words: threat and intelligence. A threat is anything that has the intent, capability, and opportunity to cause harm (Rynes and Bjornard 2011). Organizations commonly struggle with understanding what threats exist for their systems. It is not feasible to protect an organization simultaneously against every vulnerability, malicious capability, or actor. Likewise, it is incorrect to classify a vulnerability, actor, or malicious capability individually as a threat—it is only the combination of these that truly constitutes a threat (Figure 15.3).

Over the years, organizations have attempted to understand where to place the emphasis for security spending and strategies by modeling threats and performing risk management. While these processes can be effective, they are often criticized. Risk management and reduction plans often fail to accurately identify the threats specific to the organization, also known as the threat landscape. The threat landscape for one country, industry, or organization can be drastically different from others at both a macro and granular level. For example, nuclear operations centers in Iran face different threats than U.S. water utilities. This understanding of varying threats has been highlighted with the use of information sharing and analysis centers (ISACs) to encourage the sharing of threat information between different sectors of critical infrastructure (ISAC 2003). As an example, the aviation ISAC (A-ISAC) shares threat data among its member that varies greatly from the type of threat data shared by the electricity sector ISAC (ES-ISAC).

Threat-intelligence consumption operations begin with a holistic look at an organization's mission and systems. This deep internal look at the organization assists in identifying what opportunities exist for adversaries to cause harm—or in other words to determine the "operating environment." Threat-intelligence consumption personnel then apply this self-understanding to a search for information about capabilities and adversaries, or actors and groups that have the intent to harm, that could take advantage of the existing opportunities. This information can be acquired through sources such as open-source information gathering, purchased threat-data feeds, and formal threat-intelligence products from the government or private sectors. The understanding of threats facing an organization, or the threat landscape, guides what information is sought and how it is applied. Ultimately, threat-intelligence consumption personnel use this information in combination with the organization's own information gathered from past interactions with the adversary to

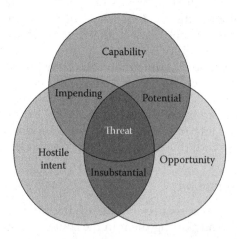

Figure 15.3 Classification of a threat. (From Courtesy of the SANS ICS515—active defense and incident response course.)

create actionable information. This actionable information is often in the form of indicators of compromise (IOCs). IOCs usually take the form of cryptographic fingerprints, or digital hashes, of malicious software, file paths and modifications to systems from malware, and Internet protocol (IP) addresses associated with malware and adversaries. IOCs can also be tactics, techniques, and procedures that indicate an adversary's presence. With the accompanying context of what the IOCs mean and what type of threat they represent, they become useful. IOCs are a meaningful and timely way for defense analysts to search networks and systems at a tactical level for indications that the systems have been breached or impacted by a threat.

It is important to note that generating threat intelligence would be an action of the Intelligence phase of the sliding scale of cyber security, whereas consuming it is in the active defense phase. Consuming this actionable information is extremely useful for ACDC personnel searching for the adversary inside the network. This hunt for the adversary in ACDC takes places through network security monitoring.

Asset identification and network security monitoring

The asset identification and network security monitoring phase of ACDC is dedicated to identifying the network topologies and monitoring the network for threats. The importance of asset identification cannot be overstated; it is not feasible to consistently ensure the security and reliability of systems if those systems are unknown. In essence, what is to be defended must be known. This is a concept familiar to many as stated by Chinese military strategist Sun Tzu: "So it is said that if you know your enemies and know yourself, you can win a hundred battles without a single loss (Sun Tzu 513BC)." This concept is also highlighted more relevantly in the critical security controls developed by the Council on CyberSecurity in 2013. The security controls total twenty recommendations for how to effectively do cybersecurity. The list was compiled by cybersecurity experts worldwide with input from various government organizations such as the U.S. National Security Agency. The number one critical control is an inventory of authorized and unauthorized devices. The second critical control is an inventory of authorized and unauthorized software.

Identification of the assets and data flows of a system should be identified and maintained with good architecture. However, in networked environments, this information is often dynamic and ever changing, even in relatively static ICS networks. For this reason, active defense personnel who monitor the network are in the best position to update this information, also identified as network topologies. These network topologies allow defenders to create a baseline of normal activity so as to quickly identify anomalies. Network anomalies are extremely useful for identifying advanced threats that passive defenses cannot identify or defend against. This search for abnormalities and other indications of adversary presence is performed through network security monitoring.

Network security monitoring is a security practice that originated from the need to move past passive defenses and actively hunt for advanced threats on a network. As a practice of monitoring networks for threats, it has no definable origin. However, the practice specifically identified as network security monitoring was created by Todd Heberlein and advanced by Richard Betjlich and BammVisscher (Bejtlich 2014). Mr. Betjlich and Mr. Visscher developed an understanding of network security monitoring in the U.S. Air Force in the 1990s as members of the Air Force Computer Emergency Response Team (AFCERT) (Beljith 2014). Mr. Betjlich then expanded on the understanding of network security monitoring in the private industry as a member of General Electric's computer security incident response team (CSIRT) and later the incident response company Mandiant (Beljith 2014). Mr. Betjlich authored two books on the subject wherein he defines network security monitoring as "the collection, analysis, and escalation of indications and warnings to detect and respond to intrusions (Bejtlich 2013)." Mr. Betjlich stated an important concept for network security monitoring: Products perform collection, people perform analysis, and processes guide escalation (Bejtlich 2004). This understanding is central to the purpose of network security monitoring and the role of the active human component keeping it in line with ACDC. The overall thought process is that defense will eventually fail, and defenders must be prepared to detect and respond to adversaries.

Network security monitoring analysts must be familiar with the network to effectively monitor it for threats. This coupling of asset identification and network security monitoring present an effective solution for identifying threats as well as contributing opportune information to the architecture and passive defenses. When asset identification and network security monitoring analysts identify a threat on the network, it is then escalated for decision makers to determine if incident response is needed. Generally, any threat that should not have reasonably been mitigated by good architecture and passive defenses will require incident response.

Incident response

Traditionally, incident response has been a process of responding to all incidents that meet a certain threshold predefined by an organization. The National Institute of Science and Technology (NIST) define a computer security incident as a "violation or imminent threat of violation of computer security policies, acceptable use policies, or standard security practices."* The goal of the response was to mitigate incidents and reduce losses from events such as security breaches. NIST categorized the phases of incident response as preparation, detection, analysis, containment, eradication, recovery, and postincident activity (Figure 15.4).

Briefly described, these phases ensure that incident responders plan ahead of time, detect the indications of an incident, analyze data to ensure that an incident has actually occurred, contain the incident before it spreads, eradicate the source of the incident, recover all systems and networks back to normal operation, and perform postincident activities such as documentation of lessons learned. This approach to incident response is a great starting place and especially made sense for networked environments when the first computer emergency response team (CERT) was established in 1988 in response to the Morris worm (West-Brown et al. 2003). However, many larger organizations do not utilize this approach to incident response for a few key reasons:

- Practices such as network security monitoring are responsible for detecting and analyzing indications of an incident as threats have become more advanced and common. Personnel on a network security monitoring team such as those found in a security operations center (SOC) may have a secondary job as an incident response team member, but incident response is often no longer responsible for detection and analysis.
- Incident responders tend to be responsible for the collection of digital evidence and information related to an incident but not the deep analysis of that data. As threats have evolved, there is more need for specialized malware analysis and forensic

---

* NIST 800-61.

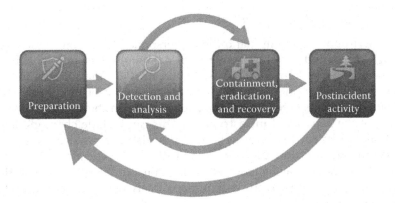

Figure 15.4 NIST's (traditional) incident response life cycle. (From Cichonski, P., et al., 2012, Computer Security Incident Handling Guide, SP 800-61 Rev. 2, National Institute of Standards and Technology. http://csrc.nist.gov/publications/nistpubs/800-61rev2/SP800-61rev2.pdf.)

approaches outside of the on-site incident responders. Likewise, as networked environments have become more complex, the skillsets of incident responders for collecting evidence have become more specialized and important.

- In many environments, it is not likely that incident responders will be performing the eradication of threats and the recovery of systems. For example, in critical-infrastructure locations, usually only certified engineers and operators of specialized control systems are allowed to access, modify, and restore systems. Incident response personnel are responsible for collecting data, giving recommendations, and providing technical assistance to the personnel performing the eradication and recovery efforts.

Incident response has changed. Likewise, incident response has also become more important as ICS organizations increasingly interact with threats that perform espionage aimed at stealing company intellectual property and state secrets. The NIST phases represent a useful framework that helps organizations start somewhere; the importance is the purpose of the framework, however, and not following specific steps chronologically and centralized to one team. Incident response in ACDC focuses on responding to threats in such a way that information and systems vital to the organization's mission are safeguarded.

Incident response's role in ACDC is to act on incidents related to threats escalated by network security monitoring personnel. These personnel acquire digital evidence from potentially compromised systems and networks as well as performing timely analysis to determine the scope and impact of a threat. Determining the impact of a threat helps decision makers make appropriate choices regarding business operations, legal and compliance requirements related to incidents, and when and where additional support may be needed. The scope of the infection allows incident response personnel to identify all the impacted systems. These systems will often be restored to normal operational status either in conjunction with the personnel responsible for the architecture or, if delegated by the architecture personnel, by the incident response members. To determine scope and impact, timely analysis is performed. This is expedited through the use of IOCs and quick verification methods on potentially compromised systems. Data collected during incident response in the ACDC are passed to the threat and environment manipulation analysts to help generate these IOCs for current and future use as well as to determine the intent of the threat.

Threat and environment manipulation

Threat and environment manipulation has personnel focus on understanding the threat through direct and safe interaction with data and adversary capabilities discovered on the network. This knowledge is used to create IOCs and information for internal threat-intelligence consumption efforts. Another key output of threat and environment manipulation personnel is recommendations for changes in the environment such as the reconfiguring of the networked infrastructure. This can include changing logical architecture such as the IP addresses of systems, administrator passwords, or actions that reroute the command and control (C2) communications of adversaries inside the network. Additionally, these efforts may include physical architecture changes such as the segmentation of systems on the network, the redefinition of network access points and pathways, or the addition or moving of defense systems.

The greatest advantage defenders have over adversaries is that they hold knowledge of and power over the network and its architecture. Threat and environment manipulation operations focus heavily on understanding the network and understanding the threat. One way to visualize a threat's phases is through the use of the Cyber Kill Chain™, which was developed by Eric M. Hutchins, Michael J. Cloppert, and Dr. Rohan M. Amin to analyze adversary campaigns (Hutchins et al. 2011). This model shows that adversaries have to first perform information gathering and reconnassiance efforts to learn about the targeted systems and networks. This allows the adversary to understand what capability will allow access to the target. Adversaries also have to perform this type of reconaissance once inside the network. Defenders start off with this knowledge as well as the ability to influence changes to the network that will confuse the adversary and force changes to their tactics, techniques, or procedures or force them to move back to the reconaissance step of their kill chain (Figure 15.5).

Threat and environment manipulation personnel are able to interact with adversary capabilities in an effort to fully understand and identify the threat. The process usually takes the form of malware analysis, as most adversaries utilize malicious software to achieve their goals (Zeltser, 2014). Reverse engineering malware, or malware analysis, is an ever-expanding field of research often identified as having a role in digital forensics. Lenny Zeltser, a noted malware analysis researcher, has focused on simplifying the complex field for the purpose of teaching others. He expanded on the traditional understanding of malware analysis to identify four simple but distinct phases: manual code reversing, interactive behavior analysis, static properties analysis, and fully automated analysis (Figure 15.6).

These phases describe malware analysts' efforts to examine and understand malware. Manual code reversing focuses on reverse engineering a malware's code to develop a full understanding of its function. Interactive behavior analysis allows malware analysts to execute, or run, the malware in safe environments so as to examine its interaction with systems. Static properties analysis gives analysts atomic identifiers related to the malware such as its digital hash and what type of file it is. Fully automated analysis attempts to

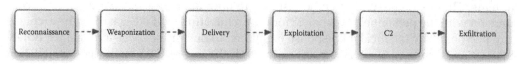

Figure 15.5 Cyber kill chain. (From Cloppert, M., 2009, Security intelligence: Attacking the kill chain. http://digital-forensics.sans.org/blog/2009/10/14/security-intelligence-attacking-the-kill-chain.)

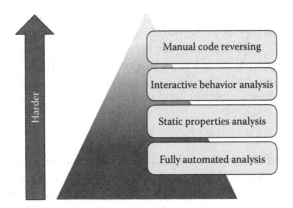

Figure 15.6 Four stages of malware analysis. (From Zeltser, L., 2014, Mastering 4 stages of malware analysis. http://blog.zeltser.com/post/79453081001/mastering-4-stages-of-malware-analysis.)

automate as much of the analysis as possible through the use of specially customized systems. These four phases give a realistic understanding of the threat and how to develop IOCs to identify it. This information, paired with an understanding of the network, allows for changes to the environment and potentially to the threat itself so as to delay, deny, counter, and confuse the adversary.

ACDC in action

Security is not a single achievable status; it is a process. Threat-intelligence consumption efforts are useful in identifying an organization's threat landscape and building on community knowledge of threats to guide the actions of others performing defense actions. Networking security monitoring personnel build on the strengths of a well-architected network to understand and map the network topologies in an effort to hunt for threats. Identified threats that become escalated to an incident, as defined by the organization, are passed to incident response personnel. Incident response focuses on obtaining digital evidence, assessing the scope of the threat, and containing it. The collected data is analyzed by threat and environment manipulation personnel to truly understand the threat and its capabilities. This understanding is useful for changing the logical or physical networked infrastructure in an active effort to delay, deny, confuse, and counter adversaries. Additionally, the information derived from this process is passed to threat-intelligence consumption personnel to centralize the information and continue the ACDC. Quick and accurate repetition of this cycle creates an active defense that can counter threats beyond the capability of traditional defense efforts. It uses the strengths of defenders to ensure the security and reliability of networked infrastructure.

Organizations that understand this process can better articulate their needs and invest in their architecture and passive defenses in a manner that will benefit active defense and security. Additionally, with an understanding of what is required for defense, organizations can better identify, define, and manage the organizing, equipping, and training of their personnel. The ACDC is one strategy for an active cyber defense that can significantly impact security. In ICS organizations, this can seem daunting to achieve. An active defense is what is required to counter advanced adversaries. There are no shortcuts. If the organization cannot achieve an active defense due to significant challenges, such as the lack of infrastructure for gathering data from the network, then there are likely issues in the architecture or passive defense phase of the sliding scale of cybersecurity that must be resolved first. It is through this understanding of what is required and what foundation must be present that ICS organizations can lay a road map for success. This allows better investments in security instead of simply investing in "security." Additionally, it helps guide processes, cultures, and technology in a way that allows defenders to get better over time in a way that adversaries cannot keep up with.

Conclusion

Executing an active defense with trained and empowered security personnel inside an organization that understands the value of security and with the appropriate foundations in place ensures the identification and countering of advanced adversaries. The best tactics, tools, and personnel adversaries can use to target ICS organizations fail when an active defense is leveraged appropriately. This is no small task or short undertaking. It requires a true security mindset and a culture of constantly pushing forward against a variety of challenges. Security will always be second place to the mission of the organization and its operations, but when done correctly it can support that mission to be safer and more reliable. For years, personnel in the community have taken a defeatist attitude toward security. Without ever taking part in actual offensive operations, many have acted as experts stating what an adversary will do, what their intentions are, and just how easy it is for them. This defender-driven narrative does not highlight the truth of the problem, however. The biggest challenge for security is not the adversary. In understanding this, in ICS networks and their personnel, and in leveraging an active defense, it can truly be stated that defense is doable.

References

Air Force Cyber Command Strategic vision (AFCYBER). (2008), U.S. Air Force.

Bejtlich, R. (2014), Taosecurity: Brief history of network security monitoring. http://taosecurity.blogspot.com/2014/09/a-brief-history-of-network-security.html.

Bejtlich, R. (2013), *The Practice of Network Security Monitoring*, No Starch Press: San Francisco, CA.

Bejtlich, R. (2004), *The TAO of Network Security Monitoring: Beyond Intrusion Detection*, Addison-Wesley Professional.

Cichonski, P., Millar, T., Grance, T., and Scarfone, K. (2012), Computer security incident handling guide, SP 800-61 Rev. 2, National Institute of Standards and Technology. http://csrc.nist.gov/publications/nistpubs/800-61rev2/SP800-61rev2.pdf.

Cloppert, M. (2009), Security intelligence: Attacking the kill chain. http://digital-forensics.sans.org/blog/2009/10/14/security-intelligence-attacking-the-kill-chain.

The Council on Cyber Security. (2013), Critical controls. http://www.counciloncybersecurity.org/critical-controls/.

Hutchins, E.M., Cloppert, M.J., Amin, R.M. (2011), Intelligence-driven computer network defense informed by analysis of adversary campaigns and intrusion kill chains, Lockheed Martin Corporation, USA. http://www.lockheedmartin.com/content/dam/lockheed/data/corporate/documents/LM-White-Paper-Intel-Driven-Defense.pdf.

DePuy, W.E. (1974), *Implications of the Middle East War on U.S. Army Tactics, Doctrine and Systems*.

DePuy, W. E. (1980), *FM 100-5 Revisited*.

Hurriyet. (2008), Turkish official confirms BTC pipeline blast is a terrorist act. http://www.hurriyet.com.tr/english/finance/9660409.asp?scr=1.

Information Sharing and Analysis Centers (ISAC). (2003), http://www.isaccouncil.org/aboutus.html.

Ismail, A. (2008), PKK claims responsibility for BTC pipeline explosion, *Today's Zaman*, August 8.

Latter, A.L. and Martinelli, E.A. (1965), *Active and Passive Defense*, RAND Corporation: Santa Monica, CA.

Lee, R.M., Assante, M.J., and Conway, T. (2014), SANS ICS Defense Use Case (DUC), ICS CP/PE (Cyber-to-Physical or Process Effects) case study paper: Media report of the Baku-Tbilisi-Ceyhan (BTC) pipeline Cyber Attack. https://ics.sans.org/media/Media-report-of-the-BTC-pipeline-Cyber-Attack.pdf.

Lee, R.M. (2015a), Closing the case on the reported 2008 Russian cyber attack on the BTC pipeline, SANS industrial control systems. https://ics.sans.org/blog/2015/06/19/closing-the-case-on-the-reported-2008-russian-cyber-attack-on-the-btc-pipeline.

Lee, R.M., (2015b), The sliding scale of cyber security: A SANS analyst whitepaper. https://www.sans.org/reading-room/whitepapers/analyst/sliding-scale-cyber-security-36240.

Lee, R.M., (2015c), Data information, and intelligence: Why your threat feed is likely not threat intelligence, Sans DFIR. https://digital-forensics.sans.org/blog/2015/07/09/your-threat-feed-is-not-threat-intelligence.

Robertson, J. and Riley, M. (2014), Mysterious '08 Turkey pipeline blast opened new cyberwar. http://www.bloomberg.com/news/articles/2014-12-10/mysterious-08-turkey-pipeline-blast-opened-new-cyberwar.

Rynes, A. and Bjornard, T. (2011), *Intent, Capability, and Opportunity: A Holistic Approach to Addressing Proliferation as a Risk Management Issue*, Idaho National Laboratory Idaho Falls, ID.

Schmitt, M.N. (2009), *The Tallinn Manual*, NATO cooperative cyber defence centre of excellence, Cambridge University Press: New York, 2009.

Schmitt M. (2014), International law and cyber attacks: Sony vs. North Korea, Just security. http://justsecurity.org/18460/international-humanitarian-law-cyber-attacks-sony-v-north-korea/.

Sun Tzu (513BC), *The Art of War.*

U.S. Department of Defense. (2013), Joint publication (JP) 3-12 cyberspace operation.

U.S. Department of Defense. (2015), Joint publication (JP) 1-02 dictionary of military and associated terms.

West-Brown, M.J., Stikvoort, D., Kossakowski, K.-P., Killcrece, G., Ruefle, R., and Zajice, M. (2003), *Handbook for Computer Security Incident Response Teams (CSIRTs)*, 2nd Edn. Carnegie Mellon University, USA. http://www.sei.cmu.edu/reports/03hb002.pdf.

Zeltser, L. (2014), Mastering 4 stages of malware analysis. http://blog.zeltser.com/post/79453081001/mastering-4-stages-of-malware-analysis.

chapter sixteen

Open-source intelligence (OSINT)

Steven Young

Contents

Introduction

The role of open-source intelligence (OSINT) in information security operations includes the identification, assessment, collection, and exploitation of information in support of corporate and public-sector technical intelligence requirements specifically in information systems (IT/IS) operations. Open-source information acquired through information security operations provides rapid performance and vulnerability assessments of potential and actual hackers, giving a critical edge to private- and public-sector current/future information technology operations.

Open-source information is publicly available information appearing in print or electronic form. Open-source information may be transmitted through radio, television, newspapers, commercial databases, electronic mail networks, or other electronic media like CD-ROMs (U.S. Department of Defense, 2006, Section 1-1-14). OSINT in IT also encompasses managed services. Managed services may aggregate information on a particular company, individual, domain, or Internet protocol (IP) address. The individual or entity that uses this information is typically a subscriber to a service. In previous years, companies that had intellectual property to protect used managed OSINT services. Industry later evolved into other forms; particularly, financial services industries began subscribing to these types of services as a subservice of fraud protection.

Why is open source intelligence necessary?

OSINT is also a means of achieving significant savings, in that many essential elements of information required by a strategic thinking leader can be acquired from commercial sources at a lower cost and in less time than from classified capabilities, with the added advantage that OSINT is often more up to date.

Whatever form they take, open sources are

- Not classified at their origin
- Not subject to proprietary constraints
- Not the product of sensitive contacts with foreign persons or U.S. citizens (U.S. Army, 2002, Sections 1-1-5-1), meaning not a documented interview with an industry contact that may have proprietary or restricted knowledge that cannot be put in the public domain

In all technical operations (public or private sector), open-source collection is a valuable addition to the overall intelligence collection effort. Open sources are evaluated and categorized as friendly, neutral, or hostile. Certain high-value open-source information sources may be identified for continuous monitoring. Other open-source information sources may be identified to screen for the presence or lack of specific indicators (U.S. Army, 2002, Section 7-2). In addition, the information obtained from open sources is extremely helpful for keeping information security and physical security teams current with the latest developments in a particular industry, location, or project. The process for conducting open-source information security intelligence operations in multiple environments begins at the sector (public or private) level.

How is OSINT positioned strategically in an organization? Most medium- and small-sized companies cannot afford a designated information "intelligence" officer. For decades, the position was set up under marketing or the public information office of a publicly traded company (McGonagle et al. 2003). Marketing staffers would use OSINT to gain a competitive advantage over another company, client, or trading partner. Likewise, the public information office of a publicly traded company would restrict information from competitors that would be publicly available. The first term that was synonymous with OSINT was competitive intelligence. Other terms encountered in the OSINT profession were knowledge management, market intelligence, and marketing research. All of these have a strategic IS/IT component; however, they did not focus on a specific technology or security threat. OSINT was not really used by other corporate departments until technology finally caught up with it. When defined through information security or corporate security departments, OSINT takes on a completely new meaning. At the private-sector level, information security teams should designate a resource to augment information security staff. This person should be an expert in open- and closed-source information that can protect IT operations. This person should also have specified training to operate in either sector. It is not enough to just be a technical expert in intrusion detection signatures or log analysis. This resource should be capable of sharing information with other companies or agencies outside their sector of expertise and operations. They should also be able to classify electronic information so as to prevent disclosure to hostile parties that may affect their IT operations or the operations of their partners.

IT professionals rely on technological advantages to successfully synchronize and execute complex modern information security operations. The introduction of a surprise technological capability by an adversary company, country, or entity causes confusion and delays project accomplishment until the capability is understood and countered. OSINT is one of the keys to the early identification of an adversary's technical capabilities, vulnerabilities, and intent. OSINT provides the information for the basic development and employment of countermeasures by corporate and public-sector leadership.

It is important to look at OSINT at a strategic level for all participating entities (both public and private sector). The United States has relied on its military and private infrastructure as a strategic deterrent to war, cyberterrorism, cybercrime, and the theft of intellectual property (U.S. Army, 2002, Section 1-1). This strength lies, in part, in the diversity and extent of its technology base. While the United States aspires to be the leader in integrating technology, the actual products are available to any buyer. An adversary can achieve temporary technological parity or advantage by acquiring modern systems or capabilities.

There are also important risks to note with OSINT. The value of the information is only as good as the people preparing it and analyzing it. There are no publicly documented or litigated cases of intentionally deceptive OSINT in supervisory control and data acquisition (SCADA) or in information security. However, it is important to note that there are plenty of publicly documented cases where public-sector groups and governments have used OSINT to disseminate deceptive or incorrect information.

The world market is willing to provide these advanced systems to countries or individuals with the resources to pay for them. A concerted OSINT program is vital to providing precise direction and purpose within the U.S. research and design (R&D) process to ensure that this cyberwarfare parity or advantage is neutralized quickly and efficiently.

It is important to look at the types of countermeasures that can be deployed against OSINT. At its most basic level, privacy laws in the European Union, Canada, and the United States offer some protection if properly enforced through a corporation counsel's office. For example, corporate attorneys may file injunctions to have names removed from databases that competitors use. Patent and trademark protections in the private sector also limit some forms for competition (and aggression). These types of actions would force competitive companies or aggressors to rethink the disposition of technology investments and projects. It would also force them to adjust their analytical and technology attack products accordingly. This in turn could lead operational planners to rethink objectives, task organizations, and many important operational control measures. In the end, enhanced understanding of aggressor capabilities in both the public and private sector would enable friendly companies and entities to plan and prepare for aggression in such a way that the enhanced aggressive capability would be negated.

Benefits from obtaining open source intelligence

Using OSINT tools and managed services, we are able to achieve the following direct information for an individual or organization:

- E-mail addresses
- Phone numbers
- Open-source (OS) info
- IP info
- Software/software versions
- Geo location
- Personal details
- Patterns of behavior in accessing files and websites
- Basically everything you can collect in a security information and event management (SIEM) tool

The value of OSINT is inherent to the missions or projects it supports. Here are a couple of examples:

- Technical reconnaissance of a competitor's new technology project
- Survey and assessment of competitor's current IT infrastructure

- Technical identification of specific products used to maintain a technology edge, as in the case of a supply-chain operation.
- Identification of technology capital purchases that will later be used to mark competitive inventory
- Threat assessment to a specific technology hosting site or corporate headquarters
- Damage assessment to a specific technology hosting site or corporate headquarters
- Misleading a competitor into making capital purchases to counter IT projects

How is open source intelligence gathered?

What are the typical activities associated with OSINT and information security operations? There are five primary OSINT collection methodologies:

- *Debriefing*: Debriefing is the questioning of individuals who are sources of information in order to obtain information in response to a program's needs. The primary categories of sources for debriefing are personnel, personnel who have been in contact with competitors and aggressors, business people who may have worked in the areas of interest, and foreigners that may be hostile to a particular industry or public-sector operation that involves information security.
- *Elicitation*: Elicitation is the gaining of information through direct interaction with a human source where the source is not aware of the specific purpose for the conversation. Elicitation is the baseline method for initiating source operations.
- *Interview*: Interview is the questioning of an individual to ascertain the individual's degree of knowledge on various topics. Interviews are also used in reference to security investigations such as a data breach or a laptop theft.
- *Screening*: Screening is the process of identifying an individual for further exploitation. Discriminators used in screening can range from appraising general appearance and attitude to asking specific questions to assess areas of knowledge and degree of cooperation. Screening is not in itself an OSINT intelligence collection technique but a timesaving measure that identifies those individuals most likely to answer.
- *Surveillance*: Surveillance is the process of keeping a person, place, or other target under physical or technical observation. Surveillance may be conducted to collect data to enhance the safety of a specific operation or to collect information to answer collection requirements. A couple of simplified examples of this method are monitoring news feeds or subscription services for changes concerning a particular individual, company, or technology. It could also mean monitoring network traffic going to or from a specific port.

How open source intelligence is analyzed and utilized

How should OSINT be analyzed? The first step is to compare business requirements or public-sector missions at a high level to the OSINT sources that are available. Part of this effort is to document requirements, mission statement, and any regulatory restrictions before beginning collection efforts. OSINT efforts may also require funding. Quality and quantitative data cost money in any sector of operation. People using OSINT should be prepared to make an investment in collection infrastructure as well as analysis for it to be of any use (U.S. Army, 2003, Section 2).

The second step is to focus on the human beings (threat, friendly, and neutral) as well as the key technology terrain. Information to monitor would include

- Demographics of both attacker and the target
- Organization and structure of all aggressors
- History of the aggressor and target
- Potential economic vulnerabilities of the target (by reviewing their balance sheet and budget)
- Key leadership (chief information officer [CIO], chief executive officer [CEO], chief information security officer [CISO])
- Financial analyst and media opinions

The third step is to determine specific tasks based on the OSINT provided. Specified tasks are those specifically assigned to an OSINT analyst after data collection or to a specific business unit that needs data to support or protect an IT capital project. The tasks are derived from information built up from the analysis of a threat situation. For example, a target company may purchase updated firewalls or a new SIEM tool to defend against an aggressor identified in a series of high-profile web attacks. At this level of task development, executive leadership must be involved. Determinations of tasks have legal obligations that could affect stockholders, for example.

The fourth step is to review available assets (U.S. Army, 2003, Section 3). Available asset analysis is a multilayer approach. For example, targets need to examine the assets they have to combat a technology threat after it has been identified in OSINT. Another way of looking to OSINT is to determine the aggressor's assets and how they can be exploited or rebuffed. For example, a target company may choose the deploy a specific application code analyzer after an aggressor brags on the web about creating a certain code attack against a specific industry.

The fifth step in the OSINT process is to determine constraints at all levels (U.S. Army, 2003, Section 3). For example, it would be important to determine the target and aggressor resource constraints as well as funding.

The sixth step in the OSINT process is to identify critical facts and assumptions derived from OSINT (U.S. Army, 2003, Section 4). For an example, are certain types of attacks only coming from one hosting provider or another? Another example of a critical fact would be a vulnerability left open by a coder or system patch that is repeatedly exploited. Critical facts and assumptions help leaders understand the risk assessment presented to them. There is a certain amount of subjectivity that needs to take place with the analysis (U.S. Army, 2002, Section 2-1). For example, OSINT information needs to be judged by consistency with other information on the same subject supplied in the past by established credible sources. It should be reviewed for completeness of detail and plausibility based on general knowledge and experience. The only people that can do this type of work are IT security engineers or security managers. Third-party reports should be examined to see whether they make sense; a self-contradictory report should be viewed with caution.

Manufactured subscription information will usually be constructed with unimpeachable logic or else it will have a set pattern of confusion. An unsound piece of information may, if taken at face value, seem consistent and logical. By contrast, a sound piece of information may contain an apparent contradiction that has crept in through clerical errors or imperfections in translation, observation, or transmission. A vague and general report may be perfectly true but useless. Detailed raw open-source intelligence that cites names and designates places can be evaluated more effectively than general statements of observations. The collector must also examine information against the background of general knowledge on the subject concerned. Information should not be rejected simply because it does not appear to be plausible.

When testing the source for reliability, security engineers need to distinguish between the actual source and the conveying source. When the originating source is not revealed, the credibility of the conveyer and the conveyer's evaluation of the originating source assume somewhat greater significance. In theory, the only absolute sources for an analyst are their own direct observations and authentic documentary evidence. Both of these sources are seldom available. Since optimum conditions are seldom working conditions, the security analyst must begin by asking many questions. Three important ones are

- Is the probable source of the report the true source?
- Has false information been released for the purposes of deception?
- Is the original source manufacturing information—that is, is the original source—a generic third-party subscription report?

The final step in the OSINT process in to develop a traditional risk assessment. There are many versions of risk assessments to use. Based on OSINT, target companies or public-sector entities should determine risk by analyzing the threat, vulnerability, cost, and probability of occurrence. There are many variations of this model shared by governments, security organizations, and insurance companies. The key aspect of the model is the incorporation of information from OSINT.

The value of open-source intelligence at any given time is determined by the situation and threat. For example, an active denial of service attack on a web page of a company is different from a pending wireless attack on a SCADA system (U.S. Army, 2002, Section 5-1). The following is a list of potential areas to look at when using OSINT for information security:

- Offensive missions/projects
  - When will our company or agency be hacked or breached?
  - What is the main objective of the attack?
  - What entities or locations will participate in the attack?
  - What tactics and tools will be employed?
  - What routes will the attackers use to cause the breach?
- Defensive missions/projects
  - How will the attacker hide? (e.g., proxy server, insider threat)
- Composition
  - What is the command and control element of the attacker?
  - What types of resources will they deploy?
  - Where are the resources located?
  - What types of skills do they have?
- Attack tools
  - What types of automated or scripted tools did will they use to attack?
  - Are the tools home grown, custom scripted, or commercial off-the-shelf ?
- Dispositions
  - Where are the attacks coming from, and where are they going?
- Special operations/physical security
  - Were employee or contractor ID cards involved?
  - Was site video surveillance involved?
  - Were site trash storage/removal capabilities compromised?
- Training
  - Has corporate training been compromised?

- Has the aggressor obtained training in a tool being used against the company?
- Can anyone (including the target company) participate in the training?
- Effectiveness
  - How many records were breached?
  - How much downtime was incurred?
  - How much time did full-time employee spend remediating a system or application?
  - Were contractors hired to supplement staff in remediation efforts?
  - Was any money stolen?
  - Was additional hardware or software purchased to defend against the attack?
  - Were any contracts or projects cancelled because of the attack?
- Technical infrastructure
  - What is the technical condition of the target company's server and network infrastructure?
  - Was it patched?
  - Are software development strategies disclosed?
  - Are there failover or mirror sites?
    - Note, the questions that can be asked regarding technical infrastructure and applications are endless.

Advantages versus disadvantages of using open source intelligence

There are many advantages and disadvantages to OSINT. The primary advantage is that OSINT offers virtually unlimited potential on any topic, particularly with use of the Internet and the managed service providers that aggregate information from it. The cost is relatively low because expertise is maintained at someone else's expense (Figure 16.1). If you use a managed service provider, the information is generally up to date.

The disadvantages include the possibility of revealing confidential plans, proprietary information, and strategic intentions. If a managed service provider is used, licensing can restrict the information from being shared. Limited security can be provided by hiding research questions through intermediaries. The time and cost associated with searching for exactly the right information within the huge volumes of public information is an issue. There is also a temptation to accept an open source at face value when it could be disinformation or simply inaccurate.

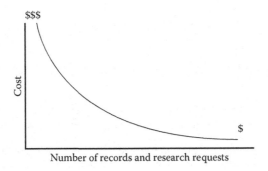

Figure 16.1 Cost vs. number of record requests.

Conclusion

It is important to add some thoughts on law and liability associated with OSINT. Identifying an individual or IP address associated with a suspected breach or system vulnerability does not mean that you can or should maintain files on that particular individual or entity. Each U.S. state and several other countries have enacted cyberstalking laws that associate potential liability for using OSINT to maintain files on an individual.* Originally, these laws were enacted to prevent cyberbullying or sexual harassment on the Internet; however, courts have taken a broader view of the definition.† Cyberstalking is defined as the unlawful act of collecting or amassing an individual's private information concerning the Internet, a computer, or alternative electronic network.‡ This can include the illegal trespass onto a computer terminal or network belonging to the victim no matter how good the intentions are thought to be. Furthermore, cyberstalking can also be defined as illicitly spying or watching another individual in which the intent is considered inherently criminal and unlawful in nature.§ Some organizations could also view their information in OSINT as a violation of their civil rights. It is recommended that investigators (public and private) and company representatives engage legal counsel before pursing information operations on a specific individual or entity.

References

McGonagle, J. J. and Vella, C.M., *The Manager's Guide to Competitive Intelligence*. p. 184. Westport CT: Greenwood Publishing Group, 2003.

U.S. Army, *Strategic Intelligence*. Washington DC: U.S. Government Printing Office, 2002. Sections 2-1–Section 5-1.

U.S. Army, *Tactical Human Intelligence and Counter Intelligence Operations*. Washington DC: U.S. Government Printing Office, 2002. Sections 1-1–5-1, 7-2.

U.S. Army, *Technical Intelligence* Washington DC: U.S. Government Printing Office, 2003. Sections 2–4.

U.S. Department of Defense, *Technical Intelligence: Multi-Service Tactics, Techniques, and Procedures for Technical Intelligence Operations*. Washington DC: U.S. Government Printing Office, 2006. Section 1-1-14.

---

* 18 U.S.C. 875(c). In addition, United Kingdom, Protection from Harassment Act, Chapter 40,1997.

† 47 U.S.C. 223(a) (1) (C).

‡ Reno v. *American Civil Liberties Union*, 521 U.S. 844, 850–852, 870. 1997; American Civil Liberties Union v. Reno, 31 F.Supp.2d 473, 476, 493. E.D. Pa. 1999.U.S. Army, *Strategic Intelligence*. Washington DC: U.S. Government Printing Office, 2002. Section 1-1.

§ http://cyber.laws.com/cyber-stalking.

section four

Commissioning and operations

chapter seventeen

Obsolescence and procurement of industrial control systems

Bernie Pella

Contents

Introduction

Obsolescence in the industrial control system has a significantly different meaning than in the enterprise network environment. Most newly installed industrial control systems are obsolete by normal IT standards. An enterprise computer system has a 3–5-year life cycle, but industrial control systems previously had a 15–30-year life cycle. Changes in computers and operating systems (OSs) and the impact of cybersecurity threats have forced changes to the industrial control system life cycle.

Initially, industrial control systems were built on proprietary hardware (e.g., IBM, DEC, etc.) and operating systems or platforms. Each vendor had customized operating systems based on VMS, UNIX, DOS, or some other custom platform. The entire system was supported only by the vendor, and the specific vendor had control of updates, fixes, patches, and upgrades. The proprietary nature of the industrial control system made the systems expensive and had significant limitations if another vendor's platform required integration from facility expansion or modification. Over time, vendors migrated from the proprietary industrial control system platforms to the more popular graphical interface used by Microsoft Windows. As the vendors migrated to Microsoft Windows, software communication connectors were built to allow the old field hardware (controllers, remote terminal units [RTUs], etc.) to communicate with the Microsoft Windows graphical interface. Using the software communication connectors allowed use of the existing, reliable, and tested software in the control modules to interface with the Microsoft Windows environment.

As many of the industrial control systems migrated to the Microsoft OS platform, the Microsoft OS support became a limiting factor for industrial control systems. Currently,

Microsoft Server 2003 and Windows XP are at end of life and are no longer supported by Microsoft. Microsoft Windows 7 is an aging operating system, with support ending in 2020.Windows Server 2008 is in the same category as Windows 7 with an end-of-support date in 2020. Microsoft Server 2012 is a mature server OS, and expected end of life or support is in 2023. Microsoft Server 2016 and Windows 10 are in the beta-testing or early-release phases. Based on current estimates, the life expectancy for future industrial control systems has been reduced to no more than 12 years. The life cycle is dependent on cybersecurity requirements and the need for support for OS updates. In some industries, without regulatory criteria or cybersecurity concerns, legacy industrial control systems are in use and have much older operating systems.

Industrial control system manufacturers wait until a new operating system has been in use for some time and has reached maturity before starting a transition to the new operating system. This is done to allow time for the bugs to be resolved. Waiting typically provides a more reliable industrial control system. Since the industrial control system is expected to operate for 15 or more years, there is no immediacy to have the latest system. The primary goal of an industrial control system is to operate a facility reliably and predictably. While the industrial control system is operating well, there is little consideration paid to replacing or upgrading the system. The old philosophy of "if it ain't broke, don't fix it" holds true when applied to industrial control systems.

This philosophy is becoming more problematic with Microsoft discontinuing patch and update support well before the previous 15–30-year life expectancy for the industrial control system. Also, the shorter end-of-support time creates an accelerated industrial control system upgrade cycle. The accelerated upgrade cycle is extremely important in the hostile malware and cyberattack environment seen today. The STUXNET malware cyberattack created a framework for future cyberattacks. Each upgrade to the OSs has resulted in improved security.

The previous obsolescence philosophy was defined to upgrade an industrial control system when repair parts are no longer available, equipment has a frequent failure rate, spare parts are supplied by refurbishing previously failed parts, or system reliability is starting to impact facility or process productivity. The time associated with obsolescence was not easily predictable. A group of equipment failures does not necessarily predict the need for replacement. A large number of similar component failures occurring within a short period of time may provide an estimate of the life expectancy of that type of component. The system may operate for many more years after the failed components are replaced. The previous philosophy was that when industrial control system components seem to fail randomly, it was time to start the process of industrial control system replacement or upgrade.

Obsolescence determination

Industrial control systems operate continuously. Most are monitored and manipulated by operations personnel on a 24-hours-a-day, 7-days-a-week basis. Since most of the systems are continuously monitored, operations personnel may observe unusual system responses, which provide clues to imminent failures. Industrial control systems are designed to log field equipment manipulations. The industrial control system logs can also provide information on unusual or unexpected equipment responses. Review of these logs is critical for establishing when an industrial control system component will fail in the near future. Network communications errors, loss-of-communications errors, and operational parameters failing high or low and then returning to normal are all preindicators of preeminent failures. Keeping a record of the failures and the components replaced is needed to build the justification for system upgrades or replacement. Failure records are also extremely useful for establishing the quantities of spare parts necessary to keep the industrial control system running.

A spare-parts inventory is necessary to support industrial control system longevity. A minimum of one or two controls of each type of control component (e.g., controllers, I/O modules, media converters, etc.) should be kept as spare parts. The quantity of spare parts is relative to the size of the system. Complete replacement of an industrial control system is expensive and happens infrequently. The majority of the replacement cost is not represented by the industrial control system hardware. The configuration of the software to make the industrial system manipulate the plant or facility is the largest expense when replacing an industrial control system. Potentially, upgrading the operating system can be performed without replacing the entire industrial control system. The choice to upgrade the operating system without upgrading the industrial control system hardware will be vendor dependent. Some vendor's industrial control systems can easily handle an operating system upgrade; others cannot. Since this is a vendor agnostic book, determining which vendors operating system upgrades are easier than others will require some research. Also, each vendor is continuously improving their industrial control system. Some vendors previous versions could not be upgraded, but newer versions can easily handle operating system upgrades.

Manufacturers will maintain an inventory of spare parts for several years. Most manufacturers do not keep spare parts available for systems more than 10 years old. Since industrial control systems are computer systems, technology improvements motivate the manufacturers to continuously improve their systems to remain competitive. With the merger or consolidation of many corporations and companies being purchased by larger corporations, legacy support is not as reliable as it was in the past. Supporting obsolete or legacy systems may not be cost effective. The potential legacy support creates a problem if spare parts are needed. Having a spare part available to replace every proprietary component in the system is necessary. A stockpile of input and output modules, controllers, power supplies, and specialty modules can significantly extend industrial control system operations. Extending the life of an industrial control system provides time to prepare, estimate, budget, and complete system replacement.

Good estimates of industrial control system component failures are initially difficult. When the system is first installed, there will be a few failures. Over the next 2 years, very few failures are expected. This initial 2 years do not provide a representative sample for spare-parts estimates. There will be a few failures, but these failures do not provide reliable data for the life of the system. The next 3 years, or the period from year 2 to year 5, provides a reliable representative sample of failure rates. This period provides a representation of the spare parts necessary to keep the system operating for 10–12 years. Manufacturers should still have spare parts available between the 5- and 8-year periods. Around the 5-year point, quantities of spare parts should be assessed. The parts should be available and estimates should be realistic to determine spare-part needs. The philosophy of only having a few spares when the system is replaced should be implemented. This is based on the 10–12 year life cycle for industrial control systems. For example, if there is only one power supply in the system, having two or three spares is not a bad inventory number, but keeping twenty-five in spare inventory is excessive. Critical spare parts require a higher inventory to ensure continued industrial control system operations. The goal of the spare-parts inventory is to keep the industrial control system operational until the facility plans to replace the system. Inadequate spare-parts inventory can have the impact of accelerating the replacement schedule, forcing system replacement before the replacement is planned. Early replacement results in additional cost.

Replacement time

Determining when to replace an industrial control system requires several factors. First, are regulatory requirements creating a need to add additional security to the industrial control system? Many industries have regulations requiring an industry to improve the cybersecurity posture of industrial control systems. There are many ways to improve the security of legacy industrial control systems and to meet the intent of the cybersecurity requirements. Changes to network infrastructure will probably be required if the system is connected to the plant business network. Regulatory requirements do not require the replacement of an industrial control system and these represent only one factor in considering whether to replace an industrial control system.

Second, does the industrial control system remain capable of continuing plant or facility operations? As facilities and processes change over time, at times efficiency of the plant or facility system are hindered by existing equipment and industrial control system capabilities. An example of the need for replacement is the addition of smart electric meters—smart grid—allowing capabilities for better power grid load regulation and control. The existing analog meters were not capable of any load regulation or of communicating the usage to a central location. The new electric meters have the capability to assist in electric grid load regulation. This improvement required new equipment. With the limits on the amount of electrical power generated due to a fixed number of power plants and power generators, plus the increase in electrical load across the country, the consumer market indirectly forced the need to change the electrical distribution strategy. The existing meters were still working well, but the market forced the need to change the meters. Regulatory requirements and government incentives accelerated this process; however, the change was inevitable.

Third, is there a need for production data or facility near-real-time information to support process improvements, which reduce costs and improve profitability? Often, information from production systems can be used to track and trend process needs. Newer industrial control systems have the ability to monitor inventories, automatically send e-mails to order more raw materials, contact shippers of ready-to-ship product, and track product delivery. Many of these tasks are currently performed by individuals with a salary and benefits. Improvements in an industrial control system can reduce the manpower required to perform repetitive predictable tasks. Additionally, the process information obtained from an industrial control system provides extremely accurate process information. The process information can be used to negotiate more accurate contracts for raw materials, reduce interprocess handling times or events, and be the impetus for process improvement. The costs saved by implementing a new industrial control could potentially pay for the system through business-cost reductions or increased production output. From the business perspective, process improvement and cost reduction are typically the primary factors determining industrial control system replacement.

Reliability is the fourth criteria to address when deciding to replace or upgrade an industrial control system. Is the industrial control system failing, causing facility or system downtime and impacting productivity? If a facility costs $1one million a day to produce a product and the industrial control system has a failure rate of 3 days downtime per year due to equipment failures, then valuable information is available to determine when to replace or upgrade the industrial control system. Analyzing the return on investment related to the cost of upgrading or replacing would be an easy analysis. The return on investment would be easy to determine, and the expectation of increased failures and downtime would justify industrial control system replacement.

An additional factor to consider when determining whether to replace an industrial control system is future capabilities. If significant facility changes are being planned, and enhanced automation capabilities can be merged with the existing facility, replacement of the entire industrial control system may be a good idea. The replacement or upgrading of the entire industrial control system would reduce any incompatibility problems with the existing industrial control system and renew the equipment failure rate of the entire industrial control system. An entire industrial control system upgrade or replacement would provide the enhanced capabilities for data and production analysis across the entire facility. The additional information is useful to optimize plant operations.

The last factor to consider is the end-of-life date of operating system support. How important are operating system patching and updates? Based on current Microsoft operating system end-of-life information, if the system is more than 10 years old, then an upgrade to the newest operating system should be considered. The 10-year point provides between a year and 18 months to budget, plan, and implement the upgrade. Please note that the end-of-life upgrade cycle may be significantly extended based on specific industry requirements or criteria.

Determining system needs

Development of an industrial control system specification is the first major task once the decision to replace the current system has been made. Creating a specification requires knowledge of the current industrial control system and of the capabilities of new industrial control systems. Consider using a vendor agnostic consultant to assist in determining the new functionality to implement since significant changes are available compared to the existing system. A vendor agnostic consultant should provide information on the capabilities of a new industrial control system and how the enhanced capabilities should be included in the new system. The consultant's recommendations should also include an assessment of current and expected future regulations to assist in regulatory compliance. Using the consultant minimizes the possibility of being influenced by convincing vendor sales personnel promoting the need for unnecessary capabilities or skewing new system capabilities. The consultant may not be able to provide specific costs associated with system replacement. However, the consultant should provide a general idea of the costs of a new system and of the various additional capabilities. The information obtained from the consultant should be used in specification development. Once the facility and business needs are accurately identified, an accurate specification can be developed.

Specification development

The specification should be explicit in defining the functionality of the current industrial control system and the potential enhancements to improve productivity, security, and system information. The replacement for the current industrial control system must match the current capabilities so that current facility operations can be continued. The knowledge of potential future expansion is also necessary. The specification does not need the specific details of potential future expansion, but the system should contain the capabilities to expand without significant rework. The specification must also include the types and connectivity of current field equipment. Equipment information is critical for maintaining the compatibility of the new industrial control system vendor equipment with existing plant equipment. The information obtained from the consultant will be extremely important in developing the specification. The specification should include an overview of the nonproprietary code used in the current industrial control system. The code-development aspect of an industrial control system is labor intensive. Conversion from existing computer code to computer code compatible with the replacement system should be within the capabilities of the new system vendor. These characteristics all need to be described in the specification.

Accurate information in the specification is critical for vendors to provide an accurate cost of industrial control system replacement. Vendors describe industrial control system components, capabilities, and field points differently. Defining critical attributes in the specification is important if bids from different vendors are to be accurately compared.

Selecting a vendor

Selecting a vendor to replace an existing industrial control system is a unique process compared to typical IT computer equipment replacement. Since the industrial control system is expected to be operational for 10–15 years, additional time and expertise is necessary to ensure the correct equipment is chosen. The specification will be submitted to the appropriate vendors. Not every vendor may reply when a request for bid is submitted. Some vendors specialize in certain industries due to familiarity with the industry. Dependent on the industry, it is possible to have a limited number of vendors to select.

Once the vendors have submitted their proposals, comparison of the proposals is necessary. The definitions in the specification are important if an accurate comparison is to be made. For example, one vendor may price their system based on the number of actual field devices. Another vendor may price on the basis of internal computer points supplied from the field device. There are many more internal computer points for a field device than actual field devices. With this difference in how two vendors define costs, understanding the price estimates is very important. The example may result in a significantly lower cost estimate if the vendor quoted based on the actual number of field devices; however, implementing the system may require a cost adjustment, resulting in higher real costs. Understanding the pricing and comparing processes accurately is critical to ensure accurate cost estimates.

Equipment reliability is an important attribute for an industrial control system. A vendor should be able to supply equipment failure rates and information on long-term spare-parts capability and the frequency of vendor supplied patching. A vendor with a history of a higher equipment failure rate than some of the other vendors should be cautiously considered. If the vendor has a record of more equipment failures but provides replacement equipment for many years, the failure-rate numbers may be skewed by equipment longevity. Additionally, if the same vendor has a record of spare-parts availability for an extended time, the vendor may be a reasonable choice based on their history of long-term product support.

If a vendor has a reputation for frequent upgrades and a short cycle for spare-parts support, then choosing the vendor has risks associated with industrial control system longevity. It is hard to plan on a 10–15 year life cycle when the vendor has significant upgrades every couple of years. This type of vendor is known to have up-to-date equipment; however, they have a tendency to continuously require equipment upgrades when equipment fails or system changes are needed. A vendor that changes equipment every few years requires additional manpower to support long-term industrial control system operations. The costs of testing new equipment and software when changes are needed will be significant.

The ideal vendor will provide long-term spare-parts support and an extended time between requiring equipment upgrades. This type of vendor typically will have a reliable industrial control system providing years of service. This vendor may not be the least expensive. However, the life-cycle costs of the more reliable vendor will typically be more economical when costs are factored over the many years of industrial control system operation.

Functional testing

Once the industrial control system specification has been developed and a vendor has been selected, the real work starts. An industrial control system is not an off-the-shelf item. Specialized equipment with specialized configurations is needed for an industrial control system. The industrial control system equipment requires testing to validate that the system operates as desired and designed. Individual components require testing of configuration settings. Network hardware requires configuration settings to ensure the correct network traffic gets to the correct equipment. Alternately, the network traffic should only be directed to the appropriate equipment, which requires more configuration settings. The verification of signals from field devices requires confirmation. Software needs to be validated to ensure the industrial control system operates as designed and within the parameters identified in the specification.

This testing is described as factory acceptance testing or functional testing. Much of the development and testing is conducted at the vendor's site. Validation of the new owner's system is performed by the owner's knowledgeable personnel. Training on the new system also occurs during the functional testing phase. This implies that the new owner's personnel who are performing or assisting in testing become system experts, or at a minimum the personnel who are knowledgeable about the new industrial control system. It is important to select the proper personnel to be associated with the functional testing phase. The personnel associated with the functional testing return to the owner's site and perform or assist in performing maintenance or modifications to the system.

Once the functional testing is complete, the new industrial control system is installed at the new owner's site or facility. Additional testing is performed at the new owner's facility. This testing is critical to make any final adjustments to the new system and validate the facility operations after installation. The postinstallation testing is an important phase of system replacement. Vendor personnel are usually available to answer questions and clarify any technical details associated with the new system. This testing and installation phase can take many months or even a few years depending on the complexity of the industrial control system. During the testing and installation time, it is important to establish a good relationship with the vendor. The relationship with the vendor should last for many years—hopefully the lifetime of the industrial control system.

Upgrading an existing system should not be as labor intensive. An upgrade should permit the reuse of much of the currently installed equipment and computer code. The system upgrade should provide needed enhancements to the system, improving system productivity. Testing and validation is required from upgrading a system. Do not be surprised if the system does not operate when first installing the upgrade. Typically, an upgrade includes faster computer equipment, which makes the process operate faster. Unfortunately, the faster processing times affect the actual timing of field devices. The field device speed does not change with the upgrade, so computer timing and wait values may require changing. The timing values are critical for the operation of the facility or system and require extensive functional testing. An upgrade requires as much functional testing as a replacement. However, much of the installed architecture may be reused. This typically means that an upgrade costs less than the installation of a new industrial control system.

Continued operations

Once the system is upgraded or replaced, minor adjustments will be required to optimize the system. This is to be expected, and a maintenance outage should be planned for several months after putting the new or newly upgraded system into operation. This allows time to identify minor changes or enhancements. This may come as a surprise to some, but some fine tuning is necessary shortly after the system is installed. This is similar to the oil change a few months or miles after buying a new car. The vendor recommends a follow-up check to ensure the system, or car in this example, is operating as expected and to allow any minor final adjustments to be made. There may have been some minor new-equipment failures during this time. It is not unusual for electronic equipment to fail shortly after installation. The vendors attempt to provide products of extremely high quality. At times, a surge created while powering up the electronic equipment causes weak internal components to fail. This is not indicative of its longevity. The failures would be covered by warranty. This is why the components or systems have a manufacturer's warranty.

Summary

There comes a time when it becomes necessary to replace an industrial control system after what has hopefully been many years of operation. Determining when to replace or upgrade the industrial control system has many factors and criteria. Once the reliability of the industrial control system becomes questionable, it is time to consider replacing or upgrading the system.

Unlike enterprise networks, servers, and desktop computers, the replacement of an industrial control system requires significant cost, labor, and time. The replacement or upgrade requires planning and many months of preparation, both at the vendor and on-site. This replacement or upgrade should provide a return on the significant investment required with increased productivity, less system downtime due to equipment failures, and improved data to provide system performance optimization.

chapter eighteen

Patching and change management

Bernie Pella

Contents

Introduction

Patching is a common term in today's computer systems. A patch is a change to the software on a computer to repair a bug in the software, remediate a vulnerability identified in the software, or improve minor aspects of the software. Most patches are installed in the background, without impacting normal operations, and once they are completely installed, the computer may need to be restarted. The restart completes the installation by modifying software or files running while the computer is operating. Some software has the capability to modify or patch the software without requiring a restart. Regardless, the patches or modified software should resolve problems on the computer system. The important security patches resolve vulnerabilities, protecting the information on the computer. Other important patches improve current functionality or add additional capabilities. As software becomes more complex and interrelated to other software on the system, more vulnerabilities are identified. The increased complexity created vulnerabilities place the computer at risk from unscrupulous individuals or organizations. When the computer is used on a network, the vulnerabilities may provide a potential-to-attack vector. The attack vector creates the potential to attack the computer, extract information on the computer, load undesirable or malicious software, or use the compromised computer as a pivot point to identify and attack other computers on the network.

Patching and vulnerability remediation is commonplace in today's computer systems. One vendor supplies patches so frequently that it is now called "Patch Tuesday." Installing patches is relatively benign on enterprise network computers. Most patches are installed with minimal, if any, testing, and the impact on normal computer operations is minimal. If a patch causes a problem, in some cases the patch is rolled back or removed, and the computer is restored to a previous known state. Not all patched systems can be rolled back, which may cause problems if the patch has undesirable affects on the system.

Unfortunately, industrial control system patching requires significantly more effort. Patching an industrial control system is not as easy a task and requires significant effort to ensure the patches do not negatively impact the system. Some facilities determine that the risk of patching is too great and employ alternative methods or architecture to protect the industrial control system. The concept of "install the patches and see what happens" has the potential for disastrous results. Also, if a patch has an undesirable impact, the process system or facility has already been impacted, which can result in downtime or equipment damage.

Patch impact minimization

To minimize the impact of patching and updating the industrial control system, the philosophy of less is better should be implemented. The less software requiring patches, the less impact patching has on the industrial control system. Since industrial control systems are not a typical enterprise computer, only the software necessary for the operation of the computer should be installed. Only the operating system features needed for essential operation should be installed. Unnecessary operating system features should be removed, or if they cannot be removed, then the feature should be disabled. Additional add-on software may be needed but only install the necessary components of the software. For example, if Microsoft Excel is needed for historian data, do not install Microsoft Office. Purchase and only install Microsoft Excel. The other components are not needed and add to patching impact. Web browsers are not needed so additional web browsers should not be installed. PDF readers may seem like a necessity; however, another nonindustrial control system computer should be available for any PDF viewing. The price of a nonindustrial control system computer for viewing PDFs is significantly cheaper than the man-hour costs of testing and patching the PDF software on the industrial control system. Report generation functions should not be performed by the industrial control computer. Install a support computer on the system to generate reports, perform backup functions, and perform other peripheral functions. Once again, the support computer can be patched without impacting the industrial control system computers. Adding another computer will have an initial cost; however, the life-cycle cost in the reduction patching will pay for the computer many times over the course of the patching cycles.

The support computer should not be on the industrial control system network. The industrial control system network transports actual field device data. Adding peripheral data on the industrial control system network may cause critical data latency. The support computer should be added on an additional network using an additional network interface card (NIC). This removes the data latency impact and enhances system reliability. Also, using the additional network provides segregation when patching the support computer or computers. Only the industrial control system computers needing connectivity to the support network should use the additional network. Minimizing the connectivity provides some enhancement to the security of the industrial control system.

Patching analysis

Patching an operating industrial control system requires risk-versus-reward analysis. If the system is operating properly, there is potentially more risk to patching the system than the reward of having an up-to-date industrial control system. Part of the risk is based on the network architecture or connectivity of the industrial control system. Additional factors to consider in determining the risk of patching are the type of operating system used, the hazards associated with the facility, and the competency of facility personnel.

Industrial control systems isolated via an air gap* from external connectivity are subject to an insider threat and the increased complexity of industrial control systems. Industrial control systems with connectivity to other networks are subject to both insider and external threats. Additional safeguards are needed to protect the system from malicious external threats. So the risk-versus-reward determination is easier to justify when the industrial control system has external connectivity.

This patching decision is obvious for industrial control systems with equipment located in areas at extended distances from the primary facility. When industrial control system components are located in areas without frequent physical monitoring, it is critical to ensure the system is properly patched. These systems require the additional security provided by the latest patches in order to remain reliable and to minimize external tampering. Having the most recent patches and well-implemented security settings enhances the security of remote or infrequently physically monitored industrial control system equipment.

Regulatory required patching

Many industries using industrial control systems have cybersecurity regulations that require system patching, or justify why the system is not patched, at some specified frequency. Meeting the regulator's industrial control system requirements creates challenges. Most patch installation requires a system restart, and industrial control systems are designed to run continuously for many years. Since industrial control systems operate equipment and facilities, an outage is usually required to safely install system patches. Most of the enterprise information technology (IT) networks patch monthly or more frequently. Conducting an outage is costly for most industries, and monthly outages are simply unacceptable. Due to the expense and downtime associated with patching an industrial control system, patching frequency is reduced. Completing industrial control systems patching less frequently may be justified if business productivity is impacted and additional security devices or procedures are strategically installed, reducing the internal or external threat factors.

An example of extending the patching frequency would be for an industrial complex that performs an annual outage to clean sediment from tanks. From a business perspective, patching during the annual outage would be cost effective. To provide an additional layer of protection to support the extended patching schedule, the industrial control system network is located behind a firewall with very restrictive communication rules. The firewall limits network traffic to the industrial control system providing an additional level of security from the corporate level. The external network is limited in its ability to communicate with the industrial control system. Information for the analysis of process parameters or system operational information is sent out to the external network, but no requests from the external network pass into the industrial control network. This level of security would be further enhanced if a demilitarized zone (DMZ) were installed between the industrial control system and the external network. A DMZ contains two firewalls or two zones in a single firewall and a DMZ server located between the two firewalls or zones to provide additional protection from the external networks.

Equipment

In most cases, only the human machine interface (HMI) is patched on an industrial control system. The HMI is best described as the computer used by operators to control the

---

* An "air gap" is a means of securely isolating two networks from each other either electronically or physically.

industrial control system. The HMI is only a small part of an industrial control system, and most modern industrial control systems use the Microsoft Windows operating system on the HMI. The other major components in an industrial control system are controllers, input modules, output modules, programmable logic controllers, managed network switches, and data converters. The other major components of an industrial control system typically use proprietary software. On older industrial control systems, the entire system contains proprietary equipment and computer code, including the HMI. An older industrial control system is only patched when the manufacturer identifies a problem with their equipment and provides the appropriate patches. The manufacturer will provide specific instructions to install the patches and which equipment requires installation of the patches.

Patching modern systems

As discussed earlier, modern industrial control systems typically use the Microsoft Windows operating system as the operating system on the HMI. To maintain the operating system up to the most recent security guidelines, frequent patching is necessary. Based on the system configuration, external network connectivity, and the industrial control system equipment installed on the system, it is possible to perform patching with minimal system impact. If the industrial control system has an installed spare HMI usable by operations personnel while patching is performed, a HMI can be isolated from the industrial control system network and patched without impacting system operations. Also, a surrogate or test system is necessary to perform patch testing prior to installation on the operational industrial control system. Additionally, only patches validated and recommended by the manufacturer should be considered. All patches should be tested on the test industrial control system before installation on the operational industrial control system is considered.

Patch testing

Preparation and planning is necessary to perform patch installation on an industrial control system. The first task is to perform a full backup or image of the system. This is necessary to establish a restore point for the system. Often, a patch may not react as expected or affects the operation of the industrial control system software. Because of specific industrial control system characteristics, rolling back the patches may not restore the system to the identical configuration established before installing the patch. In some cases, settings in the industrial control system software may not be restored, causing unexpected or undesirable operation of the industrial control system. Due to the potential inability to properly roll back the patches (or to predict if a rollback will be fully effective), the ability to restore the system to a previously known state is critical.

Industrial control system patching fundamental number one: Always perform a full backup or image prior to installing any patches on an industrial control system.

Understanding the changes caused by installing patches to the industrial control system is critical. Unfortunately, many patches do not completely describe all the files affected or changes made to the system. Knowing what was changed is important to maintain the configuration management of the system and to identify potential problems to a system. For example, a previous Microsoft Windows service pack changed how components on the network authenticate to the server. This was not a problem on an enterprise network since the service pack was typically pushed to all systems on the network. However, this service pack created numerous problems on an industrial control system network. Since most of the controllers are not Microsoft based, the change to the authentication process resulted in the controller being unable to communicate with the server or HMI. The problem was identified as a minor registry setting change but was not documented in any of the service pack information. This is an example of the need to be able to restore the system if patching creates an undesirable affect.

A good practice for industrial control system patching is to identify the file status of the computer. This is done by running a utility or batch file to create a list of all folders and files and the file size for the entire computer. A file list utility runs very quickly and is an important troubleshooting and configuration documentation tool. The utility should be run incrementally between installing patches. These tools identify the changes made to the system. If the file size changed between patches, that file was affected by the patch. The file listing utility is extremely helpful for documenting the changes made to the system during patching.

The best method for patching an industrial control system is to have a test system available to perform patch testing before installing the patches on the operational system. If a test system is not available, creating a virtual test environment is another option. With the improvements in virtual server software available, installing the image of the system on the virtual machine and then installing the patches is a good alternative to having a test system. This provides the ability to determine the impact of the patches and can identify some potential problems. A virtual machine test will not identify all possible problems but will identify a large percentage of problems associated with patch installation on an industrial control system.

Testing the industrial control system after installing patches appears to be difficult since in many cases, what to test is obscure. Actually, performing post installation testing is not difficult. Identifying what to test is where difficulties arise. Significant effort and information is necessary to establish what needs to be tested. The ultraconservative testing method is to test all the capabilities of the industrial control system. Full testing is time and labor intensive. Based on the time and additional effort needed to complete full system testing, it is not recommended unless the industrial control system performs critical or safety functions. The best testing method is to identify the files changed by the patches, determine the purpose of the changed files, and then test the attributes associated with the changed files. This focusing of the testing effort helps to reduce the scope of the effort because many of the patches may affect files or functions not used by the industrial control system.

This creates patching fundamental number two: Identify the files changed by the patch and test the affects and impacts of the changed files.

Patching minimization

Industrial control systems typically do not use all the capabilities of the installed operating system. The best method for minimizing the effect of patching is to remove any operating system software not necessary for industrial control system operation. Programs like e-mail, web browsers, drawing or painting programs, and so on can be removed without impacting the operation of the industrial control system. Removing these programs reduces the number of patches that need installing. Many of the older industrial control systems only install the operating system software necessary for system operation. When the industrial control system migrated to the Microsoft Windows environment, the entire operating system was installed. This added a significant number of programs not needed by the industrial control system. Removal of the unused programs also increases the security of the industrial control system and eases the patching effort.

This creates fundamental number three: Remove all files or programs not needed by the industrial control system.

Summary

Patching an industrial control system is different than patching an enterprise network-based system. Patches have the potential to negatively affect system operation, and patch testing is necessary prior to installation. Therefore, implementing the three fundamentals of industrial control system patching is recommended:

- Perform a full backup or image prior to installing any patches on an industrial control system.
- Identify the files changed by the patch and test the affects and impacts of the changed files.
- Remove all files or programs not needed by the industrial control system.

If the three fundamentals of industrial control system patching are followed, the problems associated with patching an industrial control system are minimized. This reduces the risk of patching the system and improves system security.

chapter nineteen

Physical security management

Allan McDougall and Jeff Woodruff

Contents

The role of physical security is to identify, establish, and maintain a predictable and controlled environment with respect to the management of acts or conditions that may, through intent or nature, pose harm to an organization's personnel, assets, and operations. When looking at supervisory control and data acquisition (SCADA) networks, this can pose a number of significant challenges to organizations that have not established clear governance structures or that have failed to look at what can be described as the *primacy of operations*. This chapter intends to look, in some detail, at how to approach those issues.

Before going too far, the reader is owed an explanation. In works like this, there are two approaches that can be taken. The first is a largely academic approach that draws on the writings and concepts of hundreds of readers, refers to arcane models and structures and, frankly, often leaves the reader confused as to what direction to take. Having managed a physical security program across forty countries, covering over 1,200 facilities (and thousands of other infrastructure points) and over 15,000 employees, for some time now, I find the above approach to be, frankly, good for academics. They can work at a certain pace that allows them to dissect the minutiae of every little thing. There is another approach. It is far more conversational in nature and is intended to walk the individual through the labyrinth of structures, models, dissertations, and so forth so that the reader has a clear path in front of him or her. As you might imagine, I tend to prefer the second approach because, there are times when a straight answer is appreciated, given the scope of my responsibilities.

Primacy of operations

As with any business effort, one needs to start with the mission of the organization. The organization does not exist to have a security program (in any discipline). The security program exists to support the organization in reaching its goals while ensuring that the risks that the organization is exposed to while doing so are controlled effectively and efficiently. Unfortunately, grand-scale efforts such as critical infrastructure protection and cybersecurity cloud this issue by suddenly declaring certain kinds of corporate assets to have additional needs and importance. But make no mistake about it; the job of the security program remains to support the organization, and, frankly, it is the role of the organization (as a whole, not just the security programs) to remain in line with those grand and overarching requirements.

So, what does the organization do? If you do not know the answer to this question, the first favor you can do yourself is to put this chapter down and find out. Being able to answer this question is the whole foundation of making sure that the physical security program (or any other program for that matter) is relevant and not simply destined for the bin when the next round of right-sizing or cost-cutting measures comes around. You can find this answer in the mission statement of the organization.

The mission statement of the organization is a simple statement that answers the exact question described above. It describes the focus, the *raison d'être* of the organization. It focuses the company's efforts in a laser-like (hopefully) direction that also provides the roots of how the company intends to measure its success.

As an exercise, just browse through your own mission statement and those of your competitors. You should see some similarities (particularly in the same industry) and there should be some differences. How these align gives you the first indicators of what you need to link back to in order to ensure that your physical security efforts are relevant.

As this point, some of the readers may be asking about whether or not we are going to talk about SCADA networks. Of course, the mission of this book is to provide guidance and information on the appropriate treatment of these kinds of networks and, in keeping with that mission statement, we are about to. We just needed some foundation material.

When we look at any networked environment, we can describe its activities in terms of a general mission statement. This mission statement was originally conceived by myself and the main author of this work some years ago when writing about the transportation-system sector, but its relevance is far broader than that application.

In the networked environment, the mission is to move something (be it persons, objects, or data) from a point of origin to its appropriate destination so that it arrives when needed, in acceptable condition, and for reasonable costs.

This can apply to transportation networks (such as shipping and public transportation), the energy sector (pipeline operations, electrical grids), utilities (water), and so on. Understanding this basic mission statement is the first step in treating SCADA networks from a physical security perspective.

When looking at how the SCADA network supports that mission, it is fairly clear. The SCADA network *enables* the organization to meet its objectives through the provision of some service or another. This may involve an *active* state wherein the network is actually causing something to happen—such as the distribution network of a pipeline. It may involve a *preparatory* state wherein the network is not causing things to move but is maintaining the conditions necessary for those things to be available when needed (such as storage tanks). It may also be acting in a *monitoring* state wherein it is watching for either (1) signs that the environment in which the active or preparatory states are taking place are moving toward unacceptable conditions or (2) that the materials involved are at certain levels or conditions themselves.

Operating environment

The architecture and topography of SCADA networks can make this a bit challenging. The optimal environment for physical security to operate in is geographically and operationally small. This is because the risk environment for physical security is subject to change as it grows larger. For example, if your physical security program operates at your factory alone, then you can generally state the following:

- I have a reasonably consistent span of control because we are the property owners and business owners.
- My outside operating environment (climate, local crime, etc.) is relatively constant and the threat is relatively homogenous (i.e., the weather on one side of the factory is most likely the weather one would find on the other side).
- My physical security environment is relatively well contained within those two factors, meaning that I can operate under one set of rules from a risk management perspective.

If, however, we expand this to a factory in another city, these three things do not apply the same way. They have to be looked at in terms of four environments:

- How it applies to each one of the two locations (environments) since those can be very different (consider the weather on the West and East Coasts this winter and spring);
- How it applies to the space in between the two locations (the third environment), which may itself have multiple environments within it (consider driving across North America on your way between the East and West Coasts); and
- The overarching or *grand* environment that describes the whole system.

Physical security environment as compared to IT network

Understanding this difference ends the first layer of doctrinal conflict between IT network security and physical security. For the IT network, the environment across the full network is relatively homogeneous as the threats to the network are usually seen as affecting the full network (and quite appropriately). This means that the controls over the network environment can be reasonably constant and consistent. They are constant in that they must remain in place at all times and under all conditions (with very rare exceptions). They are consistent in that the controls are applied universally across the full network (people need to log in no matter where they are), and they apply at each instance where something similar happens on the network (such as the restriction on removable media being applied at each USB port).

Physical security does not function this way. Whereas the sum of IT network environments may be described in terms of one environment, the physical security environment is considered to be unique at each environment. As a result, the complexity of physical security environments can be described in terms of the following:

- There are n different environments, where n represents the number of different main infrastructure points.
- If we follow laws like Metcalfe's Law, then the number of possible pair connections can be described as $n(n-1)/2$.

Consider this application and the difference between one major facility and ten major facilities. Where there is only one hub involved (such as a factory with no shipping or receiving responsibilities), then we really only need to address the main environment (n or 1 environment) and there are no connections to consider (given that $1(1-1)/2$ leads to 0). Where we consider our networked environment of ten facilities that are each connected to the other, then we have ten main environments ($n = 10$) and forty-five connected environments (as $n(n-1)/2$ will yield forty-five different environments to consider. In total, the physical security program now has fifty-five environments that it needs to monitor, characterize and manage. As the organization grows in size, the complexity of the number of environments becomes unmanageable very quickly.

Just as industrial distribution networks evolved quickly, so the physical security treatment of the various environments should focus on the same architecture as is used in the network environment. The *spoke and hub* distribution systems and their connections can be described in terms of the following:

- The number of end points (facilities or hubs) that represent one kind of item to be treated can be represented by n.
- The number of connections (between these hubs) has each peripheral hub connecting to the main hub, meaning that the number of connections in one node of the network can be described as $n(n-1)$ where it applies to that node. Each node of the network is then treated as its own hub, which is treated the same way until all the installations are treated down the line.

Consider a distribution network that has three outlying facilities that service three facilities on the perimeter of the network. In this case, we can consider the number of environments to treat in terms of $n(n-1)/2$ among the main facilities for a total of six, with each of those subnetworks being organized slightly differently in that there are four facilities (n) with the total number of connections, not including connections between, limited to ($n-1$), or three connections for a total of seven environments in each of the three networks for a total of 21 environments. The end result is that there are a total of 27 environments (as opposed to $13(12)/2$ or 78 environments) to maintain control over. The fact that each one of these environments, however, operates in the physical space and is relatively unique in nature still means that the overall physical security program has a significant challenge on its hands.

This is the reason why physical security practitioners tend to respond less than enthusiastically when the network security team asks them to do a threat and risk assessment across the organization. Where the IT network may be relatively contained, each one of the hubs and connections in the physical or operational network needs to be treated, and in larger organizations, this can very quickly become a massive undertaking.

So what does this undertaking actually look like? What mystical processes and practices happen in the dark basements where physical security offices tend to end up? The reality is that the processes are not that arcane.

PDCA model and risk management

Physical security tends to follow the same plan-do-check-act (PDCA) model that is common in many activities. This generally means that the physical security organization identifies what needs to be put in place to manage the physical security risks appropriately, then implements those controls, monitors their performance, and finally makes adjustments depending on the outcome of the monitoring.

This is an important step that needs to be taken in the physical security realm. While there is progress being made on the regulatory front and within parts of the audit community, there are still whole communities that are hanging onto the prescriptive approach to physical security. While such approaches are fine when you are dealing with noncritical systems or immature organizations, I would propose that they be categorically rejected for critical infrastructure and the auditing of larger organizations. This is for three reasons:

1. They do not assure security in that they take a broad baseline, leaving organizations exposed to the variations that are pertinent in their own environments.
2. Once the prescriptive standard is known to any adversary, then it becomes a roadmap on what needs to be in place in order to attack that particular facility (hence the not-for-critical-infrastructure statement).
3. By placing prescriptive controls as a requirement, it fails to take into account the operating environment, leaving the organization at risk of undue operational impacts—both physically and logically.

In general, I would put forward the statement that prescriptive regimes are best applied where the organizations they are being applied against are either unwilling to adopt any posture or are so undertrained that they need to have very specific things detailed for them. One would hope that, after the billions spent on security across the North American market, we are getting past that point.

Step 1: Planning, or risk assessment

The world of the modern and capable physical security organization revolves around the threat and risk assessment (TRA) and managing the outcomes of that assessment. The TRA is actually broken down into a number of subactivities, each of which is critical to the undertaking.

The first of these involves defining the scope of the activity and ensuring that it is reasonable. This can mean looking at physical security from an enterprise level—a complex undertaking in larger organizations (remember the operating environment described above). It can also focus on something as minute or small as a specific room or asset.

The scope of the TRA, however, is not best determined by saying "that room" or "that asset." It needs to take into account (directly) the *first layer of the risk environment surrounding that asset or infrastructure point* and, ideally, the *risk environment outside it that may influence that exterior environment*. This is not to say that the enterprise-level TRA has to take into account the known risks of the universe—common sense needs to be applied. It may involve the property owned by the enterprise, those properties adjacent to it, and finally those within a specific distance or that may have an impact on the infrastructure. For example, in looking at this challenge from a pipeline perspective, one might look at the property owned or controlled by the pipeline, its immediate neighbors, and then threats that appear to be operating or able to enter those spaces (such as being short car ride away, etc.). This is something that is not taught; it is something that comes from experience and careful study of past "areas of improvement."

The key here is a question of reasonability. It may be proposed that the best way to approach this scoping exercise is to consider a combination of threats (those immediately in the area, those that may enter the area, or those that may have a tangible influence in the area) and factors that have a span of influence over the infrastructure. For example, a fair percentage of the local population may pose no threat whatsoever (and therefore do not need to be studied *ad nauseam*), but upcoming regulatory changes out of the national capital may have a significant impact on operations. The key again is to use that concept of the primacy of operations as the touchstone and then work outward, identifying what can affect it.

Step 2: Identification of threats

This is a challenging exercise. For many security practitioners (IT and Physical), the identification of threats is done based on somebody else's work. It may be a report from a lead investigative body (such as the FBI, NSA, or a host of other groups in the United States; or the Royal Canadian Mounted Police [RCMP], Canadian Security Intelligence Service [CSIS], and Communications Security Establishment Canada [CSEC] in Canada), but it is ultimately produced by somebody that has, at best, a passing familiarity with your operations. The security organizations need to do better than this and need to maintain their own capability to identify *present, emerging, changing, and diminishing* threats. Present threats are fairly able to define—they are the ones that are immediately in your environment and are attempting to do you harm. Emerging threats may be the result of new operations, changing views (such as through social activism), new technology, or similar kinds of factors. Changing threats are those that are evolving, either through any of the previous conditions or because they have been ignored to the point that the kettle is about to boil over. Finally, there are diminishing threats. We have all heard about the law that that exists somewhere that you are not allowed to leave your horse on the sidewalk in some major metropolis that has not seen a horse in decades. The concept of the diminishing threat can be described in terms of making sure that you are not falling into this trap and committing resources for issues that are already handled.

Identifying threats is not enough. There has to be an understanding of that threat and how it operates. This is where the concept of *threat analysis* comes into play. This *must not* be confused with *threat assessment*, for reasons that will become clear shortly.

When looking at describing the threat, one needs to adopt a clear and systematic approach. The problem here is that, like the operating environment, there are literally hundreds of ways of doing this and, as the physical security environment evolves, there are likely to be hundreds more. The key here is to adopt the KISS principle or "Keep it simple, silly." The threat analysis needs to describe the threat. This can be done through adopting a structure such as that developed by Jeff Woodruff and myself (since we were getting a little sick of computer-generated models that seemed to come up with analyses that made little sense)—such as KSARICH. This, obviously, is not as pretty as some of the acronyms that come out but consists of the following:

- *Knowledge*: What is the knowledge base of the threat in general at the leadership, planning, and tactical levels? For example, it may have significantly educated leadership and planners, but its foot soldiers may well be desperate or disenfranchised persons that are just carrying out an instruction.
- *Skills*: What technical skills does the threat have? Does it have the skills necessary to design, build, test, emplace, and operate complex devices, or are its skills more in line with basic assault tactics?

- *Abilities*: Is the threat able to survive and thrive in the environment in such a way that it can overcome controls, apply its skills, and exploit its knowledge?
- *Resources*: What tools will it bring that will allow it to breach, bypass, or render inoperative security controls or to cause damage? Does it have inside resources (insider threats) or are its resources all exterior to the facility (meaning that access control might become a large part of the effort)?
- *Intent*: What is it that the threat actually wants to accomplish? This is going to factor significantly when looking at the threat assessment. The Physical security officer (or any security practitioner for that matter) should have an understanding of what the threats to his or her organization want to accomplish, as this will guide the threat's actions.
- *Commitment*: Just how badly does the threat actually want to achieve this goal? If the threat is rather apathetic toward a specific goal, then it is likely going to be less than completely committed to achieving it (a rather circular statement for which I apologize but some just do not seem to get this point). A threat that is totally committed and willing to sacrifice everything, however, is a far different beast to deal with.
- *History*: Has the threat ever tried anything like this in the past? Care has to be taken here. Just because it has never happened in the past does not mean that it will not happen. It may mean that it is less likely unless the threat is able to identify some vulnerability it feels it can exploit. This is where many risk structures break down—their inability to integrate intelligence-led assessment of likelihoods.

The treatment of threat is not done at this point. Remember that this is the analysis phase and not the assessment phase, which will be coming shortly.

Step 3: Asset identification and follow-the-pipe approach

When identifying the assets that need to be protected, one might adopt the approach that is part of system design and has been integrated into the overall asset protection and security community through the Masters of Infrastructure Protection and International Security (MIPIS) program at Carleton University through Dr Wayne Boone's efforts.

This approach is fairly simple: It starts with the identification of the ultimate goal of the organization (remember the mission statement—start with what achieves that). It then breaks down that ultimate goal into a number of smaller goals. Each of these smaller goals is supported by a system. For example, in order to manufacture a car, you may need your assembly processes, your human resources, your supply chains, your quality assurance, and so on. Each of these needs, however, is supported by its own systems (e.g., assembly may be supported through life-cycle management, maintenance, operations, and safety). Each of these systems is broken down until you finally reach processes.

The key difference here is granularity. The system may be described in terms of a series of processes that are organized and managed as part of a complex whole. The process itself may be defined in terms of the managed efforts of persons, materials, facilities, information, and activities toward a specific and defined purpose. These persons, materials, facilities, information, and activities can be described as the *elemental assets* in the overall structure. These elemental assets are broken down into five major categories:

- *Persons* that are capable and trustworthy to perform the work that is part of the overall organization.
- *Materials* that are used in the process or that are moved through the process. These are often subject to either quality assurance (for manufacturing) or safety controls (transportation of dangerous goods).

- *Facilities* that are used to house operations and maintain an environment wherein the work can take place.
- *Information* that is used to communicate (past and future) priorities, directions, or instructions.
- *Activities* that are needed to support the work (usually outside activities) or the provision of the services (electrical, water, energy, etc.) that are needed to perform the work.

So, this begs the question as you are standing there with the left-handed wrench (yes, I know it is fictitious)—why is it important?

When we look at these elemental assets, we have to ask ourselves, why are they important to the organization? In some cases, it may be reasonably simple—our future plans are important to us because that is how we are going to stay afloat as a company. The next question is, what is it about those assets that make them important? This might well lead to the response that "if our future plans allow us to have the sole market share in this new market, we stand to make so much." And finally, the statement that "but if our competitors find out about it, then they will enter that market earlier than we want and we will have our profits reduced." This can be broken down into the following:

- *Confidentiality*: Where the exposure of the asset (this is usually information but can be extended in terms of *unauthorized access*) results in losses due to unauthorized parties having a knowledge or awareness of something.
- *Integrity*: Where we can no longer implicitly trust an asset to perform as intended due to potential unauthorized additions, changes, or deletions or through it being handled through untrustworthy processes.
- *Availability*: Where the losses are associated with the elemental asset no longer being immediately ready for use when needed or called upon.
- *Relative Value*: Where the losses are monetary in nature; these may also be extended toward the potential losses of an organization.
- *Social Value*: Where the losses may involve injury to local communities, their identity; these may also be extended into the realm of losses associated with branding or liability.

What we are looking for is how the losses associated with these escalate up from the elemental asset level into the process level and ultimately to the highest-level goals of the organization. For this reason, bottom-up approaches to impact assessments tend to provide the clearest picture of how losses (of this type) may affect an organization.

Having this understanding of the value of the elemental assets is important as it will guide the next step in the overall planning phase.

Step 4: Threat assessment

So, we now have an understanding of the threats in our environment and the elemental assets that we need. The next question that we need to answer is, so what?

Remember that a threat exploits a vulnerability in order to cause a loss of value to an elemental asset that leads to losses and risk to the organization.

This, another phrase that one might attribute to many places but that I heard most succinctly put by Dr Boone, is a vital part of the TRA process. The security world is full of TRAs that have been exercises in the absurd because they did not follow this basic approach.

There are two steps to be taken now.

The first of these steps involves looking at the *gravity* of the threat in relation to the full suite of elemental assets. This involves drawing a line that connects the threat *directly* or *indirectly* to the elemental asset. For example, a hurricane does not affect your workstation directly. What it does do is destroy facilities, disrupt power, and flood work environments, which may indirectly impact your workstation. It is the sum total of these impacts that determine the gravity of the threat.

The second of these steps that needs to be taken involves looking at *likelihood*. Likelihood and gravity are often caught in a struggle. During periods of economic challenge, like today, we pay some attention to gravity (to avoid the absolutely catastrophic or to meet regulatory requirements) but we tend to focus on likelihood because that is where we can demonstrate efficiency. After massive attacks, however, society tends to "want to turtle up" and refocuses on gravity—meaning that there is a bit of a pendulum swing that occurs.

Likelihood has past and future connotations that need to be explored. Since examining likelihood from past events is less complex, this is the place to start.

One of the most common methods of looking at likelihood is the calculation of the *annualized rate of occurrence* or the ARO. What this basically involves is counting all of the incidents of a certain type over a period of time and then normalizing it to a period of one year. If you are having one occurrence in a month, then the ARO might lead to twelve events per year. If you have one event every ten years, then the ARO may be 0.1. There are two traps in this approach that the security practitioner in the physical realm needs to pay heed to:

- The sample of time needs to be statistically significant. Having one event in one week does not form a basis for saying that we need to consider this to be a fifty-two-event-per-year occurrence. The time considered must be relatively significant.
- The second involves shifts. This is particularly important as we look at climate change and similar factors in the physical security domain. By definition, the 100-year storm should have an ARO of 0.01. But what if we are seeing an increase in the gravity (impact) of these storms and their frequency? If using the ARO method, it is actually best to run five or six of these where you look at events from a 1-year, 2-year, 5-year, 10-year, and 25-year perspective. While this will seem to be a lot of unnecessary work, it provides an indication as to whether or not something is trending upward over time. That is particularly important if your 100-year storm is likely to happen four or five times in a decade with potentially catastrophic impacts on the organization.

The second face of likelihood involves the future. This is also where the trends of past events can become very useful. One needs to be careful to understand that such trend analysis is subject to a range of potential errors and becomes less reliable as it is projected outward, but when looking at near-term or medium-term trends (say up to five years), it does provide useful data.

The second involves the intelligence-driven likelihood. Do the factors that allow for the threat to exist, persist, and operate in the environment still present? If so, have there been any changes in terms of the intent of the threat to operate? This may be a change in any one of the *means, opportunity,* or *intent* at play. If new means are available, does that change the threat's ability to operate? Have we offered new opportunities for the threat to operate (which will become identifiable in the vulnerability assessment)? Finally, has the level of intent or commitment changed with respect to the threat's willingness to cause us injury? These are all questions that can be answered through a combination of the threat analysis and the vulnerability assessment.

A challenge in the SCADA environment

The challenge within the SCADA environment is being able to peg down the gravity of events. Some will tell you that the loss of a switch is relatively inconsequential because it is reasonably inexpensive and, as long as it is caught quickly, the system can be shut down or bypassed before something catastrophic happens. That makes an assumption that the damage is detected, the appropriate centers are notified, and the system takes the steps necessary to correct the action. On the other hand, one cannot simply leap to the absolute worst-case scenario where everything will fail to function at once (through a mystical combination of threat and bad luck). The SCADA environment may well be best served if it adopts an approach where the gravest impact and the most likely impacts are examined. This can at least provide a range within which the operations, engineering, and security personnel can all agree before approaching the senior management.

Step 5: Vulnerability assessment

Remember that vulnerabilities are exploited by threats to cause injury or damage to elemental assets. This may mean that the vulnerability is tied to a lack of something: to the incomplete application of something or the fact that something is functioning poorly (or at least below acceptable thresholds). What is also important here is that there needs to be a pairing between the threat and the elemental asset. If the elemental asset is immune to the threat (my asset is Mount Rushmore and my threat is UV radiation leading to skin cancer), then there is no real need for significant examination. Care has to be taken here, however, to ensure that the work up to this point has been suitably detailed.

The conduct of a vulnerability assessment needs an individual who not only understands operations and the threat but also how security controls function. The first step is remembering the basic mantra—that the time we force an attacker to take in order to cause the injury should be longer than the time we give ourselves in order to detect and respond to it effectively. While this is a simple statement, it can be mind-boggling to see some of the applications. To apply effective delaying measures, the following needs to be understood:

- *The intent and commitment of the threat*—particularly when looking at deterrence and point-specific defenses.
- *The knowledge, skills, abilities, and resources available to the threat*—both as part of the threat and also in terms of what can be found in the environment.
- *Appropriate design principles and practices*—particularly in environments where the threat is being couched in employee or public safety. This is not the time to guess at alternatives.

The last of these is also a factor of due diligence. For those looking at issues associated with design, identifying the appropriate testing criteria and determining whether or not something meets that criteria can be the effort that prevents the organization from significant injury—or, in more extreme cases, prevents people from getting killed. The physical security practitioner needs to have a detailed understanding of the various testing criteria that can be applied and their various limitations.

The concept of detection and response in the physical security realm is a particular challenge, particularly within the SCADA environment. Fortunately, various tests and technical improvements have been addressing some of these issues, but work still remains to be done.

It also needs to be clear that the nature of detection and notification must be clearly defined. A notification that a valve is about to fail should not go to the security office—regardless of any arguments surrounding working hours. The person who can best assess the impacts associated with that notice is one of the responsible personnel within operations or engineering. Inserting the security officer into this chain does nothing more than increase the risks associated with breaks or delays in reporting. The goal, in the operational sense, needs to be that those responsible for responding to those kinds of events are notified as quickly as possible and as accurately as possible.

Within the SCADA community, this is particularly challenging when looking at notification from remote or deployed areas. The reality is that if there is a gap in the ability to report, then it is on the organization that put the infrastructure there to find a way. The fact that something is hard does not absolve an organization of operating outside of a duty of care with respect to affected populations and environmental factors.

Adopting this structure of approach is simple. You need to be able to detect far enough out that your response capability can respond to the threat before the injury can be accomplished. This means that you may need to push back your ability to detect suspicious or potentially unwanted activity to the point where you can respond effectively. This may force the organization to get somewhat creative—ranging from the establishment of remote monitoring, the use of drones, the creation of community awareness programs, and so on. It also means that the organization will need to look at its credible effective response time analytically to determine how much time it will really take for a credible response to be put in place. Having a general security guard respond to check to see if a door is open may well be appropriate (taking into account where that door is open), but if the response is regarding the incursion of an active shooter, sending the same person out to check may well be more of a liability issue than a solution.

This also applies at the macro level outside of the facility. If the response is simply two people going to survey the damage, then the organization will likely be held to account for its lack of ability to contain the event. If it can contain the event, it may well be held to account for the cleanup costs associated with the event.

Within the context of the vulnerability assessment, the security practitioner has to take a cold and clinical view as to what the real protective posture is (will it actually deter, delay, deny, or otherwise stop a threat?) and what the actual ability to detect and respond to something (is it timely, credible and reliable?). This will be a task where the physical security practitioner needs to have solid technical knowledge and a bit of a backbone, as there will be all sorts of arguments, cajoling, or even outright threats if he or she does not represent a certain interest.

Step 6: Risk analysis and assessment

The treatment of risk has two parts. The first part is the analysis of the risk in terms of its component elements, including asset value, threat, and vulnerability. Examining how these three elements line up (remembering *the threat exploits the vulnerability to cause injury to the asset*) is important and will factor significantly when the organization starts looking at the controls or countermeasures it will put in place. The risk assessment answers the question with respect to whether or not the level of potential injury is *unacceptable, tolerable,* or *acceptable*. When the questions posed by risk assessment are answered, then the risk analysis factors in again.

These two structures, however, have to take into account some outside factors, particularly in the regulated context. First, they need to look at the broad spectrum of risks (including legal, operational, security, safety, environmental, etc.) in a manner that can be compared to other parts of the organization. This can pose a bit of a challenge in that the organization may look at certain needs and the regulator may see quite another set of needs. In this context, the high watermark principle (using the most stringent of all requirements) may prove useful, while it might also eventually be necessary to be prepared to engage (or even challenge) the regulator. To do this, risk needs to be looked at in terms of both a unit of measure and a scalar. Many organizations tend to focus on the dollar value of the event as a means of reaching a common denominator. Unfortunately, in physical security, there has been a significant push to attempt to quantify all risks, and this is frankly not possible. This is because the intangible risks (and even a fair portion of the tangible or empirical risks) are subjective in nature. Consider an event that affects a nation's national war memorial. What is the cost of the event? Does that cost touch the impacts on social sensitivities or the national conscience? Of course it does not. An attack that may involve twenty minutes and a five-dollar can of spray paint may well have in impact on a range of services and even whether or not the public access to such spaces is denied.

The other challenge is in the exactness of the response. Does this event pose a risk of value A or value B? It may well depend on whom you ask, but the reality is that many organizations will actually wait for the issue to be resolved and for an exact number to be present. This, however, is probably the worst course of action, as the risk is known, no action is being taken to mitigate the risk, and the source of the delay is in the internal processes and discussions of the organization. Even though I am not a lawyer, this still appears to be a less-than-optimal situation.

This situation can best be described in terms of the "perfect getting in the way of the good." In this context, low and high ranges may well be suitable for the purpose of assessment. In short, the lower values associated with the impact are used to calculate the low end. The higher-end estimates generate, appropriately enough, the high end, and the average is taken to provide a middle value. This can provide a relative structure within which the various risks can be assessed without having to become involved in time-consuming and counterproductive debates.

Beyond risk assessment—charting courses of action

At the end of this process, the organization should have a clear indication as to what risks it faces. It should have a clearer understanding of its vulnerability to certain kinds of threats and how those threats operate. Finally, it should have a clearer understanding of the exposure to its operations. The challenge is what happens next.

SCADA network challenge

So why is it that SCADA networks, including building automated control systems, pose such a challenge to the security practitioner? It is largely because of the relationship between the potential impacts of these networks and the interaction of the different parts of most security programs. I am certainly going to tread on some toes here where I say that we need to divide the world into the logical (network) and tangible (infrastructure) world.

Threats and risks associated with SCADA networks cross between these worlds very readily. The compromise of a sensor may mean adjusting its programming or simply hitting it with a hammer. The loss of that sensor, however, still flows back into the overall SCADA network and its operations. At the same time, a bad patch in a SCADA network can easily flow through the network and, depending on the nature of the patch, can very quickly lead to physical threats (such as an overflowing container). The problem is that we try to separate these things, and it is difficult to determine, at the working level, where that separation should be.

And this is the crux of the challenge. In most organizations, the IT security, information security, physical security, and engineering organizations are all part of separate organizations. Each one of these approaches their piece of the puzzle from its own direction, but the nature of resource allocation and business administration (in both the public and private sectors) starts to create silos of information and activity. These silos can be described in terms of gaps in the communication within the organization, not only at the basic communication level but also at the assessment and planning levels. Those who have worked where IT security and physical security domains intersect have been exposed to the challenges associated with attempting to break these challenges down.

The first problem here lies in the nature of business administration and the concept of corporate loyalty. The people within organizations tend to give their loyalty (as it is a commodity that is earned and not one that should be assumed) to those in proximity to them or to those that they see as directly affecting them. Within the administrative structures of an organization, this can mean that an individual has significant loyalty to his or her supervisor or manager but less to the organization as a whole. As this loyalty often determines what way an individual will decide to act, it can become a factor that reinforces the silo mentality within an organization.

The second aspect of this involves the management of activity within an organization, particularly during difficult economic times. These difficult economic times can be characterized by a culture that begins to demand that "more be done with less" or that managers are placed under additional accountability to "manage efficiently." Structures like "performance management agreements" or "management accountability accords" are among the ways that managers are constrained in terms of their thinking and activity. Given a list of growing accountabilities (and responsibilities) and a decreasing pool of available resources (dollars, appropriately trained staff, time) that comes from one or two layers higher in the organization, the manager may actually begin to collapse his or her activities along those controls' lines—reinforcing the various silos.

Oddly enough, these two factors play a significant part in why physical security (and the rest of the organization) has such a challenge with SCADA and other control systems. The question becomes, who owns the issue? Is it IT security because of their expertise in networks? Those in engineering or operational shops may argue that the traditional approaches to network security (heavy encryption, etc.) can actually lead to increased risk in the control system environment. Is it physical security because the impacts of primary concern operate in the tangible world? Could it be that the engineers/operators of the network are the lead because they are the ones that hold most closely the requirement for the organization to exercise due care with respect to preventing outside or external harm?

So this is the first challenge posed by SCADA and various other forms of control systems. It will generally manifest itself in one of two forms. Either various submanagers will attempt to push the issue off (too complex, no resources, etc.) to other parts of the organization and offer only their small part of it any support, or they will attempt to grab the whole portfolio (in an attempt to justify more resources) in order to shore up their own core responsibilities. Either way tends to lead to the various challenges being responded to in what might be most politely described as a "diluted" way.

Breaking the silo

In today's reality, there is little excuse for these stovepipes to exist. If we look at management in terms of the effective and efficient use of resources, we can nearly eliminate the waste associated with having to travel to meetings—teleconferencing, videoconferencing, and similar kinds of technology provide more than an adequate forum for that activity. This same technology allows managers to reach a far greater community of experts—both within trusted communities (where sensitivity of information plays a role) and globally (where information is being sought). Planning and coordination tools also allow program and project managers to share information and form collaborative networks in a way that greatly reduces the need for key persons to be present at different locations.

This technology, if leveraged right, also leads to the reduction of another challenge— that of scheduling. Highly specialized persons, managers, or key resources are all under immense time demands. Somebody once asked me, as an intermediate-level manager, how I felt working 7.5 hours a day—to which I replied that it made for a wonderful Saturday since I had my evening sort of free. The virtual meeting spaces, however, were largely designed in the IT communities where this was a problem some time ago…meaning that they have already found solutions wherein the key information can be brought together fairly quickly and without missing parts of it.

So the first step is recognizing what communication tools are present in the environment. In some organizations, the certification and accreditation (C&A) communites that oversee the network can be helpful as they already know of these kinds of tools and their respective uses. They can become an ally that you work with to overcome those challenges. It is important to recognize that this group must be engaged early in the process so that a solution can be found. When engaging these groups, however, care must be taken to ensure that the working tools (or the lack of working tools) does not become the reason for action--the focus must be on identifying and taking the right steps to protect the organization's infrastructure.

So, the next question becomes, why do we need to communicate in the first place? At an organizational level, the answer to this is simple—because you ultimately all work for the same upper-management group that will probably determine that they do not need this kind of infighting (they have bigger external problems) and will soon cast you in a negative light. This is not the position you want to be in when the next round of "right sizing" or "cuts" come down the pipe. You need to be in a position where you are firm and fair but also solution driven. The second part of the answer is that, as the skilled practitioners and managers responsible for infrastructure that, if it fails to function appropriately, can lead to significant liabilities, there should be no doubt in your mind that if you have not taken reasonable steps to address issues, you will likely find yourself in legal (criminal or civil as the case may be) peril. The last of these three equally important reasons is that you are still a member of a community and should be exercising your authority with due care to those inside and outside of your organization. If those three reasons are not enough to motivate you toward taking real steps to addressing the issue, I would propose that you may want to explore fields other than security.

Building the solution

Understanding that this is likely to be a community-driven solution (one that involves many shops within the organization) and not an individually driven solution (wherein only one shop needs to participate) and recognizing that communications should not be as limiting a factor as some portray (the problems there lie in sound management issues), then we can get down to the mitigation of the various risks identified in the risk analysis and risk assessment.

Remember, risk assessment answers the question "so what?" and risk analysis answers "how is this risk structured?" These are both important when attempting to address how to manage risks, which is what building the solution is really about. What we need to aim toward comes in two parts. The first involves understanding what we want to achieve—the "so what?" If this process is like navigating on a ship, this is the North Star you are navigating by. It may be distant, but steering according to it means less zig-zagging all over the ocean. The risk analysis ("how is the risk structured?") is important because it gives us the mechanics of what we need to fix. For example, our goal may be to prevent unauthorized entry to a control room so as to prevent untrustworthy people from having access to control panels. The risk analysis may tell us that this is an issue because we do not conduct background checks, and there are no access control measures on the space that limit access to those that have been appropriately authorized and cleared through a trusted and authorized process. Keep these two in mind.

So, the first step will be to identify the goals that need to be achieved in order to support the organization's mission. We want to reduce the risks of spills because each spill represents huge losses (real and potential) and significant legal liability that could end the company. Our control systems may allow for spills or prevent spills through having an appropriate array of sensors, controllers, switches, servers, control consoles, and user interfaces that come together to ensure that containers do not overflow, that valves are not opened or closed inappropriately, and that safety shutdowns all function appropriately through the detection of drops of pressure, and so on. As you work through this, you will find that there are a significant number of potential issues that need to be looked at.

At this point, the solution takes on a more personal aspect. I tend to look at approaching the issues from a risk management perspective. Having identified all high-level risks, I put these onto a matrix that links the infrastructure with the issue. I then look at one solution per box where these intersect and try to map out where I can use one or two measures to address a number of these appropriately. These are all identified off on the side, and then the work begins. I also identify one backup measure for each primary measure using a structure we will encounter shortly. I then work toward determining the medium and low risks.

I do not do this in isolation. This is one of the occasions where I will attempt to bring the group together because the problems are best approached from a multidisciplinary perspective. This is not to say that it is the only time the overall group will get together, but the identification of the challenges that exist and how to address them is definitely an activity best approached with the best input possible.

Following the pipe

Having identified the potential issues and the general solutions, the next challenge is identifying how to bring those into being. In this case, using a follow-the-pipe approach to identify the business lines that can lead to these challenges is useful. As noted elsewhere in the book, the follow-the-pipe approach involves identifying how persons, inputs, facilities, information, and supporting activities contribute to the existing business line (and hence the challenge) and how they can each contribute to the risk-mitigation strategy. The principles associated with identifying which characteristics of each is important to us still applies—whether that be confidentiality, integrity, availability, relative value, or public confidence (branding). This process is more fully explained in the risk management chapter.

The first step is addressing the challenge and identifying which controls can be put in place to mitigate risks to best effect. The people involved in this process should include managers (since resources need to be allocated) and their senior technical persons (since the solutions may need to be creative). This may or may not be the same person—some organizations require technical competence on the part of their management and some do not. In either case, what matters is that both the technical and management layers are well represented. Ideally, the challenges should be presented to the various members of the group some time in advance (so that groups can actually think about what they need to do) with participation being based on being solution focused. It should also allow for additional groups to be suggested to the group for inclusion where the challenges intersect with those groups. Remember that the goal of this activity is to identify the most appropriate solution sets, not simply to have a manageable mailing list.

Given this set of potential challenges, there are likely to be two levels of groups formed. These groups involve the following:

- Personnel security screening, or those involved in background checks, in order to determine what level of trust needs to be established. This group would extend into groups associated with labor relations, legal and privacy issues, and employee assistance programs.
- Asset management, and particularly controlled asset management, in order to identify controls over materials and the nature of those controls. This group will likely extend to material management, procurement, and similar kinds of shops.
- Physical security in terms of the protection of persons, assets, and operations (including facilities). This group will extend toward safety, infrastructure, facility management, and other activities.
- Information and IT security in terms not only of the protection of data moving in the system but also the instructions, plans, and other guiding material provided to persons running the system. This group will involve operations, physical security, and contracting in terms of the flow of information and its protection.
- Business continuity (or continuity of operations) and infrastructure in terms of being able to count on supporting services to be there when required. This will also extend to other shops or organizations that work either within the group or on behalf of the group to manage contracts, Memoranda of Understanding and service-level agreements.

As we can see, there is an inner ring and outer ring. For those looking for these groups, you can expect to see them handled differently between larger and smaller organizations. Smaller organizations may have individual organizations that are very refined. Smaller organizations may have several of these functions lumped into one small (and potentially overworked) group. You should start this examination with an open mind and work to get a clear sense of the organizations and how the inter-relate within your organization.

In looking at the specific controls, it is generally prudent to design controls so that they work within a system. This involves the following four elements:

- The *preventive* control, which is used to address the risk by dealing with the threat directly
- The *detection* control, which identifies that the control is at risk of failing and that there needs to be a response to prevent or control the impacts associated with the potential failure

- The *response*, which deals with stopping the forward progress of the threat (toward accomplishing its goal) through containment and ultimately halting the threat
- *Recovery*-based controls, which address any injuries caused by the threat as a result of the failure of the control

I have to confess that this structure is not my own. It is well used across both the physical security and IT communities and can be found in doctrinal manuals throughout each. What is ultimately important is that it is understood that we must be able to delay the progress of the attacker (be it deliberate, natural, or accidental) to the point that we can stop or minimize injuries through our own capacity to detect, identify, notify (making up the detection phase), and respond effectively.

The second element is to look at the kinds of controls needed. This is a combination of what needs to be accomplished, what resources are available to accomplish it, and the level of assurance needed. These can be broken down into the following:

- *Administrative controls* (such as policies, etc.), which define what is considered appropriate and what is not when making decisions or conducting activities. These controls provide limited assurance in terms of prevention but are necessary for the response and recovery phases in that they need to be presented clearly for activities like investigations.
- *Physical controls* often have the highest costs (such as guards) but can provide the greatest assurance in terms of access control, monitoring of spaces, and so on. They are the rough equivalent of the firewalls and demilitarized zones of the IT security domain. These controls, however, need to be looked at in terms of operational impacts, legal and regulatory impediments, and overall life-cycle maintenance costs.
- *Procedural controls* guide individuals by defining the appropriate steps to be taken when conducting certain kinds of activities. These, if reinforced appropriately, can help prevent issues but are often of little impact when attempting to prevent insider-threat-related issues. They do, however, provide more ammunition against this threat when combined with the appropriate administrative controls.
- *Technical controls* involve the configuration of systems (such as adjusting settings that affect the crossover error rate in access control systems), detection equipment (what level of resolution is needed for detection, recognition, or identification in normal, higher-threat, and legal contexts), and so forth. The controls are often targeted by insider threats, meaning that they need to be linked to an elevated level of checks used to determine the level of trust an individual can be given.

These controls and their focus should be determined in the group setting to make sure that the whole system is covered and with at least one level of backup. When attempting to look at when "enough is enough," Boyle's law may provide a reasonable answer by using a layers-of-protection approach.

This approach involves looking at layers of defense and the overall effectiveness of the system. If there is one layer of defense that is estimated to be 50% effective, then the overall posture can only be assured to be 50% effective under the best of conditions. If there are two layers that are each 50% effective, then the overall system can be assured to be 75% effective under the best conditions (50% of successful threats being stopped at the first layer and 50% being stopped at the next). This goes on and on until after five layers (assuming 50% effectiveness for each) finally gets you over 90% assurance under good conditions. It should be clear that these layers cannot be subject to the same vulnerabilities or means of compromise.

The final step involves looking at who will lead the challenges within the various systems. It should be clear that no part of the group can unilaterally degrade the system in this context. A logical breakdown may be having the technical (IT and similar groups) look to the design of the equipment up to the outer casing. From the outer casing and into the physical environment becomes the role of physical security. Operations and similar groups then look toward the procedural controls, while management supports the suite of administrative controls through policies.

These specific controls can be based on best practices (where suitable to the environment), risk management practices, or simple assessment. What is important is that each control aligns with risk, is weighed in terms of its impact on operations, and is based on a solid foundation of professionally accepted practices (relevant to the domain).

Managing the controls

Having established the controls, it is important to consider more than just the suite of controls (prevention, detection, response and recovery). The life cycle of these controls must be assessed on an ongoing basis through effective monitoring. This can involve the standard PDCA model used in project management. The "planning" aligns with risk assessment and security design. The "doing" aligns with the implementation of the controls up to the point that they are declared to be in force. The "checking" involves ensuring that the controls are functioning as expected and that there are no unexpected operational impacts (or unacceptable impacts). Finally, the "acting" involves making any adjustment to the controls to keep it on track with its performance and expected life cycle. This means doing more than TRAs at five-year intervals. It means ensuring that such activities may happen not less frequently than every five years but that they are subject to a continuous and risk-based (most important/vulnerable first) monitoring structure that feeds into a good information system that captures the information described in this chapter.

Conclusion

The management of physical security in this environment is forcing a number of issues—most importantly the need to communicate across the other functional groups within an organization. This is going to lead to what is called "storming" in the group dynamic mode as organizations attempt to find resources or protect mandates (as applicable to the groups within an organization). Effective communications needs to be established across administrative silos (which are as strong as ever in these economic times) so that the knowledge base and expertise within an organization can be leveraged. Ultimately, the suite of administrative, physical, procedural, and technical controls needs to address the identified risks (both in terms of assessment and analysis) so that a credible system involving multiple layers of defense can be established to protect the personnel, assets, and infrastructure involved. Depending on the complexity, national importance, and culture within your organization, this can be a challenging task, but one that can be significantly rewarding in terms of both personal and professional satisfaction.

chapter twenty

Tabletop/red–blue exercises

Robert Radvanovsky

Contents

In addition to regularly performing penetration and validation tests against critical infrastructure, it is often a good idea for organizations (both public and private sector) to plan for real-life scenarios involving either partial or totally complete infrastructure operations failures. Thus, many organizations are now implementing either "tabletop" or "red–blue team" exercises. Executing either or both of these exercises helps the organization identify any weaknesses or gaps in their procedural steps, training, or staff development, as well as their incident command response handling processes.

What is a tabletop exercise?

Put simply, a tabletop exercise is where all stakeholders of the representative organization work through one or multiple real-life scenario(s) and identify whether their organization can handle the emergency. Tabletop exercises are meant to be formally given, usually through a participatory organization (such as the Department of Homeland Security [DHS]), to step through a series of smaller, individually driven exercises to demonstrate that an organization can recover, restore, and remedy their business operations from whatever scenario was given by example. In most circumstances, the scenarios tend to be terrorist related, with an external terrorist organization or entity having an intentional goal of shutting down or creating havoc or other forms of malice against said targeted organization. The outcome is to grade and give a "win–lose" along with a scaled or percentaged grade, or a performance comparison to other enterprises within the same industry vertical. With this form of exercise, the organization can either "win" or "lose," depending on how well it has managed to handle and respond to the real-life scenario. In most circumstances, typical tabletop exercises employ everyone on the defending organization's side, usually with no one representing the attacking or offensive organization.

A tabletop exercise simulates either an emergency condition or a situation that is established in an informal and stress-free environment. The participants—usually people who are decision makers—gather around a table to discuss the general problems and procedures in a context of the presented emergency scenario. The focus of the exercise delves into specific aspects, such as training and familiarization with roles, along with procedures, processes, or functional responsibilities (FEMA, 2012).

The tabletop exercise is largely a discussion guided by a facilitator (in some circumstances, there may be two or more facilitators who may share the facilitating responsibilities). The sole purpose of this exercise is to solve problems as a group. There are no simulators, no attempts to arrange any elaborate facilities or configuration, and no communications. One or two evaluators from the group may be selected to observe the proceedings of the exercise, and note the progress made toward the outlined objectives (FEMA, 2012).

Advantages and disadvantages of tabletop exercises

The success of an exercise is determined primarily by feedback obtained from the participants; the impact of this exercise is felt through the feedback obtained, and what effect it has on the finalized evaluation and revision of the policies, plant configuration, and procedures. Thus, this exercise becomes a very useful training tool that has both advantages and disadvantages, as summarized here (FEMA, 2012):

Advantages

- Requires only a slight or modest commitment in terms of time, cost, and resources
- Provides an effective method for reviewing configurations, procedures, and policies
- Provides a very good method to acquaint key personnel with emergency responsibilities and procedures, as well with as one another

Disadvantages

- Does not provide a realistic scenario or outcome; thus, this form of exercise may not provide a true test of an emergency management system's capabilities, condition, or scenario
- Does not provide a practical way to demonstrate a dysfunctional or nonoperational system
- Provides a superficial exercise based on only the stated configurations, procedures, and personnel capabilities

How a tabletop exercise works

In many respects, a tabletop exercise is similar to a problem-solving or brainstorming session. Unlike other types of exercises, many problems of a tabletop exercise are tackled one at a time, and talked through without any stress or timing constraints. This form of exercise may not be as tightly structured as other forms of exercises, so problem statements may be handled through other methods (FEMA, 2012):

- The facilitator may verbally present general problem scenarios, which are then discussed, one at a time, by the group.
- Problems may be verbally addressed to one or more individuals first, then (eventually) opened up to the remainder of the group.
- Written detailed conditions or events (problem scenarios), along with related discussion questions, may be given to individuals to answer from the unique perspective of their own organization and role, and then discussed with the remainder of the group.
- Another approach might deliver prescribed or scripted messages to the participants. The facilitator presents them, one at a time, to individual participants. The group then discusses the issues raised by the message, using an emergency operating center (EOC) or other emergency operating plan (EOP) for guidance. The group determines what, if any, additional information is required, and then requests that information.
- Occasionally, participants receiving messages may handle them individually, making a decision for the organization they represent. Participants then work together, seeking out information and coordinating decisions with each other.

Some facilitators may like to and try to combine differing approaches, perhaps beginning the exercise with general problem scenarios directed toward specific key individuals, and then handing out messages one at a time to the other participants in the exercise (FEMA, 2012).

It is recommended that the EOC (or secondary or alternative operations center) is used for the exercise, for the following reasons:

- Utilizing the EOC (or secondary/alternative operations center) provides the most realistic setting, as this environment is what would normally be used during an emergency condition or situation.
- Necessary configurations, designs (network and operations), as well as maps, procedures, and documentation, are all available on-site.

Alternatively, any conference facility that will comfortably accommodate the expected number of participants in a face-to-face setting should be sufficiently adequate. The number of participants (along with the outlined problem scenario) will determine the number and arrangement of the tables used for the exercise. Some facilitators like to arrange small groups around separate tables, whereas other facilitators may prefer other layout configurations. Reference materials utilized should include emergency documentation, configurations, designs (networks and operations), maps, and other reference materials that would normally be available at the EOC (FEMA, 2012).

Facilitating a tabletop exercise

A tabletop exercise provides a relaxed environment for team problem solving; whereas other exercises (such as functional or full scale/full operational) tend to be more interactive, a tabletop exercise, however, is managed by one or more facilitators. The facilitator has several responsibilities that include the following:

- Providing and introducing the narrative to the participants of the exercise.
- Facilitating the problem-solving activities with and between each of the participants, as well as any fractional groups formed throughout the exercise.
- Controlling the speed (pace) and direction of the exercise; the facilitator can adjust the speed and direction according to any modified outcomes encountered throughout the exercise.
- Distributing messages to the participants of the exercise.
- Stimulating any discussion and concluding any answers or solutions from the group (rather than simply supplying them).

The facilitator must have good interpersonal and communication skills, be well informed on local configurations and organizational responsibilities, and (generally) be thought of as a discussion leader; however, this role may also include additional ideals and responsibilities, depending on the organization and type of problem scenario (FEMA, 2012).

Setting and configuring the tabletop exercise

The facilitator (generally) begins the exercise with opening remarks and outlines activities that can influence the whole experience of the exercise. Participants need to have an understanding of what to anticipate, as well as feel comfortable about participating in the exercise. Shown below are some guidelines outlined for facilitating a typical tabletop exercise (FEMA, 2012).

Guidelines for setting the stage

- *Welcoming introduction*: Begin with a sincere welcoming introduction to the participants, putting them at ease as to why they are participating in the exercise.
- *Briefing the participants*: Brief the participants about what will happen throughout the exercise, and possibly what to expect as far as outcomes are concerned. This requires a careful and clear explanation of the following:
  - Purposes and objectives of the exercise; what to expect throughout the exercise, what the anticipated outcome might be, who will be participating versus observing in the exercise, and so on.
  - Ground rules indicating the "dos" and "don'ts" of the exercise, including specific areas to avoid that are considered "off limits," as well as any timing issues or additional requirements that must be met to ensure a successful completed exercise.
  - Procedures and any supporting documentation, including configurations, designs (network and operations), maps, emergency documentation, contact lists, and so on.
- *Narrative statement about the exercise*: Start the exercise by reading (or having someone read) the narrative and introducing the first problem scenario or message. Facilitators may or may not answer any questions initially, in an effort to get the participants to begin formulating their strategies or methods of approach.

- *The "ice breaker"*: Try breaking the ice by beginning with a general question directed at one or two decision makers of the group, or to the entire group as a whole. The idea is to get the group thinking and talking about the problem scenario, and begin formulating a strategic method or solution (if possible). Later, while the exercise is underway, present other additional problem scenarios, statements, or messages that may be addressed to other individuals or organizations as part of the exercise.

Involving everyone who is participating

It is important that everyone participates and that no one person or organization dominates the topics or discussions. Some tips for involving the participants include the following:

- Organize the problem scenarios, statements, or messages in such a manner that all organizations must deal with the questions or problems outlined.
- Encourage those who are reticent or uncommunicative to be involved with the exercise; provide feedback if necessary.
- Avoid the temptation to jump in with the correct strategic solutions when participants are struggling with their own solutions; the whole premise of the exercise is to encourage and obtain strategic solutions from the participants. Providing the answers to the participating group(s) may hamper the overall outcome, ruining the entire exercise. Instead, try to draw out the answers from the participants; if necessary, encourage through the use of hints and questioning tactics. As such, the participants will more likely be willing and open to participate if they feel people are listening intently and sympathetically.
- Model and encourage the behaviors you want from the participants:
  - Give eye contact, demonstrating your willingness to listen to each participant.
  - Acknowledge comments in a positive manner; try to avoid providing any negative feedback or commentary, as this may detract from the desired outcomes of the exercise.

In-depth problem solving

The purpose of tabletop exercises usually means resolving problem scenarios or making plans as a group; this means outlining and discussing real-life scenarios (and their solutions), not artificial or improbable scenarios that would never happen within the organization.

Sometimes, facilitators make the mistake of trying to move too fast through the problem scenario, believing that they must or need to meet all of the objectives and get through all of the messages to obtain the objectives of the exercise. In most circumstances, this approach is not good, as nothing gets settled nor accomplished.

Conversely, as a facilitator, if you spend all or most of the exercise time focusing on one big problem, try to maintain interest between the participants, and reach consensus—then the tabletop will be a success; encourage and push the participants past any artificial or superficial strategic solutions. A few carefully chosen, open-ended questions can help keep the discussions going to their logical conclusion (FEMA, 2012).

Controlling and sustaining action within the exercise

To maintain a high level of interest in the exercise, and keep everyone involved, the facilitator needs to control and sustain the action. There are several methods to accomplish this:

1. *Use multiple event stages*: Develop the problem scenario narrative in event stages; for example, the initial narrative may involve a warning, in which a later stage would then deal with the remediation effort. As the discussions on a particular issue begin to wind down and come to a conclusion, introduce the next segment.

2. *Vary the pace*: Add or delete problem scenarios, statements, or messages to alter the speed and direction of the action. Mix it up; occasionally, provide one or more messages at the same time to increase the pace and interest of the exercise.

3. *Maintain balance throughout the exercise*: Maintain a balance between overly talking about a problem scenario and moving along so fast that nothing gets settled or determined. Facilitators have the responsibility to maintain and control the pace and direction of the exercise.

4. *Observe for any signs of frustration or conflict*: Facilitators need to understand that a tabletop exercise is essentially a "training exercise," not testing. Some participants of the exercise may become frustrated and irritated, thinking that the exercise is a test (of sorts). Facilitators should stop the exercise if either of these two emotional states is observed at any time throughout the exercise. Again, the whole premise is to help participants resolve any conflicts and encourage them to feel comfortable and at ease with the exercise.

5. *Keep the exercise "low key"*: The whole premise behind the exercise is to train participants and avoid any bad experiences, by keeping in mind the low-key nature of the tabletop.

Designing a tabletop exercise

A typical tabletop exercise may or may not include the following steps, depending on the problem scenarios, statements, or messages given, and the expected outcomes. Again, there is no set method of defining a tabletop exercise, but the following eight steps may help identify some, and may be expanded to improve the overall experiences encountered within and throughout the exercise:

1. Assess the needs of the exercise. What are the expected or anticipated outcomes?
2. Define the scope of the exercise, and also what limitations (if any) are (or should be) present to encourage a positive results condition of the exercise.
3. Write a purpose statement for the exercise; provide a clear set of definitions and goals from which the organization wants the participants to learn.
4. Define objectives as to how those goals and objectives will be accomplished.
5. Compose a narrative; this is where the problem scenario is presented. Ensure that the problem scenario is as real or "lifelike" as possible; use other industry examples to set the tone, pace, and direction for the initial discussions of the exercise.
6. Write significant and detailed events leading to the problem scenario; these are the facts backing the scenario, and perhaps describing how it may have become a problem in the first place.
7. List expected actions and outcomes from the exercise; more importantly, discuss what, how, and where your organization wishes to achieve those goals and objectives in the exercise. Again, expected or anticipated actions and outcomes should be positively—not negatively—reflective, further reinforcing the training aspects of the exercise.
8. Prepare any statements or messages that will be used throughout the exercise.

For most tabletop exercises, the overall process can be somewhat simplified, and as the exercise is only partially simulated, it requires little or no scripting. The only roles are the facilitator(s) and the participants (responding to their real-life roles and responsibilities), along with a scribe. The scribe takes minutes throughout the exercise and records the decisions determined; the scribe does not usually need to fill out or complete any formal evaluation forms.

Applying the design steps

The following steps outline how the exercise is (typically) designed and implemented:

- *Narrative statement*: The tabletop exercise narrative is generally shorter than most other exercise narrative statements. It is usually given to the participants in printed form, although it can be presented through other methods, such as radio, television/video, or some combination involving all three delivery methods. The primary purpose of the exercise is to discuss general responses; thus, the narrative may be presented in parts (as the exercise happens, so does the presentation of the narrative in stages for each section) with a discussion of problem scenarios after each section.
- *Statements or events*: Put simply, statements or events should be closely related to the objectives of the exercise. Most exercises require only a few major or detailed statements or events, which can then easily be turned into problem scenarios.
- *Expected or anticipated actions or outcomes*: A list of expected or anticipated actions or outcomes is useful for developing both problem scenarios. It is always important to be clear about what facilitators want participants to do. However, in a tabletop exercise, sometimes the "expected action" will be a discussion that will eventually result in consensus or ideas for change.
- *Messages*: A tabletop exercise can succeed with just a few carefully written messages or problem scenarios. Messages should be closely tied to the overall exercise objectives, and should anticipate giving all participants the opportunity to take part. The messages might relate to a large problem (almost like an announcement of a major event) or a smaller problem, depending on the purpose of the exercise. Usually, they are directed to a single individual or organization, although others may be invited to join in the discussion.

What is a red–blue team exercise?

With the red–blue exercise, the organization is given a scenario similar to that which may be given in the tabletop exercise, but with one exception: members of the defending organization are split into usually two (perhaps three) teams: offensive (attacker, called the red team), defensive (defender/target, called the blue team), and neutral (referee, called the white team). The objectives of each team are similar, but each side knows little to nothing about what the other is going to do, how they are going to perform, their tactics, and so on. The objective is for the participants to work through the attack model as either defenders or attackers. The objective is simple: either the red team or the blue team will win; there is not always a clear winner, in which case there may be a tie, or both teams may lose. The red team's objective is usually to gain a foothold on the target's system, modifying the system operation or shutting it down or destroying it, and generally creating havoc for the defending blue team; while the blue team must utilize every method to defend against the attacking red team. The white team usually referees each side, and determines (or can even modify) the rules of engagement for the exercise, and can even modify the rules while the exercise is proceeding, if they feel that one side is winning unfavorably over the other team.

Advanced DHS red–blue training course

The U.S. DHS Cyber Security Division's Control Systems Security Program (CSSP) employs an advanced red–blue exercise method with the intent to provide education and awareness to asset owners/operators of critical infrastructures, as well as military, intelligence, regulatory/compliance, and law enforcement organizations. The main goal and objective of the CSSP is to reduce industrial control system risks within and across all critical infrastructure and key resource sectors by coordinating efforts among and between federal, state, local, and tribal governments, as well as industrial control systems owners, operators, and vendors (ICS-CERT, 2015). The CSSP coordinates activities to reduce the likelihood of success and severity of impact of a cyberattack against critical infrastructure control systems through risk-mitigation activities. The red–blue exercise is just one part of this effort, and is an important and vital educational effort to make all interested parties aware of potential threat and attack vectors—meeting other people with similar interests, networking, and, overall, just having some fun.

The advanced training course provides an intensive hands-on training on protecting and securing industrial control systems from cyberattacks, through a red team–blue team exercise that is conducted within an actual control systems environment. This exercise provides an opportunity to network and collaborate with other colleagues involved in operating and protecting control systems networks, and consists of five days of intensive training on cybersecurity for industrial control systems, along with the red team–blue team exercise (CSSP, n.d.):

- *Day 1*: The first day provides an overview of the DHS CSSP, a brief review of cybersecurity for industrial control systems, a demonstration showing how a control system can be attacked from the Internet, along with hands-on classroom training specific to network discovery techniques and best practices.
- *Day 2*: The second day provides continued hands-on classroom training involving network discovery, the use of tools, and separating into red-team and blue-team participants.
- *Day 3*: The third day provides continued hands-on classroom training on network exploitation and more advanced network defense techniques and practices, as well as allowing both the red team and the blue team to formulate separate individual team strategies.
- *Day 4*: The fourth day represents the actual exercise, representing an exhaustive and intense 12 h exercise where participants are either attacking (red team) or defending (blue team). The blue team is tasked with providing the cyberdefense for a corporate environment, as well as with maintaining plant operations to a batch process plant, and an electrical distribution SCADA system.
- *Day 5*: The final day provides a red team–blue team review of the exercise, where the facilitator fleshes out lessons learned from the participants, and a round-table discussion with presentations given by the red, blue, and white teams, from a designated representative of each team.

Lessons learned through a tabletop or red–blue team exercise

Overall, either the tabletop exercise or the red–blue exercise tests the defending organization's cybersecurity incident response plan with specific objectives to

- Test the team members' understanding of the policies and procedures for handling a cyberincident.
- Review the effectiveness and suitability of the policies and procedures.
- Evaluate coordination with federal, state, and local government.
- Identify any gaps and mitigate them (if possible) against the response plan.
- Educate, educate, educate—the overall exercise is to provide takeaway lessons learned for each participating team member (including both red and blue teams for the red–blue exercise).

The facilitators of the training exercise utilize the playbook in hand and release a series of "injects" or story lines throughout the day. These "injects" are designed to test the defending organization's response to internal and external cyberattacks on its control systems and supporting networked environments. The facilitators conduct a follow-up discussion, with probing questions designed to generate discussions on how the participating team members would handle the topic at hand. A variety of subjects are covered, including traditional cybersecurity issues of access control, remote access, perimeter defenses, logging, auditing, and so on. The exercise also covers non-information-technology (IT) subjects, such as SCADA and control systems.

For example, one of the "injects" may produce conversations on the human resources policies and procedures for dealing with an employee suspected of an internal cyberattack. Another "inject" might force the defending organization to think about recommended practices for handling media coverage caused by any disruption of services due to the cyberattack. The participating team members can hold "hot washes" that would highlight key points—perhaps any takeaways—following the completion of each scenario. Any notes or hot washes generated that are used by the defending organization's team members would be incorporated to further develop any action plan modifications used for the next scenario.

Incident response is crucial to the defending organization: how an incident is responded to, how quickly, and whether it can be remedied (especially today), can make—or break—an organization. During a real incident, organizations do not want to discover any major gaps in their policies or procedures, as well as their technology tools. The collaboration that occurs during either a tabletop exercise or a red–blue exercise helps everyone within the defending organization to understand roles and responsibilities in accomplishing their overall goal; thus, this allows participating team members to leave the exercise with a fresh, new approach as to how to handle probable, real-life scenarios.

How to prepare for an exercise

If you are interested in conducting either a tabletop exercise or a red–blue exercise to test your organization's response to a cyberattack on your SCADA/control systems enterprise, here are a few ideas for organizing the exercise:

- Identify the goals and objectives for the exercise; for example, testing an incident response plan, determining weaknesses in outer defense layers, or determining gaps in defense-in-depth equipment.
- Develop relevant and realistic scenarios (perhaps looking at recent news about incidents involving similar organizations that were attacked) and incorporate those scenarios to achieve similar goals, by preparing a situation manual or play book documenting the scenario.

- Prepare briefing slides to guide the participating team members through the exercise; explain the rules of engagement—what the "dos" and "don'ts" are.
- Generate a facilitator's handbook that provides instructions to guide the facilitator during the exercise, capturing any relevant information; document any action items, then develop an action report or plan.
- Invite all crucial stakeholders to the exercise, including technical as well as nontechnical staff and managers.
- Determine which facilitator will draw out comments from the participating team members, and include a note as to who will capture the key points of the exercise.

Conclusion

Whether your organization utilizes either a tabletop exercise or a full-blown red–blue exercise, ensuring that your organization is ready against a cyberattack always demonstrates good preparedness. As outlined in the red–blue exercise, "expect the unexpected"; what this translates to is to prepare and anticipate worst-case scenarios and outcomes for your organization, so that you and your organization can be ready. As outlined for the tabletop exercises, encourage your participants to "think outside the box" by delving into and promoting open discussions as to how to obtain and achieve the overall goals and objectives of the exercise. Depending on the scenario, either method will help your organization achieve its goal of awareness and training of your key staff and personnel responsible for your SCADA and control systems environments.

References

Federal Emergency Management Agency (FEMA). (2012). The table top exercise. Emergency Management Institute. http://training.fema.gov/emiweb/downloads/is139unit5.doc.

Industrial Control Systems Cyber Emergency Response Team (ICS-CERT). (2015). http://www.us-cert.gov/control_systems.

Cybersecurity for Control Systems Engineers & Operators (CSSP). (n.d.). http://www.us-cert.gov/control_systems/cstraining.html#workshop.

chapter twenty one

Integrity monitoring

Craig Wright

Contents

Integrity

Data needs to be accurate and processed correctly to be able to be relied upon. This warrants that objectives such as access rights, the integrity of operations, and data and reporting are both valid and consistent.

One of the most critical aspects of supervisory control and data acquisition (SCADA) security is to ensure that the system has not been compromised and altered. The need for system integrity includes both the software and the data sent and received. It is easy to imagine that if an attacker manages to place hostile code onto a system that this will enable the alteration and control of a system, but the network traffic is just as important.

If the network is compromised and an attacker can inject traffic from even an untrusted port, the lack of native authentication and protections on the MODBUS protocol,* for instance, would allow all communications to be altered and subverted, not only changing the reports to a monitor but also possibly leading to physical system damage. No integrity checks have been incorporated into the MODBUS application protocol previously mentioned. This leaves the lower-layer protocols with the task of preserving integrity, something that is rarely achieved in SCADA systems unless IPSec is enabled. When configuring integrity controls in a SCADA environment, it is necessary to incorporate both the network and system level.

Some of the key checks include the following:

- *Protect the audit trail*: Has the organization protected the audit trail so that audit information cannot be added, changed, or deleted without being recorded and logged?
- *Audit normal activity*: The process of gathering historical information about particular system activities that may be reviewed as a baseline. Knowing the baseline provides a starting point to find changes that are out of the ordinary.
- *Protect the network path*: Using protocols such as IPSec (in AH mode) can allow for the protection of traffic as it travels between nodes in the network ensuring that traffic has not been altered or injected on route.

Integrity controls aid by protecting data from unauthorized use and update. There are numerous tools that can be used to take samples of the integrity controls used across a SCADA system and to ensure that these match the security and integrity requirements. These include commercial tools but may be as simple as a manually created script that

---

* MODBUS is an application-layer messaging protocol which is situated at level 7 of the Open Systems Interconnection (OSI) model, see http://www.modbus.org/specs.php.

compares cryptographic hashes of firmware, configuration, and binary files used by the system over time. Integrity controls can be used to limit the values a field may hold and also the actions that may be performed on the data. They may also trigger the execution of other procedures. For instance, integrity controls may be used to place an entry into a log to record access to particular systems. In this way, user access may be recorded.

One way of monitoring changes to a system even by the administrative staff would be to have separate logging and monitoring servers with restricted access. These servers could be mirrored on another system and accessible only by security and audit staff. An example of this would be to record all changes made by the system administrator to such a server and have them as a record for posterity.

System triggers are also effective in adding security controls to a system. A trigger can include an event, condition, and action and can be run on external servers and logging systems and can be automated. Triggers may be complex and can allow the system to automatically prohibit inappropriate actions, to automatically start handling events using stored procedures and/or scripts or other processes, or to write an entry to a log file. This may be used to reflect information about the user and the transaction that has been created. This log may then be displayed in a format that can be read by humans or using automated procedures and tools. Triggers can be used to enforce controls for all users and all system activities.

These controls do not have to be coded into each query or program. They can even be formulated on separate systems (such as a network intrusion detection system [NIDS]) that monitor intersystem traffic. This makes it difficult for individual users or even malicious code to circumvent controls around the system. Even with assertions, triggers, and stored procedures on a system, other forms of integrity control are necessary. It is still not possible to stop all malicious or unauthorized access to a system. As such, a change audit process is still necessary. To do this, all user activity should be logged and monitored. The reason for this is to check that all policies and constraints are being enforced across the system.

The difficulty in this method is that every system query and transaction needs to be logged to record the characteristics of all data use. It is essential that all modifications to the system include who accessed the data, the time the data were accessed, and, if a program or query was used to run this process, what that query or program was. It is also essential to log the network address or location where the request was generated from. There are also other parameters depending on the business and system structure that may be used to aid an investigation of a suspicious data change. The problem with this sort of structure is that it creates extra data and extra maintenance.

With the drop in the cost of storage continuing, however, the ability to record and store all network traffic to and from a critical system is becoming simpler and less difficult all the time. A complete network capture allows an incident handler to reconstruct past events using recorded data, including any firmware changes and updates, and even to carve malicious code out of network streams.

This additional cost often puts people off this. However, the savings in the long run and the increased ease with which systems may be verified can make it worthwhile.

SCADA systems are generally run as a distributed environment. In the past, systems were configured on mainframes, and while a mainframe mentality still permeates the SCADA world, unfortunately the controls associated with mainframes have long since disappeared. Worse, the controls available in mainframe systems (other than perceived isolation) never existed or were never implemented on many SCADA systems. Networks are often not secure, and the system administrator cannot control all aspects of the path from a sensor to the database or collector. In particular, many modern applications involve users and sensors at remote destinations, even on the other side of the world. SCADA security is thus a combination of system security, the security of the hosts themselves, web security (when used as a human interface), and the security of the network between the client and the server. As a consequence, database security is not just about the aspects of the system itself covered in this chapter. It must also involve aspects of security concerning the network, routers, firewalls, and systems that the SCADA system is involved with.

One of the key tenets of SCADA security is availability. To ensure the availability of a system, it is important to maintain backup and recovery processes. SCADA systems recovery involves including mechanisms to restore the system quickly and accurately after loss or damage. This ensures availability in the case of an outage and also, more importantly, data integrity. The basic recovery facilities for a SCADA management system should include the four basic facilities for backup and recovery of any system:

1. *Backup facilities*: Backup facilities provide periodic backups or images of either the entire system or selected portions thereof.
2. *Journaling facilities*: Journaling facilities maintain an order trail of transactions and changes.
3. *Checkpoint facilities*: These provide the system with a point-in-time control, designed to stop processing periodically, suspending and synchronizing all its files and journals, and establishing a recovery point.
4. *Recovery manager*: A recovery manager provides the ability to restore the system to the correct functioning condition and restart processing transactions.

The goal of maintaining transaction integrity is to ensure that no unauthorized changes occur either through user interaction or system error. This is important not only in managing databases associated with the SCADA system but also in the configuration and versioning within the environment. In general, the process of following well-accepted properties is called the ACID principle.

The ACID principle stands for

- Atomic
- Consistent
- Isolated
- Durable

This means that the individual transactions cannot be subdivided, hence atomic. A process must be included in its entirety or not at all. Next, it needs to be consistent; this means that any database constraints used by the SCADA systems must be true. What is true before the transaction must also be true after the transaction. Next, the transaction should be isolated. This means that changes to the database are not revealed to users until the transaction is committed to the database. And finally, transactions need to be durable, meaning that the change has to be permanent. Once a transaction is committed, no subsequent failure of the database will end up reversing the effect of the transaction. This is important in case of failures where transactions may be lost.

System integrity

Monitoring the state and integrity of the files on the system (including the binaries and configuration files) is a core aspect of system integrity in SCADA systems that is commonly overlooked in programmable logic controllers (PLCs), remote terminal units (RTUs), and other sensor devices. In many cases, a flash or other image of the host can be taken at periodic intervals and a cryptographic checksum generated using a hash function. This process can be automated to download a read-only copy of the firmware and other files and to compare the hash created to a known value. Linux tools such as MD5Summ are freely available for this purpose as are several specialized tools such as Integrit, advanced intrusion detection environment (AIDE), and TRIPWIRE (Kemp, 2011).

Other tools such as Osiris (Wotring et al., 2005) can be easily extended to work seamlessly within a standard SCADA environment and to provide integrity monitoring services.*

In addition to creating your own signature repositories, the National Software Reference Library (NSRL) (http://www.nsrl.nist.gov/) maintains a list of common signature repositories that can be used to validate software versions. They also maintain links to processes and sources that can aid in

- File integrity monitoring
- Host integrity monitoring
- Kernel monitoring

Network traffic analysis

There are a number of freely available intrusion detection system (IDS) and network capture products available that can help capture and maintain a complete network trail of all traffic entering and leaving a SCADA network. Some of these programs include the following:

- Snort: An open-source NIDS
- TCPDump: The standard for packet capture
- NGrep: Network Grep and filter
- Etherape: GUI Network traffic monitor
- Wireshark: Network traffic analyzer

Network intrusion detection

The number one fallacy about intrusion detection is that IDSs prevent intrusions. They do not prevent or deter intrusions in any way; they only report that an intrusion occurred or was attempted.

Snort is an open-source IDS that has become one of the standards against which other commercial systems are compared. You can use Snort (which is available from www.snort.org) to capture network traffic and alert you concerning traffic analysis. You can even configure it to be a true intrusion prevention system (IPS) that can stop malicious traffic. It can also create a forensic repository of all traffic.

To accomplish these tasks, Snort uses rule sets that are compared to incoming traffic. These rule sets are available from the Snort site or other security sites and are updated regularly with new attacks. If you are considering using Snort, you should definitely read and understand the documentation prior to installation. The more advanced rule sets can be quite complex and may not apply to your network configuration.

* Linux Security (http://www.linuxsecurity.com/content/view/101884/49/) has a configuration and deployment guide for OSSIM freely available.

Using Snort as a live traffic-analysis tool is common, and you can also use a known good Snort installation to evaluate captured traffic files. You can tell Snort to read any cap (TCP dump-formatted) file and generate warnings from the file. Snort will typically output any warnings or alerts to the screen unless you designate an output file in which to save them.

Encryption

Data encryption is one of the many features that is necessary to protect information and may be necessary for many compliance requirements. Most modern network devices (including many switches) include procedures for the encryption and decryption of data. In addition to this, most systems include functions for hashing data.

Hashing and encryption are similar and related but not the same thing. Hashing is a one-way function that takes data, provides a cryptographic fingerprint of the data that cannot be reversed, and uniquely identifies the information to the fingerprint. Encryption is reversible. The use of a key will either lock or unlock the data, protecting them from prying eyes.

IPSec

IPSec adds a means to send data across networks without the details being visible or open to change or compromise. There are a couple of protocols in IPSec:

- AH: Authentication header
- ESP: Encapsulating security payload

AH and ESP may be applied alone or in combination with each other.

- AH provides
- Integrity
- Data origin authentication
- Optional (at the discretion of the receiver) antireplay features
- ESP provides
- Integrity
- Data origin authentication
- Optional (at the discretion of the receiver) antireplay features
- Confidentiality (*not* recommended without integrity)

ESP does add many privacy benefits but at the expense of not being able to validate the packets or record these forensically, and it makes the network and system more complex. It should be used for authentication traffic. With the dearth of authentication traffic in existing SCADA networks (with many Windows-based object linking and embedding [OLE] systems left unauthenticated) many of the benefits of using ESP vanish.

Conversely, AH does not encrypt the traffic, allowing it to be captured and stored, analyzed, and examined without decryption while still adding a layer of packet validation. AH ensures the integrity of packets sent within SCADA networks and stops replay and injection attacks.

Building and deployment

The key to developing a secure system is to start secure. To do this, always build new or replacement systems in a trusted network or environment first. Patch or lock down the systems before deployment.

Read-only agent and systems

One means to ensure the ongoing state of the system is to write the files in read-only mode. Many believe that this will stop an attacker changing system files and configuration data. The truth is that an attacker can load modules into a running system without changing the firmware and other read-only systems. This is one of the reasons to audit and validate in-memory processes (as noted earlier).

The same dynamic link library (DLL) injection (Shewmaker, 2006), buffer overflow (Foster et al., 2005), and call hooking (Kuster, 2003; Madshi, 2012; Wright, 2012) attacks work against many SCADA systems, and many control systems are based on either Linux/Unix or Windows and hence face all of the common attacks.

With many SCADA systems now using common but insecure operation systems, including Windows CE and Linux derivatives, attacks against memory become even simpler.

Auditing the deployment

The SCADA system environment should be evaluated in an ongoing manner, not just as it is implemented. This involves the identification and prioritization of the users, data, applications, and activities to be validated. The Internal Audit Association (IIA) defines the key components of a system audit to include (Ndiaye, 2009)

1. Creating an inventory of all system structures, systems designs, and usage classifications. This should include production and test data. It needs to be maintained and to be up to date.
2. Classifying data risk within the system systems. Monitoring should be prioritized for low-, medium-, and high-risk information.
3. Implementing access request processes that require data owners to authorize the "roles" (through role-based access) granted to accounts in the system.
4. Conducting an analysis of access authority. User accounts that have a higher degree of access or permissions should be under higher scrutiny. Any account for which access has been suspended should be monitored to ensure access is denied and attempts are identified.
5. Assessing application coverage. Determine what applications have built-in controls and prioritize system auditing accordingly. All privileged user access must have audit priority. Legacy and custom applications are the next highest priority to consider, followed by the packaged applications.
6. Validating technical safeguards to ensure that they are in place and enforced with access controls having been set appropriately.
7. Auditing activity and access. It is necessary to monitor data changes and modifications to the system structure, permission and user changes, and data viewing activities. Where possible, use network-based system activity monitoring appliances instead of native system audit trails.

8. Ensuring that processes are in place to archive, analyze, review, and report audit information. Reports to reviewers and IT managers must communicate relevant audit information, which can be analyzed and reviewed to determine if corrective action is required. Organizations that must retain audit data for long-term use should archive this information with the ability to retrieve relevant data when needed.

Steps 1–6 are most effectively performed by the reviewer manually. Reperformance can be completed using baselines. Steps 7 and 8 are most effectively achieved with the implementation of an automated solution.

The best approach to auditing system activity is through the use of nontrigger audit agents connected to every system server. Nontrigger audit agents capture all significant actions that occur on the system without concern as to what application is used. These differ from system triggers in that system administrators cannot disable nontrigger audit agents without setting off alarms and raising alerts that may tip off security administrators to these actions. Also, the disabling of a nontrigger audit agent is an event in itself. Triggers are automatic procedures that occur when data have been altered in a table. Nontrigger system audit agents are uncommon at present. They work thus:

1. Gathering information from the system transaction log. Systems maintain transaction logs in the course of normal operation. Nontrigger audit agents gather data modifications and other activity from these sources directly.
2. Systems have inbuilt event notification systems. Nontrigger audit agents acquire supplementary records, including permission changes and data access, which are used to record the events occurring within the system.

Using logs

Logging is an oft-overlooked but critical component of maintaining a secure SCADA system. The issues associated with logging that need to be considered include the following:

- Log analysis and correlation
- Log signatures
- Archiving

Log and record data changes to objects

These requirements are very application and installation specific. This is where the security implementer needs to know what they are doing and why. This type of review needs to be purposeful and objective.

Monitoring any use of system privileges

It is one thing to check the configuration of a system; it is another altogether to validate that access has been the same as a configuration file over time, or indeed if the system is reacting as it should. Logging to a separate system is critical for this reason. If the system administration and audit function lie with the same person, it is possible to remove evidence of changes to the system.

Separate logs provide the capacity to check if either an attacker or a rogue administrator has made any changes to the system.

System logs

Most systems can be configured to generate numerous log files. Many of them provide useful information that can assist in an audit or review of the SCADA system. An alert log (for instance) can be used to provide evidence of system start-up and shutdown events. More crucially, it will provide details of structural changes (such as adding or changing a configuration data file or changes to the firmware).

Failed log-on attempts

Check for attempts to gain unauthorized access the system (and ensure the logs are available).

Attempts to access the system with nonexistent users

This could be an attempt to bypass the controls in place around the system.

Attempts to access the system at unusual hours

Check for any attempts to access the system outside working hours in environments where this is feasible. Otherwise, validation of access patterns over time may be completed using a baseline.

Checking for users sharing system accounts

Nonrepudiation hinges on not sharing accounts and access. Shared accounts are the anathema of a secure system, and there is no compliance regime that allows this practice. As common as this practice is within many SCADA environments, it is possible to "wrap" use authentication into an external system where older SCADA systems do not support multiple users.

Multiple access attempts by different users from the same terminal

Check if multiple system accounts have been used from the same terminal. This can indicate compromised access or shared access.

Auditing for integrity

System access auditing is a surveillance control as well as an integrity control. By monitoring access to all sensitive information contained within the system, suspicious activity can be brought to the reviewer's awareness. Data access auditing should address six questions:

1. Who accessed the system?
2. When was the system accessed?
3. How was the system accessed? (i.e., What computer program or client software was used?)
4. Where was the system accessed from (i.e., the location on the network or Internet)?
5. Which query, view, or client was used to access the data?
6. Was it the attempt to access the system successful? (And if yes, how much data were retrieved? What may have been changed?)

The evidence available to the reviewer is provided

- Within the client system (this may be infeasible—such as in web-based commerce systems)
- Within the system (including the logs produced by the system that are sent to a remote system)
- Between the client and the system (such as firewall logs, IDS/IPS devices, and host-based events and logs)
- More and more we need to start looking to network-based controls to protect and log SCADA systems.

Auditing within the client entails using the evidence available on the client itself. Client systems can hold a wealth of system access tools and the logs that these create. These logs may contain lists of end-user activity that a user has performed on the system. In terms of web-based systems, the web server itself may be treated as a client of sorts.

To obtain an adequate audit trail from client systems alone, all system access must have occurred using client tools under the control of the organization conducting the audit or review. In the event that data access can transpire using other means, it is rare that sufficient evidence will be available. This option by itself is entirely the worst option available to the reviewer, but it can provide additional evidence in support of the other methods. This is chiefly used in the event of a forensic investigation.

Auditing within the system is often problematic due to

- The limited audit functionality of many system management systems used within SCADA environments
- Inconsistent configurations and types being deployed throughout an organization
- Performance losses due to enabling the audit mechanisms

Auditing within the system is without doubt better than auditing within the client; however, the best approach is a combination of auditing the client, the network, and the system.

Auditing between the client and the system entails monitoring the communication between the client and the system. This involves capturing and interpreting the traffic between the client and the system. Software is available for this, and it may be used to provide data access auditing. The biggest issues with this type of data access auditing are as follows:

- Encryption between the client and the system server when configured poorly
- Privacy considerations and rights to view data (as well as the ability to capture sensitive system information and access controls)
- Correlating large volumes of data that also need to be parsed and processed to be useful

A baseline audit process may be created using tailored scripts that the audit team can save to a CD or DVD with statically linked binaries. Each time there is a requirement for an audit, the same process can be run. The benefits of this method are twofold. First, subsequent audits require less effort. Next, the results of the audit can be compared over time. The initial order can be construed as a baseline and the results compared to future audits to both verify the integrity of the system and to monitor improvements. A further benefit of this method is that a comparison may be run from the tools on the system against the results derived from the tools on the disk.

The creation of a set of test scripts allows the system security tester to have validation scripts run, which send information at preset times. These scripts can be configured to load into a database and validate any changes to the system. Any variation from the baseline or from the results of the previous security test or penetration test creates an automated change alerting system and helps to maintain the integrity of the system.

Attacks and integrity

We can see from the example attack trees and the associated table of attacker goals against MODBUS systems (Byres et al., 2004) that a combination of a lack of authentication and a corresponding lack of session structure in MODBUS systems can lead to a severe loss of system integrity and even to the loss of control in a SCADA environment. One of the issues with common SCADA protocols (such as MODBUS [Real Time Automation, 2009]) is a lack of authentication and packet integrity checking (Table 21.1).

Control categories

There are many types of controls. In maintaining the integrity of a system, controls need to be enforced. The following section will introduce a number of these control categories. When designing a control framework, it is necessary to include multiple levels of controls. For instance, either preventative or detective controls alone are unlikely to be effective in stopping attacks.

When these operate together they create an effect that is greater than its sum.

Deterrent (or directive) controls

Deterrent controls are administrative mechanisms (such as policies, procedures, standards, guidelines, laws, and regulations) that are used to guide the execution of security within an organization. Deterrent controls are utilized to promote compliance with external controls, such as regulatory compliance. These controls are designed to complement other controls (such as preventative and detective controls). Deterrent and directive controls are synonymous.

Preventive controls

Preventive controls include security mechanisms, tools, or practices that can deter or mitigate undesired actions or events. An example of a preventive control would be a firewall. In the domain of operational security, preventative controls are designed to achieve two things:

1. To decrease the quantity and impact of unintentional errors that are entering the system
2. To prevent unauthorized intruders (either internal or external) from accessing the system

Table 21.1 Attack tree analysis of SCADA systems

Attacker goal	Technical difficulty	Severity of impact	Prob. of detection	Underlying critical vulnerabilities	Comments
Gain SCADA system access	1–3	Very low	Low	Wireless PCN Third-party access Remote field sites SCADA transmission media	Critical precursor for all other attack goals Difficulty highly dependent on point of access and security measures in place
Identify MODBUS device	2	Very low	Low	Lack of confidentiality	Critical precursor for other goals
Disrupt master–slave communications	2	Moderate	High	Lack of authentication Lack of session structure Simplistic framing tech	
Disable slave	3	Moderate	High	Lack of authentication Lack of session structure Simplistic framing tech	
Read data from slave	2	Moderate	Very low	Lack of confidentiality Lack of authentication	
Write data to slave	**2**	High	Very low	Lack of authentication Lack of session structure Lack of integrity	
Program slave	2	High	Low	Possible lack of authentication Lack of session structure Lack of integrity	
Compromise slave	3	Very high	Low	Lack of integrity Possible lack of authentication	
Disable master	2	Moderate	High	Lack of authentication Lack of session structure	

Table 21.1 (Continued) Attack tree analysis of SCADA systems

Attacker goal	Technical difficulty	Severity of impact	Prob. of detection	Underlying critical vulnerabilities	Comments
Write data to master	3	High	Low	Lack of authentication Lack of session structure	
Compromise master	2	Extreme	Low	Lack of authentication Lack of session structure	Very useful precursor to other attack goals

Source: Byres, E., et al., The use of attack trees in assessing vulnerabilities in SCADA systems. Paper presented at the IISW 2004. Institute of Electrical and Electronics Engineers, Lisbon, Portugal.

An example of these controls would include firewalls, antivirus software, encryption, risk analysis, job rotation, and account lockouts.

Detective controls

Detective controls are designed to find and verify whether the directive and preventative controls are working. Detective controls are designed to detect errors when they occur and operate after the fact. They include logging and forensic controls, which are used to collate unauthorized transactions for purposes such as the prosecution of the offender or to lessen the impact of the attack or error on the system. Examples of this category of control include audit trails, logs, closed-circuit television (CCTV), and IDSs.

Corrective controls

Corrective controls comprise the instructions, procedures, or guidelines that are used to overturn the consequences of an incident. Corrective controls are put into practice in order to alleviate the impact of an event that has resulted in a loss and also to respond to incidents in a manner that will minimize risk. Examples include manuals, logging and journaling, incident handling, exception reporting, and fire extinguishers.

Recovery controls

Recovery controls are designed to recover a system and return it to normal operation following an incident. Examples of recovery controls include system restoration, backups, rebooting, key escrow, insurance, redundant equipment, fault-tolerant systems, failovers, and contingency plans (BCP).

Application controls

Application controls are designed into applications in order to minimize and detect operational irregularities that may occur within the application. Transaction controls are a type of application control.

Transaction controls

Transaction controls are utilized in order to afford a level of control over the various stages of a transaction as it is processed. Transaction controls are implemented from the first stages when the transaction is initiated through to when the output is produced. Comprehensive testing and change control are also types of transaction controls. A number of these controls have been included below.

Input controls

Input controls are used to make certain that transactions are correctly inputted into the system only on one occasion. An element of input control could include the counting of data or the time stamping of data with the date they were entered or edited.

Processing controls

Processing controls are used to certify whether a transaction is valid and accurate. These controls are also used to find and reprocess incorrectly entered transactions.

Output controls

Output controls are designed to protect the confidentiality of output and to verify the integrity of output using a comparison of the input transaction to the output data.

Change control

Change control is implemented to preserve data integrity in a system as changes are made to the configuration. Procedures and standards have been created to manage the change and modification of a system and its configuration.

Test controls

Test controls are designed to prevent violations of confidentiality and to ensure transactional integrity. Test controls are often included as a component of the change control process. An example of this category of control is the appropriate use of sanitized test data.

Transaction operational controls

Operational controls include those methods and procedures that afford protection for systems. The majority of these are implemented or performed by the organization's staff or outsourced entities and are administrative in nature. Organizational controls may also include selected technological or logical controls.

Hardware inventory and configuration

It is important to keep an inventory of the hardware and software used and deployed within the organization. To do this, the following control should be implemented:

- *Hardware inventory*: This is an inventory of all assets owned by the organization. It provides an overview of the hardware installed on any automated system and may also be used to track the ownership and status of an asset.
- *Hardware configuration chart*: This document provides details of the configurations that are deployed on each of the individual systems in use within the organization. This document should contain a detailed breakdown of the components installed on each host.

Hardware operational controls

Operational controls are implemented to protect the day-to-day running of the organization. These involve everything from hardware controls (such as maintenance) through to controls designed to monitor privileged entities (there are administrator or system operators who have access to exceptional, high-order functions and capabilities that normal users cannot access). Operational controls include the monitoring and general review of systems.

Media controls expand on the idea of controls that cover the handling of sensitive information. Secure media should never leave a secured environment. This involves using secure transport to move this type of media from one location to another. In a similar fashion, media that is brought into a secure environment must always be thoroughly checked to ensure that it does not contain malicious code such as malware or other hostile applications.

Trusted recovery makes certain that the security of the organization is not breached if a discontinuity (this is a system crash or other system failure) occurs. Trusted recovery needs to incorporate processes that are designed to restart the system without compromising the protection scheme that is applied to the system. For instance, CheckPoint Firewall-1 can be started in a manner that allows the passing of packets before the firewall rule set is applied. This would not be a trusted recovery.

It is also essential to ensure that the system of use after the failure can be recovered and complete a rollback without being compromised subsequent to the failure. Trusted recovery is derived from the U.S. "Rainbow Workshop" series where it is required for B3 and A1 level systems. A system failure characterizes a severe security risk as security controls that are applied to the system may be bypassed due to the abnormal functioning of the system.

Hardware controls

All applications and systems run on hardware. This is an obvious statement but one that is often overlooked. The physical controls surrounding hardware and the processes used to maintain those systems are critical to the continued operation of any organization.

Hardware maintenance

System maintenance necessitates that either physical or logical access to a system is granted to support and operations staff, vendors, or service providers. Maintenance can be performed through a combination of on-site and remote means. From time to time, hardware will need to be relocated to a repair site. When transporting hardware systems, controls need to be put in place to ensure the integrity and confidentiality of data.

It may be necessary to conduct background investigations into the history of the service personnel that are repairing the system. Alternatively, supervising and escorting the maintenance personnel off-site may be an option. It is essential to always supervise and escort external personnel when they are on-site.

Maintenance accounts

Many operating systems have been configured with default maintenance accounts (this was a common attack vector against DEC VAX equipment in the 1980s). Maintenance accounts are generally configured to be supervisor-level accounts. The problem is that they are generally factory preset with widely known user names and passwords that are rarely, if ever, changed. It is vital that these maintenance account passwords changed or disabled. If the account is disabled, the passwords could be reenabled if and when the account is needed.

In the event that a maintenance account is used remotely (virtual private networks [VPN], secure shell [SSH], modem, and even Telnet), it should be protected using additional controls (such as application firewalls, authentication gateways, and other methods).

Diagnostic port control

Many systems have diagnostic ports that are designed to allow system administrators to troubleshoot hardware issues or failures through direct access to a port on the machine. Diagnostic ports are generally not well secured and should only be accessible by authorized personnel.

Hardware physical control

It is essential that secure systems are contained within an environment that has implemented physical security controls (such as locks and alarms). The following are some examples of possible physical controls:

- Sensitive operator consoles and keyboards
- Media storage cabinets or rooms
- Server or communications equipment
- Data centers
- Wiring panels
- Modem pools or telecommunication circuit rooms

Protection of operational files

It is important to protect operational files. The maintenance of critical data and systems files is commonly known as library maintenance. This process involves using strong backup and restoration procedures that are tested thoroughly. Selecting the "verify" option during a backup is not a control. A control would include a process where a tape is randomly selected from a storage location, restored, and verified against the original data or a hash.

On live systems, data integrity procedures such as hashing (using software such as AIDE or Tripwire) are essential to ensure the integrity of data.

Some other considerations include the following:

- The protection of *source code* using source safe technology and escrow
- The protection of *object code* using code libraries and hashing techniques and
- Ensuring the integrity of system *configuration files*

Configuration change management

Configuration management is the practice of tracking and approving changes to a system. The change process incorporates the identification, control, logging, and auditing of all changes made to a system. Change management applies to the following:

- Hardware and software changes
- Networking changes
- Any other change concerning the security of the organization

Configuration management may be deployed in order to defend a trusted system during the process of design and development. The primary security objective associated with configuration management is to ensure that any change to a system does not unintentionally diminish the security of the system. Change management also acts as a detective control to find unauthorized changes that could be the result of an attack.

For instance, change and configuration management could prevent a previous version of an operating system from being installed and run as a production system. Configuration change management (CCM) introduces the ability to effectively roll back to a prior version of a system. This is generally deployed when an update to a system is found to be faulty. An additional objective of CCM is to make certain that system changes are documented.

There are seven primary phases to operational change management or CCM:

1. *Requesting* the change to be made
2. Conducting an *impact assessment* to determine the effects of the change
3. Gaining *approval* for the change
4. *Building and testing* the system that has been changed in a development environment
5. *Implementing* the change within the production environment
6. *Monitoring* the change to ensure that it has been successful
7. *Reporting* on the status of the change to the system owner and CCM board

This process should be managed by a formal CCM board. This board does not need to be large but should involve multiple parties such as those whom the change will impact. The final report should be a lessons-learned document containing anything that did not work or that could have been done better. Small and insignificant changes could be reported using informal processes such as e-mail.

References

Byres, E. J., Franz, M., and Miller, D. (2004). The use of attack trees in assessing vulnerabilities in SCADA systems. Paper presented at the IISW 2004, Institute of Electrical and Electronics Engineers: Lisbon.

Foster, J., Osipov, V., Bhalla, N., and Heinen, N. (Eds). (2005). *Buffer Overflow Attacks: Detect, Exploit, Prevent*. Rockland, MA: Syngress.

Kemp, S. (2011). Monitoring your filesystem for unauthorised change. Debian Administration. Retrieved June 10, 2012, from http://www.debian-administration.org/articles/49.

Kuster, R. (2003). Three ways to inject your code into another process. Code Project. Retrieved May 15, 2012, from http://www.codeproject.com/Articles/4610/Three-Ways-to-Inject-Your-Code-into-Another-Proces.

Madshi. (2012). API hooking methods. Retrieved May 20, 2012, from http://help.madshi.net/ApiHookingMethods.htm.

Ndiaye, F. (2009). Audit manual, Internal Audit Division, Office of Internal Oversight Services. United Nations.

Real Time Automation. (2009). Modbus TCP/IP unplugged—An introduction to Modbus TCP/IP addressing, function codes and Modbus TCP/IP networking. Retrieved June 10, 2012, from http://www.rtaautomation.com/modbustcp/.

Shewmaker, J. (2006). Analyzing DLL injection. Paper presented at the NS2006, GSM Presentation.

Wotring, B., Potter, B., and Ranum, M. J. (2005). *Host Integrity Monitoring Using Osiris and Samhain*. Rockland, MA: Syngress.

Wright, C. S. (2012). Taking control, functions to DLL injection. *Hakin9, Exploiting Software*, 2(4), 22–27.

chapter twenty two

Data management and records retention

Jacob Brodsky and Robert Radvanovsky

Contents

With any cybersystem, acknowledgment that processes occurred, or have occurred, is important, especially to those who operate in regulated industries (energy, water, transportation, etc.). As this not only affirms but also confirms that a process has completed its task (or suite of tasks), it is important from a regulatory as well as a legal perspective, ensuring that minimal requirements are being adhered to and are in compliance with those requirements. Essentially, what we are talking about are logs and their creation. Mind you, data management can also include stored or transferred data, but for the majority of organizations out there, this usually translates to plant data and log retention.

The term *data* represents a collection of qualitative or quantitative variables or something of significance, usually belonging to a set of items, assets, and objects. Data in terms of cybersystems are oftentimes represented by a combination of items that are sent and/or received by an organization's process or operation, which collects, consolidates, and organizes said items into a construct with meaningful context. Data generally are the result of measurements taken from a process or operation and are represented in columnar or noncolumnar format; they can also be graphically represented in the form of charts, graphs, or other meaningful graphical representation. Data can be described in an abstracted context, being thus viewed in their lowest level of abstraction from which information, and eventually knowledge (to some, *intelligence*), is obtained and derived.

Data comes in a variety of differing types—*meta, raw, processed, field,* and *experimental*:

- *Metadata*: Represents data about data (direct translation), in which data are generated from or about other data; this is usually a descriptive construct that identifies form and factor to either contextual or raw data (in some slightly meaningful form).

Essentially, this form of data is used descriptively to refer to content, structure, or representations used to manage other metadata that describes statistical data, graphical representations, and/or processes.

- *Raw data*: Represents the unconfirmed, unverified, unprocessed data that have come directly from a given process or operation and have yet to be further processed, correlated, consolidated, and organized. Because data in this form are not yet organized, it can prove to be challenging to the organization if they are acquired in large quantities or amounts as well as rapidly produced.
- *Processed data*: Represents "raw data" being processed, or slightly processed, and are data in which processing may be organized by stages. This represents data that are still "in process" and may not be completely finished as part of their processing or ingestion process.
- *Field data*: Refers to the "raw data" collected in an uncontrolled operation or environment. This generally refers to data being collected from a distributed operation into a centralized collection point or through a tiered collection method and is associated with sensory equipment that may or may not produce data based on trigged occurrences, events, or situations.
- *Experimental data*: Refers to data generated or collected within the context of a scientific experiment or investigation (which can include forensics investigation, pre- or postmortem) through the method of observation and third-party recording (which means observing a situational circumstance or event and reporting on it accordingly).

The term *information*, in its most technical sense, is an interpretation of data, a message, or a visual (graphical) representation. This level of interpretation represents that those items, assets, and objects identified are arranged and organized in a particular, specific sequencing of symbols, constructs, or an array of constructs in such a manner that interpretation of that ordering process is received, understood, and comprehended. Information may be identified and transferred without storage as signals, may be recorded and stored as a series of signs or symbols, or may be an event or circumstance that affects the state or transition of an operational system. Information may be part of a greater construct or an array of constructs or (perhaps) may even be the construct itself, in which the message being conveyed is the message unto itself (information about someone or something in and of itself is construed as a form of information).

Most information requires proper management from its creation, through (and including) its authorized use, to its eventual disposal and deletion. Thus, different kinds of information require different levels of protection. In most aspects, information needs to be classified on an ongoing basis ("as needed" or "as necessary") and managed based on its confidentiality, integrity, and availability characteristics specific to the organization concerned. The classification of information is usually pursuant to whatever law or policy exists that has determined the levels of importance of that information, as well as its application of controls with the retention and disposition requirements of those records. Quite simply put, how information is defined, determined, and managed depends on its applicability, where it is being used, who is using it, how often it is being used, and when it is being used.

It is the responsibility of most records-management administrators to make records available for inspection and copying under the provisions of the Freedom of Information Act (FOIA), or depending on how their requirements are worded, specific or pursuant to their infrastructure-based regulation requirements or compliance guidelines. The process of classifying information serves as a basis on which the information owner can evaluate its retention and disposition schedules, what processes are currently in effect for its records and, most important, where accurate and efficient records of the exemptions from disclosure are enumerated within the written requirements by providing a framework for the comprehensive assessment of said information.

In order to provide a comprehensive data-management and records-retention-management program, organizations first need to identify several components specific to their organizational structure—and ensure that these are adhered to. Without this adherence, the organizations will become lost within the mountainous amounts of data, and as a result, much of these data and information will become *unmanageable*. Therefore, several areas of responsibility must be established within the organization; otherwise, the correspondence (and, more importantly, the commitment to and responsibility for maintaining such records) is pointless.

Information consists of assets (items that either generate data/information or retain data/information), records (the actual data/information), and logs of those records (records of records). In most circumstances, information assets should have an information owner established within the confines of the organization; essentially, someone will have to take ownership of and maintain the data/information for the organization. One point that should be noted is that there can be more than one "information owner." Oftentimes, information owners within a critical infrastructure organization will be categorized by its stakeholder or by the group specifically responsible for that specific activity within the plant and its operation. Typically, your stakeholders will generally include (but are not limited to) the following:

- *Engineering*: Responsible for controlling and maintaining plant equipment; this especially includes supervisory control and data acquisition (SCADA) and control-systems equipment that are vitally important to the security, safety, and safety of operations of the plant operating the equipment. It is engineering's responsibility to ensure that plant equipment is operational "within specification"; that is, that the plant equipment is producing the data and information accordingly, and there are no erroneous conditions or states, nor are the data themselves erroneous.
- *Information technology (IT)*: Responsible for most of the remaining cybersystems within the plant and its operations. This can include systems to which the plant systems connect, such as the data historian or logging servers used to control access to systems vital to the plant and its operations. In some circumstances, IT and engineering may share this responsibility, especially if it pertains to plant systems; some of this depends on the organization's culture/subculture, how stakeholders view their data and information, and to what degree they feel that their data and information need (or require, if regulated or governed) protecting.
- *Security*: Responsible for controlling (usually) physical and electronic access to plant systems throughout the plant and its operations. In some industries, security works cooperatively with IT, but security usually represents the owners of the security information, while IT represents simply the custodians of the data and information. Again, this depends on the organization's culture/subculture, how stakeholders view their data and information, and to what degree they feel that their data and information need (or require, if regulated or governed) protecting.
- *Operations*: Responsible for the overall management and administration of the plant systems throughout the plant and its operations. Realistically, the operations group coordinates all the plant systems and activities that operate within the confines of the plant and will often liaise with engineering, IT, and security, depending on the issue. The operations group oversees and manages all plant systems, usually from a centralized control room; thus, its role in what data and information are shared, and how they are shared, is critical to this group.

- *Other groups*: Other stakeholder groups, such as risk management, maintenance, and emergency management, have some interest in how data and information is accumulated, stored, and disseminated. These stakeholders, although important, usually have a slightly less indicative role in securing plant data and information and their operations.

For the most part, the information owner will be responsible for assigning, prioritizing, and classifying information; determining the access privileges of users or groups of users based on their job duties; and overseeing daily decisions regarding information asset management. Periodic reviews generally are performed by the information owner to confirm the classification of, or to reclassify, the information asset.

Third-party maintenance of data

Each classification generally has an approved set of controls that are applied to the data/information being recorded and maintained. If the data/information are stored by a third party, the information owner is responsible for communicating those requirements based on the organization's policy, or as required by law through regulation or governance, to the third party and then addressing them through third-party agreements as they relate to the information owner's data. This avoids any legal issues with the third-party organization and ensures that the requirements relating to the data/information that are either stored with, transferred through, edited, audited, logged, or maintained by the third-party organization are known by that organization and have been explained by the information owner. In most circumstances involving laws and regulations/governance, it is usually left to the information owner to administer and enforce data/information classification policies with any third-party organizations, and probably rightfully so; it is the information owner's data/information.

Records retention: How much is too much?

With any effort involving data/information records management, the more important question is how much data an organization will retain. Depending on the infrastructure sector and its industries, in many circumstances, retention may be defined for the life of plant (LOP), meaning that any and all relevant data and information identified as "critical" is retained for the entire life of the plant's operation. If the plant were to operate for several decades (such as the case with oil and chemical refineries, water treatment facilities, and power generation facilities), such an undertaking would be costly (time to store and process the data/information, storage of the data/information, archiving retrieval of the data/information, etc.). Several industries have opted to reduce this requirement to a more manageable timeframe of only several years. An example would be the nuclear power generation industry, as indicated within the Nuclear Regulatory Commission (NRC) Regulatory Guide (RG) 5.71 (U.S. NRC, 2010), which states

> 10 CFR 73.54(h) The licensee shall retain all records and supporting technical documentation required to satisfy the requirements of this section as a record until the Commission terminates the license for which the records were developed, and shall maintain superseded portions of these records for at least three (3) years after the record is superseded, unless otherwise specified by the Commission.

Additionally, the NRC further clarified the types of data/information to be retained (U.S. NRC, 2010):

C.5 Records Retention and Handling

In accordance with 10 CFR 73.54(h), the licensee must retain all records and supporting technical documentation required to satisfy the requirements of this regulation until the Commission terminates the license for which the records were developed. Furthermore, the licensee must maintain superseded portions of these records for at least 3 years after the record is superseded, unless otherwise specified by the Commission.

An acceptable method for complying with this requirement is for the licensee to maintain records or supporting technical documentation so that inspectors, auditors, or assessors will have the ability to evaluate incidents, events, and other activities that are related to any of the cyber security elements described, referenced, and contained within the licensee's NRC-approved cyber security plan. Records required for retention include, but are not limited to, digital records, log files, audit files, and nondigital records that capture, record, and analyze network and COA events. Licensees should retain these records to document access history and discover the source of cyber attacks or other security-related incidents affecting COAs or SSEP functions. Section 5 of Appendix A to this guide includes a template for the licensee to use in preparing the cyber security plan regarding records retention and handling of security controls.

Reasons why we store mountains of data

One of the more significant issues with data/information generation, recording, and retention is whom the organization shares this data/information with. More importantly, it can be asked what data/information is shared, how often is it shared, by whom, and to whom?

A festering concern among many plant/operator owners is the growing amounts of data/information that are required to be recorded, logged, stored, and retained for extended periods of time. In the majority of these circumstances, IT does not know much about the process data being collected—to them, it represents a "black box" of sorts and is a process maintained by engineering or operations; IT's role is that of "data custodians," ensuring that data/information flows from one source or location to another or to its final destination. IT does not ask what the data/information are or why they are being recorded, logged, stored, or retained; and in those same circumstances they are told by engineering that they need to simply maintain the data/information repositories with no logical explanation whatsoever.

From another perspective, engineering does not know all that much about how IT gets things done. To them, IT staff are technological wizards who perform wizardry/witchcraft of sorts and simply—as if by magic—make data/information move from one place or location to another place or final destination. Similarly, engineering staff regard the technological aspect as the "black box," and as such, they cannot explain technically how the process is performed, why it is being performed, and so on. They simply know that they need to perform a task, and that it is required as part of their operational process or is critical to a function or factors required for a vital processing step.

Lastly, there are operators who know the process very well but often lack the context to understand it. From their perspective, they see two "black boxes," as they do not know the reasoning behind the data/information requirements provided by engineering, nor do they know any of the technical specifics as to how the data/information are generated, recorded, logged, stored, and retained. For those industries that are regulated, such as the oil and chemical refinement industries, the water and wastewater treatment industry, and the power generation and transmission industry, regulatory requirements and/or compliance guidelines may have been provided under the following pretenses:

1. Use of, and availability to, said data/information can and will be utilized for postmortem analysis following a cyberrelated event or incident involving the infrastructure.
2. Use of, and availability to, said data/information may be utilized for investigative purposes by the regulatory or compliance organization to determine adherence (or lack thereof) to regulatory requirements and/or compliance guidelines as set forth by the regulatory or compliance organization.
3. Use of, and availability to, said data/information may be utilized for criminal investigative purposes by law enforcement in order to determine criminal intent and/or acts of terrorism.

Thus, generating, recording, logging, storing, and retaining said data/information may be a good thing for analysis, regulatory, and law enforcement reasons, or that data/information may be stored because you just never know when you might it. Therein lies one of the issues surrounding the growing heaps of data and information being collected every minute, hour, day, week, month, and year and tucked away until requested: manageability and its ability to be shared once it becomes necessary to review it.

Share data, not headaches

Believe it or not, sharing information is a social thing; we adapt to yearning to share information about our expertise, our experiences, our past and our own history, and so on. In many regards, we become both *teachers* and *students*, both describing to others what has been experienced or learned (as the teacher) and embracing and understanding new concepts, methods, and theories (as the student). Thus, the sharing of information, and of knowledge, reenforces the social exchange of our knowledge and experiences.

Sharing data/information also involves communicating the goals, priorities, and constraints not just of individuals but of entire organizations, conveying the strategic objectives and directions of such an organization. Having knowledge and access to such data/information would prove to have a level of value far beyond any price that could be placed, as having access to that data/information could either make or break the organization.

So—when someone comes along and asks for data from the SCADA system, what do you do? More importantly, what do you give them? And, even if they have a valid purpose or reason for acquiring access to such data/information, how do you get them to them? Do we just give them the data to "shut them up"? Or do we offer services to help them understand what they have? Lastly, why are they even asking for the data in the first place? These are just a few of the puzzling questions that many critical infrastructure organizations are facing today. It is a valid and growing concern among critical infrastructure organization owners and operators; and with the mounting heaps of growing terabytes—and in some circumstances, petabytes—of data/information, how do you address these data-management issues?

Like everything that has some level of importance to society, everything has a cost, including data/information. Some of the costs attributed to data management include the following:

- Processes that generate and record data/information from an operation.
- Processes that log that data have been generated and recorded against a logging server.
- Processes that archive once "active data" that now become "archived data"; determine archival points (when should data be archived and how often?)
- Processes that store the generated, recorded, and logged data/information: First, do you keep the logged transactional data on a separate data store or include it as part of the massive data respository? Second, is archival data stored on a separate data repository, and if so, how are the data transferred—when, where, and by what method?
- Processes that review, categorize, and report summaries on the "active data": Do we create alerts based on the "active data," and again, what data are alerted, who gets this data/information, and how often are they alerted?
- Processes that back up the "active data."
- Processes that back up the "archived data."
- Processes that allowing searching and review of plant/operations data/information.

Again, information sharing has a cost: the social cost of communicating the context in which those data were collected. It has the social risk that data/information could be misused. For example, sending unreviewed data to the accounting division of the company might be very bad. They could use them to quietly make policy (through memos) without an organizational committee.

Issues with sharing information

Sharing information has a price

- Someone who really understands the data can also misuse them in order to cause harm. The demonstration at one of the U.S. national labs several years ago is an example of how inside information can be used to effect a great deal of harm; in this case, a simulated operation caused a cataclysmic failure of the infrastructure. This too is a concern not only for critical infrastructure organizations but also for regulatory and compliance organizations, policy management organizations, and politicians and political groups. Having control over an organization's data/information operations process flow could be devastating to society, especially where the critical infrastructure organization is either (highly) dependent upon other critical infrastructures, or where other critical infrastructure organizations are (highly) dependent on this critical infrastructure organization (e.g., water cannot operate without electricity; transportation cannot operate without fuel; financial trading firms cannot operate without IT and telecommunications, etc.). This strong set of dependencies can lead to a "domino effect"; having access to one critical infrastructure's key critical data/information can potentially cause this cascading (or "domino") effect.

Sharing data can mislead and confuse

- Some manager within the plant's facilities may ask IT for the average, minimum, and maximum of a particular piece of data over the period of an entire season (several months, several quarters, etc.). IT may then provide the manager with exactly that. Do you see the problem with this scenario? The issue here is that the minimum and maximum data points might be reported at both full and minimum scales each and every single time. Why? One reason might be that the instrumentation producing all of these data is calibrated only quarterly. What the manager wanted was the data without any calibration artifacts, but as the manager did not think of this scenario, and did not ask IT for that, IT (probably) was not aware of this issue and thus simply provided what was requested. Thus, the principle of the "black box" processing concept applies here.

Sharing information costs time

- It is expensive, as it takes and consumes time to generate, record, log, store, and retrieve/retrieve those data/information. Often the people asking for the data/information do not understand what they are asking for, nor do they have any comprehension of the net result of the heaping amounts of data being presented to them. In many circumstances, this comes down to simply communicating what they are requesting, which, for most managers and executives, is simply a summarized report indicating the status or condition of a given plant or operations, rather than volumes of raw data. Because there is processing that must be done, both by the devices generating the data and the individuals processing those requests to management, a simplified process request for plant/operational data to be presented in a concise manner would significantly reduce the amount of time required to process the volumes of data/information collected and stored.

Sharing information has a risk

- Again, we as humans would rather openly share and distribute information than restrict it. In today's state of world affairs, the sharing of data needs to be guarded. Sometimes, individuals share them without giving much thought to whom they may have given them to, thinking that it was someone that they knew or had reasons for requesting access to that data/information. Thus, the use of spear-phishing techniques to acquire plant/operational data/information provides a threat vector that was unheard of only a few years ago. For example, an executive for a major corporation loses his tablet on a flight during a business trip. The tablet had either some critical data on it, or worse yet, had access codes, passwords, and software that would allow someone who found the tablet unfettered access to the corporation's internal network, thereby allowing external third parties access to corporate intellectual property, and so on. From that perspective, most individuals do not think of the ramifications behind the simple loss of a tablet. Such a loss could allow a third party, or worse yet, one of the competitors of that corporation, to potentially put the targeted company out of business.

Conclusion

Although not entirely conclusive, the growing problem (and threat) of data management within our critical infrastructures is (quickly) becoming increasingly more important to the success and very survival of our society. How data/information are collected and manipulated, where they are stored, and who has access to them can either make or break a company. Having a suitable data-management and retention strategy is important based on these factors.

Reference

U.S. Nuclear Regulatory Commission (U.S. NRC). (2010). Public meeting: Records retention requirements to support cyber security. U.S. NRC. December 16. http://pbadupws.nrc.gov/docs/ML1035/ML103550533.pdf.

section five

Conclusion

chapter twenty-three

The future of SCADA and control systems security

Jacob Brodsky and Robert Radvanovsky

One of the increasingly visible issues of supervisory control and data acquisition (SCADA)/control systems security deals with the disclosure of vulnerabilities; whether the vulnerabilities are disclosed within a public venue, or in closed confinement, continues to be a heated debate of those close to this effort. As this community continues to evolve, many are observing some progress being made regarding security-related vulnerabilities, research, and disclosure, along with the many interesting issues that have come and gone. Clearly, this community's understanding of security-related issues has matured significantly over the past decade, and thus appears that it has made great advancements in recognizing that consequence has a great deal of importance as far as risk is concerned.

Since late 2008/early 2009, there appears to have been some consensus regarding what defines the terms *severe* or *important* regarding vulnerabilities (and their disclosure to and within this community), and that this has (somehow) matured from a state of thinking that each and every security-related issue discovered is the equivalent of a Stuxnet scenario to one in which we can now consider that particular security-related issue or vulnerability in the context of its operational domain. More specifically, this community has come to recognize that the security requirements of a SCADA/control systems environment never have been, nor ever will be, defined similarly to those security requirements used for the information technology (IT) domain. Unlike the IT domain, in which the primary security principles apply unilaterally, only the availability and integrity principles apply within the SCADA/control systems domain.

What many have failed to recognize is that this community has reached a point where it can now better classify SCADA/control systems vulnerabilities into distinctively unique categories, while also matching what is being mitigated against what is vulnerable (perhaps, even, against what is being exploited). Although many of the recent vulnerabilities being discovered may be considered generic by some community experts, when exploited and utilized for nefarious purposes even the simplest of vulnerabilities can result with potentially devastating consequences.

To some, this comparison would be no different than an insider threat vector being exploited, either utilizing insider knowledge of a plant's configuration, or knowing the internal capabilities of a given system to perform tasks that otherwise would not normally be allowed to be performed. Through this, the reader should ask the question: How does a device—one that was designed to support a repetitive process (safety, security, etc.)—become the target of a given vulnerability if an adversary assumes the role of an inside operator, while performing tasks that, again, would not normally be performed?

At some point in time, in the not too distant future, this community has to agree on the more troublesome issues regarding these newly discovered vulnerabilities and begin to develop mitigation strategies that are more than simply patching or updating a device. On a more chilling thought, there is a significant difference between unsecured legacy designs or communications protocol flaws versus an application, programming, or coding error for a specific product that can be patched and remedied relatively quickly. This issue continues to plague this community, as the lines of communication, responsibility, and coordination have become blurred.

This perspective is not meant to negate the efforts of researchers, policy makers, manufacturers, engineers, and so on—their dedication to this effort has been vitally essential in the advancement of SCADA/control systems security. The real issue is more about attempting to add some depth to the vulnerabilities being discovered, understand their meaning and context, and, if possible, mutually agree on a common disclosure process framework. If a given security-related discovery has an extensive impact on a large community (perhaps more than one industry—say a vulnerability affecting both the energy generation and water treatment industries), and the issue requires either significant or complete rework of the technology currently in production within those communities, then the process becomes highly complicated and very political.

Over time, one of the largest challenges (realistically, *the* biggest challenge) is to educate all stakeholders within this community such that they recognize the complexity of many of these issues, while assuming responsible courses of action and continuously improving the security posture of their systems, regardless of whether they are an owner/operator, an integration vendor, a SCADA/control systems manufacturer, or an independent researcher performing analysis against these systems. Ideally, the responsibility falls on all of us.

From another perspective, the future of control systems and SCADA security has several areas of significant development.

While the lack of control systems protocol authentication is well known, and the development of standard secure authentication features are just starting to reach the SCADA market, there are still many questions regarding access control and key management. For instance, how should one build a network of resilient certificate authorities and keep them synchronized? Similar questions concern the use of Institute of Electrical and Electronics Engineers (IEEE) 802.1x, remote authentication dial-in user service (RADIUS), terminal access controller access control system (TACACS), Kerberos, and other authentication/access tools.

In addition to the problems of authenticating human–machine interface (HMI) traffic, there is also a problem with existing embedded systems that were not designed to "play nicely" with these network standards.

This problem is part of a much larger issue that involves patch management and upgrades in general. Most people seem to forget that the SCADA or industrial control system is not the plant itself. It is analogous to the autopilot of an aircraft. One does not redesign the aircraft around the autopilot. Control system upgrades and patches present the same problem: A control system has to work within the confines in which it was designed. The process actuators and sensors may not be secure to operate, but there is little that can be done about this in a timely fashion by the control systems engineers or process IT specialists.

The whole issue comes down to the issue of how best to manage complexity. In effect, we have been using the processing equivalent of a large steam turbine to move a sports car. Perhaps the answer is to size the processor to the process.

Many are starting to reexamine what a control system is, and ask why we have been using conventional microprocessors, software, and the like. It is entirely possible that the control system may fragment into several directions: field-programmable gate array (FPGA) chips, simple microcontrollers, and complex embedded processors with extensive real-time operating systems. The latter exist, but the other two have largely been forgotten. Newer technologies, such as FPGA chips with significant processing power,* and simple, low-power microcontrollers, have changed the scope of technical costs. It is time to reexamine the field.

It is not too hard to see why some are starting to reexamine the need for large, bloated, real-time operating systems. The alternative of using defensive coding with small microcontrollers or FPGA-based designs may be better suited to meeting the needs of this market. Indeed, while there is somewhat less work when an operating system performs input/output (I/O) handling, the vulnerabilities that can creep in are starting to make many wonder at the efficacy of relying so heavily on the work of those unknown. A small team of hardware and software engineers, working with simple equipment, can produce very tight designs that may be better suited to the demands of industry. Furthermore, having everyone sign off on their work and maintaining full traceability of that work may make these designs much tighter and more resilient, and reduce the opportunity for dead code to host some sort of malware.

As a community, our work is cut out for us, which means more education and awareness training courses, instructing owners/operators about unknown threats through simulated scenarios, improving designs of those control systems that control just about everything that is repetitive and automated, and establishing greater flexibility and cooperation between governments and researchers; hopefully, the SCADA/control systems community continues to evolve and transform in a positive direction.

* Chris Fenton is well known for having implemented most of a Cray-1A supercomputer on to a single FPGA chip.

Appendix I: Listing of online resources of SCADA/control systems

There are several organizations that exist to support the security efforts of supervisory control and data acquisition (SCADA) and control systems. Some of these organizations are specifically chartered for securing our cybersecurity infrastructure, while others simply include it as a subset of their overall charter. As such, not all organizations listed provide primary guidance in the areas of securing and safeguarding SCADA and control systems but are included as a courtesy because of their involvement and commitment to SCADA and control systems development and support. Additionally, as this community continues to evolve, more organizations specific to SCADA and control systems (cyber) security will emerge.

Please note that many descriptions of organizations (and their related information) provided in this appendix have been drawn primarily from the listed organizations and their websites and from other public sources; however, not all the information has been verified. Readers are encouraged to contact the organizations directly for the most up-to-date and complete information.

The *American Gas Association (AGA)*,* representing roughly 200 energy utility organizations that deliver natural gas to almost 60 million homes, businesses, and industries throughout the United States, advocates the interests of its energy utility members and their customers and provides information and services. The AGA 12 series of documents recommends practices designed to protect SCADA communications against cyberincidents. The recommended practices focus on ensuring the confidentiality of SCADA communications. The document series titled Cryptographic Protection of SCADA Communications will, when complete, consist of the following four documents:

1. AGA 12-1—Background, Policies, and Test Plan
2. AGA 12-2—Retrofit Link Encryption for Asynchronous Serial Communications
3. AGA 12-3—Protection of Networked Systems
4. AGA 12-4—Protection Embedded in SCADA Components

The purpose of the AGA 12 series is to save SCADA system owners' time and effort by recommending a comprehensive system designed specifically to protect SCADA communications using cryptography. The AGA 12 series may be applied to water, wastewater, and electric SCADA-based distribution systems because of their similarities with natural gas systems; however, timing requirements may be different. Recommendations included

---

* http://www.aga.org.

in the AGA 12 documents may also apply to other industrial control systems (ICSs). Additional topics planned for future addendums in this series include key management, protection of data at rest, and security policies.

The *American Petroleum Institute** represents more than 400 members involved in all aspects of the oil and natural gas industry. API 1164 provides guidance to the operators of oil and natural-gas pipeline systems for managing SCADA system integrity and security. The guideline is specifically designed to provide operators with a description of industry practices in SCADA security and to provide the framework needed to develop sound security practices within the operator's individual organizations. It stresses the importance of operators understanding system vulnerability and risks when reviewing the SCADA system for possible system improvements. API 1164 provides a means to improve the security of SCADA pipeline operations by

- Listing the processes used to identify and analyze the SCADA system's susceptibility to incidents
- Providing a comprehensive list of practices to harden the core architecture
- Providing examples of industry recommended practices

The guideline targets small to medium pipeline operators with limited information technology (IT) security resources. The guideline is applicable to most SCADA systems, not just oil and natural gas SCADA systems. The appendices of the document include a checklist for assessing a SCADA system and an example of a SCADA control system security plan.

The *Centre for the Protection of National Infrastructure (CPNI)*† provides integrated security advice (combining information, personnel, and physical) to organizations that make up the national infrastructure. Its advice helps to reduce the vulnerability of the national infrastructure (primarily the critical national infrastructure) to terrorism and other threats to national security. CPNI is an interdepartmental organization, with resources from industry, academia, and a number of government departments and agencies (including the Security Service, Communications-Electronics Security Group [CESG], and departments responsible for national infrastructure sectors). CPNI sponsors research and work in partnership with academia, government partners, research institutions, and the private sector to develop applications that can reduce vulnerability to terrorist and other attacks and lessen the impact if an attack does take place.

The *Netherland's Centre for Protection of National Infrastructure (CPNI.NL)*‡ (not to be confused with the United Kingdom's CPNI organization) provides similar functions to the United Kingdom's CPNI but is located within the Netherlands and is a dedicated resource for the cybersecurity of Netherland's critical infrastructure. The organization was incepted (circa 2006) through a grant via the Ministry of Economic Affairs, Agriculture and Innovation (EL&I). One of the functions of CPNI.NL is the development of a roadmap for securing process control systems.§

The *Center for SCADA Security* (Sandia National Laboratories n.d.) is composed of several test-bed facilities that allow real-world critical infrastructure problems to be modeled, designed, simulated, verified, and validated. These labs are integrated into a research

---

* http://www.api.org.
† http://www.cpni.gov.uk/about.
‡ https://www.cpni.nl/cpni.
§ https://www.cpni.nl/projecten/nationale-roadmap-voor-veilige-procescontrolesystemen.

effort focusing on solving current control system security problems and developing next generation control systems. These facilities include the following:

- *Distributed Energy Technology Laboratory (DETL),* which provides a platform to test the control of operational generation and load systems
- *Network Laboratory,* which provides network visualization and wired and wireless network modeling
- *Cryptographic Research Facility,* which supports the research and development of encryption for applications in control system networks
- *Red Team Facility,* which provides a suite of tools to attack and analyze control system vulnerabilities
- *Advanced Information Systems Lab,* which is used to research intelligent technologies for development of the infrastructures of the futululre

The *Chemical Sector Cyber Security Program** is a strategic program of the Chemical Information Technology Center (ChemITC®) of the American Chemistry Council. The Chemical Sector Cyber Security Program focuses on risk management and reduction to minimize the potential impact of cyberattacks on business and manufacturing systems.

The Department of Homeland Security (DHS) *Control Systems Security Program (CSSP) (U.S. DHS,†* part of the U.S. Department of Homeland Security's National Cyber Security Division (NCSD), was created to reduce industrial control system risks within and across all critical infrastructure and key resource sectors by coordinating efforts among federal, state, local, and tribal governments, as well as industrial control systems owners, operators, and vendors. The CSSP coordinates activities to reduce the likelihood of success and severity of impact of a cyberattack against critical infrastructure control systems through risk-mitigation activities.

The Department of Homeland Security (DHS) *Control Systems Security Program (CSSP) Recommended Practices‡* website provides a current information resource to help industry understand and prepare for ongoing and emerging control systems cybersecurity issues, vulnerabilities, and mitigation strategies. The CSSP works with the control systems community to ensure that recommended practices, which are made available, have been vetted by subject-matter experts in industry before being made publicly available in support of this program.

Recommended practices are developed to help users reduce their exposure and susceptibility to cyberattacks. These recommendations are based on understanding the cyberthreats, control systems vulnerabilities and attack paths, and control systems engineering. The practices recommended on this site are focused on increasing security awareness and providing security practices that have been recommended by industry to aid in a secure architecture. Additional recommended practices and supporting documents that cover specific issues and associated mitigations will continue to be added.

The Department of Energy (DOE) *Cybersecurity for Energy Delivery Systems (CEDS)§* designed the CEDS program to assist the energy sector asset owners (electric, oil, and gas) by developing cybersecurity solutions for energy delivery systems through integrated planning and a focused research and development effort. The program cofunds projects

---

* http://www.chemicalcybersecurity.com.
† http://www.us-cert.gov/control_systems.
‡ http://www.us-cert.gov/control_systems/practices.
§ http://energy.gov/oe/services/technology-development/energy-delivery-systems-cybersecurity.

with industry partners to make advances in cybersecurity capabilities for energy delivery systems and emphasizes collaboration among the government, industry, universities, national laboratories, and end users to advance research and development in cybersecurity that is tailored to the unique performance requirements, design, and operational environment of energy delivery systems. The aim of this program is to reduce the risk of energy disruptions due to cyberincidents as well as help the energy sector survive an intentional cyberassault with no loss of critical function.

The *Electric Power Research Institute (EPRI)** conducts research and development relating to the generation, delivery, and use of electricity for the benefit of the public. An independent, nonprofit organization, EPRI brings together its scientists and engineers as well as experts from academia and industry to help address challenges in electricity, including reliability, efficiency, health, safety, and the environment. EPRI also provides technology, policy, and economic analyses to drive long-range research and development planning, and it supports research in emerging technologies. EPRI's members represent more than 90% of the electricity generated and delivered in the United States, and international participation extends to 40 countries.

The *European Network and Information Security Agency (ENISA)*† is the European Union's (EU) response to cybersecurity issues within and throughout the European Union.‡ Its objective is to make ENISA an exchange of information, best practices, and knowledge in the field of information security. ENISA's website provides an access point to the EU member states and other actors in this field. The agency's mission is essential to achieving an effective level of network and information security within the European Union. Together with EU institutions and member states, ENISA seeks to develop a culture of network and information security for the benefit of citizens, consumers, businesses, and public-sector organizations within and throughout the European Union. ENISA is helping the European Commission, the EU member states, and the business community to address, respond to, and especially prevent network and information security problems.

The *European Network for the Security of Control and Real-Time Systems (ESCoRTS)*§ is a joint endeavor among EU process industries, utilities, leading manufacturers of control equipment and research institutes, under the lead of the European Committee for Standardization (CEN),¶ to foster progress toward the cybersecurity of control and communication equipment in Europe. ESCoRTS is an intersector organization embracing the following industrial fields: power, gas, oil, chemicals and petrochemicals, pharmaceuticals, and manufacturing.

The *European SCADA and Control Systems Information Exchange (E-SCSIE)*** makes use of commercial off-the-shelf (COTS) products, including Ethernet and desktop and workstation computers. Running Microsoft Windows within the domain of control systems has put these systems at the same risk to disruption as desktop workstations but with potentially much more serious consequences. The E-SCSIE is a working group formed from European industry, government, and research in order to benefit from the ability to collaborate in a formally controlled context on a range of common issues and to focus efforts and share resources where appropriate.

The *Forum of Incident Response and Security Teams (FIRST)*†† is a private-sector organization that was created approximately one year after the CERT® Coordination Center,

---

* http://www.epri.com.
† http://www.enisa.europa.eu.
‡ http://sta.jrc.ec.europa.eu/index.php/cip-action-menu?start=10.
§ http://www.escortsproject.eu.
¶ Comité Européen de Normalisation; http://www.cen.eu/cen/AboutUs/Pages/default.aspx.
** https://espace.cern.ch/EuroSCSIE/default.aspx.
†† http://www.first.org.

which was established after the infamous Internet worm incident (circa 1989–1990). FIRST coordinates several security and incident response teams that include product security teams from public, private, and academic sectors.

The *Government Forum of Incident Response and Security Teams (GFIRST)** (not to be confused with the private-sector organization FIRST) is a group of technical and tactical practitioners from incident response and security response teams responsible for securing government information technology systems while also providing support for private sectored organizations. GFIRST members work together to understand and handle computer security incidents and to encourage proactive and preventative security practices across government agencies while promoting cooperation among federal, state, and local agencies, which include defense, civilian, intelligence, and law enforcement organizations.

The *Industrial Control Systems Cyber Emergency Response Team (ICS-CERT),*† in coordination with US-CERT, operates as a functional component of the National Cybersecurity and Communications Integration Center (NCCIC), provides focused operational capabilities for defense of control system environments against emerging cyberthreats, and coordinates control systems–related security incidents and information sharing with United States–based federal, state, and local agencies and organizations, the U.S. intelligence community, private sector constituents including vendors, owners, operators, as well as international and private sector computer security incident response teams (CSIRTs).

ICS-CERT provides a control system security focus in collaboration with US-CERT to

- Respond to and analyze control systems–related incidents
- Conduct vulnerability and malware analysis
- Provide onsite support for incident response and forensic analysis
- Provide situational awareness in the form of actionable intelligence
- Coordinate the responsible disclosure of vulnerabilities/mitigations
- Share and coordinate vulnerability information and threat analysis through information products and alerts

The ICS-CERT serves as a key component of the *Strategy for Securing Control Systems,* which outlines a long-term, common vision wherein effective risk management of control systems security can be realized through successful coordination efforts.

The *Industrial Control Systems Joint Working Group (ICSJWG)* was created by the Department of Homeland Security (DHS) Control Systems Security Program (CSSP) to facilitate information sharing and reduce the risk to the nation's industrial control systems. The ICSJWG is a collaborative and coordinating body operating under the Critical Infrastructure Partnership Advisory Council (CIPAC) requirements, and it provides a vehicle for communicating and partnering across all Critical Infrastructure and Key Resources Sectors (CIKR) between U.S. federal agencies and departments as well as private asset owners/operators of industrial control systems. The goal of the ICSJWG is to continue and enhance the collaborative efforts of the industrial control systems stakeholder community in securing CIKR by accelerating the design, development, and deployment of secure industrial control systems.‡

* http://www.us-cert.gov/GFIRST.
† https://ics-cert.us-cert.gov/sites/default/files/FactSheets/ICS-CERT_FactSheet_ICS-CERT_S508C.pdf.
‡ http://www.us-cert.gov/control_systems/icsjwg.

The *Institute of Electrical and Electronics Engineers (IEEE)** is the world's largest professional association dedicated to advancing technological innovation and excellence for the benefit of humanity. IEEE and its members inspire a global community through IEEE's highly cited publications, conferences, technology standards, and professional and educational activities. There are two relevant documents that involve IEEE (NIST, 2011):

1. *IEEE 1686-2007—Standard for Substation IED Cyber Security Capabilities* (IEEE 2008). IEEE 1686-2007, Security for Intelligent Electronic Devices, establishes a minimum set of requirements for tools and features to allow a user to implement an intelligent electronic device security effort in accordance with NERC Critical Infrastructure Protection (CIP) requirements. This standard defines the functions and features to be provided in substation Intelligent Electronic Devices to accommodate critical infrastructure protection programs. IEEE 1686-2007 introduces a table of compliance, which vendors and other suppliers that claim to comply with the 1686 standard must generate to indicate a "level of compliance" with the requirements in every numbered paragraph.
2. *IEEE P1711—Trial Use Standard for a Cryptographic Protocol for Cyber Security of Substation Serial Links.* This trial use standard defines a cryptographic protocol to provide integrity and optional confidentiality for cybersecurity of serial links. It does not address specific applications or hardware implementations and is independent of the underlying communications protocol.

The *Institute for Information Infrastructure Protection (I3P)*† is a consortium of leading national cybersecurity institutions, including academic research centers, government laboratories, and nonprofit organizations. It was founded in September 2001 to help meet a well-documented need for improved research and development (R&D) to protect the nation's information infrastructure against catastrophic failures. The institute's main role is to coordinate a national cybersecurity R&D program and help build bridges between academia, industry, and government. The I3P continues to work toward identifying and addressing critical research problems in information infrastructure protection and opening information channels between researchers, policymakers, and infrastructure operators. Currently, the I3P does the following (NIST, 2011):

- Fosters collaboration among academia, industry, and government on pressing cybersecurity problems
- Develops, manages, and supports national-scale research projects
- Provides research fellowship opportunities to qualified postdoctoral researchers, faculty, and research scientists
- Hosts workshops, meetings, and events on cybersecurity and information infrastructure protection issues
- Builds and supports a knowledge base as an online vehicle for sharing and distributing information to I3P members and others working on information security challenges

Membership in the I3P consortium is at the institutional level; individuals are not eligible. Membership is open to not-for-profit research and academic institutions actively

* http://www.iee.org.
† http://www.thei3p.org.

engaged in research and policy focused on cybersecurity and information infrastructure protection.

The International Society of Automation (ISA), formerly known as *The Instrumentation, Systems, and Automation Society,* is a nonprofit technical society consisting of engineers, technicians, business managers, and academics who are interested in industrial and process automation. Originally known as the *Instrument Society of America,* the society become more commonly known by its acronym, ISA, and now includes many technical and engineering disciplines, including the securing of automation systems, as part of its scope and charter. ISA is one of several professional organizations worldwide for setting standards and educating industry professionals in industrial and process automation, of which security has becoming an emerging issue. Subset to the organization, ISA has two standards relevant to SCADA and control systems, ISA99 and ISA100:

- The ISA99 committee is establishing standards, recommended practices, technical reports, and related information that will define procedures for implementing electronically secure industrial automation and control systems and security practices and assessing electronic security performance. Guidance is directed toward those responsible for designing, implementing, or managing industrial automation and control systems and shall also apply to users, system integrators, security practitioners, and control system manufacturers and vendors. The committee's focus is to improve the confidentiality, integrity, and availability of components or systems used for automation or control and provides criteria for procuring and implementing secure control systems. Compliance with the committee's guidance will improve industrial automation and control system electronic security, and it will help identify vulnerabilities and address them, thereby reducing the risk of compromising confidential information or causing industrial automation control system degradation or failure. There are several standards in the ISA99 series; some are complete and some are in development. Each will cover a specific aspect or subset of the subject of industrial automation and control systems security. The documents have been broken down into four main categories (NIST, 2011):
  - *ISA-99.01.xx: General Security Requirements for Industrial Automation and Control Systems.* The first set of documents in the ISA99 series contains requirements that span the rest of the documents in the ISA99 series. The documents explain terminology, concepts, and models that apply to the whole series and metrics that can be used to measure the performance of the security program and countermeasures (NIST, 2011).
  - *ISA-99.02.xx: Security Program Requirements for Industrial Automation and Control Systems.* The second set of documents in the ISA99 series concerns the establishment, operation, and certification of security programs and is generally end-user focused. Much of the material in the ISA-99.02.xx set of documents is based on management systems from information technology that has been adapted to industrial automation and control systems (NIST, 2011).
  - *ISA-99.03.xx: System-Level Technical Requirements for Industrial Automation and Control Systems.* The third set of documents in the ISA99 series specifies technical capabilities and requirements for systems used in automation and control. These stem from the security program requirements in the ISA-99.02.xx series but are focused on the technical requirements needed to meet the security program requirements. The scope of this series is very broad and contains everything

from end-user requirements for setting up their industrial networks to vendors combining multiple features into a larger product (NIST, 2011).

- *ISA-99.04.xx: Component-Level Technical Requirements for Industrial Automation and Control Systems.* The fourth set of documents in the ISA99 series specifies technical capabilities and requirements for individual components used in automation and control. These stem from the system-level technical requirements in the ISA-99.03.xx series but are focused on the individual components that make up full systems. The components may be things such as embedded devices, network hardware, computers, and software packages (NIST, 2011).
- The ISA99 committee was formed in 1992, and at the time this document was published it had produced two technical reports and two standards documents, one of which superseded one of the technical reports. In 2009, IEC TC65/WG10 began working with ISA99 to publish the ISA99 document series internationally (NIST, 2011).
- The ISA100 (1945) committee will establish standards, recommended practices, technical reports, and related information that will define procedures for implementing wireless systems in the automation and control environment with a focus on the field level. Guidance is directed toward those responsible for the complete life cycle, including the design, implementation, ongoing maintenance, scalability, and management of industrial automation and control systems and shall apply to users, system integrators, practitioners, and control systems manufacturers and vendors (ISA, n.d.).

NOTE: Rather than risk duplication of effort, ISA100 will contribute to the efforts of existing committees (e.g., ISA84, ISA99) that wish to incorporate wireless technology in future revisions of their work (ISA, n.d.).

The *International Council on Large Electric Systems (CIGRE)** is a nonprofit international association based in France. It has established several study committees to promote and facilitate the international exchange of knowledge in the electrical industry by identifying recommended practices and developing recommendations. Three of its study committees focus on control systems (NIST, 2011):

1. The objectives of the *B3 Substations Committee* include the adoption of technological advances in equipment and systems to achieve increased reliability and availability.
2. The *C2 System Operation and Control Committee* focuses on the technical capabilities needed for the secure and economical operation of existing power systems, including control centers and operators.
3. The *D2 Information Systems and Telecommunication for Power Systems Committee* monitors emerging technologies in the industry and evaluates their possible impact. In addition, it focuses on the security requirements of the information systems and services of control systems.

The *Linking the Oil and Gas Industry to Improve Cybersecurity (LOGIIC)*[†] program is an ongoing collaboration of oil and natural gas companies and the U.S. Department of Homeland Security, Science and Technology Directorate. LOGIIC was formed in 2004 to facilitate cooperative research, development, testing, and evaluation procedures to improve cybersecurity in petroleum industry digital control systems. The program undertakes

---

* http://www.cigre.org
† http://www.dhs.gov/science-and-technology/csd-logiic.

collaborative research and development projects to improve the level of cybersecurity in critical systems of interest to the oil and natural gas sector. The program objective is to promote the interests of the sector while maintaining impartiality, the independence of the participants, and vendor neutrality. After a successful first project, the LOGIIC consortium was formally established as a collaboration between DHS, the Automation Federation, and five of the major oil and gas companies.*

The *National SCADA Test Bed (NSTB)* (Energy.gov, 2003; Sandia, n.d.) is jointly managed and executed by Idaho National Laboratory (INL) and Sandia National Laboratories (SNL). Other partners include the Pacific Northwest National Laboratory, Argonne National Laboratory, the National Institute of Standards and Technology, and contractors. Using the testing facilities within the NSTB, researchers have made significant accomplishments in securing control systems for the energy sector. The NSTB provides a variety of realistic testing environments to help industry and government identify and correct vulnerabilities in control systems including SCADA, energy management systems (EMS), and DCS.

The *NIST Special Publication 800 Series Security Guidelines†* for documents on information technology reports on the NIST Information Technology Laboratory (ITL) research, guidance, and outreach efforts in computer security and its collaborative activities with industry, government, and academic organizations. Focus areas include cryptographic technology and applications, advanced authentication, public key infrastructure, internetworking security, criteria and assurance, and security management and support. In addition to NIST SP 800–82, the following is a listing of some additional 800 series documents that have significant relevance to the ICS security community. These as well as many others are available through the URL listed above.

- NIST SP 800-18 Revision 1, Guide for Developing Security Plans for Federal Information Systems
- NIST SP 800-37, Guide for Applying the Risk Management Framework to Federal Information Systems: A Security Life Cycle Approach
- NIST SP 800-39, Managing Information Security Risk: Organization, Mission, and Information System View
- NIST SP 800-40 Version 2, Creating a Patch and Vulnerability Management Program
- NIST SP 800-41, Revision 1, Guidelines on Firewalls and Firewall Policy
- NIST SP 800-48, Wireless Network Security: 802.11, Bluetooth, and Handheld Devices
- NIST SP 800-50, Building an Information Technology Security Awareness and Training Program
- NIST SP 800-53 Revision 3, Recommended Security Controls for Federal Information Systems and Organizations
- NIST SP 800-53A, Guide for Assessing the Security Controls in Federal Information Systems and Organizations, Building Effective Security Assessment Plans
- NIST SP 800-61, Computer Security Incident Handling Guide
- NIST SP 800-63, Electronic Authentication Guideline
- NIST SP 800-64, Security Considerations in the Information System Development Life Cycle
- NIST SP 800-70, Security Configuration Checklists Program for IT Products—Guidance for Checklists Users and Developers
- NIST SP 800-77, Guide to IPSec VPNs

---

* http://www.dhs.gov/science-and-technology/csd-logiic.
† http://csrc.nist.gov/publications/nistpubs/index.html.

- NIST SP 800-83, Guide to Malware Incident Prevention and Handling
- NIST SP 800-86, Guide to Integrating Forensic Techniques into Incident Response
- NIST SP 800-88, Guidelines for Media Sanitization
- NIST SP 800-92, Guide to Computer Security Log Management
- NIST SP 800-94, Guide to Intrusion Detection and Prevention Systems (IDPS)

The *NIST Industrial Control System Security Project* represents the continuing effort to provide effective security standards and guidance to federal agencies and their contractors in support of the Federal Information Security Management Act (FISMA) and, as part of the effort to protect the nation's critical infrastructure, NIST continues to work with public- and private-sector entities on sector-specific security issues. Industrial and process control systems are an integral part of the U.S. critical infrastructure, and the protection of those systems is a priority for the federal government. This project intends to build on the current FISMA security standards and provide targeted extensions and/or interpretations of those standards for industrial and process controls systems where needed. Since many industrial and process controls systems are supporting private-sector organizations, NIST will collaborate with ongoing standards efforts addressing these sector-specific types of systems (NIST, 2014).

The mission of the *North American Electric Reliability Corporation (NERC)** is to improve the reliability and security of the bulk power system in North America. To achieve that, NERC develops and enforces reliability standards; monitors the bulk power system; assesses future adequacy; audits owners, operators, and users for preparedness; and educates and trains industry personnel. NERC is a self-regulatory organization that relies on the diverse and collective expertise of industry participants. As the Electric Reliability Organization, NERC is subject to audit by the U.S. Federal Energy Regulatory Commission and governmental authorities in Canada. NERC has issued a set of cybersecurity standards to reduce the risk of compromise to electrical generation resources and high-voltage transmission systems above 100 kV, also referred to as bulk electric systems. Bulk electric systems include balancing authorities, reliability coordinators, interchange authorities, transmission providers, transmission owners, transmission operators, generation owners, generation operators, and load serving entities. The cybersecurity standards include audit measures and levels of noncompliance that can be tied to penalties. The set of NERC Cyber Security Standards includes the following (NIST, 2011):

- CIP-002 Critical Cyber Asset Identification
- CIP-003 Security Management Controls
- CIP-004 Personnel and Training
- CIP-005 Electronic Security Perimeter(s)
- CIP-006 Physical Security of Critical Cyber Assets
- CIP-007 Systems Security Management
- CIP-008 Incident Reporting and Response Planning
- CIP-009 Recovery Plans for Critical Cyber Assets

The standards can be downloaded at http://www.nerc.com/page.php?cid=2|20.

The *Nuclear Regulatory Commission (NRC) Regulatory Guide 5.71 (RG 5.71)* describes a regulatory position that promotes a defensive strategy consisting of a defensive architecture and a set of security controls based on standards provided in NIST SP 800-53 and NIST SP 800-82, *Guide to Industrial Control Systems Security,* dated September 29, 2008. NIST

---

* http://www.nerc.com/pa/Stand/Pages/CIPStandards.aspx.

SP 800-53 and SP 800-82 are based on well-understood cyberthreats, risks, and vulnerabilities, coupled with equally well-understood countermeasures and protective techniques. Furthermore, NIST developed SP 800-82 for use within ICS environments, including common ICS environments in which the IT/ICS convergence has created the need to consider application of these security controls. RG 5.71 divides the above-noted security controls into three broad categories: technical, operational, and management (NRC, 2010).

The *Office of Critical Infrastructure Protection and Emergency Preparedness** was originally created to work within the Department of National Defense but was later integrated into the Public Safety and Emergency Preparedness Canada portfolio in order to streamline emergency preparedness and responses to natural disaster and security-related issues. The office provides national direction assurance of Canada's critical infrastructures specific to both physical and cyber-related issues. OCIPEP is also the Canadian government's primary agency for ensuring national civil emergency preparedness, providing close cooperation and information sharing capabilities within the security and intelligence communities, particularly in relation to threat assessments for information systems (and their operations), which includes cyberwarfare, cybersabotage, and cybercrime.

The *Repository of Industrial Security Incidents (RISI)*† organization has a history dating back to early 2001, when Eric Byres, Justin Lowe, and David Leversage developed a database called the *Industrial Security Incidents Database (ISID)* while working on an academic research project. ISID tracked industrial security incidents affecting control systems, allowing its developers to identify trends and patterns in support of their research project. In 2006 BCIT, Eric, Justin, and David discontinued ISID.

Sometime in 2008, Eric Byres of Byres Research Inc. and Mark Fabro of Lofty Perch Inc. began a collaboration on a project to develop the RISI with the goal of making RISI available to the entire industrial automation community. On March 31, 2009, exida acquired Byres Research and in July 2009 created the Security Incidents Organization™, a 501(c)(3) nonprofit corporation, to operate RISI and fulfill the vision of Eric, Justin, David, and Mark in the hope that one day this important information would be available to the community. The spirit of ISID and RISI has always been about exemplary research and a sharing of information amongst a community of people who value this information. The Security Incidents Organization™ was established to maintain this spirit and to be a self-sustaining organization focused on performing research in the public interest and making the results of that research available to the public on a nondiscriminatory basis. Its success is dependent not only on the financial support of member companies but also, more importantly, on the willingness of those affected by industrial security incidents to share their experiences for the benefit of the community.

The *SCADA Perspective Mailing List*‡ (formerly known as the "SCADA Gospel Mailing List") was created by Ian Wiese around early 1997 and has since changed owners; its new owner and moderator is Ronald Southworth, who is currently working in the water sector for a public utility based out of Australia. The SCADA perspective mailing list was established as a forum to allow information exchange between all interested parties regarding SCADA systems to discuss standards in the SCADA industry, with the aim to achieving the acceptance of standards that will improve the understanding, operation, and interoperability of equipment and systems.§

* http://www.publicsafety.gc.ca/cnt/ntnl-scrt/crtcl-nfrstrctr/index-en.aspx.
† http://www.securityincidents.org.
‡ http://www.scadaperspective.com.
§ http://scadaperspective.com/SCADAMAIL.html.

The *SCADA and Control Systems Security Mailing List* (aka "SCADASEC")* was created by Bob Radvanovsky, Jake Brodsky, and Mark Fabro back in early 2008. It is currently owned and maintained by Bob Radvanovsky and is moderated by both Bob and Jake. The SCADASEC mailing list was created to fill a niche area not currently covered by either public- or private-sector interests and provides an "open source" venue where individuals can openly discuss security-related events, issues, situations, and methods pertaining to industrial and process automation, SCADA, and control systems.

The primary goal of the *Smart Grid Interoperability Panel (SGIP) Cyber Security Working Group (CSWG)* is to develop an overall cybersecurity strategy for the smart grid that includes a risk mitigation strategy to ensure the interoperability of solutions across different domains/components of the infrastructure. The cybersecurity strategy needs to address prevention, detection, response, and recovery. Implementation of a cybersecurity strategy requires the definition and implementation of an overall cybersecurity risk assessment process for the smart grid (NIST, 2013).

The *Trusted Information Sharing Network (TISN)*[†] for Critical Infrastructure Resilience provides an environment for sharing information between private and public sectors specific to security issues that are relevant to critical infrastructure and its continuity of operations. TISN is coordinated by several critical-infrastructure owners and operators from seven sectors. Additionally, advisory groups provide strategic advice specific to aspects on critical infrastructure, which includes cybersecurity.[‡] Subset to the TISN, the *IT Security Expert Advisory Group (ITSEAG)* provides strategic direction to the TISN on emerging IT security issues that impact on Australia's critical infrastructure sectors. It also provides oversight for the TISN's *Supervisory Control and Data Acquisition (SCADA) Community of Interest (COI)*, which consists of IT security experts from industry and Australian academia as well as the Australian government and was formed to facilitate emerging IT security issues pertinent to critical infrastructure.

The *Werkgroup voor Instrument Beoordeling (WIB)*[§] (English: *Working-Party on Instrument Behavior*) provides process instrumentation evaluation and assessment services for and on behalf of its industrial user member companies. WIB operates in close collaboration through the "SWE" federation with its "sister" associations EXERA in France and SIREP/EI in the United Kingdom. A cooperation agreement exists with the NAMUR organization in Germany.

References

Energy.gov. (2003). National SCADA test bed (NSTB). http://energy.gov/oe/technology-development/energy-delivery-systems-cybersecurity/national-scada-test-bed.

IAS100. (1945). Wireless system for automation. http://www.isa.org/isa100.

IEEE. (2008). 1686–2007—Standard for substation IED cyber security capabilities. http://ieeexplore.ieee.org/iel5/4453837/4453852/04453853.pdf?arnumber=4453853.

National Institute of Standards and Technology (NIST). (2011). Guide to industrial controls systems (ICS) security. NIST. June. http://csrc.nist.gov/publications/nistpubs/800-82/SP800-82-final.pdf.

National Institute of Standards and Technology (NIST). (2013). NIST smart grid collaboration wiki for smart grid interoperability standards. http://collaborate.nist.gov/twiki-sggrid/bin/view/SmartGrid/CyberSecurityCTG.

---

* http://www.scadasec.com.
† http://www.tisn.gov.au/Pages/default.aspx.
‡ http://www.tisn.gov.au/Pages/Cyber_security.aspx.
§ http://www.wib.nl/about_his.html.

National Institute of Standards and Technology (NIST). (2014). Industrial control system security (ICS). http://csrc.nist.gov/groups/SMA/fisma/ics.

Nuclear Regulatory Commission (NRC). (2010). Regulatory guide. January. http://nrc-stp.ornl.gov/slo/regguide571.pdf.

Sandia National Laboratories. (n.d.). National supervisory control and data acquisition (SCADA). http://energy.sandia.gov/energy/ssrei/gridmod/cyber-security-for-electric-infrastructure/scada-systems.

The International Society of Automation (ISA). (n.d.). ISA100, wireless systems for automation. ISA. https://www.isa.org/isa100/.

Appendix II: Terms and definitions

Many terms and definitions that are specific to the supervisory control and data acquisition (SCADA) and control systems community may conflict with other industrial terms, definitions, acronyms, and so on. The following glossary is meant to provide a useful reference of terms, definitions, and acronyms that are specific to this community. Please note that several of the glossary items listed may be indicative of other communities, such as information technology (IT) (e.g., *local area network* or *LAN* is IT specific).*

AC drive Alternating current drive; synonymous with *variable frequency drive (VFD)*.

Application server A computer responsible for hosting applications to user workstations.

Backup domain controller Backup to the *primary domain controller*.

Control server A server hosts the supervisory control system, typically a commercially available application for DCS or SCADA systems, and communicates data between the peer-to-peer network and the LAN.

Data A repository of information that usually holds plant-wide information including process data, recipes, personnel data, and financial data.

DC servo drive A specific type of drive that works specifically with servo motors. Transmits commands to the motor and receives feedback from the servo motor's resolver or encoder.

Distributed control system (DCS) A supervisory control system that typically controls and monitors set points to sub-controllers distributed geographically throughout a factory.

Distributed plant A geographically distributed factory that is accessible through the Internet by an enterprise.

Domain controller A Windows server responsible for managing domain and authentication information, which includes login user names and passwords.

Enterprise A business venture or company that encompasses one or more factories.

Enterprise resource planning (ERP) system A system that integrates enterprise-wide information including human resources, financials, manufacturing, and distribution; it also connects the organization to its customers and suppliers.

Fieldbus A category of network that links sensors and other devices to a PC or PLC-based controller. Use of Fieldbus technologies eliminates the need for point-to-point wiring between the controller and each device. A protocol is used to define messages over the Fieldbus network with each message identifying a particular sensor on the network.

---

* Some terms and definitions (along with our thanks) have been taken courtesy of a NIST white paper (Falco et al. n.d.).

Firewall A device on a communications network that can be programmed to filter information based on the information content, source, or destination.

Human–machine interface (HMI) The hardware or software through which an operator interacts with a controller. An HMI can range from a physical control panel with buttons and indicator lights to an industrial PC with a color graphics display running dedicated HMI software.

Internet A system of linked networks that are worldwide in scope and facilitate data communication services. The Internet is currently a communications highway for millions of users.

Input/output (I/O) A module relaying information sent to the processor from connected devices (input) and to the connected devices from the processor (output).

Light tower A device containing series of indicator lights and an embedded controller used to indicate the state of a process based on an input signal.

Local area network (LAN) A network of computers that span a relatively small space. Each computer on the network is called a node, has its own hardware, and runs its own programs, but it can also access any other data or devices connected to the LAN. Printers, modems, and other devices can also be separate nodes on a LAN.

Machine controller A control system/motion network that electronically synchronizes drives within a machine system instead of relying on synchronization via mechanical linkage.

Modem A device that allows a computer to communicate through a phone line.

Management information system (MIS) A software system for accessing data from production resources and procedures required to collect, process, and distribute data for use in decision making.

Manufacturing execution system (MES) Systems that use network computing to automate production control and process automation. By downloading "recipes" and work schedules and uploading production results, an MES bridges the gap between business and plant-floor or process-control systems.

OPC client/server A mechanism for providing interoperability between disparate field devices, automation/control, and business systems.

Peer-to-peer network (P2P) A networking configuration where there is no server and computers connect with each other to share data. Each computer acts as both a client (information requestor) and a server (information provider).

Photo eye A light-sensitive sensor utilizing photoelectric control that converts a light signal into an electrical signal, ultimately producing a binary signal based on an interruption of a light beam.

Pressure regulator A device used to control the pressure of a gas or liquid.

Pressure sensor A sensor system that produces an electrical signal related to the pressure acting on it by its surrounding medium.

Primary domain controller A Windows server that is responsible for managing domain and authentication information, including login user names and passwords, and is the primary controller for security functions, usually paired with a secondary (or backup) domain controller. (See *backup domain controller*.)

Printer A device that converts digital data to human readable text on a paper medium.

Process controller A proprietary, typically rack-mounted, computer system that processes sensor input, executes control algorithms, and computes actuator outputs.

Programmable logic controller (PLC) A small industrial computer used in factories; originally designed to replace the relay logic of a process control system, they have evolved into a controller having the functionality of a process controller.

Proximity sensor A noncontact sensor with the ability to detect the presence of a target within a specified range.

Redundant control server A backup to the control server that maintains the current state of the control server at all times.

Remote terminal unit (RTU) A computer with radio interfacing used in remote situations where communications via wire is unavailable. It is usually used to communicate with remote field equipment. PLCs with radio communication capabilities are also used in place of RTUs.

Servo valve An actuated valve whose position is controlled using a servo actuator.

Sensor A device that senses or detects the value of a process variable and generates a signal related to the value. Additional transmitting hardware is required to convert the basic sensor signal into a standard transmission signal. A sensor is defined as the complete sensing and transmitting device.

Single-loop controller A controller that controls a very small process or a critical process.

Solenoid valve A valve actuated by an electric coil. A solenoid valve typically has two states: open and closed.

Supervisory control and data acquisition (SCADA) system Similar to a *distributed control system* with the exception of subcontrol systems being geographically dispersed over large areas and accessed using *remote terminal servers*.

Temperature sensor A sensor system that produces an electrical signal related to its temperature and, as a consequence, senses the temperature of its surrounding medium.

Variable frequency drive (VFD) A type of drive that controls the speed but not the precise position of a nonservo AC (alternating current) motor by varying the frequency of the electricity going to that motor. VFDs are typically used for applications where speed and power are important but precise positioning is not.

Workstation A computer used for tasks such as programming, engineering, and design; the computer may or may not be network connected or may be isolated from any network (telephone or Ethernet based).

Wide area network (WAN) A network that spans than a LAN, consisting of two or more LANs connected to each other via telephone lines, other networked connections, or very large area networks such as the Internet.

Wireless device A device that connects an automation system via radio frequency (RF) or infrared (heat) waves; it is used to collect and/or monitor data but may also modify control set points of control systems.

Reference

Falco, J., Stouffer, K., Wavering, A., and Proctor, F. (n.d.) IT security for industrial control systems, NIST white paper, Intelligent Systems Division, National Institute of Standards and Technology (NIST).

Index

A

Acceptance testing, 190
Accidental threats, 57, 59, 60
ACDC, *see* Active cyber defense cycle (ACDC)
ACID, *see* Atomic, Consistent, Isolated, Durable (ACID) principle
Activation criteria, and procedure, 137
Active cyber defense cycle (ACDC), 279, 285–286
Active defense
    active cyber defense cycle (ACDC), 279, 285–286
    and architecture, 271–272
    asset identification and network security monitoring, 281–282
    description of, 274–275
    foundation, 269–270
    incident response, 282–283
    intelligence, 275–277
    offense, 277–278
    overview, 267–268
    and passive defense, 272–274
    and sliding scale of cybersecurity, 270–271
    threat and environment manipulation, 284–285
    threat-intelligence consumption, 279–281
    working in ICS, 268–269
Address resolution protocol (ARP), 262
Administrative law, 207
Advanced DHS red–blue training course, 338
Advanced intrusion detection environment (AIDE), 345
AGA, *see* American Gas Association (AGA)
AIC, *see* Availability, integrity, or confidentiality (AIC)
AIDE, *see* Advanced intrusion detection environment (AIDE)
Air traffic control (ATC), 97
Algorithmic classification, 196–197
Alternate sites, 127–129
Alternate storage, and processing facilities, 146–147
American Gas Association (AGA), 375–376
American National Standards Institute (ANSI), 213
American Petroleum Institute, 376
ANSI, *see* American National Standards Institute (ANSI)
#AntiSec movement, 39

B

Backup methods, 126, 142
Bash interface shell, 88
BCP, *see* Business continuity plan (BCP)
Behavior-based IDS, 179
BIA, *see* Business impact analysis (BIA)

AP&S risk management, 42, 43, 44, 49, 50, 62, 64, 69, 72, 76
APCERT, *see* Asia Pacific Computer Emergency Response Team coalition (APCERT)
APIs, *see* Application programming interfaces (APIs)
Application controls, 353
Application programming interfaces (APIs), 32
Architecture, active defense, 271–272
ARP, *see* Address resolution protocol (ARP)
Asia Pacific Computer Emergency Response Team coalition (APCERT), 100
Asset identification
    and network security monitoring, 281–282
    and physical security, 319–320
Asset valuation, 53–57
    considerations for, 55–57
    in support of mission success, 54–55
ASTM Dictionary of Engineering Science and Technology, 58
Astroturfing, 35, 39
Asynchronous transfer mode (ATM), 152
ATC, *see* Air traffic control (ATC)
ATM, *see* Asynchronous transfer mode (ATM)
Atomic, Consistent, Isolated, Durable (ACID) principle, 345
Attack group knowledge, 251
Attacks, and integrity, 351
Auditing
    deployment, 347–348
    for integrity, 349–351
Aurora generator test, 107–114
    controversy surrounding the disclosure of, 111
    images of test site, 111–114
    mitigation of aurora effect, 110–111
    overview, 107–109
Availability, integrity, or confidentiality (AIC), 45, 47, 48, 50, 51, 53, 57

Printed in the United States
by Baker & Taylor Publisher Services